London
A Musical Gazetteer

Lewis Foreman
and
Susan Foreman

BROMLEY PUBLIC LIBRARIES	
02519518	
Bertrams	24.03.07
780.9421	£15.99
BECAPB	

Yale University Press
New Haven and London

© 2005 Lewis Foreman and Susan Foreman

All rights reserved. This book may not be reproduced in whole or in part, in any form
(beyond that copying permitted by Sections 107 and 108 of the U.S. Copyright Law and
except by reviewers for the public press), without written permission from the publishers.

For information about this and other Yale University Press publications, please contact:
U.S. Office: sales.press@yale.edu   www.yalebooks.com
Europe Office: sales@yaleup.co.uk   www.yalebooks.co.uk

Designed by Sandy Chapman

Library of Congress Cataloging-in-Publication Data

Foreman, Lewis.
London : a musical gazetteer / Lewis Foreman & Susan Foreman.-- 1st ed.
p. cm.
Includes bibliographical references (p.   ) and index.
ISBN 0-300-10402-2 (cl : alk. paper)
1. Musical landmarks--England--London--Guidebooks. 2. Music--England--London. I.
Foreman, Susan. II. Title.
ML286.8.L5F67 2005
780'.9421--dc22

2004021370

A catalogue record for this book is available from the British Library.

10 9 8 7 6 5 4 3 2 1

Front cover: (left to right from the top): A National Concert (1851) at Her Majesty's Theatre;
The Tallis Window at St Alfege, Greenwich; Sir Henry Wood at Queen's Hall; Royal Festival
Hall; Royal Albert Hall in summer: the queue for the arena promenade at the Proms;
Members of the Ballets Russes with Stravinsky outside the Alhambra; The Promenade at the
Empire Theatre; The Wigmore Hall.

Back cover: The Royal Opera House, Covent Garden.

Frontispiece: Sir Henry Wood, with Australians Hubert Clifford (BBC Empire Director of
Music) and (with beard) John Gough (BBC Pacific Director of Music) survey the ruins of
Queen's Hall, May 1941. Later the picture became celebrated when, as a photograph of Wood
heroically surveying the ruins of his life's work, his two companions were airbrushed out.

Contents

Acknowledgements and Sources

One of the pleasures when finishing any book is to thank the enormous number of people who have helped in varying ways, and this is no exception. First we have to thank Christina Bashford whose idea it was; we hope she likes what she started, and finds it useful. Then we have to thank Nigel Simeone for his infectious enthusiasm and his constructive reading of our first draft, and for the helpful example of his book *Paris: A Musical Gazetteer* which we have found an inspiration in so many ways. Graham Parlett's close reading of the first draft was invaluable and we are grateful for his host of literary and editorial suggestions. Sections of the page proofs were read by John Abbott, Margaret Fingerhut, Garry Humphreys, Leanne Langley, Tony Payne, Mike Purton, Edward Sargent and Hannah Shield; we thank them for their time and expertise. The book is immeasurably better for their contributions – so many potential infelicities removed – but as always for what remains you have to blame the authors.

Many helpful friends put their memories and specialised knowledge at our disposal, notably Felix Aprahamian on 'thirties London, Dame Jennifer Bate on Messiaen, Lionel Carley on Grieg and Delius, Tony Catterick on orchestral life, Gavin Henderson on the Savile Club and Trinity College of Music, Peter Horton on the Royal College of Music and Victorian music, the late John Huntley on films and filming, David Knight on cathedral music, Stephen Lloyd on Lambert and Walton, Rodney Newton on opera, recording sessions and film music, Anthony Pollard on the record industry, Mike Purton on the Savage Club and on military music, the late Kenneth Roberton on Curwen and music publishing, Janet Snowman on the Royal Academy of Music, Richard Turbet on Elizabethan music, and, finally, Malcolm Walker who compiled the original of the list of recording halls on page 158. To all heartfelt thanks.

Without many libraries and archives we could not have achieved the coverage we have, and librarians and archivists were helpful as only librarians can be, notably at: the Barbican Music Library (Robert Tucker), the BBC Written Archives Centre at Caversham (Jeff Walden and Jacquie Kavanagh), EMI Archives (Ruth Edge), the Henry Watson Music Library Manchester (Martin Thacker), the London Library, the Royal Academy of Music (Bridget Palmer), Royal College of Music (Peter Horton), Sheffield University Special Collections, Trinity College of Music (Rosemary Firman), Westminster Abbey Library (Tony Trowles), Westminster Music Library (Central Music Library)(Ruth Walters) .

Last, but far from least, the following have all contributed in their various ways. They are here listed in alphabetical order. We have to thank: Michael Allis, John Amis, David Baldwin, Stephen Banfield, Paul Banks, Tony Boden, Tony Catterick, Judith Deschamps, Jeremy Dibble, Mike Dutton, Alistair Ferguson, Christopher Fifield, Sir Anthony Figges, Howard Friend, Leslie Head, Edward Johnson, Nick Kenyon, Paul Kirwan, David Kremer, Martin Lee-Brown, John McCabe, Simon McVeigh, Anthony Pollard, Hon Laura Ponsonby, Tully Potter, Stephen Rinker, Evelyn Rothwell (Lady Barbirolli), Patrick Russell, Malcolm Smith, Diana Sparkes (Foss), Bradley Strauchan, Philip Stuart, John Tyrrell, Timothy Walker, Joanne Watson and Adrian Yardley. The maps were specially drawn by Phil Longford.

The quotations from Martin Lee-Brown's book *Nothing So Charming as Musick!* are reproduced by kind permission of the author. The quotations from the writings of Sir Arnold Bax, principally his autobiographical *Farewell, My Youth*, are printed by permission of A. B. Rye representing the Estate of Sir Arnold Bax. For Henry Wood's speech to the Columbia Graphophone Company we are grateful to Anthony Pollard, and to Kay Dreyfus for her list of Percy Grainger's London addresses formerly published in the *Grainger Society Journal*. The quotations from Eric Coates are made by permission of the late John Bishop and Thames Publishing. For short extracts we must acknowledge the Estates of J. B.Booth (for *Palmy Days*), Sir Henry Wood (for *My Life of Music*) and Arthur Jacobs (for *Henry J. Wood Maker of the Proms*).

This is not intended as a conventional scholarly study, though as the fruit of much original research and first-hand knowledge not otherwise documented in the literature we hope it will find a useful place. However, for this reason we have not used footnotes, which seemed inappropriate in a guide book, albeit an historical one. All printed sources consulted other than concert reviews appear in the bibliography. Those most frequently cited are by Barnett, Bax, Berger, Cowen, Klein, Mackenzie, and Moscheles.

The only extensively used archive sources are from the BBC Written Archives Centre at Caversham (in their RCONT1 series for each composer) and the EMI Archives at Hayes for the Columbia recording ledgers from the 1920s. These are not quoted verbatim but have largely been used to document dates of performances, addresses and visits to London, notably in many composer entries in Part II. We have also consulted the various BBC historical files on BBC buildings. Quotations from BBC files are reproduced by permission of the BBC Written Archives Centre at Caversham, and remain BBC copyright.Press cuttings were consulted in the Central Music Library Edwin Evans Collection at Westminster Music Library. The transcripts from Parry's diaries (in the Wagner section) were made at Shulbrede Priory by courtesy of the Hon. Laura Ponsonby and are printed with her permission. The quotation from an interview with George Lloyd is reproduced by permission of William Lloyd.

The text briefly re-visits several of Lewis Foreman's previous publications. These are *Lost but Only Sometimes Found* (used with acknowledgements to the British Music

Society); the entry on Webern was first written for Murray Khouri and the Testament CD label and comes from the booklet notes for their issue of the archive recording of Berg's Violin Concerto conducted by Webern (Testament SBT 1004); *Oh My Horses! Elgar and the Great War* (used with acknowledgements to Elgar Editions and the Elgar Society); the article 'Watford sur Gade: Delius in Watford' published in the *Delius Society Journal* (with thanks to the editor and the Delius Society); finally the discography from the article on Queen's Hall in *ICRC* No 10 Autumn 1997 and 'Crystal Palace on Shellac' in *CRC* No 26 Autumn 2001 (both with thanks to Tully Potter).

Illustrations   Most of the illustrations are from the authors' collections. These consist of historical engravings, photographic picture postcards and printed ephemera. We thank the many dealers in and out of London, and in the USA, Australia and New Zealand from whom these have been accumulated over the years. Special thanks to the unknown compiler of a wonderful 1920s music scrapbook, purchased at Sotheby's for just one pound in 1969, for an invaluable compilation.

Modern photographs of buildings, graves and memorials have been specially taken by Lewis Foreman. Tamsin Roberts took the photograph of the 2004 Proms queue (illus 10 and cover). These have been supplemented by: Brian Denington's portrait of Sir John Barbirolli (82) at Trinity College of Music reproduced by kind permission of Trinity College of Music; the group photograph of Edwin Evans, Walton, Hubert Foss etc at Nightingale Corner, Rickmansworth (78) provided by the Foss's daughter Diana Sparkes; the photograph of Olivier Messiaen in Felix Aprahamian's garden (93) kindly supplied by Dame Jennifer Bate and reproduced by permission of the photographer Yvonne Loriod; and the photograph from the first UK performance of Siegfried Wagner's opera *Der Friedensengel* (9) kindly supplied by Leslie Head. We are grateful to Lionel Carley, the owner of Henry Wood's painting of the inside of the barn at Chorleywood (79), for allowing us to photograph his painting and reproduce it. Our frontispiece, the original of the well-known picture of Sir Henry Wood in the ruins of Queen's Hall is reproduced from Hubert Clifford's original by kind permission of his daughter Sue Fawkes. Documents and ephemera are all from the authors' collections except 2 and 89, for which we thank the Edwin Evans Collection at Central Music Library, and 106 kindly supplied by John Norris and reproduced by permission of him and the Elgar Society.

At Yale we have to thank Harry Haskell for commissioning our book and giving us such friendly support; Robert Baldock in the London Office for his encouragement and finding the book's present shape; Sandy Chapman for designing the book, managing the production process and bringing it to reality, and last, but by no means least, Stephen Kent for his cover design.

Lewis Foreman and Susan Foreman
Rickmansworth
December 2004

Preface: The Scope and Use of the Gazetteer

This historical gazetteer was commissioned to be a companion to Nigel Simeone's pioneering *Paris – a musical gazetteer* (Yale, 2000), and accordingly we have followed his general approach, including the disposition of the text between the long section dealing with individual musicians and earlier chapters on more places, buildings and organisations. However, unlike Nigel, we have taken an interest in that characteristically twentieth-century development, recording, with a chapter on an idiosyncratic London activity, freelance recording sessions in churches and lesser-known halls.

The book reflects our personal interests and enthusiasms and we hope will usefully provide insights, memories and information not available elsewhere. Various anecdotes record the London music we have witnessed over nearly half a century, and also reflect the reminiscences of many orchestral players and recording personnel who have confirmed and amplified our impressions.

The musicians in the second and longest section of the book include not only some of the British composers of the past three or four hundred years, but also many of the musicians who were attracted to the unique musical market that has been London since the seventeenth century. Inevitably the musicians section is far shorter than we would wish, and many deserving names are not mentioned; but the only alternative to our selective treatment would be to make it a separate book. Thinking back to London concerts we have attended over the years conducted by distinguished visitors, we might have included, say, Bernstein or Khachaturian – or Copland, whose curious jerky beat and rhythmic head wagging, at the Royal Festival Hall in April 1960, is still a vivid memory. Nor have we been able to find space for Bernard Herrmann, celebrated film composer, whose residence in London (at 11 Cumberland Terrace, Regent's Park) so entranced those privileged to know him here in his last decade. We have not dealt with pop music or jazz in the musicians section, nor other than in passing in the sections on publishers or recording studios. No addresses have been given for living musicians.

We have followed the second edition of *New Grove* for the spelling and transliteration of names, which means, for example, that we render Scriabin as Skryabin, Wassily Safonoff as Vasily Safonov, and Tchaikovsky's Christian names are Pyotr Il'yich. Otherwise we have used the RED *Classical Catalogue 2003* for composers and performers not found in *New Grove*, and the second (1910) edition of *Grove* for earlier names not in either. However, we have preferred Rachmaninov to alternatives.

While this is an historical gazetteer it should not be forgotten that London is a vibrant and very active musical city and its present-day bustle is but a reflection of its life in the past. Attending a concert or service in, say, Westminster Abbey or St Paul's, means one is immediately sharing the acoustic enjoyed by musicians of the past. The range and quantity of music performed in London must be wider than any other city of the world, and accordingly we have mentioned in passing some of the more practical aspects of accessing London's music of today, including such matters as music in city churches and free tickets for BBC recording sessions, which are not widely publicised to visitors. Inevitably the internet looms large for all researchers today, and almost all present day institutions and establishments, including churches, have their own web sites. We have provided a select list of those which readers may find useful; others can doubtless be traced using one of the well-known search engines such as Google.com.

Privately owned buildings identified in the gazetteer are not open to the public unless otherwise stated. Many older buildings have been demolished, were bombed or have been rebuilt beyond recognition. Many survive, however, and the period of writing this book seems to have coincided with an unprecedented period of refurbishment of many of London's major musical landmarks. In discussing London we do not always preface familiar buildings such as the Festival Hall or the Albert Hall with their formal appelation 'Royal'. All visitors to London are advised to obtain a free London tube map from London Transport. (Otherwise view on the web at www.thetube.com/content/tubemap.)

Finally, for those new to London, here are our personal top ten musical bargains:

• The arena promenade at the 'Proms' during the summer (join the queue on the steps opposite the Royal College of Music or in Prince Consort Road up to an hour and a half before the concert);

• Free or inexpensive BBC orchestral concerts at Maida Vale or elsewhere (find what's on from the BBC Radio Three website);

• Any end of term opera production at the conservatoires (Guildhall School of Music and Drama; Royal Academy of Music; Royal College of Music; Trinity College of Music), not forgetting the many free concerts and lectures during term time;

• Ballet matinees and lunchtime events at the Royal Opera House, Covent Garden;

• Lunchtime concerts at any of the City churches (inexpensive or free, pick up a leaflet at any of them or at the Tourist Information Office opposite St. Paul's cathedral);

• Wigmore Hall celebrity recitals and Sunday morning coffee concerts;

• Free Christmas performance of Handel's *Messiah* at St. Paul's (needs early booking);

• The Handel House Museum, the only composer museum in central London;

• Choral evensong mid-week, late afternoon, or Sunday morning services at the major religious centres (see the *Daily Telegraph* on a Saturday for times and places);

• Sung Eucharist on the first Sunday of the month at the Chapel Royal, St James's Palace (not in summer, usually at 11.15 a.m.; free)

Greater London: Some Places of Interest out of the Centre

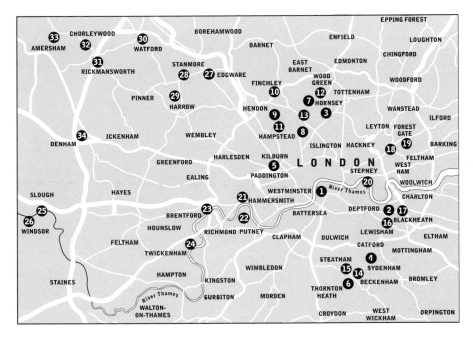

1 Morley College
2 Trinity College of Music
3 Fenton House
4 Blackheath
5 Kensal Green Cemetery
6 West Norwood Cemetery
7 Highgate Cemetery
8 Hampstead Cemetery
9 Golders Green Crematorium
10 East Finchley Cemetery
11 Golders Green Hippodrome
12 Alexandra Palace
13 Kenwood
14 Crystal Palace/Sydenham
15 Norwood
16 Blackheath
17 Greenwich
18 People's Palace
19 Theatre Royal Stratford
20 Whitechapel Bell Foundry
21 Lyric Hammersmith
22 Barnes
23 Musical Museum, Brentford
24 Kneller Hall
25 Eton College
26 Windsor
27 St Lawrence Whitchurch
28 Grim's Dyke
29 St George's, Headstone
30 Watford
31 Rickmansworth
32 Chorleywood
33 Amersham
34 Denham Studios, site of

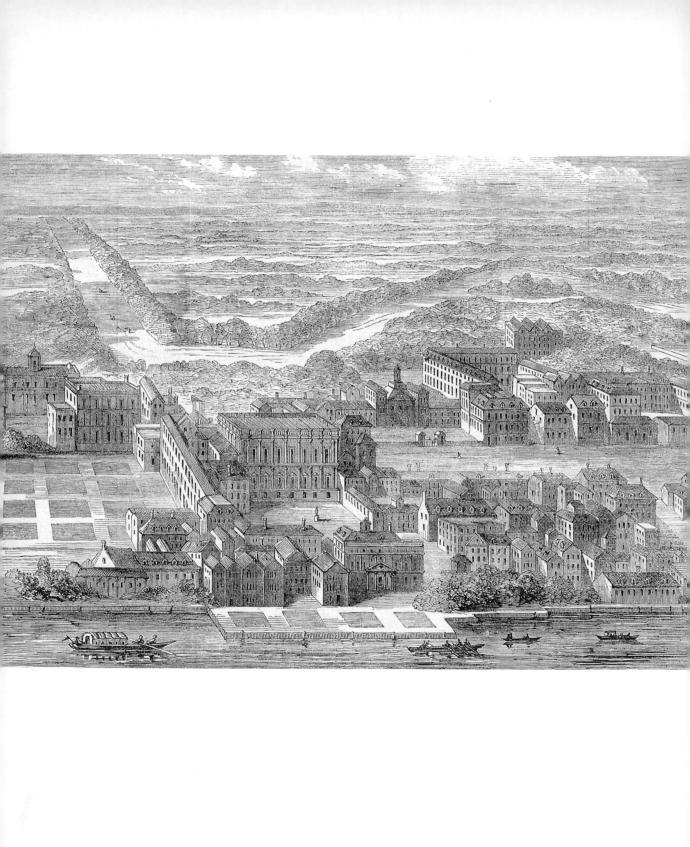

Introduction • Five Centuries of Music in London: An Outline

1500–1660

For the purpose of any history, London comprises all the places adjacent to the City, including Westminster to the west and Greenwich to the east, which are part of the modern conurbation that constitutes the capital. The confluence of musical traditions arising from ecclesiastical institutions, the large number of co-located city churches, the Court (the Palace of Whitehall was burned down only in 1698), and wealthy residents at a major European port and centre of trade, combined with a vigorous tavern culture have made London a significant musical centre from earliest times.

There was a great expansion of music in the City churches in the early fifteenth century, and music was lavish, notably in processions. Throughout that century there was a growth in musical activity both at Court and in church, and the first organ in a London church is recorded at St Peter Cheap in 1433. A new organ in Westminster Abbey (earlier organs go back to the previous century) was completed in 1442. With the growth of polyphonic music the demand for singers increased, as did the possibility of making a professional career as a singer. In 1500, London music was focused on the court, the aristocracy and the church, at least as far as that which was written down and survives is concerned; there must have been a considerable oral tradition. The need for ceremonial on public occasions seems to have been a particular feature of the age. During the marriage of Prince Arthur with Katherine of Aragon in 1501, for example, the Court was taken down the Thames to Greenwich in a water pageant accompanied by a large mixed instrumental ensemble.

It is convenient to start an overview of London's musical history with the accession of King Henry VIII in 1509, a significant event in the musical life of the English Court, for the king was not only a musical enthusiast and performer but also a composer. In that year he increased the royal trumpets from nine to fifteen. Music played an important role in establishing the standing, the authority and mystique of the throne. Typical of this was the high profile role of music at the Field of the Cloth of Gold in 1520; it was a significant element in the French and English kings' competition to impress each other. It is clear that Henry had a considerable musical establishment, in which he took a personal interest, and in due course Henry's

1 (facing page) The Palace of Whitehall as Purcell would have known it. Only the Banqueting House (centre) now survives. A Victorian artist's impression, from the *Illustrated London News* in 1862.

funeral procession in 1547 included nearly sixty musicians. In many ways Henry VIII's enthusiasm is the most important single factor generating the growing infrastructure in London, not only for his musical activities in his lifetime, but also for the fact that he passed on this passion to his children, who were successively monarchs for the remainder of the century.

This was an age of teeming musical vitality that was driven by the Court and developed across a wider and wider audience as the century passed, music being one of the interests in which aspirational members of the upper echelons of society needed to excel if they were to be accepted. This was fuelled by the enormous growth of London residences of the nobility and important provincial figures. During the second half of the century the rise of the London bourgeoisie provided a growing market for music which expanded with the population over the succeeding centuries.

The style of church music was materially influenced by the religious turmoil of the mid-century. The early Tudors are celebrated for the development of a glorious polyphonic repertoire, but this was cut short by the dissolution of the monasteries and then the death of King Henry VIII. Edward VI and his protectors had a more puritan view of the role of music in church, and sympathetic to Calvinistic sentiment, took a critical stance on elaborate polyphony. But after seven years Mary Tudor came to the throne and restored Roman Catholicism and the music that went with it. In 1554 Mary's marriage to Philip II saw the Spanish king bring with him a large retinue of musicians, the actual ceremony being at Winchester.

Four years later Mary died and Elizabeth came to the throne and remained there for forty-five years, finally establishing a distinctive non-Roman Catholic religion (she was excommunicated in 1570). During her lifetime music developed and expanded enormously and church music created an English-language working synthesis of the earlier styles in the hands of many musicians who had continued to serve the varied demands of the previous twenty years. Yet it was only in the Chapels Royal and Westminster Abbey that the much trumpeted Elizabethan golden age took place. Thus London saw both sides of these sensibilities: in most London churches congregational singing of metrical psalms replaced organ music and contrapuntal choral music, and large crowds gathered at Paul's cross and elsewhere for mass singing.

The Chapel Royal (which was a mobile organisation serving the sovereign, not primarily a building) operated during her reign and had considerable status. Musicians from it had a wide influence across Westminster, St Paul's and the City. While all singers at services were English (culled from institutions all over the country), many foreign musicians arrived in London throughout the century to satisfy the demand for top-line players at court.

In the early 1500s music in the city churches developed significantly with the growth of polyphony, though this was checked by the religious upheaval of the mid-century which resulted in a decline and the removal of many organs.

Essentially the dissolution of the monasteries changed the musical world, but during Henry VIII's lifetime his enthusiasm for music transcended this cataclysmic change. The eventual arrival of Elizabeth, herself an enthusiastic performer at the keyboard, saw a musical compromise that allowed the growth of centres of Puritan teaching. This sentiment came from the continent, and in London it had an impact on the style of church services and reduced the role of music, though requiring that which was sung to be given in English. London as a significant centre of Puritan feeling found its apogee a hundred years later in the Commonwealth.

The reign of Elizabeth (1558–1603) was a period of remarkable stability. In an age of religious ferment, despite having the trappings of what we might now regard as a police state, it saw an unprecedented flowering of the arts, notably the theatre and music. Music was supported by an active printing trade and was not only disseminated to a growing market of affluent music lovers, but because it was printed, it also survived to the present day more successfully than in previous generations.

We are told the queen was an avid dancer and would have required her musicians to provide the music. It may well be that the galliards that inspired the queen and her court were improvised, though in *My Ladye Nevell's Booke* we find William Byrd presenting a sequence of stylised galliards and pavans that probably only distantly reflects what was actually played for the dance. At the end of Elizabeth's reign various instrumental works have individual aristocrats' names associated with them, suggesting perhaps that they constituted a species of 'theme' music.

Outside the Court the developing musical infrastructure led to the growth of musicians' guilds, and the Company of Waits, who were the premier non-court musical body. They provided the music for civic ceremonial and, informally, played in the theatres of the day. Henry VIII had established the roles of instrumental consorts in Royal Music, and the shawms and sackbuts, recorders, viols and later violins appeared in court as groups, only coming together for lavish entertainments such as masques. Separate were functional musicians such as trumpeters and drummers.

The 'orchestra' grew during the century, starting with shawms, and successively adding viols, sackbuts, recorders, cornets and the latest fashionable instruments as they became available. In 1571 they were required to play from the turret of the Royal Exchange every Sunday, and on holiday evenings in the summer, in a striking precursor of what much later became public concerts. The interplay of popular ballads in the theatre and other music of the day can best now be heard in a modern period group such as The Musicians of Swanne Alley, who demonstrate the range and virtuosity of the 'broken consort' with voices in their recordings, featuring instruments such as lutes, viols, pandora, recorders, cittern and violin.

William Byrd was the predominant composer of his age, and, despite his Catholic sympathies, he had the protection of the queen. Born in 1539 or 1540 near Lombard Street, he was technically a cockney. Trained as a chorister, as a child at St Paul's, and probably in the Chapel Royal, he grew up with the religious unrest involved in the succession from Queen Mary to Queen Elizabeth. In Richard

Turbet's phrase 'all previous musical streams flowed into his music, and he had a massive influence as a teacher'. His pupils included John Bull, Thomas Morley and Peter Philips. The religious music written for the Chapel Royal and St Paul's had Byrd at its centre and he was the driving force in English music. Yet Byrd was and remained a Roman Catholic and his most celebrated polyphonic works were written for private performance by the great families who protected him.

In 1575 Byrd and Tallis were granted an exclusive licence to print not only music but also music manuscript paper, and in 1598 Thomas Morley, successively organist of St Giles, Cripplegate and St Paul's cathedral, received a twenty-one-year licence. Thus from shops near various City churches and legal establishments a wide variety of printed music, both imported and locally printed, could be purchased. Between 1587 and 1630 many collections of secular part songs appeared, totalling nearly two thousand individual pieces. The last twenty years of Elizabeth's reign constituted a golden age of composition, including many of the most celebrated names in British music, most of whom are featured in the collection of madrigals *The Triumphes of Oriana* that Morley issued in 1601.

The development of consort music for domestic use was also a significant movement late in the sixteen century, again developed in court circles, and in the music of Coprario, Alfonso Ferrabosco and Orlando Gibbons. The rise and fall of the madrigal, adding English words to Italian models, in just thirty years at the end of the century, created a body of work that is the most frequently remembered by a wide audience today.

During the latter part of the sixteenth century popular and increasingly sophisticated London theatre developed, and with it a requirement for music. We hear it in the songs in Shakespeare's plays. The Jigg, a popular dramatic form dating from the mid-sixteenth century, encompassed music, dancing and comedy and was widely seen, incorporating popular and traditional tunes and dances. At the end of the century and during the following years serious entertainments often ended with them, though Jiggs were frequently the feature of the more rowdy popular theatres, such as the Fortune.

The flowering of the lute song at the end of the century, in the music of John Dowland, Thomas Campion and others, produced a significant body of work still sung today. The musical culture of the late sixteenth century continued into the reign of James I. Round the Prince of Wales, Prince Henry, there developed an active musical circle, including the Italians Angelo Notari and Alfonso Ferrabosco, which was cut short by Prince Henry's premature death at the age of eighteen in 1612. (Prince Henry's Room at 17 Fleet Street, EC4, a timber framed house built in 1611, escaped the Fire of London and is open to the public.)

In addition to church music in English and the secular madrigal, there was keyboard and lute music, dance music and song. Songs and dance music for strings or ensemble were written for Court masques which date back into the reign of Elizabeth, but which saw their zenith in the 1630s. These were elaborately staged musical entertainments, in which royalty and the nobility usually participated, involving dance and complex scenery with music. From masques emerged traditions that would later evolve into the theatre and opera. In 1633 *The Triumph of Peace*, a masque by William Lawes and Simon East, was produced in the Banqueting House, Whitehall.

During the Commonwealth, music, at least public music, was much reduced. Church music was silenced, organs removed (though paradoxically Cromwell himself loved organ music), the theatres closed and with the Court in exile only cultured merchant and aristocratic families enjoyed the former repertoire, in private.

1660–1790

After the Restoration in 1660, music flowered as an apparent reaction to the austere regime that had preceded it. Samuel Pepys's diary makes clear that music played an active role in the lives of the educated classes, at least. The theatres reopened and Charles II brought with him from exile the example of the musical practices of the French court; London was open to the music of Europe. The rise of an aristocratic and a commercial musical theatre, with the development of the court masque and soon opera and the expansion of music in every walk of life, made London a magnet for continental musicians, notably after the reign of Queen Anne and throughout the eighteenth century and into the nineteenth. The untimely death of Purcell in 1695 may be taken as a convenient dividing line between one generation and the next. In fact, after the death of both Queen Mary and Purcell in 1695, the short reign of William and Mary was not a musical high point. It was Handel's arrival in London in 1710 that was symptomatic of a century when almost all the leading musicians of Europe came to London.

The growth of concerts in London was in advance of similar activities in Europe and originated both in tavern culture and the enthusiasm of connoisseurs, both bourgeois amateurs and aristocrats. These included private and public concerts and eventually became a feature of smart West End society. This was largely an audience for the latest music from the leading composers of Europe disseminated by the equally active music publishing trade.

As early as the Restoration, concerts were being given in taverns; Pepys noted one by John Bannister at the Mitre Tavern in Fleet Street, and by 1672 such events were being advertised in the newspapers. Thomas Britton, the 'musical small coals man' is best remembered for regular concerts in his attic in Clerkenwell. These ran from 1678 to 1714, and despite cramped and insalubrious premises attracted an audience of leading musical lights of the day, including aristocrats and musicians and, not least, towards the end, Handel.

After the establishment of Handel in London in 1713, the Italian opera became the focus of musical life for the aristocracy and Handel remained pre-eminent for

2 Westminster Abbey: the performers at the 1784 Handel Festival as shown in a contemporary print.

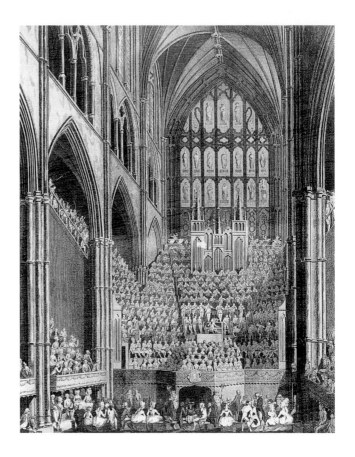

at least two decades, establishing what was a new art for London society audiences. However, there was also a more popular constituency that was created by the invention of the ballad opera by John Gay, and the enormous popularity of his *The Beggar's Opera*, first seen at Lincoln's Inn Fields on 29 January 1728.

The active concert life and the brilliant operatic seasons became more and more formalised and structured during the eighteenth century, while the development of pleasure gardens facilitated an ever broadening audience. The coronation of King George II in October 1727, in Westminster Abbey, was a magnificent musical event given a high profile for modern audiences in the reconstruction by the King's Consort, directed by Robert King, which has been widely performed throughout the UK and abroad, and at a spectacular Prom at the Royal Albert Hall in 2002, available to all on Hyperion CDs (CDA 67286). There would not be another coronation of such influential musical importance until the early twentieth century.

The oratorio tradition that dominated nineteenth-century British music developed after 1732 when the Bishop of London banned Handel from a proposed stage presentation of *Esther*; it was from this that Handel's Lenten oratorio series grew.

There was an oratorio season every year thereafter, which did not end with Handel's death. The Handel commemoration in Westminster Abbey in May 1784, featuring large forces and leading soloists, at a guinea a ticket (half price at dress rehearsals), attracted an enormous well-heeled following and was repeated over the following years, ending in 1791 on which occasion Haydn was in the audience and was enormously impressed, and was soon gestating *The Creation*.

In 1784, when the total performers numbered 513, the orchestra included 25 bassoons and 12 horns. In subsequent years the numbers grew and by 1788 the forces had grown to 712. The Handel festivals were emulated in various provincial festivals over the next thirty years, but it would be over sixty years before the tradition was renewed by the enormous Handel Festivals at Crystal Palace (from 1857) where thousands of singers took part.

By the late eighteenth century there was an active and regular pattern of concert-giving, various mechanisms being used either to restrict or expand the audience, including house concerts, subscription performances, benefit concerts, music societies and oratorio concerts. Halls used included The Pantheon, the Hanover Square Rooms, the Tottenham Street Rooms, the Freemason's Hall, Willis's Rooms and the King's Theatre, while oratorios were heard at Covent Garden, the Drury Lane Theatre and the King's Theatre. Music was also heard extensively at the pleasure gardens at Ranelagh and Vauxhall Gardens and elsewhere.

1790–1851

The rise and development of concerts continued through the years of the Napoleonic wars and after, with the enormous success of Haydn in the 1790s, and the establishment of the Concerts of Antient [Ancient] Music in 1776 and the [Royal] Philharmonic Society in 1813. Haydn's residence in London in 1791–2 and 1794–5, promoted by Salomon, signals the high point of eighteenth-century London music. In the nineteenth the appearances of Spohr, Mendelssohn and a host of touring virtuosi, including Paganini, Moscheles and the young Liszt, and the continuing activity at the Italian Opera provided a London focus for its ever-growing reputation as an active and burgeoning musical market where many artists and composers came hoping to make their fortune; Weber died in London in 1826 while seeking to earn a capital sum; Paganini unsuccessfully attempted to double ticket prices; Liszt came as a young prodigy; and Chopin made a largely unsuccessful appearance that passed almost unnoticed.

Musical London from the end of the Napoleonic Wars to the Great Exhibition in 1851 saw the successive appearances of the latest operas and the leading singers of the day, including works by Bellini, Donizetti and Verdi that quickly established iconic status which in many cases survives. 'English opera is more a drama with songs', wrote Weber as he prepared to compose *Oberon* in 1825, and a German visitor was appalled by the 'coarseness and brutality of the audiences'. English opera

3   Possibly the earliest programme notes, by John Ella for his Musical Union Concerts at the Princess's Rooms. This example is from 1 April 1845.

developed from the ballad operas and stage burlesques familiar from the late eighteenth century, and even Mozart's operas (as in *Figaro*, arranged by Bishop) appeared with the leading characters as speaking roles, the arias sung by other singers and with interpolated popular English songs. With the appearance of composers such as Balfe and Wallace who produced new scores on an annual basis from the 1830s onwards, English opera appeared to flourish. Other once successful British operas of the period, including those by Macfarren, have been forgotten.

The development of concerts where those attending did so anonymously came gradually. The Philharmonic Society, which promoted concerts for an audience limited by seat prices, tended to be focused on a musical public that included some of the leading figures of the day. The success of provincial choral festivals was only occasionally replicated in London, and in December 1840 *The Musical World* could lament that the development of choirs in the industrial north meant that 'hundreds of Lancashire weavers . . . can be found possessing a better knowledge of Handel's works than a majority of London professors'. By the 1850s London choral societies grew up in which amateurs sang the new music as well as the now established classics of Handel, Haydn and Beethoven. The Sacred Harmonic Society appeared in 1832 with a nonconformist religious sympathy, and sang regularly at the Exeter Hall in the Strand. Consisting of a wide spectrum of social classes and with admission at affordable prices it was a significant mechanism for the development of London audiences. It stimulated the development of amateur choral singing that was also facilitated by the sol-fa movement. At the Handel Festival in 1859 the Sacred Harmonic Choir fielded over 2,750 singers. The establishment of Novello as a source of cheap music, particularly of vocal scores (*Messiah* was sold in sixpenny weekly parts in the 1840s), indicates the potential popular demand.

Concert series began to be established, competition to the Philharmonic being provided by the New Philharmonic Society, while music by British composers was featured by the Society of British Musicians founded in 1834. Chamber music and the etiquette concerning its presentation came particularly as a consequence of the activities of John Ella and his Musical Union, which was launched in 1845. (Incidentally, Ella's last house at 9 Victoria Square, off Buckingham Palace Road, is a remarkable survival in an unspoilt corner, though without a plaque.)

The marriage of Queen Victoria brought Prince Albert as a youthful and energetic performing musician and composer to the centre of court life and over the next twenty years he gave court status to a wide variety of musical initiatives.

The increasing consumption of popular music fuelled the London publishing industry, and as early as September 1840, *The Musical World* could write 'the world is mad for waltzes and quadrilles' and these not only appeared at balls and dances but as the backbone of Promenade concerts that became the entrée to selling a wide audience a more serious repertoire. To quote *The Musical World* again 'Take the late Concerts d'Ete, for example; there was a great deal of Strauss and Musard it is true . . . but there was [the] *Pastorale* . . . the C minor, and the *Eroica*, of Beethoven . . .'

1851–1900

From 1850 the modern concert finally evolved in most of its familiar elements, and the demand for musicians grew very significantly. The dissemination of music was aided by the widespread and growing ownership of upright pianos and increasingly affordable sheet music and vocal scores. Developments in engraving music, particularly in Germany, made possible the printing of the most complex modern scores.

During the 1850s two concert halls were established that would dominate London music for the next half century: the Crystal Palace at Sydenham held concerts from 1855, and the St James's Hall in Piccadilly opened in 1858. Otherwise for choral music there was the Exeter Hall and St Martin's Hall, and, until 1874, for concerts the Hanover Square Rooms. There were also London theatres including

4 Covent Garden: the interior view of the theatre before the fire of 1856 destroyed it.

5   A precursor of the Proms. Programme for a Riviere's Promenade Concert at Covent Garden 27 September 1873.

Covent Garden, which although burned down in 1856 was soon rebuilt. Concert series heard during this time included the continuing Philharmonic Society; the Society of British Musicians' concerts between 1834 and 1865; the newly established Crystal Palace Saturday Concerts; and the concerts of the New Philharmonic Society set up in competition with the Philharmonic in 1852. The inauguration of the enormous Crystal Palace organ gave impetus to the popularity of organ recitals which, by including transcriptions, were often a substitute for orchestral concerts. Later came a much smaller organ installed in the Concert Room inside the Crystal Palace. This was built by J. W. Walker (whose workshops were at 27 Francis Street, Tottenham Court Road) and inaugurated on 14 March 1868. In 1870 the opening of the Royal Albert Hall with its huge organ gave added impetus to this public enthusiasm.

Taking the season of 1855 as an example, immediately before Crystal Palace or St James's Hall became significant venues, London musical life was focused on the opera season at the Royal Italian Opera, Covent Garden, which in that year opened on 12 April and closed on 9 August. The repertoire was one we would readily recognise today, including *Le Comte Ory*, *Fidelio*, *Il Trovatore*, *Ernani*, *I Puritani*, *Norma*, *The Barber of Seville* and three operas by Meyerbeer. There were seven major series of concerts, the pre-eminent one being the Philharmonic Society's, of which in 1855 Wagner was the visiting conductor. In strong competition was the recently formed New Philharmonic Society, while other series included those at the Royal Academy of Music, the Amateur Musical Society, Mr Hullah's Concerts at St Martin's Hall, Alfred Mellon's Concerts and Jullien's popular Promenade Concerts at Covent Garden. These tended to feature the lighter end of the repertoire disseminated by Jullien's music publishing interests through his shop in Regent Street.

By this time there was also a significant stream of choral concerts with amateur choristers, including the Sacred Harmonic Society, the Harmonic Union and Salomon's Amateur Choral Society. At Exeter Hall there was a celebrated annual performance of *Messiah* with big-name soloists, conducted by Michael Costa, while the Bach Society, already known for pioneering the modern acceptance of Bach's 'Passions-Musik', was rehearsing the Mass in B minor. The Royal Society of Musicians under the batons of Sterndale Bennett and Cipriani Potter promoted its 170th anniversary festival at the Freemason's Tavern. Choral singing was socially inclusive and brought music to a wide variety of participants and during the late nineteenth century was a significant aspect of the temperance movement.

Chamber music concerts that had been pioneered by Ella's Musical Union (which continued for an exclusive audience) developed in Ella's Musical Winter Evenings, the Society of British Musicians' concerts, William Sterndale Bennett's

Classical Pianoforte Soirées, Mr Dando's Quartet Concerts and soirées by Hallé, Goffrie and Cooper. The Monday Popular Concerts at St James's Hall presented chamber music at affordable prices to a wide audience between 1859 and 1876, when many of the leading players of the day, including the young Joachim appeared. Subsequently the Saturday Popular Concerts that ran from 1865 to 1904 continued this tradition.

Opera in London for much of the nineteenth century was dominated by the Italian opera, which meant that in 1843 Wagner's *Der fliegende Holländer* received its first British stage performance at Drury Lane sung in Italian as *L'Olandese Dannato*. Opera was driven by the competition between Covent Garden and Drury Lane sung in Italian under letters patent, though as the nineteenth century passed other theatres sprang up in competition, notably the English Opera House at the Lyceum. The monopoly was abolished by the Theatre Regulation Act of 1843.

Opera continued at Covent Garden and the King's Theatre, later known as Her Majesty's, advantage passing from one to the other, conspicuously when theatres were destroyed by fire. The champions of Italian opera were obsessional in their devotion, destroying Berlioz's *Benvenuto Cellini* on its first night in 1853 by heckling and booing. There were also foreign touring operas, and later in the century English touring companies such as Carl Rosa and Moody-Manners presented opera in English as well as commissioning a constant flow of new British operas. Earlier this tradition had been launched by the Pyne-Harrison administration at Covent Garden which flourished from 1858 to 1864. Success was focused on big-name singers and the public enthusiasm to hear, for example, Jenny Lind in the late 1840s was still in evidence sixty years later when the objects of their affection were Tetrazzini and Melba.

6   Paderewski at St James's Hall; front cover of *The Graphic*, 17 December 1892.

All these musical activities were constantly widening the audience, a process that continued throughout the nineteenth century and was greatly developed by the introduction of the Queen's Hall Promenade Concerts from 1895. This was also the time of the introduction to London audiences of many of the works by Tchaikovsky, Brahms, Dvořák, Saint-Saëns, Wagner, Max Bruch and others, which soon assumed iconic status as the classics of the repertoire. In 1895 August Manns held a plebiscite concert at Crystal Palace in which the audience voted for their favourite works, and it is remarkable how similar the chosen list was to what might have been produced by a similar exercise today, the principal requested works in the programme consisting of Beethoven's *Pastoral* Symphony, Mendelssohn's Violin Concerto, Liszt's *Hungarian Fantasia* and Wagner's *Tannhäuser* Overture. Russian music became increasingly popular in the 1890s, with the widespread acceptance of

Tchaikovsky, Rubinstein (his Fourth Piano Concerto had appeared at Crystal Palace as early as 1872) and the early performances of Rimsky-Korsakov in London (the first performance of *Scheherazade* was in 1895). The late 1890s were dominated by Wagner, the 1898 cycles of *The Ring* attracting huge interest, while performance of orchestral excerpts were widespread, extracts from *Parsifal* being heard among others at the Church of the Annunciation, Marble Arch and St Margaret's Westminster. The emergence of a generation of virtuoso conductors was heralded by Hans Richter and the young Henry Wood, who were soon joined on the London concert platform by Mottl, Strauss, Weingartner, Nikisch and English conductors including Landon Ronald and Thomas Beecham. In the late nineteenth century London suburban amateur choral and orchestral societies proliferated, nearly fifty being listed in 1898, and more in the period to the First World War.

1900–1914

In the fifteen years or so before the outbreak of the First World War, London become a frenetic market for music, with an enormous increase in the numbers of concerts of all sorts. With the demise of concerts at Crystal Palace and the demolition of the St James's and Exeter Halls, concert-giving focused on the newly opened Queen's Hall, and for smaller concerts the Bechstein Hall (later Wigmore Hall) in Wigmore Street. The orbit of concert-giving had therefore moved north in London, and would now be very close to the showrooms of most music publishers and piano retailers, indeed many smaller halls were actually run by piano manufacturers to demonstrate their own instruments. Thus the Bechstein, Steinway and Erard halls all envisaged pianists largely at the centre of their business, while even in Queen's Hall, the lease-holder, Chappell, a piano manufacturer, ensured that a Chappell piano appeared there in advertisements.

All the leading musicians of the day came to London, and in addition to those documented in detail in Part II three legendary pianists deserve mention: Paderewski, Rachmaninov and Skryabin. Paderewski first appeared in 1890 and was lionised from the start, public support and takings at his concerts reaching unprecedented levels. He was one of only two foreign musicians to receive a British knighthood (much later the other would be Georg Solti) from King George v in 1925. Rachmaninov first came as a composer in 1899, when his tone poem *The Crag (The Rock)*, was given at a Philharmonic Society concert. The Society was assiduous in asking him back, subsequently as a pianist, and in 1911 he presented his then new Third Piano Concerto. Rachmaninov always had an enormous public following, though the critics could be dimissive of his music. In 1932 he received the Gold Medal of the Royal Philharmonic Society and his last visit to London was on the occasion of Sir Henry Wood's Jubilee Concert at the Royal Albert Hall on 5 October 1938 when he played his own Second Piano Concerto. Skryabin had a much shorter acquaintance with the London public,

for his music was first played in 1913 and he was dead in 1915, but in February 1914 he appeared in his own *Prometheus (Poem of Fire)* and his Chopinesque Piano Concerto and played two recitals of his solo piano music.

It is also worth considering the practical difficulties that faced audiences living increasingly away from the centre, of attending some concert venues in the days of horse buses and winter fogs. This was before the opening of tube stations at Oxford Circus (1900) and Piccadilly Circus (1907), and the introduction of the Central line through Oxford Circus in 1906, yet during its pre-eminence the Crystal Palace had its own railway station and arranged special fares for its audiences.

In the early years of the twentieth century many talented British performers appeared who would dominate the next half-century. These included the pianists Mark Hambourg, Myra Hess, Irene Scharrer, York Bowen, Moiseiwitsch and Solomon, the latter both appearing in their teens. This was a time when a succession of young prodigies found a large following in London owing to their youth. Visitors included the violinists Mischa Elman, Joska (later Joseph) Szigeti, Florizel von Reuter, Franz von Vecsey and Jan Kubelík, not all of whom managed to continue their sailor-suited early teen celebrity into mature careers. Young British string-players included the sisters May and Beatrice Harrison on violin and cello, and Lionel Tertis who, based at the Royal Academy of Music, single-handedly would transform the status of the viola as a solo instrument. Very much a London musician was the self-taught violinist Albert Sammons; discovered by Beecham at the Waldorf Hotel he found fame overnight in Beecham's orchestra.

There was also an unprecedented development in musical styles in this period. Strauss, who had been first heard in the 1890s, visited London repeatedly to con-

7 *Punch* notes the competition between the leading operatic sopranos of the day as expressed in their recordings.

8 A child prodigy arrives by hansom cab to play: Mischa Elman and his impresario Herr Direktor Grosz. His sensational London debut was on 21 March 1905 when he was just fourteen, the sailor suit emphasising his youth.

duct his works and his operas *Salome* and *Elektra* created their own scandals. Elgar, finding his maturity, produced almost all his most celebrated works in London and was knighted. Two coronation ceremonies, in 1902 and 1911, introduced a new repertoire of British ceremonial music. British composers who would dominate the early twentieth century began to emerge, notably Delius, Vaughan Williams and Holst, while the Patron's Fund at the Royal College of Music enabled a wide conspectus of student composers' music to be performed in leading London halls.

Debussy and Ravel began to be heard in London, and between 1911 and 1914 the visiting Ballets Russes introduced a new repertoire and dazzled a generation with its brilliant colours in both settings and music. New composers as varied as Sibelius, Mahler, Skryabin and Schoenberg were heard, often under the baton of Henry Wood, while all the leading conductors of the age appeared at Queen's Hall. The opera, too, enjoyed a glittering and unprecedented success, with Beecham first appearing at Covent Garden in 1910 with two seasons, funded by his father, Joseph Beecham. They included new operas such as Delius's *A Village Romeo and Juliet* and Ethel Smyth's *The Wreckers*, as well as Strauss's *Elektra* and mainstream repertoire. In a summer season at His Majesty's Beecham included a pioneering Mozart Festival, scores such as *Cosí fan Tutte* then being little-known. These riches continued over the remaining seasons before the war, and attracted substantial audiences. This activity came to a climax in the summer of 1914, which, in retrospect, Arnold Bax described as 'that sinister carnival time'.

1914–1945

The outbreak of war in August 1914 resulted in a temporary cessation of musical life, but one which was speedily restored, though quickly exhibiting the anti-German sentiment that would characterise the war. Thus artists with German names, musical institutions organised by those of German extraction, and the new German music, were all targeted by over-zealous patriots. But it is notable how quickly the accepted masterpieces of the German repertoire, including Beethoven and Brahms, returned to the concert hall. However, the break in the former integration of musical life between Germany and England was permanent.

The period after the First World War was a time of sudden change. It was dominated by the loss of a huge number of musical jobs with the advent of the talkies in 1927, by the rise of electrical recording after 1925, by the decline of the pianola after 1929, and by broadcasting, which started nationally in 1922 and by the 1930s was the principal musical employer in the UK. It soon became the mechanism by which performance standards and repertoire across the country were raised and standardised. It also became an unprecedented medium for presenting new music. The BBC's concerts at Queen's Hall and elsewhere became the most important strand of the development of new music in the UK. Queen's Hall saw all the leading conductors of the day and most of the composers.

Remarkably, the interwar period saw the first performances of a significant repertoire of new music by British composers, many of them given at Queen's Hall, and these within a few years constituted the iconic British repertoire by composers such as Vaughan Williams, Holst, Bax, Bliss, Walton and Moeran, though many would not be finally established until recorded during the last third of the twentieth century.

The rise of British ballet in the 1930s, building on the enthusiasm for the Diaghilev Ballet in the 1920s, was crowned by the establishment of the Sadler's Wells Ballet. Constant Lambert was a prime mover in this, as a conductor and composer. The music specially written for ballets included some of the most characteristic of the period, including Lambert's *Horoscope* (1938), Vaughan Williams's *Job* (1931), Gavin Gordon's *The Rake's Progress* (1935) and Arthur Bliss's *Checkmate* (1937).

The Second World War was another divide, but after a brief hiatus at the outbreak of war a significant audience for music grew, not only as a consequence of BBC broadcasting, but of the cinema. The popularity of Rachmaninov-style piano concertos followed the success of the films *Brief Encounter* (Rachmaninov's Second) and *Dangerous Moonlight* (Addinsell's *Warsaw Concerto*). The lunchtime National Gallery Concerts that ran throughout the war providing chamber and instrumental music at a low, fixed price, and touring companies, notably the Sadler's Wells Ballet, which outside London brought the arts to local halls at a time of austerity, attracted a growing audience. The Promenade Concerts, although the 1939 season was truncated, also continued throughout the war, first at Queen's Hall and after it was destroyed by bombing, at the Royal Albert Hall.

During the war the British Council began a programme of subsidising recordings of the new British music on the HMV label and there were discs of Bax's Third Symphony, Moeran's Symphony in G minor, Walton's *Belshazzar's Feast* and Elgar's *The Dream of Gerontius*, among others. This was a time when once again the latest German music was unheard, and the infrastructure of the new music that would achieve wider significance after the war was developed. This was focused on London's Morley College, which was badly bombed early on. Even so, through the direction of Michael Tippett, and the interest of Britten and Pears (back from the USA in 1942), it became the focus of the revival of an earlier repertoire by Monteverdi, Purcell and the English Madrigal School, this given added character by the discovery of the counter-tenor voice of Alfred Deller, who became widely known as one of their key performers.

1945–2003

The London musical world after 1945 was different in kind from previous generations owing to the state funding of the arts, and the enormous development of extramural teaching. Practically, the post-war period of London musical life is chiefly characterised by the existence of five permanent orchestras (London Symphony Orchestra, London Philharmonic, Philharmonia, Royal Philharmonic and the BBC Symphony Orchestra). There were also other permanent orchestras, notably the Royal Opera House Covent Garden Orchestra and the BBC Concert Orchestra. In addition there emerged various ad hoc orchestras such as the City of London Sinfonia, the Academy of St Martin-in-the-Fields, the London Festival Orchestra and the London Mozart Players; there were also specialist groups such as The Fires of London and the London Sinfonietta formed to play avant garde music. The Fires were founded as The Perriot Players by Harrison Birtwistle and Peter Maxwell Davies, but changed to their later name when Maxwell Davies took control. Later came the establishment of various period instrument ensembles, starting with the London Classical Players founded by Roger Norrington, who eventually extended the concept of period performance into the nineteenth century. That orchestra was disbanded in 1997 and succeeded by the Orchestra of the Age of Enlightenment. Exploring a pre-Classical repertoire, David Munrow was the most successful in establishing a significant following for his concerts and recordings with the Early Music Consort of London, and after his untimely death in 1976 he was followed by a growing number of early music groups of ever greater virtuosity. They found an active following from London audiences and London record companies, particularly Hyperion.

Over the fifty years after the coronation in 1953 London became, de facto, one of the freelance musical capitals of the world, where a remarkable number of fine players could be available for recording sessions. Possibly the first celebrated example of this came with Sir Charles Mackerras's recording of an authentic version of Handel's *Music for the Royal Fireworks* which drew on every top-line wind-player in London and as a consequence was made at night. A freelance orchestra of front-desk players would appear for recording from time to time under the name the National Philharmonic, organised and led by the violinist Sydney Sax. Conductors who used them included Bernard Herrmann, Leopold Stokowski and the film composer Miklós Rósza. This concentration of top-line performers stimulated the conservatoires to produce a new generation of highly trained players and singers and also made possible an enormous expansion of the recorded repertoire, largely by smaller specialist record labels, as artists diversified to promote their careers, and companies looked for ever more unfamiliar potential successes.

Opera and ballet were also active immediately after the war, and Sadler's Wells' premiere production of *Peter Grimes* within weeks of the end of the war in Europe has become a legendary occasion. At Covent Garden, which had been a dance hall during the war, opera and ballet were again seen. Karl Rankl was appointed musical director at Covent Garden with a remit to rebuild the old international seasons while the Sadler's Wells Ballet under the inspiring direction of Constant Lambert appeared at Covent Garden with *The Fairy Queen*, said to be one of the most adventurous and lavish productions ever attempted there. It was followed by a repertoire in which new ballets with new music by British composers were a high point. London has had two continuously active opera companies since 1945 – the Royal

9   The London 'Fringe' (here at the Queen Elizabeth Hall): the British premiere of Siegfried Wagner's opera *Der Friedensengel* given by Pro Opera. Conductor Leslie Head leads the bows with (left to right) Valerie Hill, Hanne-Lore Kuhse, Raffaele Polani, Martha Mödl, Vivienne Bellos, Valerie Morgan, Raimund Herincx, Raymond Whitely, Christopher Adams, David Bacon and Alan Judd.

Opera House, Covent Garden (sharing the platform with the Royal Ballet), and Sadler's Wells Opera (later English National Opera at the Coliseum).

During this time there was also an unprecedented expansion of the London musical fringe, again exhibiting an ever-rising general technical competence, as semi-professional opera companies and orchestras became more and more numerous, stimulated in the 1960s by Jennie Lee when Minister of the Arts, as a consequence of her policies on funding evening classes. However it faded in the last decade of the century as conditions caused by adverse government policies in the 1990s and the rise of inflation made such initiatives less and less viable. These companies generally concentrated on revivals, and in the 1970s and early 1980s many of their productions were broadcast on BBC Radio London. Before the growth of provincial opera companies in the UK, fringe companies in London became one of the routes through which future stars could obtain the necessary stage experience to launch their subsequent careers. Probably the most notable example was the conductor Sir Colin Davis, professional clarinettist and a charismatic young conductor of the Chelsea Opera Group in the late 1950s until he was propelled to overnight stardom when he substituted for Beecham at short notice. As well as the Chelsea Opera Group, such opera companies included the John Lewis Partnership Opera Company, University College Opera Company, Opera Viva, Fulham Municipal Opera and the productions of all the London colleges of music.

The growth of recording, the appearance of LPs in 1950, followed by stereo around ten years later and the introduction of compact discs in 1983, all stimulated recording and enabled the rise of the independent record labels. As the major companies dispersed their in-house recording teams, London became a centre where world class technical staff and equipment were available for freelance dates with a succession of employers. However, the orchestras were heavily unionised, the soloists, conductors and recording professionals were not. Eventually the orchestras succumbed to the competition from East European orchestras in the 1990s and record companies were less and less willing to pay the full union rate for recordings in London. Financial packages adopted to keep work in London included 'shared session' deals with BBC orchestras and orchestras starting their own labels of live recordings of their performances. The London Symphony Orchestra was notably successful in this with their prize-winning budget price recordings largely conducted by Sir Colin Davis.

After the war London's principal concert hall, Queen's Hall, was a bombsite and it took ten years before the final decision not to rebuild. At first the Royal Albert Hall provided an unsatisfactory alternative, supplemented by concerts given at Central Hall Westminster and in various cinemas and theatres. During the late 1940s the Royal Festival Hall, then a startlingly modern shape, had been built on the South Bank as part of the Festival of Britain and opened in 1951. It was the only building from that event to survive the Conservative government that came to power immediately after the Festival. Later various churches that had been damaged during the war were rebuilt. St John's Smith Square was deconsecrated and used as a concert hall, allowing a range of concerts that demanded smaller and less analytical acoustic to take place. Other deconsecrated churches were refurbished for musical use, including St Luke's, Old Street, now the home of the London Symphony Orchestra; Trinity Church, Borough, now the Henry Wood Hall as a recording studio and rehearsal hall; Cadogan Hall, Sloane Terrace, now the home of the Royal Philharmonic Orchestra; St Mark's, Silvertown, now the Brick Lane Music Hall; and St Augustine's Haggerston Park, E2, now 291 Gallery.

With the building of the Barbican complex in the City of London, the Barbican Centre with its associated concert hall was established from the outset as the permanent residence of the London Symphony Orchestra. From then on competition for concert audiences became intense with the Barbican, the Festival Hall and its smaller halls, the Queen Elizabeth Hall and Purcell Room, St John's Smith Square, and other venues in churches and local halls, all offering concerts on most nights.

The music lover is more generously provided for in London than in any other city in the world. At the beginning of a new century, with the contraction of the recording industry and the loss of traditional music teaching and singing in schools, with a basically musically philistine wider public (and government), its long-term viability has many question marks. We hope to have revealed something of its fascination and magic. Enjoy it while you can.

Part I

1 • Theatres, Concert Halls and Watering Places

The sheer size of London has resulted in a multiplicity of arts activities developing in different areas of the capital at different times. Even in the eighteenth century visitors remarked on the size of the city, the frenetic bustle of the streets and the scale of musical activity. At the present time concert life is focused on many centres. On the South Bank, the Arts complex at Waterloo (encompassing the Royal Festival Hall, the Queen Elizabeth Hall and the Purcell Room) is engaged in replanning the facilities, which will probably see the Festival Hall closed for refurbishment when this book first appears in 2005. Musical performance is also centred on the Barbican Centre in the City of London, at Wigmore Hall behind Oxford Street, at a variety of churches and former churches, notably St John's Smith Square, and at the Royal Albert Hall at South Kensington and the adjacent Royal College of Music and the other conservatoires, not to mention the BBC. Opera may be seen not only at Covent Garden and the Coliseum but at the conservatoires and in fringe productions. A host of amateur entrepreneurs present choral society and orchestral concerts and stage productions across the capital.

Over the centuries the centre of concert life has tended to move across the city as new concert halls and theatres have been built and have superseded their predecessors. Thus, at the end of the eighteenth century, the Hanover Square Rooms just south of Oxford Street together with the Pantheon in Oxford Street provided this focus for concerts. With the building of Regent Street completed in 1820, this moved to the Argyll Rooms in two successive concert spaces on the same site near to the present-day Oxford Circus. The activity returned to Hanover Square before the opening of the much larger St James's Hall near the present-day Piccadilly Circus signalled a new centre for concert life that would dominate the second half of the nineteenth century.

Musical activity moved north of Oxford Street with the opening of the larger Queen's Hall in 1893 at Langham Place and the nearby Wigmore Hall in 1901. (Earlier the Beethoven Rooms in Harley Street had also been a concert-givers' option in the mid-nineteenth century.) The destruction of the Queen's Hall in the Blitz changed the face of London concert life, making the Royal Albert Hall the temporary centre before the opening of the Royal Festival Hall on the South Bank

10 (facing page)   London music in summer: the queue for the arena promenade at the Proms (August 2004).

in 1951, and subsequently a variety of other halls, churches and deconsecrated churches and the Barbican complex in the City.

A number of less prestigious halls deserve passing mention, and those active in 1900 included the Princess's Concert Room, which was situated at the rear of the Princess's Theatre at 150 Oxford Street, to the east of Oxford Circus, which had been rebuilt in 1880; the International Hall, above the Café Monico at 19 Shaftesbury Avenue; and the Salle Erard at 18 Great Marlborough Street. The pianist Francesco Berger makes reference to the London Tavern, where in the 1840s he made his debut. Later, the Royal Horticultural Halls (which are still *in situ*) off Vincent Square, Westminster, appear as the occasional location of choral concerts.

Though not extensively discussed below, it should also be remembered that up to the Second World War, and particularly before the First, many concerts were given in the various mansions in the West End owned by the musical aristocracy. That useful musical chronicler Francesco Berger particularly remembered in the nineteenth century 'the Dowager Marchioness of Downshire in Belgrave Square, Lord Dudley in Park Lane, and the Duke of Westminster in Grosvenor Street. Somewhat later this number was increased by Mrs Freake in Cromwell Road and Mrs Lewis in Campden Hill'.

We might add that notable twentieth-century patrons included Lord Howard de Walden (who as T. E. Ellis funded Holbrooke to set his own libretti), Mrs Samuel Courtauld at 20 Portman Square and Walton's later companion Alice, Lady Wimborne who presented the new music at Wimborne House, Arlington Street. Other rich patrons presented concerts in West End hotels – for example in 1924, Arnold Bax's Oboe Quintet was first heard at one of the regular chamber concerts given by Mrs Adèla Maddison (Fauré's mistress) at the Hyde Park Hotel.

*   *   *

Halls are listed by district (West End; Westminster; Covent Garden and Holborn, City and East End; Kensington and Chelsea; and Vauxhall and South Bank) and then alphabetically.

West End

Æolian Hall
135/7 New Bond Street, the rear of the premises on Bowdon Street
Tube: Bond Street

The Æolian Hall was opened in 1903 by the American Orchestrelle Company. It had originally been the Grosvenor Gallery, built in 1876, an art gallery that was used for concerts until forced to close by legal action. Other art galleries also acted as substantial concert halls in the late nineteenth century, the Piccadilly Art Galleries being depicted by the *Illustrated London News* when royalty attended. In 1903 the Æolian Hall was reopened by the Æolian Company as a concert-hall and showroom for instruments, notably pianos and pianolas, which were an Æolian speciality, and until the late 1920s were for many the preferred reproducing medium for music in the home. The history, repertoire and story of the sudden demise of the pianola or player piano has yet to be adequately told. The main concert hall was on the first floor with a balcony, and with organ pipes to the rear of the platform. The stage and organ pipes were decorated in black and gold, with a glazed arched roof. The hall measured 78 by 35 feet, seated 400 to 500 and was a favoured place for chamber concerts and recitals. These might sometimes be for a larger ensemble, the Oriana Madrigal Society giving concerts there in the 1920s and Schoenberg's *Kammersymphonie*, Op. 9, for fifteen solo instruments having its first British performance in May 1921. On the second floor there was a smaller concert hall measuring 23 by 50 feet. On 27 February 1909 Debussy was there as the guest of the Music Club, where a programme of his music was played and Arnold Bax was the accompanist in a selection of the composer's songs. Bax remembered Debussy's 'thick-set clumsy figure, the huge greenish, almost Moorish face beneath the dense thicket of black hair'. These were not the only Debussy premieres in London: various piano pieces and songs were first heard between 1906 and 1913, when the second book of *Préludes* was played complete by Walter Morse Rummel.

11　The surviving façade of the Æolian Hall in Bond Street.

Later, during the First World War, the latest music by the allies would feature in programmes, including the first English performances of Debussy's Cello Sonata and Sonata for flute, viola and harp in 1916 and 1917 respectively. New music also heard during the war included Ravel's *Deux Mélodies Hébraïques* and, in 1915, his Piano Trio. The first public performance of *Façade* was given here on 12 June 1923. A regular location for chamber concerts up to the Second World War, the Æolian Hall saw no less than twenty-eight premieres of chamber music and songs by Arnold Bax, the last, of two fanfares for the BBC programme *Show Business* recorded there by Billy Ternent and his orchestra in April 1950, by which time the hall had become a BBC studio. Here many British chamber works of the time had their premieres, from Stanford's *Serenade* (for nonet) in January 1906 and his song cycle *Cushendall* in June 1910, to his pupil Vaughan Williams's early Piano Quintet in December 1905, and a wonderful concert on 15 November 1909 when his First String Quartet and *On Wenlock Edge* were both first heard in the same concert. After the war Elgar's Violin Sonata was given in public for the first time in March 1919. Other notable premieres include the first London performance of Fauré's Piano Quintet No. 1 in March 1907 and Bartók playing in his own Violin Sonata on 22 March 1922. The hall was taken over by the BBC, and in 1943 they had it refitted as offices and studios. The original façade remains, as does the glazed arched roof internally, but it has been renamed

Renoir House. Now it is the home of Sotheby's London Collectors division, with access from the former side door.

The Alhambra
Leicester Square
Tube: Leicester Square

The Alhambra first opened in 1854 as the Royal Panopticon of Science and Art, when it was used for lectures and musical performances. Its site is now the location of the Odeon Cinema. As its later name implies, it was extravagantly Moorish in design. The organ of the Royal Panopticon was built by Hill & Son in 1853 and had three consoles so that three organists could play. The organ was later bought by St Paul's cathedral, where it was in use from about 1860 to 1873. The building was converted into a music hall in 1860 and was the first music hall to be registered as a limited company. The Alhambra was destroyed by fire on 7 December 1882, rebuilt, and reopened on 3 December 1883. It was home to actors, singers, musicians and acrobats – and also a notorious haunt of prostitutes, being on the boundary of Soho. The Alhambra was known in the 1860s for ballet and dancing. Its presentation of the can-can was responsible for it losing its licence in the 1870s, when there were objections to one of the dancers raising her foot higher than her head when facing the public, and being enthusiastically applauded. The first performance of Sullivan's setting of Kipling's song 'The Absent-Minded Beggar' was sung there in November 1899 by John Coates.

It was a popular rendezvous for soldiers on leave from the trenches in the First World War, hosting what was reputedly the most popular show of the war, *The Bing Boys are Here*, with its hit song 'If You were the only Girl in the World' sung by George Robey. Robey reigned for years as the Alhambra's star artist.

The Alhambra made a feature of spectacular Christmas pantomimes, traditional in treatment and lavish in production. It was owned by Sir Oswald Stoll, who wanted to improve the quality of acts there. When the Diaghilev Ballet returned to London, after appearing at the Coliseum for its first season, Stoll put it in the Alhambra for the April to July 1919 season, with two new ballets *La Boutique Fantasque* (music by Rossini arranged by Respighi) and *The Three Cornered Hat* (music by de Falla), as well as revivals of most of the celebrated pre-war Diaghilev ballets. Stoll was Chairman and Managing Director of both the Coliseum and the Alhambra, and of the four directors of each company three were common to both, so that the placing of shows was very much guided by commercial considerations. The Alhambra had half the audience capacity of the Coliseum, presumably the reason for Stoll placing Diaghilev at the latter for four of his thirteen London postwar seasons. The Ballets Russes appeared at several London theatres, and they returned to the Alhambra on 2 November 1921 for a three-month season featuring Diaghilev's most celebrated ballet, *The Sleeping Princess*, the Alhambra's Christmas spectacular that season.

12   The Alhambra as shown on an Edwardian postcard. This example is postmarked 29 July 1908.

However, the big audiences preferred variety acts. In the 1930s, after the death of Diaghilev, the Ballets Russes appeared several times; but during the Depression, and with the advent of radio, variety became less popular and the Alhambra closed for economic reasons; it was demolished in 1936, the Odeon Cinema opening on the site on 2 November 1937.

No representation of the Alhambra has been found in a feature film. British Pathé list a three-minute clip (tape PM 1170) from 1929 said to be of Mavis Chaney and Edward Fox dancing on its stage.

Almack's Assembly Rooms, later called Willis's Rooms
28 King Street, St James's
Tube: Green Park

The suite of rooms at first called Almack's Rooms was designed by Robert Mylne in 1765, the building surviving until it was bombed in 1940 and 1944, the site now being occupied by an office block that commemorates its origin as Almack House. It was first opened by William Almack, formerly major domo to the Duke of Hamilton. The guest list was controlled by seven society ladies and there was a rigid dress code. The accommodation was spacious, focused on a ballroom 100 by 40 feet in size, decorated with columns and mirrors. Adjoining rooms were used for dining. When Almack died in 1781 the rooms became the property of his niece, Mrs Willis, and became known as Willis's Rooms. Here the Bach–Abel Concerts took place from 1768 to 1773, and later the Vocal Concerts that continued to 1821, the 1792 series launched by the singer Samuel Harrison. Concerts continued during the

13   Almack's (later Willis's) Rooms: the opening of the 1843 season.

nineteenth century with subscription concerts and benefits, chamber concerts and piano recitals with artists such as Ernst Pauer, Charles Hallé and Sterndale Bennett from 1852 to 1855. The rooms ceased being a focus for music in the 1890s, part becoming a restaurant and part auction rooms. Bombed during the Second World War, the building, opposite Christie's, was not demolished until 1949.

Argyll Rooms
Regent Street at Little Argyll Street
Tube: Oxford Circus

There were two Argyll Rooms in succession. The original building was opened in 1806 and pulled down in 1819 to make way for Regent Street and a new concert hall for the Royal Harmonic Institution built by John Nash at the corner of Regent Street and Little Argyll Street. It had a domed roof and seated 800.

The Philharmonic Society gave its inaugural concert in the original premises on 8 March 1813. During its heyday it saw performances by Liszt, Mendelssohn and Weber, and was a notable source for the purchase of printed music. A fire in 1830 destroyed the building. The site is marked by the domed building next to 246 Regent Street in Little Argyll Street, now the Natwest Bank.

14   Thomas Shepherd's view of the Argyll Rooms – the Harmonic Institution – in 1828, two years before it was destroyed by fire.

Bechstein Hall
see Wigmore Hall

Café Royal
68 Regent Street
Tube: Piccadilly Circus

Now 'The Café Royal by Le Méridien', the Café Royal was founded in 1865 and became synonymous with a fine wine cellar. As a French-style restaurant in the 1890s it attracted many of the most celebrated artists of the day – visitors to the Domino Room including the painters Whistler and Augustus John, the writers Oscar Wilde, Bernard Shaw, and Frank Harris, and the music hall singer Marie Lloyd. *London of Today* commented in 1897: 'Daily at mid-day and the dinner-hour, you will find no inconsiderable proportion of the better class of foreigners – French, Italian, and others commingling'. 'If you want to see English people at their most English', remarked Sir Herbert Beerbohm Tree, 'go to The Café Royal where they are trying their hardest to be French'.

Rebuilt in 1923–4 it maintained its former celebrity, musical patrons including Peter Warlock; but although after the Second World War many of the literati were seen no more, it became the haunt of a new group of younger Bohemians who were or had also been habitués of The George and Pagani's Restaurant. These included Constant Lambert, Michael Ayrton, Cecil Gray, Dylan Thomas and their BBC and Covent Garden cronies, who met at the back bar in the 1940s. 'While they were about, they were the best company I ever knew', remarked Ayrton, going on to describe Cecil Gray and Dylan Thomas dancing a hornpipe there after a few drinks. Here Ayrton was introduced to William Walton by Lambert. 'When Constant was present', remembered Ayrton, 'it was unparalleled conversation'.

The ornate mirrored Grill Room, which stands on the site of the former Domino Room, remains, with its painted ceiling, an extravagant rococo experience even before the food. This modern incarnation of the restaurant was masterminded by Charles Forte, who restored it in the early 1950s and introduced extensive conference and banqueting facilities.

Today the Green Room at the Café Royal is famous for cabaret, and it is associated with the Soho Jazz Festival in October, hosting the festival ball.

Carlisle House
Soho Square
Tube: Tottenham Court Road

In 1760 Mrs Theresa Cornelys, a colourful entrepreneur and one-time opera singer, bought a mansion on the east side of Soho Square and in the garden she built a two-storey Chinese pavilion for entertainments. These included subscription concerts – Bach and Abel directed them from 1765 – and fifteen of these 'Soho Square concerts' were given per season for a subscription of five guineas for gentlemen and three for ladies. She attempted to put on operas in 1771 but could not get a licence and was fined and then indicted for keeping a disorderly house (some of the audience were not quite as they should have been). The opening of the Pantheon (see below) in Oxford Street nearby took away much of her clientele, and in November 1772 she went bankrupt. However, the building was still used for benefit concerts until 1778 when it was demolished. The site became the location of the present St Patrick's Roman Catholic chapel, which dates from 1893. Theresa Cornelys's mansion, destroyed in 1941, is remembered by Carlisle Street on the opposite side of the square.

London Coliseum
St Martin's Lane, near St Martin's-in-the Fields
Tube: Charing Cross or Leicester Square

The Coliseum was built in 1904 by Frank Matcham for Sir Oswald Stoll. It has long been London's largest theatre. It was designed on Romanesque lines, as its name suggests, with columns and arches. The globe on the top of the building was designed to revolve but it was judged illegal to make it move, though in 2004 this restriction was again being addressed. It was originally used for variety, and during one show in 1912 Elgar's pageant *The Crown of India* attracted enthusiastic crowds the year after the celebrated Delhi Durbar. During the First World War Elgar's wartime song cycle to words by Kipling, which he called *Fringes of the Fleet*, was featured in another show, the four singers appearing in costume as four old tars round a table at a coastal hostelry.

Diaghilev's Ballets Russes returned to London before the end of the war, opening on 5 September 1918 with *The Good Humoured Ladies*, music by Scarlatti. Oswald Stoll put the show into the Coliseum, presumably because of its enormous audience capacity. Other ballets new to England included *Sadko*, *Midnight Sun* and *Les Contes Russes*, as well as revivals of ballets seen before the war. The Ballets Russes returned to the Coliseum in November 1924, their first visit to London since 1922, with a programme that included Milhaud's *Le Train Bleu* conducted by its composer and the last act of *The Sleeping Princess* as 'Aurora's Wedding'. They remained until 10 January 1925, but returned twice during 1925, with Poulenc's *Les Biches* in May and Dukelsky's *Zephyr and Flora* in October, both with a large programme of revivals.

In 1931 the theatre was used for musical performances and, later, American musicals. It is the largest proscenium theatre in England, and seats over 2,300. It was restored in 1968 and reopened as the London Coliseum – the home of English National Opera. Here there is a conscious attempt to keep ticket prices low (at least when compared with Covent Garden) by a programme of generous subsidies. Since then English National Opera has built a vibrant tradition of radical opera productions using a strongly developed in-house team and sung in English. This notable tradition has included such remarkable achievements as the British premiere of Prokofiev's *War and Peace* (1972), Ligeti's *Le Grand Macabre* (1982), Busoni's *Dr Faust* (1986) and Philip Glass's *Akhnaten* (1985), as well as strikingly different stagings of repertoire works such as Jonathan Miller's gangland *Il Trovatore* and his black and white *Mikado*. Because it has a stage door opening direct onto the street many large stage properties can be used. The opening scene of Ligeti's *Le Grand Macabre* featured a splendid 1920s Rolls Royce car. This had no engine in it and was manhandled onto the stage each evening, being otherwise parked on the kerb outside. One evening it was given a ticket by an over-zealous traffic warden. The ticket office took some persuading that while it looked like a car, without an engine it technically was not one.

This is also the home of a long tradition of new British operas, the most memorable including David Blake's *Toussaint* (1977, revised 1983) and Mark-Anthony Turnage's *The Silver Tassie* (2000). In the Blake one remembers the stunning *coup de théâtre* after the noisy crowded battle scenes of Act I, of Teresa Cahill as Napoleon's sister Pauline Leclerc, in a spotlit slowly swinging hammock on an otherwise blacked out stage, apparently completely nude.

A £41-million large-scale restoration project was completed by the end of 2003, improving public facilities and front of house. The internal decoration has been transformed and the original gold, cream and white colour scheme has been reinstated, with purple drapes and gold tassels round the boxes. Upstairs, the Edwardian curved glass roofs that had been destroyed in the Second World War bombing have been restored. Announced to reopen on 7 February 2004, its intended first production of John Adam's *Nixon in China* had to be abandoned. The theatre opened late on 21 February with a gala concert. The first production was Wagner's *The Rhinegold*, first seen on 27 February.

15 The London Coliseum 24 November 1924: Leon Woizikowsky and Lydia Sokolova in *Le Train Bleu*, music by Milhaud, costumes by Chanel.

Empire Leicester Square
Leicester Square
Tube: Leicester Square

On the site of the former Savile House, the Empire Theatre opened on 17 April 1884 and was registered as a music hall on 12 October 1887 with a capacity of about 1,500. The theatre was set up to rival the nearby Alhambra. As well as the theatre it offered a billiard room, coffee shop and wine vaults. In its early days it featured ballet. Its

16   The Empire Promenade as depicted in 1897, suggesting to gentlemen visitors what they might expect. This post-dates the licensing objection of 1894.

promenades were conducive to soliciting as well as strolling and listening to music, and W. Macqueen-Pope tells us 'there was no secrecy about it, there was indeed nothing to hide. The Ladies were there for all to see and a great portion of the world went to see. They made no secret of their profession . . . the promenade was unique – and the Ladies of the Empire were unique too'. However a court case for renewal of the licence in 1894 demanded that the promenades be abolished. In 1895 the Empire put on the first public film show in London, and it is still used as a cinema today.

The George Public House and Pagani's Restaurant
Great Portland Street
Tube: Great Portland Street or Oxford Circus

The George is on the corner of Mortimer Street and Great Portland Street, Pagani's was diagonally opposite in Great Portland Street. The composer Elisabeth Lutyens referred to The George as 'the focal point of both my social and professional life for some nine years'. An apparently chance meeting with BBC producers in the pub would result in their commissioning her on a seemingly casual basis. This was her principal means of getting work, and was true of many of the composers and musicians, producers and writers who crowded the bar. Humphrey Searle, in his memoirs, *Quadrille with a Raven*, remembers the George very well as 'a famous hostelry ... mainly frequented by BBC producers, writers and actors ... and orchestral players from the nearby Queen's Hall'. Sir Henry Wood named it 'The Gluepot' as his players were always stuck there. Other nearby pubs that had a similar role included The Stag's Head on the corner of New Cavendish Street.

Close by, the other rendezvous frequented by musicians and the literati was Pagani's Restaurant at 42–50 Great Portland Street. Designed by Beresford Pite, it opened in 1904 and quickly became the focus for musical diners, especially those going to and playing at Queen's Hall. Its imposing exterior was notable for the use of tiling and the elaborate decoration of the upper floors in art-nouveau style. It was the venue in 1940 for a lunch, typical of many such occasions, given by the PEN Club for Myra Hess, instigator of the lunchtime concerts in the National Gallery during the war.

J. B. Booth remembered how

> One evening I was quietly supping in the big restaurant on the ground floor, with its brown walls, and its mirrors with their painted trellis-work, when I became aware of a suppressed excitement amongst the Italian waiters. Through the glazed screen which cut off the dispense bar and the entrance to the kitchens I could see chefs in white caps bobbing their heads excitedly round the kitchen doors, and then, as excitement grew, service of every kind ceased, and amid a hum of excitement and faint cheering, a befurred Caruso, smiling and gesticulating, followed by his little court, burst into the restaurant. He had been singing at Covent Garden, in *La Bohème*, with Melba, and an atmosphere of excited triumph still enveloped him.
>
> On the second floor of Pagani's was the Artists' Room, one of the most interesting rooms in any London restaurant, for the walls were covered with autographs, caricatures, sketches, and musical notes.

In his autobiography, the composer Eric Coates recalled the musicians' table at Pagani's, pointing out that 'especially on Symphony Concert days at Queen's Hall, would foregather every musician of note in London at that time. Sometimes you would see world famous artists sitting at other tables about the restaurant, if they were desirous of talking over some private business or other, the musicians' table not being the place where you could talk in an undertone.'

Coates highlighted some of the musicians to be seen there, including John McCormack, Moiseiwitsch, Kreisler, Mark Hambourg, Cyril Scott, Percy Grainger, Norman O'Neill, Roger Quilter, Herman Finck, Edward German, Mengelberg, Ysaÿe, Nikisch, Raoul Pugno, Moriz Rosenthal, Mischa Elman, Jacques Thibaud, Alfred Cortot, Casals, Delius, Solomon, Pachmann, Rachmaninov, Ben Davies, Peter Dawson, Plunket Greene, Santley and Gervase Elwes. As he said, 'There was not another place like it in the whole of London'. Over this 'great and fluctuating

17 (right)   Pagani's restaurant before the First World
War showing the distinctive
tiling and decoration.

18 (far right)   Caricature of
Ysaÿe by Busoni in 1901 from
the Artists' Room at Pagani's,
destroyed in the bombing in
1941. Note in the bottom left-
hand corner: Percy Pitt is
depicted showing him
negotiating with Busoni.

family' Coates tells us how 'Maschini, the proprietor and most perfect of hosts . . .
went from table to table followed closely by his little bulldog'.

In his autobiography *Farewell, My Youth* Arnold Bax describes walking from
Pagani's to Queen's Hall with Balfour Gardiner, with whom he had been dining
before going to a Philharmonic Concert at Queen's Hall. 'As we turn into Riding
House Street my heart beats faster . . . The light of a street lamp reveals the rain-
drops glistening on the ends of my black evening-dress trousers . . . At the orchestra door the players are arriving, cursing at the weather, and chaffing one another
with the obscure type of banter apparently peculiar to bandsmen.' Like Queen's
Hall, Pagani's was bombed the same night. It carried on as a bar with restaurant
above for a while. It is no longer there, although the similar existing façade of 50
Great Portland Street gives a feel of what it must have been like. The George continues in business, and still attracts musical and artistic drinkers, although with the
old musical associations distinctly muted.

Hanover Square Rooms
Hanover Square
Tube: Oxford Circus or Bond Street

These concert rooms lasted for about a century, from 1775 to 1874, though by the
end they had been superseded by the very much larger St James's Hall. These fashionable 'New Assembly Rooms' were built on a garden by Giovanni Gallini, who
was the licensee and manager of the King's Theatre. He bought 4 Hanover Square,

19 The Hanover Square Rooms as shown in the *Illustrated London News* dated 24 June 1843, possibly depicting a Philharmonic Society concert.

on the east side of Hanover Square. The principal room seated up to 900. The opening concert was in February 1775 – a J. C. Bach and Carl Friedrich Abel subscription concert, so very exclusive. In 1791 Haydn, persuaded by the violinist J. P. Salomon, agreed to a series of twelve concerts, for which he composed and conducted from the keyboard six new symphonies.

A hundred years of music at the Hanover Square Rooms included the Professional Concerts, those given by the Concert of Ancient Music from 1804 onwards, vocal concerts, Philharmonic Society concerts, and they were also used by the Royal Academy of Music (then off the square in nearby Tenterden Street), who gave the last concert of all in December 1874. At the mid-nineteenth century they were colloquially referred to as 'The Queen's Concert Room'. The rooms were restored and redecorated in 1862 but converted into a club in 1875. Now the site is occupied by two banks and there is no indication that the rooms were ever there.

Her Majesty's Theatre
see King's Theatre

Hickford's Rooms
63–5 (formerly 41) Brewer Street
Tube: Piccadilly Circus

The first Hickford's Room was John Hickford's Dancing School at Panton Street and James Street, SW1, later the site of the Comedy Theatre, and was used for concerts between 1697 and 1738. Hickford's Rooms in Brewer Street were built in 1738 and flourished as a concert centre until the 1760s, after which the building survived until 1934, when it was demolished for the construction of the annexe to the Regent Palace Hotel.

The Rooms are best remembered for the concert given by the nine-year-old Mozart with his sister Nannerl on 13 May 1765.

King's Theatre
Haymarket
Tube: Piccadilly Circus

The first theatre on this site was designed by Vanbrugh and opened in 1704, specifically for operas. It was the first of four, and was the home of Italian opera in London for nearly two centuries. Handel's *Rinaldo* was performed there, as was his oratorio *Esther*. In the nineteenth century Mendelssohn appeared frequently, as composer (his *Italian Symphony* and *Fingal's Cave* were first heard at the King's Theatre), and as conductor and pianist. The theatre was burnt down in 1789 and rebuilt in 1791. From 1837 to 1847 it was known as the Italian Opera House. It was destroyed by fire again and rebuilt in 1868. A series of promenade concerts directed by Balfe were performed in 1850. However, it did not regain its former popularity until the present theatre – Her Majesty's Theatre – was built in 1897, designed by C. J. Phipps. This was founded and directed by Herbert Beerbohm Tree until his death in 1917. Plaques on the side walls tell the story of the theatre. In the twentieth century there have been several very long-running musical shows, starting with *Chu Chin Chow*, which opened in 1916 and ran for 2,238 performances. Its recent history

20   Her Majesty's Theatre, showing the disposition of the staging for use as a concert hall. This National Concert dates from 1851.

has been dominated by the seventeen-year run of Lloyd Webber's *Phantom of the Opera* and before that for the much shorter first London run of Stephen Sondheim's *Company*.

Langham Hotel
Portland Place
Tube: Oxford Circus

The Langham Hotel, sumptuously decorated and appointed, was opened by the Prince of Wales on 10 June 1865, and was the first luxury hotel of its size to be built in London. Although it went bankrupt within three years, new management established it as a pre-eminent institution of its day. It was long associated with rich American visitors, while celebrated literary names included Oscar Wilde, Ouida, Longfellow and Mark Twain. St George's Hall across the road generated a musical clientele before Queen's Hall appeared nearby in 1893 and the BBC in 1931.

For many years after the war it was used by the BBC as an annexe, but is now a hotel again, the Langham Hotel, London, opened in May 2004. It is owned and managed by the Great Eagle Hotel Group.

When it was first a hotel, visiting conductors used to stay because of its proximity to Queen's Hall. Among the more famous musical guests were the knights Thomas Beecham and Edward Elgar, as well as visiting composers such as Dvořák in the 1880s, long pre-dating Sibelius, and Delius during the 1929 Delius Festival. In its present refurbished state the musical connection is emphasised with rooms named after distinguished former visitors, including, for example, Toscanini and Noël Coward Suites.

London Pavilion
Coventry Street
Tube: Piccadilly Circus

Opened in 1861 as a music hall, it was sold in 1878 to the Metropolitan Board of Works for demolition and improvements to Piccadilly. A second Pavilion opened in 1885. It was later used as a theatre and cinema, and now houses a shopping centre and amusement arcade in Piccadilly Circus called the London Trocadero. Until recently its original name, 'London Pavilion', could still be seen in Art Deco lettering on the portico.

Marylebone Gardens
Marylebone High Street
Tube: Baker Street

The site is now covered by Devonshire Street and its environs. The entrance was at what is now 35 Marylebone High Street (later the address for the BBC Third

Programme and BBC Publications). Opened in 1650 for leisure activities such as cock-fighting and bear-baiting, boxing and bowling and other sporting pursuits, it became more exclusive in 1738 when it was enlarged, 'low life' banned and an entrance fee charged. In 1769 it was leased by composer and musician Dr Samuel Arnold and the gardens thereafter used more for music of quality. In 1773 the orchestra was conducted by Thomas Arne. The gardens closed in 1778.

National Gallery
Trafalgar Square
Tube: Charing Cross or Leicester Square

The National Gallery is one of London's most familiar landmarks, dominating the north side of Trafalgar Square. The building, by William Wilkins, dates from 1831 and has been several times extended. Evacuated on the outbreak of war, in 1939, the empty gallery was the home of popular wartime lunchtime concerts organised by concert pianist Myra Hess, assisted by composer Howard Ferguson and with the enthusiastic backing of the director of the Gallery, Sir Kenneth Clark. The concerts took place in gallery 36, a large octagonal space with a dome, and the surrounding rooms. Numerous artists, including the RAF Orchestra, performed there, and the lunchtime concerts were held every weekday. A canteen was provided for the audience, with 'the best sandwiches in London', and the atmosphere was relaxed and appreciative of the varied programmes. (During the war the paintings were removed and stored in the country for safety.) The concerts finally came to an end on 10 April 1946 after six and a half years, with a performance by the Griller Quartet playing Beethoven and Haydn. There had been 1,698 concerts. The file of concert programmes and related papers is in the British Library (see p. 236).

The National Gallery concerts were a significant musical icon of London life in the Second World War, evoked on film in the wartime documentary *Listen to Britain* (1942), which includes Myra Hess in Mozart's Piano Concerto K. 457 playing at the actual National Gallery Concerts. The opening sequence of the postwar film *Man of Two Worlds* is set at a concert at the National Gallery with Bliss's music *Baraza*.

Palace Theatre
Cambridge Circus
Tube: Leicester Square or Tottenham Court Road

The foundation stone of the Palace Theatre on Cambridge Circus at the then recently completed Shaftesbury Avenue was laid by Helen D'Oyly Carte on 15 December 1888. It was conceived by Richard D'Oyly Carte as the Royal English Opera House, opening with a spectacular royal gala on 31 January 1891 with Sullivan's specially composed grand opera *Ivanhoe*. The design and detailing of the theatre, including the lobby and the ornate plasterwork on pillars and walls, were all intended to reflect the Saxon theme of Sullivan's opera and survive today. Frederic H. Cowen remembered 'the first night well, the crowd of fashionable and musical people, the admiration expressed for the charming building, and the enthusiastic applause with which the new work was greeted.' *Ivanhoe* ran for a remarkable 155 performances, the record for an English opera until Rutland Boughton's *The Immortal Hour* in the 1920s. Unfortunately, Carte had expected an even longer run and had engaged two casts, the first of which came to be seen by the public as the one to be preferred and when the second cast was billed the audiences stayed away. Under these circumstances the run was not long enough to recoup Carte's enormous investment.

When *Ivanhoe*'s intended successor, Cowen's opera *Signa*, was not ready, Carte followed it with an English version of André Messager's light opera *La Basoche* as a stop-gap, and when that failed to run Carte gave up his scheme and sold the theatre, which reopened as the Palace Music Hall. The appearance here of lavish musicals in the 1980s was crowned by Claude-Michel Schönberg's quasi-operatic

21   The Palace Theatre, then The Royal English Opera House, featured in *The Graphic* for the opening on 31 January 1891 with Sullivan's *Ivanhoe*. The theatre is little changed over a hundred years later; the interior was refurbished in the summer of 2004.

through-composed setting of Victor Hugo's *Les Misérables* transferring from the Barbican. This succeeded where Carte had failed, and when it closed on 27 March 2004 to transfer to The Queen's Theatre it had been running at the Palace for over eighteen years – a total of 7,602 performances.

The Pantheon
Oxford Street
Tube: Oxford Circus

The Pantheon, which opened in January 1772, was on the site of what is now a large branch of Marks and Spencer. A sign high up on the façade reads 'The Pantheon'. Widely admired, it was designed by the architect James Wyatt as an indoor Ranelagh or Vauxhall pleasure garden with provision for balls and masques. It also hosted some of the performances of the large-scale 1784 commemoration of Handel's sacred and instrumental music. It boasted a dome, statues and columns, and gilded decorations, and could hold up to 1,600 people. But its popularity declined and in 1789 it was used as an opera house after the King's Theatre burnt down and after conversion took the theatre's name as well. In January 1792 it too burnt down. In April 1795 it reopened to the public as Claggett's Great Room. The lease was sold in 1812 and the Pantheon became a theatre again, run by N. W. Cundy, but closed two years later. It was rebuilt as a bazaar in 1832 and lasted until 1937 when it was demolished.

Queen's Hall
Langham Place
Tube: Oxford Circus or Great Portland Street

Queen's Hall was located in Langham Place on Upper Regent Street, adjacent to All Souls Church, and lasted from 1893 to 1941. It was designed by architects C. J. Phipps and T. E. Knightley and had a large curved frontage on the corner of Riding House Street, which provides a thoroughfare to Great Portland Street. The building adjoined St George's Music Hall. It had large and small halls with capacities of 3,000 and 500 people respectively. The upper, small hall was used for lectures, dances, recitals and chamber music. The hall was originally leased to Robert Newman and, after his bankruptcy in 1902, by Chappells. It opened in November 1893 with a children's party and a miscellaneous concert followed by dancing. The first concert was on 27 November 1893, a smoking concert given by the Royal Amateur Orchestral Society attended by the Prince of Wales. The official opening came on 2 December with Mendelssohn's *Hymn of Praise* and Beethoven's *Emperor* Concerto played by Frederick Dawson. By the following year many choirs and orchestras had moved to Queen's Hall from other London halls. These included the Philharmonic Society, which transferred there from St James's Hall, the Bach Choir, Henschel's London Symphony concerts and the Wagner concerts (previously given at the Hanover

Square Rooms), the London Music Festival, Promenade concerts (from 1895) and Balfour Gardiner concerts. Prices for the Proms ranged from one shilling to five shillings for best Grand Circle seats. The Promenade concerts were established by Newman in 1895 with the objective of developing an audience.

Arnold Bax vividly described the short walk from Pagani's to Queen's Hall, which must have been a familiar journey for many playing and attending Queen's Hall.

> The principal entrance is thronged with taxis and motor broughams, and under the brightly lit portico red-faced men in evening dress and gibus hats and expensive and glittering dowagers are ascending the steps with that air of self-conscious and dignified complacence natural to the Britisher patronizing one of the more abstract and serious arts. Clustering volubly in the vestibule or lurking in the dark corners amongst the hoardings around the entrance are bevies of students from the various colleges of music. Their chatter is so mercurial, and so electric are their movements, that they produce the illusion of diving in and out among the legs of the steady procession of elderly magnificence that the motors continuously pour forth. These youngsters make but little effort to check the abandon of manners usual in their school refreshment rooms, and every new arrival of their own kind is hailed with shrieks and colloquial sallies – whilst the girls, if sufficiently attractive, are greeted with pinches and proddings from their high-spirited admirers.
>
> Also are to be remarked those aesthetic and foreign-looking young men darkly efflorescent of hair, their pince-nez only serving to heighten their eyes' fine melancholy, a class that would seem to have been born and bred in concert halls and opera houses, for they are never to be seen anywhere else – except perhaps in the Café Royal. They carry, a little ostentatiously, miniature scores of the symphonies or overtures to be played, and there are but two varieties, the dapper and the grubby. It is five minutes to the hour, and we pass quickly up the steps, Balfour's round blue eyes peering shortsightedly through their glasses, and my own glance roaming restlessly from corner to corner. I notice some of the newspaper men, with most of whom I am merely on terms of distantly nodding acquaintance.

The inception of Queen's Hall was one of the principal drivers of the enormous expansion of musical activity in London in the fifteen years before the First World War. By a combination of innovatory planning, by the provision of a cheap summer concert series (the Proms), by systematically presenting the best international artists (in many cases controlling their exclusive appearance) and by focusing on a charismatic young Londoner in Henry Wood, Newman and Wood built a new audience. Having this available in central London eclipsed the Crystal Palace as London's popular concert hall and meant that getting home was easier for a suburban audience, though the Central line tube (Oxford Circus station opened in 1900 for Bakerloo only) was not opened until 1907. Sir Henry Wood remarked in a BBC radio feature in 1941 'They said there wasn't a public for great music forty-seven years ago. The critics wagged their heads. But Robert Newman said we'd *make* a public, and we did . . . It was a bold venture in 1895.'

In that same programme the commentator evoked the appearance of the hall on entering: 'Blue and silver and a towering organ: that was your first impression of Queen's Hall. It was a place of warmth and life and light and colour.' The overwhelming affection that all who knew it seem to have had for Queen's Hall was not only owing to careful marketing but also to its central location and to its intrinsic architectural virtues. The composer Dr Thomas Wood was typically emotive in his memories of it: 'I knew Queen's Hall in most of its moods, but I like to think of it best on some autumn evening, when the sun was setting over London and all the West was a glory. The big lamps down Regent Street would be lighting up. The pigeons had gone to bed. You'd arrive late, for there was one particular work, and only one, that you wanted to hear; so you'd tiptoe along the corridor that went curving round the Grand Circle.'

Queen's Hall was the focus for London orchestral concerts for the first four decades of the twentieth century. All the principal artists of the day appeared there, and conductors included Richter, Nikisch, Mengelberg, Safonov, Młynarksi, Beecham and Landon Ronald, as well as Elgar, Parry, Walford Davies and Coleridge-Taylor. Beecham kept the London Symphony Orchestra going in the 1914–15 season in the early days of war. It saw all the important London premieres from the 1890s to the outbreak of the Second World War. Acoustically it was equally a rewarding hall for the sumptuous orchestral demands of Strauss, the impressionism of Debussy and the modernism of Stravinsky. It saw the first London performances of Elgar's first two Pomp and Circumstance marches in 1902, Vaughan Williams's *A London Symphony* in 1914 and two generations of new music during its relatively brief lifetime. Other distinguished conductors were Damrosch, Goossens, Busoni, Weingartner and Toscanini. It was also the hall in which two generations of British composers first heard their music, and it has been suggested that the sound in the hall materially affected the way the British composers of Vaughan Williams's generation actually scored their work.

After the formation of the BBC Symphony Orchestra in 1930, Queen's Hall (which was across the road from Broadcasting House, which opened in 1931) became the focus of BBC concerts, which was one of the most prominent and consistent aspects of the hall's activities in the 1930s. Starting in 1935 the Queen's Hall was the location of Toscanini's celebrated series of concerts with the BBC Symphony Orchestra, during which he described the orchestra as the world's best. Many of these concerts were recorded and are available on CDs today. Queen's Hall was destroyed by the Luftwaffe on the night of 10/11 May 1941, in the same raid that destroyed the Temple Church, when the actual targets were presumably the BBC at Broadcasting House and Bush House. The last work heard in the hall was Elgar's *The Dream of Gerontius*.

The interior was gutted and only the outer shell remained, rather like a bizarre ancient Roman arena. Now the St George's Hotel is on the site. A green plaque was

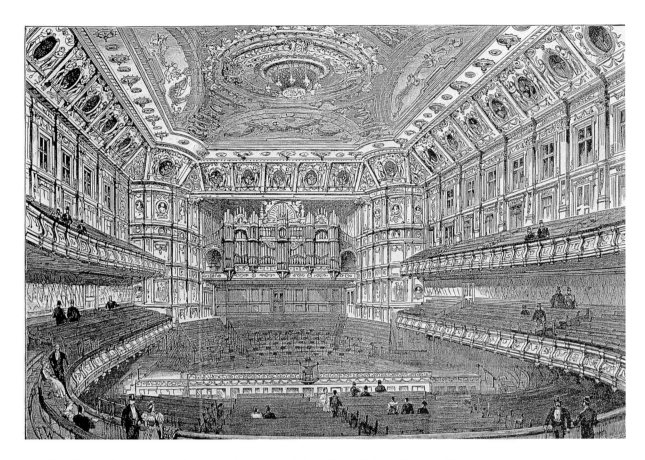

unveiled by conductor Sir Andrew Davis on one of the pillars of the adjacent office block on 13 July 2000.

Queen's Hall features surprisingly little on film. British Pathé have a two-and-a-half-minute clip (tape PM 1540) from a newsreel of 1942 showing the hall before and after it was bombed. It includes extracts from the BBC Symphony Orchestra playing the overture to Wagner's *Die Meistersinger* and close-ups of the statues of Wagner, Weber and Handel in the walls and the ruined hall after the bombing. From 1938 survives a comparatively well-known short clip of Vaughan Williams sitting on steps leading to the platform as Sir Henry Wood rehearses his new *Serenade to Music* for Wood's Jubilee concert in October 1938. Another newsreel (nearly three minutes long) shows Sir Adrian Boult conducting the BBC Symphony Orchestra in the hall in Elgar's *Pomp and Circumstance* March No. 1 (tape PM 1068).

Film of the exterior of Queen's Hall in its hey-day does not appear to have survived. Paul Czinner's 1937 film *Dreaming Lips*, with music by William Walton, includes an extended sequence apparently shot in Queen's Hall during a concert, though as Boyd Neel the conductor on that occasion (his only film appearance) tells us in his autobiography even this actually consisted of a reduced scale model of portions of the hall

22   Interior view of Queen's Hall, pictured by *The Illustrated Sporting and Dramatic News* in December 1893 to mark the opening.

built on the lot at the Elstree Studios. The key scene comes early in the film when Boyd Neel conducts fragments from the first movement of the Beethoven Violin Concerto, the end of the Tchaikovsky violin concerto and the waltz from the *Serenade for Strings* arranged for violin and orchestra. Raymond Massey 'plays' the violin, but

---

Live recordings from notable concerts at Queen's Hall that have been issued commercially

(*Many of these were of Toscanini's concerts with the BBC Symphony Orchestra which were recorded by landline to the HMV Studios at Abbey Road. A few performances were recorded off-air. A variety of further short extracts recorded off-air from Queen's Hall may be found in the Leech Collection, now in the National Sound Archive.*)

15 May 1933 Sibelius: Symphony No 7 BBC SO/Koussevitsky Pearl GEMMCDS 9408

4 June 1934 Sibelius: Symphony No 4 Finnish National Radio O/Schnéevoigt LP World Records SH 237

3 June 1935, Brahms: *Tragic* Overture BBC SO/Toscanini EMI CDH 7 69783 2

3 June 1935, Elgar: *Enigma Variations* BBC SO/Toscanini EMI CDH 7 69784 2

3 June 1935, Cherubini: *Anacréon* Overture BBC SO/Toscanini BBC Legends BBCL 4016-2

5 June 1935, Brahms: Symphony No 4 BBC SO/Toscanini EMI CDH 7 69783 2

5 June 1935, Wagner: *Siegfried's Death and Funeral March* BBC SO/Toscanini. Grammofono AB 78611

5 June 1935, Wagner: *Faust Overture* BBC SO/Toscanini. Grammofono AB 78611

5 June 1935, Wagner: *Parsifal Prelude and Good Friday Music* BBC SO/ Toscanini. Grammofono AB 78611

12 June 1935, Rossini: Overture *Semiramide* BBC SO/Toscanini Testament SBT 1015

12 June 1935, Beethoven: Symphony No 7 BBC SO/Toscanini BBC Legends BBCL 4016-2

12 June 1935, Debussy: *La Mer* BBC SO/Toscanini EMI CDH 7 69784 2

14 June 1935, Mendelssohn: 'Nocturne and Scherzo' from *A Midsummer Night's Dream* Testament SBT 1015

14 June 1935, Mozart: Symphony No 35 *'Haffner'* BBC SO/Toscanini BBC Legends BBCL 4016-2

10 November 1935, Delius: *Appalachia* Cuthbert Matthews (bar)/ Royal Opera Amateur Chorus/ LPO/Beecham EMI Classics 7243 5 75938 2 3

10 November 1935, Weber: Der Freischütz Overture LPO/Beecham EMI Classics 7243 5 75938 2 3

3 January 1936, Beethoven: Symphony No 8 BBC SO/Wood Symposium 1253

8 September 1936 [Proms], Mozart: *Sinfonia Concertante*; 'L'amerò, sarò constante' (*Il re pastore*); *Exsultate Jubilate*. Jean Pougnet (vln), Bernard Shore (vla), Elisabeth Schumann (sop) BBC SO/Wood Symposium 1150

19 March 1937, York Bowen: Piano Concerto No 4. Bowen (pf)/BBC SO/Boult *World premiere* Connoisseur Cassettes CPL 4

1 May 1937, Beethoven: Symphony No 9 Soloists/Bruno Kittel Choir/Berlin PO/Furtwängler Music & Arts CD 818 EMI ED 270123-1

25 Oct 1937, Beethoven Symphony No 1 BBC SO/Toscanini Dutton CDEA 5004

17 November 1937, Tovey: Cello Concerto Casals (cello)/BBC SO/Boult *World premiere* Symposium 1115

9 January 1938, Mendelssohn: Music for a *Midsummer Night's Dream* BBC SO/Mengelberg Archive Documents Mengelberg Edition ADCD 111

15 April 1938, Elgar: *The Dream of Gerontius*: Muriel Brunskill/Parry Jones/Harold Williams/BBC Chorus & SO/Wood (extracts from Part II only), 'The crown is Won' on Dutton CDLX 7044

19 May 1938, *God Save the King* [together with a minute of hall ambience] BBC SO/Toscanini Symposium 1253

27 May 1938, Verdi: *Messa di Requiem* soloists/BBC Choral Society/BBC SO/Toscanini Melodram MEL 28022

10 June 1938, Brahms: Symphony No. 2. BBC SO/Toscanini Testament SBT 1015

28 May 1939, Beethoven: *Missa Solemnis* soloists/BBC Choral Society/BBC SO/Toscanini BBC Legends BBCL 4016-2

10 June 1938, Sibelius: Symphony No 2 BBC SO/Toscanini EMICDH7 63307-2

10 June 1938, Brahms: Symphony No 2 BBC SO/Toscanini Testament SBT 1015

2 June 1938, Mozart: *Die Zauberflöte* Overture BBC SO/Toscanini Biddulph WHL 008/9

9 March 1939, Bloch: Violin Concerto Szigeti/London Philharmonic O/Beecham *European premiere* Beecham Society WSA 5

1 June 1939, Beethoven: *Leonora Overture No 1* BBC SO/Toscanini Dutton CDEA 5004

1 June 1939, Beethoven: Symphony No 4 BBC SO/Toscanini Dutton CDEA 5004

we do not see him actually play but rather view over his shoulder as he watches Elisabeth Bergner in the audience, and we see both auditorium and audience. As Boyd Neel recounts in his autobiography, Massey was unmusical and the violin was actually being 'played' by two members of the orchestra, only the fingering being authentic. More recent films have tried to evoke the atmosphere of Queen's Hall, notably the celebrated concert sequence in the Merchant-Ivory film *Howards End*.

St James's Hall
Piccadilly
Tube: Piccadilly Circus

Situated on a site between Air Street, Vine Street, Regent Street and Piccadilly, there were entrances from Piccadilly and the Regent Street Quadrant. Built by Chappell and Co., to designs by Owen Jones, it was opened in March 1858 and consisted of a Great Hall (measuring 140 by 60 feet and 60 feet high) and two smaller ones. It became the home of London orchestral concerts for the next forty years, and produced a chamber concert on Mondays. The Monday Popular concerts started in February 1859 and were unique in promoting chamber music played by leading artists to an increasingly large audience, the prices being affordable by more impecunious music lovers, with gallery seats at a shilling. From March 1865 there were chamber concerts on Saturday afternoons as well. The acoustics of the hall were found to be especially good for chamber music, and with its capacity of 2,000 it had a financial basis that allowed low prices to be maintained.

The backbone of the ensemble were the cellist Alfredo Piatti and Louis Ries on second violin, who remained for nearly forty years. The focus of the series over many years was the violinist Joseph Joachim. Herman Klein remembered how he dominated the ensemble

> by his rhythmic energy and decision, by the completeness and grandeur of his conception, rather than by temperamental warmth and passion . . . one rival, and only one, ever challenged the supremacy of Joachim at St James's Hall. That was Wilma Norman-Néruda (Lady Hallé) . . . as a rule, she led the Quartet from the opening of the season until he arrived; sometimes also at the Saturday 'Pops', when he was playing at the Crystal Palace or elsewhere. The contrast between their styles was very marked; her exquisite silvery tone and delicate artistry reminding one more of Sivori or Sarasate.

The concerts ended in March 1902 when there had been an unbroken series of 1,552 performances.

The Philharmonic Society moved to St James's Hall from the Hanover Square Rooms in 1869. This was a low point in the Philharmonic Society's fortunes with only occasional packed houses for visiting celebrities, such as Hans von Bülow's performance of Beethoven's *Emperor* Concerto in April 1873. By 1880 the concert halls at Exeter Hall and Hanover Square had gone and St James's became the pre-

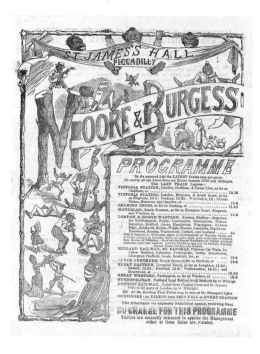

23 (above)   The other side of St James's Hall: Moore and Burgess's popular minstrel shows. This programme is from 26 October 1887.

24 (right)   The Piccadilly entrance to St James's Hall, drawing by Howard Penton.

mier concert hall in central London, putting on the emerging romantic repertoire of Brahms, Saint-Saëns and Tchaikovsky and British works by Mackenzie, Stanford, Cowen, Parry and Sullivan, among others.

When the Richter Concerts started in 1879, Londoners were aware of a new standard of orchestral direction, becoming the backbone of the concert life of the period up to 1896. There were London Symphony concerts from November to March each year from 1886 to 1897. Here, too, on successive Wednesday evenings during the autumn and spring seasons, were given Boosey's London Ballad Concerts.

One of the smaller halls was used almost exclusively from September 1865 for the Moore and Burgess Minstrels, the successors to the celebrated Christy Minstrels, giving nine performances a week and in December migrating upstairs to the larger main hall for each Christmas season. When it first opened the company consisted of eight members, by 1888 it numbered forty-two.

The opening of Queen's Hall in 1893 moved the focus of London concert-giving north of Oxford Street. St James's Hall had its limitations, and Mackenzie remarked on the cooking smells apparent during rehearsals. The hall was ultimately demolished in 1905 to make way for the Piccadilly Hotel, now Le Méridien, and the Queen's Hall was left as the unquestioned focus of London orchestral music until the Second World War.

Another St James's Hall opened in Great Portland Street on 25 April 1908 with a series of promenade concerts conducted by Lyell Tayler which lasted until 23 May. It featured a variety of new works, many by now forgotten composers including Henry Waller, Edith Swepstone, Stephen Phillips and Algernon Lindo. With a capacity of 1,100 it failed to establish a high profile in London musical life.

Savile Club
69 Brook Street, W1
Tube: Bond Street

London gentlemen's clubs constitute the largely undocumented networks where influence is discreetly exercised and musical plots are hatched face-to-face. The Savile is the pre-eminent musical club first founded at Savile Row, then briefly at 100 Piccadilly before moving to its present address after the First World War. One cannot apply to join such institutions, but rather is proposed by two existing members.

In the nineteenth century Joseph Barnby was an active member and on one occasion he brought Dvořák as a guest. Stanford, Parry, Mackenzie and Elgar were all members. The story is told that when Elgar first entered the Club, Mackenzie found him in the smoking-room, looking rather lost. Mackenzie, trying to put the younger man at his ease, proposed that they should lunch together. It was an uncomfortable meal, but things were beginning to go tolerably when the cheese arrived. 'You know the ropes of this place, Mackenzie. What cheese do you advise?' appealed Elgar. 'I think I know your taste,' was the instant reply. 'Why not try a little port Salut d' Amour?'

Later influential figures both from the BBC and the film world were members, the latter including Sir Michael Balcon, Sydney Gilliat, Michael Powell, Ernest Irving, Hubert Clifford and Dallas Bower. Bower, as well as being the pioneer of music and opera on BBC television was an important radio producer, his most iconic radio achievement probably being Louis MacNeice's wartime play, *Christopher Columbus*, with music by Walton. Muir Mathieson, the driving force behind British film music in the 1940s and '50s was also a member. Walton himself was an active member, as also were Sir Adrian Boult, Sir Arthur Bliss, Francis Chagrin, Herbert Howells, Richard Arnell, William Alwyn, Bernard Herrmann and Sir Malcolm Arnold, who actually lived at the Savile from time to time.

Steinway/Grotrian Hall
15 Lower Seymour Street, Portman Square
Tube: Bond Street

The principal piano manufacturers tended to have London recital halls in which their pianos could be shown off under concert conditions, examples including the

Bechstein (later Wigmore) Hall and the Salle Erard, Great Marlborough Street. In the 1860s the Collard Concert-Room, Grosvenor Street, was depicted in the *Illustrated London News*. Further west down Wigmore Street and on the opposite side of the road was the hall for the Steinway company. This was opened as the Steinway Hall in 1875 with seating for 400. The inaugural concert was given by Hans von Bülow. It was closed when the lease expired in 1924 and reopened as the Grotrian Hall in 1925, but closed again in 1938. Grotrian Hall handbills were in a strikingly similar style to the Wigmore Hall and gave its address as simply 'Wigmore Street'. The building was badly damaged in the Second World War and then demolished.

Tottenham Street Rooms
Tottenham Court Road
Tube: Tottenham Court Road

Also known as the New Rooms or Antient Concert Rooms and standing on the site of what was later the Scala Theatre, the rooms were built in 1772 by Francis Pasquali, a musician. They became the first home of the Concert of Antient [Ancient] Music, established by the Earl of Sandwich and various other aristocrats in 1776, to preserve by means of regular performances the great works of the older masters. Subscribers were nearly all peers. Programmes for many years consisted mainly of Handel's music plus a little Purcell, Corelli, Gluck, Pergolesi and the like. Under the patronage of George III, the rooms were enlarged and improved, and concerts were known as the 'King's Concerts'. In 1794 the Concert of Antient Music moved to the King's Theatre, Haymarket, and in 1804 to the Hanover Square Rooms. It was dissolved in 1848. The Tottenham Street Rooms also put on concerts of music and singing.

In 1800 the rooms were taken by a trumpeter, John Hyde, and became briefly known as Hyde's Rooms. Later they became used for amateur dramatics, a circus and then theatrical performances. In 1822 the rooms closed after a landlord/tenant dispute, and later the premises were occupied for some years by the Salvation Army. The building fell into disrepair and was sold for demolition in 1902. The Scala Theatre was built on the site in 1904.

Wigmore Hall (at first Bechstein Hall)
Wigmore Street
Tube: Bond Street or Oxford Circus

This 'new, handsome and commodious concert hall' opened on 31 May 1901. It was in the renaissance style, with alabaster and marble walls designed by Thomas Collcutt, and had seating for around 550. It was thus small enough to be used comfortably for recitals, but in no way replicated the economics of St James's Hall, demolished in 1905. Until the First World War it was known as the Bechstein

Hall and was erected for the piano manufacturers of that name whose showrooms adjoined the hall.

The opening concert on 31 May 1901 featured Busoni and Ysaÿe, and other leading musicians of the day were soon heard there, including Schnabel and Percy Grainger. It was used for chamber music and recitals, as it is today. However, it also soon became known as the hall at which young hopefuls would make their debuts, seeking attention, press coverage and out of town dates. Among those who succeeded were pianists such as Frank Merrick and Myra Hess making their first impact there. The hall was also used by small orchestras who felt they could not justify a larger venue, and thus Thomas Beecham gave four of his earliest London concerts between May and December 1906 (a final concert announced for January 1907 was cancelled) playing miscellaneous selections of what he would later call 'lollipops'.

25   The Wigmore Hall.

The outbreak of war in 1914 was nearly the end of the Bechstein Hall, for as a German-owned enterprise it was placed in the hands of an official Receiver and Manager. It continued, though soon without Bechstein pianos. However, during the First World War many markedly good musical activities that had a Germanic input found themselves the victim of super-patriots who used the press to attack them. Thus the renewal of the hall's London County Council licence in November 1915 was opposed by the journal *The Pianomaker* and in November 1916 everything was auctioned. The hall was rescued by being bought by Debenham's store together with the offices, studios and pianos. It reopened as the Wigmore Hall in 1917 with a recital by the young Albert Sammons and Vasily Safonov. Its former character continued and all manner of special musical events took place there. A notable occasion between the wars was the memorial concert for Peter Warlock in 1931.

One of the Hall's most striking features is the painted cupola above the stage. Designed by Frank Lynn Jenkins in arts and crafts style, it strongly recalls the then fashionable symbolist art of figures such as Jean Delville who were on the fringes of the Theosophical movement in London. The central figure represents the Soul of Music gazing at the Genius of Harmony (represented by a ball of eternal fire). On the left a musician plays and on the right Psyche encourages a composer. This mural was restored as part of the refurbishment of the Hall in 1991–2.

The appointment of William Lyne as director in 1966 resulted in the gradual evolution of the prestige the hall enjoys today. His bust, sculpted by Irena Sedlecka-Belsky, now faces the box office. The miscellaneous nature of its programmes, with many debuts, has changed and it has become the place where Londoners may hear the leading singers and recitalists of the day. The Hall currently puts on over 400 concerts a year, the innovation of Sunday morning coffee concerts being particularly popular. Further development took place in the summer of 2004, and it was reopened by Dame Margaret Price on 11 October 2004.

Westminster

Banqueting House
Whitehall
Tube: Westminster or Charing Cross

The Banqueting House, designed by Inigo Jones for King James I, was completed in 1622 and from the first was used for masques and ceremonial occasions. It was built in Palladian style in the form of a double cube, with a spectacular ceiling boasting nine magnificent paintings by Rubens, commissioned by Charles I, depicting the peace and prosperity of James's reign. The Banqueting House is the only surviving building to remain after the great fire of 1698 that destroyed Whitehall Palace. It has witnessed tragedy and triumph, from the regicide to the victory celebrations after the Second World War, from Royal Maundy rites to royal funeral processions.

King Charles I was executed in front of the Banqueting House by order of Cromwell and Parliament on 30 January 1649 and it was not used for festive occasions again until the Restoration. During the nineteenth century it became a venue for charity concerts. Regular lunchtime concerts are still held.

Buckingham Palace
SW1
Tube: Victoria; Buses 11, 211, 239, C1, C10

The Concert Room at Buckingham Palace, extensively used as such during Queen Victoria's reign, we now know as The Ballroom. While the largest multi-purpose room in the Palace it is today rarely used for concerts. It is the usual location of investitures and formal occasions and may be seen during summer openings of the public rooms.

26   An Edwardian tourist postcard of the platform in the Concert Room at Buckingham Palace as it was before the First World War.

Methodist Central Hall
Westminster
Tube: Westminster or St James's Park

The hall stands on the site of the Royal Aquarium (see below). It was completed in 1912, funded by money raised to commemorate the centenary of the death of John Wesley, founder of Methodism. The organ was also constructed in 1912 with 3,695 pipes. It now has 4,731 pipes, the tallest of which are thirty-two feet high. Organ recitals are frequently given. It was used for festivals, notably the Bach Festival of 1920, and choral concerts. Children's concerts, organised by Sir Robert Mayer, took place there for many years. Recordings were made there between the wars, notably by Columbia, and it was used as an alternative venue for concerts after Queen's Hall was destroyed. This continued until the Royal Festival Hall was opened in 1951. The hall was the scene of the first-ever performance of Havergal Brian's massive *Gothic Symphony* on 24 June 1961, a concert that started late owing to the unexpected queue that formed round the hall, on a steaming hot night. The box office staff could not cope. In the end, in desperation, a member of the organising committee called out 'half a crown and no change given'.

Audiences at concerts are aware of the passing rumble of the District and Circle lines running below. For this reason it is rarely used for recordings today. (See also Chapter 2.)

National Opera House
Embankment
Tube: Westminster

No trace now remains of the Opera House that was conceived by the colourful impresario Colonel James Mapleson. It was designed by Francis Fowler on a site acquired

27   A contemporary artist's impression of Mapleson's proposed National Opera House of 1876 which he started building on the Thames Embankment next to the House of Commons, but went bankrupt before it was finished. It was demolished soon after.

in 1875 on land later occupied by New Scotland Yard, backing on to Cannon Row. It was to have had access from the river as well as from the adjacent District Railway station and with a tunnel under the road direct from the House of Commons. It had been planned to be bigger than the Royal Opera House Covent Garden and as splendid as La Scala Milan, but proved to be so expensive that after £103,000 had been spent there was no money left for the roof, and the project had to be abandoned.

Royal Aquarium
Westminster
Tube: Westminster or St James's Park

Built in 1875 on a site now occupied by Methodist Central Hall, Westminster, at the junction of Tothill and Victoria Streets at Broad Sanctuary, opposite Westminster Abbey, the Aquarium was built of glass, red brick and Portland stone by A. Bedborough and had a 600-foot frontage occupying most of the present north side of Tothill Street. Sir Arthur Sullivan was engaged as conductor for the inaugural concert in February 1876, but resigned that August. British music performed included works by Macfarren, Sterndale Bennett, Balfe and Wallace. An 1884 promenade concert began with the band of the Grenadier Guards under Dan Godfrey (whose son was later founder of the Bournemouth Symphony Orchestra). By 1887 standards had fallen and more popular music was being played. It closed in 1903 and was demolished after only twenty-eight years to be replaced by the Methodist

28 The Royal Aquarium, the front of the site later occupied by Central Hall Westminster. Howard Penton's view is seen across Broad Sanctuary outside Westminster Abbey. Victoria Street runs to the left. Neither building in the drawing survives.

Central Hall. Howard Penton remarked, sadly, it was 'a place for high-class music and refined entertainments'.

St John's, Smith Square
Smith Square
Tube: Westminster or St James's Park

The large baroque church in the middle of Smith Square was built between 1713 and 1728. In the Second World War it was severely damaged by an air raid in 1941. It was desconsecrated and restored as a concert hall, featuring both lunchtime and evening concerts. It is also used for recording sessions. (See full account in Chapter 2.)

The Savage Club
at the National Liberal Club, 1 Whitehall Place, SW1
Tube: Embankment

Founded in 1857, the Savage Club became the leading Bohemian gentleman's club in London, members referring to each other as 'Brother Savage'. Membership falls into six categories – art, music, drama, literature, science and the law. It is perhaps more down to earth than the competing Savile Club, musical members tending to be active performers. The club owns a piano donated by the celebrated pianist Benno Moiseiwitsch, himself a member.

Musical members included instrumentalists, singers, conductors, arrangers, trustees of musical societies and opera groups, jazz musicians and others who can show genuine musical attainment. Member musicians have included the conductors Sir Henry Wood and Sir Charles Groves, composers Leonard Salzedo and Richard Arnell, while Sergei Rachmaninov would be seen at the Club in the 1930s.

The club enjoys the facilities of the National Liberal Club, activities featuring regular entertainments, after dinner, given by distinguished members and their guests.

Conway Hall
Red Lion Square, near Holborn
Tube: Holborn

Covent Garden and Holborn

The Conway Hall Humanist Centre has been the headquarters of the South Place Ethical Society since 1929. The main hall is used for regular chamber music concerts early (usually 6.30 p.m.) on a Sunday evening. It is also used for recordings and rehearsals during the daytime. The name was chosen in honour of Moncure Daniel Conway, anti-slavery advocate, outspoken supporter of free thought and biographer of Thomas Paine. The concert series has taken place on Sunday evenings for over a hundred years. They were first called 'People's popular concerts', which still describes

29   Conway Hall, Red Lion Square, today.

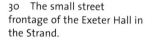

30   The small street frontage of the Exeter Hall in the Strand.

their character today, now promoted by the London Chamber Music Society. The architect's brief was to design an acoustic specifically for the string quartet. A plaque in the lobby of the hall commemorates Alfred J. Clements, the secretary from 1887 until his death in 1938. From time to time the hall is also used for piano auctions.

Exeter Hall
The Strand
Tube: Charing Cross or Embankment

Opened in March 1831, the Exeter Hall was built on the site of the gardens of the former Exeter House in an area bounded by Covent Garden to the north, the Strand to the south, Wellington Street to the east and Southampton Street to the west. The main entrance was in the Strand. Conceived as a meeting place for religious and charitable organisations, it is probably most generally known as the focus of anti-slavery meetings in the 1830s and 1840s. It was a big space, 76 feet across, 131 feet long and 45 feet high. With its large balcony it could hold 3,000 people. Like the St James's Hall in Piccadilly, it had a narrow frontage onto the street consisting of two Corinthian pillars with a flight of steps from the street. It became the home of important choral performances for nearly fifty years and was used for choral singing from the 1830s by the Sacred Harmonic Society. As such it was particularly associated with the music of Mendelssohn after the success of *Elijah* in 1846. A permanent organ was installed in 1840 and more improvements carried out in 1850 when a new roof was constructed, intended to improve the sound.

The New Philharmonic Society's first concert was held here in March 1852. The hall was notably the location of Berlioz's concerts in 1852 when the leading instrumentalists in the country were assembled in an orchestra of 110 players, then reputed to be the largest ever brought together in London. Here were given Berlioz's *Romeo and Juliet* (24 March) and possibly the first fully adequate performance of Beethoven's *Choral Symphony* in London (9 June). (See also p. 210.)

Sir Frederic Cowen tells the story of a rehearsal at the Exeter Hall for one of the Crystal Palace Handel festivals. He reminds us that on the organ was the name of the maker, John Walker. After a rehearsal one very hot evening in June, Cowen received a note from one of the tenors saying that having to sing in such a warm atmosphere facing the name 'Johnny Walker', that of a well-known brand of whisky, was more than he and his thirsty companions could bear. Cowen obligingly had the name covered.

Exeter Hall was also the place where 'Monster Concerts' were given that lasted for four or five hours. These consisted of forty or fifty items, including a few by big names, but most of the performers were unknowns who were satisfied by seeing themselves on a West End bill with the elect. The hall was bought by the YMCA in 1881 and musical performances were banned. Exeter Hall was pulled down in 1907 and the site used for the Strand Palace Hotel.

31 The Great Anti-Slavery demonstration at Exeter Hall gives a better idea of the capacity of the hall than later illustrations of concerts given there. The organ, to the right, was the focus of the platform for chorus and orchestra when used for concerts. This illustration from the *Illustrated London News* is dated 7 February 1863.

Freemasons' Hall
Great Queen Street
Tube: Covent Garden or Holborn

Designed by Thomas Sandby, Freemasons' Hall and Tavern in Great Queen Street opened in May 1776 and is remembered as the home of the Academy of Ancient Music, and in July 1864 for the inaugural meeting of the College of Organists. Above the main entrance was a gallery with an organ. Benefit concerts and meetings and performances of the Academy of Ancient Music were held there. The hall was rebuilt in the 1860s and later burnt down. The present hall was erected between 1927 and 1933 but gives no feel for the style and scale of its earlier incarnation.

Gaiety Theatre
Aldwych
Tube: Charing Cross or Temple

The theatre's original site was between the Strand and Catherine, Exeter and Wellington Streets. The Strand Music Hall had stood here but the site was developed in the 1860s. It opened as the Gaiety in 1868 and saw performances of W. S. Gilbert's *An Old Score* (1869) and *Ganymede and Galatea* (1872), and the specially commissioned Gilbert and Sullivan's *Thespis*, conducted by the composer in 1871, the music of which is now lost. The theatre closed in July 1903 for the Strand improvement scheme and reopened facing up the Strand on the corner of Strand

32   The Gaiety Theatre, Strand. This postcard is postmarked 7 November 1911.

and Aldwych in October the same year. It closed in 1939, though it was not demolished until 1957. It is now replaced by Citibank House. A plaque marks the site.

Lyceum Theatre
Wellington Street
Tube: Charing Cross, Covent Garden or Holborn

The Lyceum was originally built in the Strand in 1772 and used for opera, ballet, puppet shows, conjuring, panoramas and similar entertainments. In 1794 the lease was taken by the composer Dr Samuel Arnold, who had the auditorium reconstructed to stage opera, but failed to secure a licence, and so the theatre was used for a circus and performances by horses. In 1802 it housed Madame Tussaud's waxworks, but it was finally licensed for musical works in 1809 when the company of the Theatre Royal across the street in Drury Lane took up residence after fire had destroyed their theatre. In 1816 it was rebuilt as the New Theatre Royal English Opera House, retaining the frontage to the Strand. It was the first stage to be lit by gaslight. Concerts and operas were performed until it was destroyed by fire in 1830.

It was rebuilt again, now as the New Theatre Lyceum and English Opera House on a site in Wellington Street and there were winter seasons of Italian opera and promenade concerts, and in the 1850s French and English operas. In the 1870s and '80s Verdi and Wagner operas were given and the Carl Rosa Opera appeared.

After a dip in its fortunes the theatre regained its popularity as the Royal Lyceum Theatre with Leopold Lewis's *The Bells*, produced by Henry Irving, who took on the management in 1878 with Ellen Terry as his leading lady. At the same time, Bram Stoker (author of *Dracula*) gave up his job in the civil service to become Irving's business manager. Irving commissioned some of the leading British composers of the day to write incidental music, including Stanford for Tennyson's *Becket*, a very young Edward German for Shakespeare's *Richard II* and *Henry VIII* and Mackenzie for Herman Merrivale's *Ravenswood*. In the 1880s and '90s, Irving would entertain to supper the leading personalities of the day at the Beefsteak Room at the Lyceum and Stoker tells how Boito, Paderewski, George Henschel, Hans Richter, Liszt and Gounod were all his guests.

The theatre also had a long association with Gilbert and Sullivan. Gilbert's first stage work, *Uncle Baby*, was performed there in 1863, and Sullivan was commissioned by Irving to write incidental music for a production of *Macbeth* in 1888 and also for *King Arthur* in 1895. In 1899 the D'Oyly Carte Company had a brief run of *The Mikado*. The Lyceum was demolished in 1902 and in 1904 reopened after Sir Oswald Stoll redesigned the theatre as a music hall. Later it put on variety shows, music and ballet performances – some by the Carl Rosa company, others by Diaghilev's Russian Ballet and by Chaliapin. During the Second World War, like Covent Garden up the road, the theatre was used as a ballroom for troops on leave.

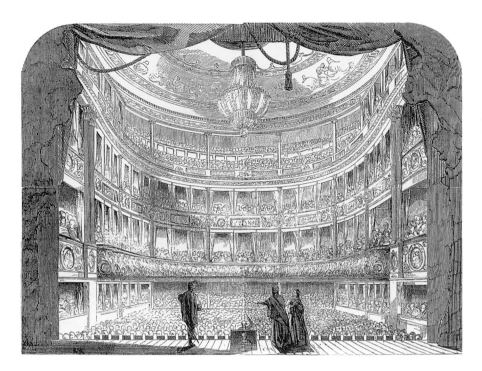

33   The Lyceum Theatre auditorium viewed from the stage: this engraving shows it on opening as the Royal Italian Opera after the destruction of the Royal Opera House by fire. From the *Illustrated London News*, 19 April 1856.

More recently the Lyceum has been restored to its former glory by Andrew Lloyd Webber as a home for musicals, reopening in 1996 with *Jesus Christ, Superstar*.

New London Opera House
Kingsway
Tube: Holborn

The Opera House was opened at a cost of £200,000 by Oscar Hammerstein (father of Oscar Hammerstein II of *Oklahoma* fame) in November 1911 with the British première of the spectacular opera *Quo Vadis?* by the French composer Jean Nouguès. Hammerstein was determined to make a big splash with this sumptuous production in luxurious surroundings. The opera house was large, with seating for 2,700, and lavishly decorated. 'The company descended the stairs flanked with marble balustrades to settle themselves in the ample armchairs officially called stalls, or passed through charming little private ante-rooms into spacious boxes', reported one commentator. It closed in 1913, to be bought by Oswald Stoll, who reopened it, staging variety shows and in 1915 an opera season. The following year it was renamed the Stoll Picture Theatre. From 1952 onward it was used for ballet, opera and plays but was pulled down in 1958, and in 1960 an office block was built on the

34　The London Opera House, later the Stoll Theatre, in 1912.

site. The new building incorporated the Royalty Theatre. It was eventually bought by the London School of Economics.

Opéra Comique
Strand
Tube: Charing Cross or Embankment

The Opéra Comique lasted for less than thirty years: opening in 1870 and closing in 1899, it was demolished soon afterwards. The building was first occupied by French companies, but reopened in 1877 with D'Oyly Carte's Comedy Opera Company performing a clutch of Gilbert and Sullivan operettas: *The Sorcerer*, followed by the premiere of *HMS Pinafore* (1879) and then *The Pirates of Penzance* (1880) and *Patience* (1881). The last opera performed there was the run of Stanford's *Shamus O'Brien*, in 1896, conducted by a youthful Henry Wood.

The Regent
37–43 Euston Road
Tube: King's Cross

On the site of what is now the Town Hall extension, opposite St Pancras Station, the hall opened as the Euston Palace Music Hall in 1900, and was later acquired by Nigel Playfair and reopened in August 1922 as The Regent. It is principally remembered for Rutland Boughton's opera *The Immortal Hour*, which opened there on 13

October 1922 with a young Gwen Ffrangçon-Davies as Etain. After a slow start it became an institution, fans returning many times to see it. It ran for 216 performances and returned in November 1923 for another 160. It is thus the longest-ever running opera by a British composer. Boughton's Christmas drama *Bethlehem* was also staged at this time. Later the theatre was reconstructed as the Century Cinema, becoming the Granada in 1967 before closing in 1968.

Royal Opera House, Covent Garden
Bow Street/Covent Garden Piazza
Tube: Covent Garden, Charing Cross, Embankment or Leicester Square

There have been four theatres at Covent Garden, as the Royal Opera House is still familiarly known. In the eighteenth and early nineteenth centuries operas, pantomimes, plays and dance were put, on with seating for around 2,000, from the time of its opening in 1732 with Congreve's *The Way of the World* to its destruction by fire in 1808. In 1728 John Rich, actor–manager, commissioned *The Beggar's Opera* from John Gay. The profits went towards building the Theatre Royal. Handel operas were performed there between 1735 and 1759, and in 1743 *Messiah* had its first London performance.

In 1846, after a disagreement with the management of Her Majesty's Theatre, home of opera and ballet then, Michael Costa, its conductor and musical director, moved to Covent Garden and brought several members of his company with him. The interior of the theatre was reconstructed and a grand reopening in April 1847 saw a performance of Rossini's *Semiramide*. Thereafter opera by Italian composers alternated with works translated into Italian. The theatre was destroyed by fire in 1856 and rebuilt. It reopened in 1858 with Meyerbeer's *Les Huguenots*.

In 1888 Augustus Harris, the son of a former stage manager of Drury Lane, became manager of Covent Garden and supported by aristocratic backers brought a new life to the opera season, which had been in decline, bringing the leading singers and conductors of the day to London. Covent Garden continued to be known as the Royal Italian Opera until 1892. After Harris's death in June 1896 the Grand Opera Syndicate, well-off opera lovers who guaranteed any losses, took over his interests under the chairmanship of H. V. Higgins.

During the quarter-century before the First World War, stars of the opera house included not only the leading British singers of the day but also such legendary names as Mattia Battistini, Emma Calvé, Caruso, Eduard and Jean de Reszke, Emmy Destinn, Emma Eames, Mary Garden, Nellie Melba, Adelina Patti, Tetrazzini and Giovanni Zenatello. Debussy's *Pelléas et Mélisande* reached London in May 1909 and was staged under the personal supervision of the composer. It returned in the summer seasons of 1910 and 1911. Beecham's spring season in 1910 attracted notoriety for nine performances of Strauss's *Elektra*, two of them conducted by Strauss himself. This was a season of pioneering repertoire with

35   The view from the audience: *Lohengrin* opens the 1902 opera season in the presence of the king and queen on 8 May that year.

Debussy's *L'Enfant Prodigue* done in costume, and operas by Delius and Ethel Smyth. *Elektra* returned in the winter season of 1910 with Strauss's *Salomé* with the Finnish singer Aino Ackté in the title role, and attracted much comment.

The summer 1914 season was a glittering one, and during July it included the three-hundredth performance of *Don Giovanni* at Covent Garden and the hundredth of *Le Nozze di Figaro*.

The opera house was closed during the war and was used by the Ministry of Works as a furniture repository. After the war, short opera seasons resumed under Thomas Beecham, and the opera house reopened on 12 May 1919 with Melba as Mimi in *La Bohème*. Opera was supplemented with dance, circuses, films, pantomimes and cabaret. The interwar revival was led by many famous names – Clara Butt, Melba, Eva Turner, Kirsten Flagstad, Isobel Baillie, Gigli, Tauber and Heddle Nash.

In the Second World War the building was leased to Mecca Cafés and used as a dance hall for the forces. Towards the end of the war, government patronage for music and the arts was promoted (later to be embodied in an official organisation – the Arts Council). Boosey and Hawkes, music publishers, acquired the lease after the war, and the opera house reopened in February 1946 under David Webster and Ninette de Valois with the ballet *Sleeping Beauty* conducted by Constant Lambert. Lambert was also the principal instigator of the sumptuous Covent Garden staging of Purcell's *The Fairy Queen*, presented on 12 December 1946 at the start of Covent Garden's first season of opera in English, equally involving the Sadler's Wells Ballet and the Covent Garden Opera.

The resident opera company was directed by Karl Rankl, and *Carmen* was performed in 1947, followed by new operas such as Britten's *Peter Grimes*, *Billy Budd* and *Gloriana*, Walton's *Troilus and Cressida* and Tippett's *Midsummer Marriage*. Opera and ballet companies still shared seasons at the Royal Opera House. The history of Covent Garden since the war is, of course, the history of the singers who have appeared there. As in earlier generations this has been highlighted by the constant procession of big names such as Maria Callas, Joan Sutherland, Luciano Pavarotti and Plácido Domingo.

The government gave land for an extension in 1975 and this opened in July 1982. With the help of National Lottery funding a wide-ranging refurbishment programme was carried out by Dixon Jones BDP and completed in 2000. A major feature of this was the incorporation of the Vilar Floral Hall into the complex. As the highest subsidised arts facility in the UK, the Covent Garden refurbishment generated a widely publicised financial row that extended over several years and has been the subject of several books and a TV documentary. Since the reopening, however, a measure of stability seems to have been restored.

Backstage and front-of-house tours lasting an hour and a quarter are available at 10.30 a.m., 12.30 p.m. and 2.30 p.m. Monday to Saturday. The unsurpassed archives include prints, photographs, programmes, song sheets and files on the Royal Ballet and Diaghilev's Ballet Russes. The cuttings scrap books are an invaluable resource. In the main foyer is a large statue by Prinz von Gleicken of Frederick Gye in court dress dating from 1880. Gye was manager of the Royal Italian Opera (1848–1878). Gye built the present opera house. To the right on entering we see the sculpture of the head and hands of Beecham by Michael Rizzello, OBE. Among the many works of art throughout the building are busts of Melba (by Bertram Mackenna, undated) and Patti (by Ludovic Durand, 1869) both at the top of the Crush Bar steps, and Hockney's commissioned portrait of administrator Sir David Webster in the Ampitheatre Bar, while Yolande Sonnabend's oil portrait of Kenneth Macmillan, on loan from the Garrick Club, is to the left in the foyer.

36 *The Sphere* spotlights a high-society view of the 1900 opera season.

St Martin's Hall

Long Acre
Tube: Covent Garden or Holborn

The hall, designed by Richard Westmacott, was opened in 1850 on a site at Long Acre at the junction with Endell Street. It was used for classes and concerts and provided John Hullah, champion of the Hullah-Wilhem method of teaching singing, with a venue for his singing classes. The hall seated 3,000 and was used for both concerts and classes at very reasonable fees. Sterndale Bennett's cantata *The May Queen* received its first London performances here in December 1858, a work that at the time helped to stimulate the growing tradition of amateur choral societies by giving an extended score that all could manage and also by providing an example to other composers. Here Charles Dickens's first public readings from his books were given, and Mr and Mrs German Reed's then noted dramatic/musical events were held from 1855. The hall was burnt down in 1860, rebuilt in 1862 and reopened for concerts until 1867, when it became a theatre. Later it was the printing works of the Odhams Press Ltd, but although the building survived the Second World War, the former appearance of the whole area has now been swept away and redeveloped under new office buildings.

37   The opening of St Martin's Hall, Long Acre, in February 1850. John Hullah is conducting.

Savoy Theatre

Savoy Court, Strand
Tube: Charing Cross

When his lease on the Royalty Theatre expired, Richard D'Oyly Carte built his own theatre as a permanent home for Gilbert and Sullivan operas. The architect, C. J. Phipps, also co-designed Queen's Hall with T. E. Knightley. The Savoy Theatre was the first public building to have electric lighting and opened in 1881 with *Patience*. It continued to stage the Savoy operas until the 1890s when a dispute with Gilbert caused a breach that ended in court. For twenty years (1909–29) no Gilbert and Sullivan works were performed. Instead the theatre was used for plays and three seasons of opera. In 1929 the theatre was refurbished and reopened with a gala performance of *The Gondoliers*. The centenary of *Trial by Jury*, the first Gilbert and Sullivan opera performed under D'Oyly Carte's management, was celebrated in

1975. The celebration consisted of a complete cycle of Gilbert and Sullivan operas, including the rarely heard *Utopia Ltd* and a concert performance of *The Grand Duke*. In 1990 a fire gutted the auditorium but the Savoy reopened three years later with a charity ballet gala. It is now the venue for a variety of stage productions, including Gilbert and Sullivan operettas. In 2003 Raymond Gubbay attempted to promote popular seasons of opera but in less than a year the initiative had failed. The composer Peter Warlock (Philip Heseltine) was born in 1894 at the adjoining Savoy Hotel.

Theatre Royal, Drury Lane
Drury Lane
Tube: Covent Garden or Holborn

Three successive theatres were destroyed by fire before the fourth and current one opened in 1812. The stalls foyer contains a large statue of Michael Balfe by Leo A. Malempré. Balfe's early operas were successfully performed there, a regular feature of the time (see Part II). These included *The Siege of Rochelle*, which ran for seventy-three performances in 1835. Other statues include a bronze of Ivor Novello by Clemence Dane and, facing the doors, a statue of Noël Coward by Angela Conner which was donated by Graham Payn and unveiled by the Queen Mother in December 1998. Outside is a bust of Augustus Harris.

Musicals were launched in the 1920s and '30s with a succession of hits such as *Rose Marie, Desert Song, Showboat, Cavalcade*, and the Ivor Novello favourites from 1933 onwards. During the Second World War it became the headquarters of ENSA (Entertainments National Service Association). After the war Rodgers and Hammerstein took over, and the theatre is still host to long-running lavishly staged musicals.

Already known for scores such as *Rose Marie* in the 1920s, after the Second World War Drury Lane became the home of musicals, and a wooden plaque informs us in gold lettering that 'Miss Saigon produced by Cameron Mackintosh became the longest running musical in the history of this theatre on the 19 December 1994 with 2282 performances'. When it finally closed it had almost doubled this number.

Musicals at the Theatre Royal Drury Lane with over 700 performances		
1989	Miss Saigon	4,263
1958	My Fair Lady	2,281
1984	42nd Street	1,824
1947	Oklahoma	1,375
1976	Chorus Line	1,113
1953	The King & I	947
1974	Billy	904
1925	Rose Marie	851
1965	Hello Dolly	794
1951	South Pacific	792
1970	The Great Waltz	705

Barbican Hall
Barbican Centre, Silk Street
Tube: Barbican or Moorgate

City and East End

The Barbican Hall was opened in March 1982, and a redesign of the foyer took place during 2003. The unexpectedly wide hall with its extensive use of woods on the stage makes for a striking impression. Generally a warmer acoustic than the Royal Festival Hall, it is also noted for its good sightlines from most parts of the house.

38   The Barbican today.

The hall seats 2,000 and has been home to the London Symphony Orchestra from the outset. When the LSO is not performing, the hall is host to a wide range of concerts, ranging from recitals and symphony concerts to jazz, including the world's leading orchestras.

Financially supported by the City of London, the hall's very existence spurred competition in London's already well-provided concert life, and thus injected a new vitality into London musical activity, with thematic programming and series devoted to the leading artists of the day. In their ongoing 'Great Performers' series, period instrument ensembles such as Les Arts Florissants have had a notable following. Many BBC Symphony Orchestra concerts also now take place in the Barbican, and the BBC now has a permanent installation there. Other London orchestras that appear regularly include the City of London Sinfonia and the English Chamber Orchestra.

With Colin Davis the London Symphony Orchestra has made an internationally acclaimed series of CDs, recorded live during Barbican concerts, including all the major works of Berlioz, which have been issued on the orchestra's own label 'LSO Live'.

Crosby Hall
Tube: Liverpool Street

A private mansion called Crosby Place was built by merchant John Crosby in the fifteenth century at Bishopsgate and was, when new, the tallest house in London. The original site was in a passage leading from Bishopsgate to Crosby Square. Part of the building was destroyed by fire, and by the nineteenth century only the three largest rooms survived. In 1842 the violinist J. H. B. Dando secured a lease on the Great Chamber or Throne Room and after restoration opened it as a concert and assembly room. With its organ, it was used for numerous concerts, many of chamber music, of which it was a notable pioneer. Mendelssohn played at one of the concerts and in 1845 the programme included Purcell and Mendelssohn anthems and a chorale by Prince Albert. At this concert Mendelssohn's *Hear My Prayer,* which had been written for Crosby Hall, was first heard.

In the late nineteenth century the premises were converted into a restaurant. In the face of threatened development in 1910 the Great Hall – but not the Throne Room – was re-erected in Cheyne Walk, Chelsea. It survives, is now privately owned and is undergoing complete restoration and rebuilding, a process widely reported in the press, though not expected to be finished until 2010.

Eagle Tavern
City Road/Shepherdess Walk
Tube: Old Street

Dating from the early 1820s, the tavern had a Grecian Theatre attached to it and was famous for ballet and dancing. Dickens left a vivid description of the entertainment as it was in 1836 in 'Miss Evans and The Eagle' in *Sketches by Boz.*

> As to the concert-room, never was anything half so splendid. There was an orchestra for the singers, all paint, gilding, and plate-glass; and such an organ! . . . The audience were seated on elevated benches round the room, and crowded into every part of it; and everybody was eating and drinking as comfortably as possible . . . The concert commenced – overture on the organ. 'How solemn!' explained Miss J'mima Ivins . . . Comic song, accompanied on the organ. Miss J'mima Ivins was convulsed with laughter – The concert and vaudeville concluded, they promenaded the garden.

Marie Lloyd is said to have made her debut at the Eagle in 1885. It features in the song 'Pop Goes the Weasel' ('Up and down the City Road, In and out the Eagle . . .'). The Eagle also staged classical opera such as *Don Giovanni, The Barber of Seville* and *La Sonnambula* in the 1840s. The building was demolished in 1901 after a spell as a Salvation Army rehabilitation centre, but it was rebuilt as a pub and is still in use. It sports a plaque, and the well-known lines from the nursery rhyme quoted above are written on an outside wall.

Mermaid Theatre
Puddle Dock, Upper Thames Street
Tube: Blackfriars

Developed from a bombed Thames-side warehouse, the Mermaid was the brainchild of Bernard and Josephine Miles and opened as a permanent theatre in May 1959 with Laurie Johnson's musical *Lock Up Your Daughters* (a production issued on LP), followed by Purcell's opera *Dido and Aeneas*, with Kirsten Flagstad in the main role, which instantly put the theatre on the map with the *cognoscenti.* The Mermaid developed the format of shows featuring the words and music of celebrated popular entertainers with *Cowardy Custard* (Noël Coward) in 1972. Later, in 1974, came *Cole*, featuring the words and music of Cole Porter, and in 1976 *Side by Side by Sondheim.* All are remembered on original cast recordings made at the time. The Mermaid was conspicuous for its brickwork walls, which celebrated its origin as a warehouse, and the lack of a raised stage, which meant that audience and actors were much more integrated than was usual at that time. It closed in 1979 but was modernised and reopened in 1981. It is still sometimes used for recording sessions, BBC invitation concerts and the BBC's regular popular programme *Friday Night is Music Night.*

Sadler's Wells Theatre
Rosebery Avenue, Islington
Tube: Angel

Sadler's Wells has its roots in the seventeenth century. It was built by Thomas Sadler in his pleasure gardens as an opera and ballet house. The name derives from that of the proprietor and his discovery of a well, thought to have had healing properties, in the grounds of his house. By the end of 1685 hundreds were taking the waters and enjoying the musical performances. The theatre was rebuilt in 1765 and staged topical shows. It was bought in 1802 by a consortium that improved it and put on exhibitions and extravaganzas.

Later, Shakespeare plays were performed in the mid-nineteenth century but the theatre went downhill. Music hall performances were given in the 1880s onwards – at one period (1876) it became the New Spa Skating Rink and Winter Garden, but was shut down in 1906 for a long time. Sadler's Wells was eventually rebuilt in 1927 and reopened under Lilian Baylis in 1931 with *Twelfth Night*. From 1934 onwards it was used for opera, and for ballet under Ninette de Valois's direction. Britten's *Peter Grimes* was first performed there on 7 June 1945. Sadler's Wells escaped the wartime bombing and de Valois kept performances going throughout the war.

39   Sadler's Wells Theatre in the late eighteenth century.

The opera company moved to the Coliseum in 1968 and Sadler's Wells then put on many and varied attractions. The new building was started in 1996, with refurbishment completed in 1998, and it now hosts many ballet companies and is still used for opera. In 1999 the Birmingham Royal Ballet's London season featured John McCabe's full-length ballet *Edward II* (by David Bintley), and in 2001 *Arthur*, the two parts of the McCabe/Bintley ballet about King Arthur, were given on the same day, as a matinee and evening performance.

Kensington and Chelsea

Ranelagh Gardens
Chelsea
Tube: Sloane Square

The gardens were active from 1742 to 1803. Promenade concerts, where people could stand or walk while listening to music, were held here and Ranelagh was unusual in that both performers and audience could be under cover. It was generally considered to be more 'proper' than Vauxhall, possibly because it was higher priced.

40   The inside of the Rotunda in Ranelagh Gardens, 1754.

Mozart, as a child prodigy, appeared there in 1764. The site of Ranelagh Gardens is now part of the grounds of the Royal Hospital, Chelsea.

Royal Albert Hall
Kensington Gore
Tube: South Kensington or Kensington High Street

The inscription that extends round the outside of the hall at roof level reads: 'THIS HALL WAS ERECTED FOR THE ADVANCEMENT OF THE ARTS AND SCIENCES AND WORKS OF INDUSTRY OF ALL NATIONS IN FULFILMENT OF THE INTENTION OF ALBERT, PRINCE CONSORT'.

The hall was built with the proceeds from the Great Exhibition of 1851, funding also coming from selling boxes to private owners. Work stopped with Prince Albert's death in 1861 but restarted in 1865 and the massive hall, seating up to 8,000, was opened in March 1871. A mosaic frieze 800 feet long encircles the building 100 feet up and consists of various allegorical groups. To the right of the porch facing Hyde Park is the group representing music, designed by F. R. Pickersgill RA. This includes a harper playing to a medieval group, followed by a musician leading a joyful bridal procession and finally a representation of music as the messenger of love.

The hall had a somewhat miscellaneous feel to its lettings from the outset which continues to today, events promoted there not only include concerts, especially choral concerts, but also exhibitions, banquets, boxing matches and events of a national character, of which the Festival of Remembrance is probably the most recognised today. A series of celebrated European composer-organists were invited to give recitals to mark the occasion (see Part II) on the great organ when the hall first opened. Wagner's concert series, notionally conducted by the composer, took place in 1877 (see p. 304) and the soprano Adelina Patti concerts in 1886.

Between the wars the hall was the home of the Royal Choral Society's popular performances of Coleridge-Taylor's *Hiawatha*, in costume, the arena full of wigwams, conducted by Malcolm Sargent. After the war the Albert Hall became synonymous with the ubiquitous Sunday evening Tchaikovsky nights, which always attracted a large audience, though standards were decidedly variable. Today this same mass audience responds to seasons of popular operas promoted by Raymond Gubbay, visiting East European opera companies and large-scale popular ballet performances.

Since 1941 the Royal Albert Hall has been the home of the Promenade concerts, and in recent years an open-air prom in Hyde Park has been held at the same time as the Last Night of the Proms. For twenty years after the war a small number of conductors, notably Sir Malcolm Sargent, conducted night after night, often with the same orchestra. Concerts at this period have been accused of being unadventurous and lacking in charisma, but an examination of the programmes and revisiting those that survive in sound archives shows this to be unfair. A generation was educated to know a wide repertoire at very small cost, new British music was consistently played, while the leading British composers of the early twentieth century had a wide exposure leading to their later celebrity on LP records and CDs.

Possibly the brightest flame from that period was the young cellist Jacqueline du Pré (see Part II) who appeared regularly from 1962, particularly with the Elgar Concerto, her appearance generating enormous queues for the promenade. Since the mid-1960s the Proms have been built up to be a great international festival with a huge variety of visiting orchestras, the presentation of concert performances of operas and an enormous repertoire (constantly the subject of criticism from this group or that). As the only growing classical music series in London it performs a vital role in developing audiences and has achieved an international reputation owing to the dissemination of recordings of the concerts via the BBC Transcription Service. It is now the only major arts event where a ticket for the promenade is still only £4, possibly a major reason for its continuing success with a young audience.

The Royal Albert Hall is familiar from television broadcasts of the Last Night of the Proms, and several years have appeared on videos. In feature films the most celebrated Albert Hall sequence is to be found in *The Man Who Knew Too Much* where the Albert Hall passage comes towards the end, in the 1934 version in black and white, in Hitchcock's 1956 version accurately reflecting the appearance of the hall in colour. Between the two, in the wartime film *Love Story*, featuring Hubert

Bath's score *Cornish Rhapsody*, the music (for piano and orchestra) is seen being played at the Albert Hall.

The Albert Hall acoustic was a problem from the outset, the echo resulting in the gibe that it was the only place where many British composers could hear their music twice. This was only adequately tackled after the Second World War with the installation of the canopy over the orchestra and the 'mushrooms' suspended from the ceiling. When the latter were first installed it was found they tended to fill with condensation and holes had to be drilled in them to prevent this happening.

The Royal Albert Hall organ was out of action from 2002 to 2004 for restoration by Mander Organs, reopening with an Inauguration Concert on 26 June 2004 with the Royal Philharmonic Orchestra conducted by Richard Hickox at which organists David Briggs, Thomas Trotter and John Scott all appeared. On this occasion David Briggs improvised a set of variations on the tune from Purcell's *Abdelazar* used by Britten in his *Young Person's Guide to the Orchestra,* to demonstrate the stops, in what he called 'the young person's guide to the organ'. When first built, it was claimed to be the biggest in the world, and despite refits over the years, notably in the 1920s, it had deteriorated, suffering in particular from the hall's heating system, which had dried out and split much of the original internal woodwork. All the pipes remain but most of the mechanism has been replaced, together with a new electrical system. The reopening was widely reported in the press, the statistic that the organ contains 9,999 pipes being often cited.

Royal Festival Hall
South Bank Centre, Belvedere Road
Tube: Waterloo or Embankment

Vauxhall and South Bank

With the loss of Queen's Hall there was no adequate concert hall in London suitable for symphony concerts, the Royal Albert Hall and Central Hall Westminster being unacceptable acoustically and the Albert Hall being too large for most events. The Royal Festival Hall, the vision of the then Home Secretary, Herbert Morrison, with the motto 'let the people sing', was built as part of the arrangements for the Festival of Britain in 1951. Designed by a team led by Leslie Martin, the hall was based on the London County Council (LCC) and embraced the latest architectural philosophies. It was regarded from the first as a distinctive modernist building. Seeking to exclude external noise, in conception it is a box within a box, John Pudney calling it 'an egg poised on stilts and partially enclosed . . . the casing itself is largely transparent'.

The foundation stone was laid by the Prime Minister, Clement Attlee, in 1949 and the building opened with a dedication concert on 3 May 1951 followed by a concert the next day, conducted by Sir Malcolm Sargent and attended by the king and queen. This was the first purpose-built concert hall of its size in London since the Queen's Hall was opened in 1893. It cost £2 million and had seating capacity for about 2,900 people. For its time it was very acoustically advanced, though it was criticised as 'dry'.

41   Royal Festival Hall from the Hungerford Footbridge across the River Thames.

There were acoustic tests including performances by a student orchestra in which the conductor Leslie Head, then a student horn player, remembers how cold the sound seemed to be. Certainly with its small reverberation time even today the sound is considered analytical and the hall is rarely used for recordings. The organ, designed by Ralph Downes, was installed in 1954.

Specially commissioned works for the opening of the hall included Rubbra's *Festival Te Deum*. There was also a composition competition whose winning entry was Peter Racine Fricker's Violin Concerto. The Royal Festival Hall remained the pre-eminent London concert hall, seating 2,900 people, until the 2,000-seat Barbican Hall opened in 1982. As such the hall hosted all the major orchestras, both British and foreign, and all the principal musicians of the day when visiting London. Although the various orchestras, including the BBC Symphony Orchestra, had regular series during the season, it was unusual to find themed series or events until the 1980s. Following the success of the London Symphony Orchestra making the Barbican its home, the other London orchestras have sought residency status at the Festival Hall, currently enjoyed by the London Philharmonic Orchestra, the New London Consort and the Philharmonia Orchestra.

The letting policy in the 1970s was notably unadventurous, and when in 1977 the conductor Bryan Fairfax tried to hire the hall for the revival of Elgar's *King Olaf*, he was refused until he could obtain 1,500 signatures from an intending audience (which he obtained – the concert sold out). With the abolition of the Greater London Council, successor to the LCC, the centre was no longer treated as a space for hire but an integrated arts complex, the South Bank Centre.

The South Bank Centre music complex was completed in 1967 with the opening of the adjacent smaller Queen Elizabeth Hall and Purcell Room, holding 900 and about 360 respectively, and built in the notably brutalist style of the 1960s with much use of raw concrete. However, the Queen Elizabeth Hall in particular has been used for much pioneering programming and, for example, over the years has been home to many concert performances of rare operas put on by such fringe companies as the Chelsea Opera Group and Opera Viva. Here Berthold Goldschmidt's opera *Beatrice Cenci* had its first concert performance in 1988 and was broadcast, with extracts shown on television. The Purcell Room became the regular alternative venue to the Wigmore Hall, and for many performers preferable, owing to the inclusion of the hall in the South Bank Centre's publicity literature.

The Royal Festival Hall, as it was when it first opened, with the main entrance on the opposite side to the River Thames and raised walkways enabling patrons to cross to the hall without being on the same level as the traffic, is vividly and extensively recorded in the otherwise rather feeble black and white thriller *The Long Arm* (1956) featuring Jack Hawkins as the detective and Herbert Howells's daughter Ursula Howells. Much later the hall is briefly seen in the film *A Touch of Class*, with George Segal rushing between a concert at the hall and his mistress's flat in Soho.

Vauxhall Gardens

Vauxhall Gardens lasted for nearly two hundred years, from 1660 to 1859. The gardens were located off Kennington Lane, and north of where Vauxhall Station is now. They were laid out in 1661 and were converted into pleasure gardens in 1732 by Jonathan Tyers. Particularly popular in the eighteenth century, they encompassed all musical tastes, from classical to modern, sacred to secular, symphonies to songs. At a time when the new music was largely imported, many featured composers and performers were English. The Gardens were written about by several authors and diarists such as Pepys and Evelyn. Composers who wrote songs for Vauxhall included Arne, Hook and Bishop, the last writing five operas for Vauxhall. A statue of Handel by Roubiliac stood at the entrance and is now in the Victoria and Albert Museum.

In *Sketches by Boz*, Dickens described the gardens as being revealed as tawdry when daytime opening was inaugurated in the mid-1830s. The gardens closed in 1840 when the owners went bankrupt. They reopened shortly afterwards only finally closing in 1859. The site has now been heavily built on, with Kennington Lane to the south and Tyers Street (in memory of Jonathan) in the middle.

42   The 'Moorish-Gothick' orchestra (or bandstand) in Vauxhall Gardens, 1784: the celebrated soprano Elizabeth Weichsel (later Billington) is singing with orchestra. Engraving after Rowlandson.

2 • Choirs and Places Where They Sing

The City is full of churches, some hidden unobtrusively down alleyways, others squeezed between office blocks, some even standing proudly within their own grounds. These churches have a long musical history in the story of London. Today, many offer lunchtime concerts and recitals, some evening concerts as well. Indeed the churches of London offer an enormous amount of music on their own accounts and many also host a variety of choirs, orchestras and concert-giving organisations on an ad hoc basis. In the summer the City of London Festival takes place across many of these churches and halls. The variety is amazing, as are the memorial windows, plaques and kneelers commemorating London's musicians and composers. This also means that there is an active concentration of professional and semi-professional singers and a large number of organists and musical directors within a very small area. The following thumbnail sketches of a select list of favourite churches should be read in conjunction with the account of churches in Chapter 6. For opening hours see their respective websites.

City Churches

St Andrew's, Holborn
Holborn Circus
Tube: Chancery Lane or Farringdon; train: Farringdon

St Andrew's was the headquarters of the Royal College of Organists between 1991 and 2003, when they moved to Birmingham. The earliest mention of the church is in 951 and in the twelfth century a Norman stone church was built. Sir Christopher Wren designed a new building in 1686. While the present interior dates back to the mid-fifteenth century, the actual fabric of the interior was destroyed in a 1941 air raid. The restored church was reconsecrated in 1961 and the tomb of Thomas Coram, benefactor and founder of the Foundling Hospital, was placed at the west end. The organ was built by Mander in 1990 within a case whose upper part is mid-nineteenth century from the chapel of the Foundling Hospital; the supporting columns and lower part of the case are a restoration following an eighteenth-century drawing showing the organ as it stood in the Foundling Hospital chapel.

43 (facing page) Westminster Abbey on the scale Purcell would have known. The view from the cloisters garden today.

St Botolph's

Aldgate

Tube: Aldgate

What is reputed to be the oldest working organ in the City, dating from 1676, is to be found here. The church was completely rebuilt in 1744 when the organ was reinstated, though it was rebuilt again by Hill in 1867. The church was badly damaged by fire in 1966 and Mander restored the organ using the original pipework and refurbished the case with gilding but left the pipes ungilded. The church is occasionally used by the BBC for choral programmes, and it is also used for concerts, notably during the summer City of London Festival.

St Bride's

Fleet Street

Tube: St Paul's or Blackfriars; train: Blackfriars

The distinctive tower, by Wren, resembles a wedding cake with its tiers. The present building, also by Wren, was begun in 1673 and completed in 1703. It was badly damaged in a Second World War air raid, but has been restored. An exhibition in the Crypt relates the fascinating history of the eight churches that have stood on this site. Musical associations are strong. Thomas Weelkes, madrigal composer and organist, was buried here in 1623 and a memorial plaque to him can be found in the Crypt, erected to commemorate the tercentenary of his death. The organ was destroyed in the 1940 bombing and as a gift from Lord Astor a new instrument was built in 1957 by the John Compton Organ Co. Today there are numerous recitals and a well-known choir.

St Giles, Cripplegate

On the piazza facing the Barbican Centre

Tube: Moorgate or Barbican

A church has occupied this site for nearly a thousand years. The present church was built in 1394 but has been extensively restored after fire damage and bombing raids. After the Second World War it was rebuilt by Godfrey Allen.

Oliver Cromwell was married here and Ben Jonson, Daniel Defoe and Holman Hunt were baptised in the church. Shakespeare was a parishioner and John Milton is buried here – his statue is within the church. The original organ was by Renatus Harris (1704). The current organ was originally built for the redundant St Luke's Church, Old Street, and was installed in St Giles by Mander in 1971. It had been first built by Jordan and Bridge and rebuilt by Gray and Davison and later Henry Willis in the nineteenth century. In 1947 it was repaired by Mander. The church has a modern window of the Fortune Theatre, Golden Lane. St Giles has an honourable history of recording (see Chapter 6) and is still used for recording sessions, the most recent at the time of writing being that of choral music by Cecilia McDowell for the Dutton Epoch label in May 2004. St Giles is now the headquarters of the St Giles International Organ School.

St Lawrence Jewry
Gresham Street
Tube: Bank or St Paul's

This twelfth-century church stood on the east side of the City on a site then occupied by the Jewish community, hence the name. Like so many others it was almost destroyed in the 1940 air raids, but restored and reopened in 1957. It contains a grand piano that previously belonged to Sir Thomas Beecham, and an organ by Noel Mander with fifty speaking stops. There are regular recitals – piano on Mondays and organ on Tuesdays, with occasional special lunchtime and evening concerts.

St Mary-le-Bow
Cheapside
Tube: St Paul's or Mansion House

The first mention of Bow bells is in 1469 when the Common Council ordered a curfew to be rung at 9 p.m. each evening, and this continued until 1876. Bow bells are celebrated in song and story, from the tale of Dick Whittington to the nursery rhyme 'Oranges and Lemons'. Pepys occasionally refers to Bow bells in his diaries. By 1881 there were twelve bells, but in 1926 they were declared unringable and did not sound again until restored and recast in 1933 through the generosity of Gordon Selfridge, founder of Selfridges, Oxford Street.

The bells were destroyed in a May 1941 air raid. Now there is a new peal of twelve bells, cast in 1956 at the celebrated Whitechapel bellfoundry (see p. 181) and rung regularly. The tune used to strike the quarters and hour was composed by Sir Charles Villiers Stanford in 1904. The organ is by Rushworth and Dreaper, Liverpool, with a case by Dove Brothers who rebuilt the church in the mid-1960s following the war damage. Much of the cost of rebuilding and recasting the bells was the gift of the Bernard Sunley Charitable Foundation and Holy Trinity, Wall Street, in New York.

St Mary Woolnoth
King William Street on the corner with Lombard Street
Tube: Bank

The church, with its very unchurchlike façade, stands on the apex between the two streets. It was rebuilt by Hawksmoor and reopened in 1727. It contains a seventeenth-century Schmidt organ, built by 'Father' Smith. Of particular musical interest is the incumbent from 1780 until 1807, who was John Newton, formerly vicar of Olney, Bucks, and collaborator with William Cowper on the *Olney Hymns*.

St Michael's
St Michael's Alley, Cornhill
Tube: Bank

The entire church, except the tower, was destroyed in the fire of London in 1666. It was rebuilt by Wren in 1669–72. The earliest pipes of the organ date from 1684. It was built by Renatus Harris and the opening recital was given by Henry Purcell. The organ has been enlarged many times, most recently by Rushworth and Dreaper.

Directors of music have included some most distinguished musicians, including William Boyce, Richard Limpus (founder of the Royal College of Organists) and Harold Darke, the latter in post for almost fifty years and composer of, among other pieces, 'In the Bleak Midwinter'. Jonathan Rennert celebrated his silver jubilee as organist in 2004.

The church is noted for the St Michael's Singers, the choir that Harold Darke founded in 1919 and conducted until his retirement in 1966. It established a reputation for the performance of Bach Cantatas and of new British music of the day, first performances including Parry's *The Vision of Life*, Britten's *Te Deum*, W. H. Harris's *Michael Angelo's Confession of Faith*, Dyson's *Hierusalem*, Vaughan Williams's *A Vision of Aeroplanes* and Howells's *An English Mass*. The choir was dormant after Darke left but was re-established in 1979 by the new Director of Music Jonathan Rennert who immediately promoted a series of performances, though with the original choir of eighty halved and on some occasions smaller than that. An example of that choir may still be heard on the LP they made in 1981 of music by Parry with George Thalben-Ball at the organ (Antiphon ANTI 2503). An organ recital is given every Monday at 1 p.m. except on public holidays, in a long-running series that started in 1916.

St Paul's Cathedral
St Paul's Churchyard, EC4
Tube: St Paul's; or walk up Ludgate Hill from Blackfriars

Built by Sir Christopher Wren to replace the cathedral destroyed in the Great Fire of London, St Paul's has always been a significant musical centre in the City. Handel and Mendelssohn both loved playing the grand organ, which was at that time the one commissioned in 1694 and built by 'Father' Smith inside the case designed by Wren and decorated with carvings by Grinling Gibbons. The organ was rather too big for the case and several pipes projected at the top, later screened by extra carvings. The pedals were added later. This organ was designed for services within the quire, but as the nave began to be used for services a newer and larger instrument was needed. In the same year – 1872 – that it was built, by Henry Willis, John Stainer

Organists of St Paul's	
1530	John Redford
1549	Thomas Giles
1591	Thomas Morley
1622	John Tomkins
1624	Adrian Batten
1638	Albertus Bryne
1687	John Blow
1695	Jeremiah Clarke
1707	Richard Brind
1718	Maurice Green
1756	John Jones
1796	Thomas Attwood
1832	John Goss
1872	Sir John Stainer
1888	Sir George Martin
1917	Charles Macpherson
1927	Stanley Marchant
1936	John Dykes Bower
1968	Christopher Dearnley
1990	**John Scott**
2004	Malcolm Archer

44 St Paul's from the Millennium footbridge.

was appointed organist and carried out many reforms, including enlarging the choir. The organ's Wren case was split in half, modified and put against the pillars supporting the dome on either side of the quire, as it still is today. The organ was reconstructed in 1972–7 by Mander and was ready for the Queen's Silver Jubilee in 1977. Organ recitals are held on Sunday afternoons at 5 p.m., and celebrity recitals on the first Thursday of the month from May to October. An annual free performance of Handel's *Messiah* attracts an enormous following. The choir consists of thirty choristers, eight probationers and eighteen men. They give concerts and broadcasts as well as taking part in all the choral services. There was long a tradition for charity children to sing at St Paul's, and the massed singing of several thousand children from the so-called Free Schools was one of the city's musical marvels to visiting composers as varied as Haydn, Berlioz and Liszt (see Part II).

In the Crypt can be seen the graves or memorials of many distinguished organists and musicians associated with St Paul's. (These are discussed in Chapter 4.) There are countless guide books about St Paul's, but of particular interest is the booklet entitled *Music at St Paul's: the story of the choir, organ and school* which is generously illustrated. It is on sale in the cathedral bookshop.

St Sepulchre-without-Newgate
Giltspur Street
Tube: Farringdon or St Paul's

St Sepulchre looks forbidding from the outside, as well it might, for its Great Bell was rung on the mornings of executions at the nearby Newgate Prison, and the handbell rung outside the condemned cell at midnight. Inside, however, its treasures are worth a visit from anyone musically inclined. It is the largest parish church in the City and its name derives from its title during the Crusades – St Edmund and the Holy Sepulchre. The main part of the church was gutted in the great fire of 1666 and rebuilt 1670–71, though the porch, tower and outer walls date from about 1450. The roof and plaster ceilings date from 1834. The interior was remodelled in 1932.

Sir Henry Wood learned to play the organ from the age of ten and was appointed Assistant Organist at fourteen. His ashes were buried in the church in 1945 and lie beneath the central St Cecilia window in what is now the Musicians' Chapel. Below it hangs a laurel wreath and at one side of the window Wood is shown as a youth playing the organ. In the other, as Sir Henry, he is shown conducting a Prom at Queen's Hall. The Musicians' Chapel was dedicated in 1955. Stained glass windows depict John Ireland and Dame Nellie Melba. Above the altar is the 'Magnificat' window in memory of the children's composer Walter Carroll. Kneelers in the church are embroidered with musical themes and dedicated to musicians, composers and conductors. A glass fronted case contains the Musicians' Book of Remembrance.

45 An example of the kneelers in St Sepulchre's Church dedicated to specific composers.

The tower has a peal of twelve bells, restored as recently as 1985. These were made famous by the nursery rhyme 'Oranges and Lemons' as 'The Bells of Old Bailey'. The organ is particularly fine, originally built by Renatus Harris in 1670, and played by Mendelssohn and Samuel Wesley, father and son. It was removed from the west gallery under the tower in 1932 and was rebuilt by Harrisons. In the Sanctuary the carpeting, some kneelers and an altar frontal were given in memory of Sir Malcolm Sargent. There are many kneelers dedicated to specific composers. The church was closed for several years in the early 1990s but was reopened as a place of regular worship and prayer, and a concert and recital venue. The annual Musicians Benevolent Fund St Cecilia Day service which started in 1946 became so large it transferred to Westminster cathedral in 1990. It is now held at the cathedral, Abbey and St Paul's in rotation and is a unique ceremonial and musical occasion strongly recommended to read-ers. Concerts are frequently held here, especially for St Cecilia's Day. Opening hours tend to be limited - check on the church's website before a visit.

Temple Church
In a courtyard reached via Middle Temple Lane off Fleet Street
Tube: Temple

The church is twelfth century and was built by the Knights Templar. It consists of two parts – the round church, consecrated in 1185, and the chancel, built 1240. It is famed for its music and the long line of distinguished organists serving there. In the seventeenth century the church became the arena for a battle of organ-builders: the Inner and Middle Temples both wanted an organ but disagreed as to who should build it – Bernard Smith (Middle Temple favourite) or Renatus Harris (Inner Temple). Both employed distinguished organists to show off the instruments – Smith had Blow and Purcell, Harris had Giovanni Battista Draghi. Smith finally won after five years' wrangling and a ruling by the then Lord Chancellor, the notorious Judge Jeffreys. The organ underwent many restorations over the centuries and was played by various eminent organists, the more recent of whom stayed at the church for many years. These included Dr Edward John Hopkins from 1843 to 1896, then (later Sir) Henry Walford Davies until 1923, and Dr (later Sir) George Thalben-Ball from 1923 to 1982. During Walford Davies's stewardship the organ was rebuilt by Frederick Rothwell.

During Thalben-Ball's incumbency the famous record of Mendelssohn's *Hear my Prayer*, sung by Ernest Lough, was made and issued by HMV. Between 1927 and 1932 many recordings were of the Choir with the organ as rebuilt by Rothwell, several with Ernest Lough as treble soloist. Both church and organ were almost destroyed by incendiaries in 1941, on the same night that Queen's Hall was destroyed.

Restoration took many years. The chancel's vault sur-vived and the rebuild culminated in the rededication of the choir in 1954 with a Harrison & Harrison organ donat-ed by Lord Glentanar. The round church was rededicated in 1958.

On Friday 27 June 2003 the Temple saw the world pre-miere of Sir John Tavener's all-night vigil *The Veil of the Temple*, which started at 10 p.m. and ended at 5.30 a.m. the following morning. It was given by the choir of the Temple

---

City Churches, all with interesting organs, and other halls with organs, not discussed above

All Hallows, Barking
All Hallows, London Wall
St Andrew, Holborn
St Andrew-by-the-Wardrobe
St Annes and St Agnes
St Bartholomew-the-Great
St Bartholomew-the-Less
St Benet, Paul's Wharf
St Botolph, Aldersgate
St Botolph, Bishopsgate
St Clement, Eastcheap
St Dunstan-in-the-West
St Edmund the King, Lombard Street
St Helen, Bishopsgate
St James Garlickhythe
St Katherine Cree
St Magnus-the-Martyr
St Margaret, Lothbury
St Margaret Pattens
St Martin, Ludgate Hill
St Mary Abchurch
St Mary Aldermanbury
St Mary-at-Hill
St Michael Paternoster Royal
St Nicholas, Cole Street
St Olave, Hart Street
St Peter, Cornhill
St Peter-ad-Vincula, Tower of London
St Stephen, Walbrook
St Vedast, Foster Lane
The Dutch Church, Austin Friars
St Mary Moorfields
The Chapel of the Worshipful Company of Mercers
The Hall of the Worshipful Company of Merchant Taylors

church and the Holst Singers conducted by Stephen Layton. The soprano soloist was Patricia Rozario. A reduced concert version was later given by the same performers at the Royal Albert Hall during the 2004 Proms.

Wesley's Chapel
City Road
Tube: Old Street

John Wesley, founder of Methodism and prolific hymn writer, built this chapel as his London base. It was designed by George Dance the Younger, surveyor to the City of London, and completed in 1778. It stands opposite Bunhill Fields Nonconformist Cemetery (see p. 116), which contains the grave of Susanna Wesley, mother of John and Charles. A statue of John Wesley dominates the courtyard. Charles Wesley's organ is on this site, as are John Wesley's tomb and pulpit.

Strand/ Covent Garden/ West End/ Westminster

Banqueting House/Chapel Royal
Whitehall
Tube: Charing Cross, Westminster or Embankment

The Banqueting House, designed by Inigo Jones and completed in 1622, is the only outward remnant of Henry VIII's Whitehall Palace. It was in the time of the Stewarts used for lavish receptions, masques and musical performance. From 1698, the year of the fire that gutted most of the palace, the Banqueting House was used as the Chapel Royal and the first service was on Christmas Day. New fittings included an organ against the west wall and an altar at the northern end. This was, however, only a temporary measure and the Chapel Royal moved to St James's Palace in 1702, although Royal Maundy services were still often held in the Banqueting House. In 1808 it was used as a military chapel for the Horse Guards and balconies were put up to allow for a larger congregation. Charity concerts were held there in 1814. Towards the end of the nineteenth century use of the building as a place of worship was discontinued and it became the United Services Museum. Today it is again used for large state occasions and for concerts, including a regular lunchtime series.

Chapel Royal, St James's Palace
St James's Palace
Tube: Green Park

One of the least-known architectural and musical jewels in London, and open to the public at specified times, is the Chapel Royal at St James's Palace. There are two historic chapels in the palace – the Chapel Royal and the Queen's Chapel. The chapel, built with mellow Elizabethan bricks, has a board on the left of the doorway that reads: 'This chapel formed part of Henry VIII's palace. The ceiling, traditionally attributed to Holbein, bears the date 1540. The chapel was enlarged in 1837.' It also tells of King Charles I receiving Holy Communion in the chapel on the morning of his execution, 30 January 1649, before walking across St James's Park to Whitehall, where he was beheaded.

Royal weddings took place in the chapel, notably those of Queen Victoria to Prince Albert in 1840, and of King George V, when Duke of York, to Princess May of Teck in 1893. In more recent times the choir of the Chapel Royal combined with that of St Paul's cathedral at the wedding of the Prince of Wales and Lady Diana Spencer in 1981. In September 1997 the coffin of Diana, Princess of Wales rested before the altar in St James's Palace before her funeral.

The Chapel Royal is really a body of priests and singers rather than a building and would accompany the monarch on ceremonial occasions, in particular the annual ceremony of the Royal Maundy and at all coronations. In 1702 Queen Anne had the chapel moved from Whitehall Palace, where the Banqueting House had been fitted up for use as the Chapel Royal, to St James's Palace after the great fire that destroyed Whitehall.

In the vestibule of the present Chapel Royal can be seen the names of deans, sub-deans, organists and musicians. The organists represent the finest of composers and musicians, including Tallis, Byrd, Gibbons, Blow, Purcell (who shared lodgings with Dryden in the gatehouse which survive), Greene and Boyce. Handel was appointed 'Composer of Musick to His Majesty's Chapel Royal' in February 1723. King George II requested him to compose the anthems for his coronation in 1727 and one of these was the dramatic *Zadok the Priest*, sung at every coronation since.

The choir of the chapel consists of the same numbers as it had in Byrd's day and constitutes six men (Gentlemen in Ordinary) and ten boys (Children of the Chapel). The boys still wear scarlet and gold state uniforms reminiscent of the more familiar 'beefeaters' uniforms at the Tower of London. These date from the reign of Charles II. The boy choristers are Queen's Scholars at the City of London School.

Walking into the chapel itself one notices that it is surprisingly small and light. The pews, seating perhaps a hundred, set against the side walls, were installed in 1876 and the pulpit removed in 1893. Painted panels, attributed to Holbein, commemorate the short-lived marriage of Henry VIII and Anne of Cleves in 1540. The altar was bought at the Queen Mother's (then queen) command during the Second World War to replace that destroyed during an air raid. Tapestries hang on each side. The organ was given to the chapel by George V in 1925 – a large three manual

46   The Chapel Royal in St James's Palace in the late nineteenth century.

and pedal instrument, built by Hill, Norman and Beard and rebuilt by Mander in 1980. The public have access for the services of Holy Communion and Sung Eucharist, which are celebrated in the chapel on the first Sunday of the month and at Great Festivals. From Easter Day to the end of July services are held in the Queen's Chapel, Marlborough Road, and the Chapel is closed during August and September.

Other Chapels Royal based in or near London are at St Peter ad Vincula in the Tower of London and at Hampton Court Palace. All three are what are called 'Royal Peculiars' and have owed their allegiance directly to the Queen, though this is to change. St Peter ad Vincula is open to the public as part of a guided tour of the Tower and is in regular use for worship. Its organ was originally by 'Father' Smith (1699) and has been restored by Létourneau. It has a choral foundation. The permanent choir at Hampton Court Palace was established in 1868 and consists of fourteen boys and ten gentlemen who sing on Sundays and for major feasts. Musicians who played there included Tallis, Byrd and Purcell. The organ was built by Schrider in 1712 and restored most recently by Hill, Norman and Beard in 1993.

Methodist Central Hall
Westminster (facing Westminster Abbey)
Tube: Westminster or St James's Park

The hall was built to commemorate the centenary of the death in 1791 of John Wesley, founder of Methodism. A quarter of 'The Million Guinea Fund', raised by one million Methodists, paid for the building, which opened in 1912 on the site of the old Royal Aquarium (see p. 50). A highlight of the building is its organ, constructed in 1912 with 3,695 pipes. It now has 4,731 pipes, the tallest being thirty-two feet high. The hall was used for recording sessions, especially in the days of 78s before the building of Abbey Road Studios in 1930, and concerts and organ recitals are still held there from time to time, particularly when large choral forces are required. Built over the district line tube, the rumble of trains can be distantly heard from time to time, which must be the prime reason the hall is now infrequently used for recordings. (See also Chapters 1 and 6.)

St George's, Hanover Square
Corner of Maddox Street and the east side of St George Street
Tube: Oxford Circus or Bond Street

Built in 1721–4 by James Gibbs, this was one of the fifty new churches then voted by Parliament and dedicated, in compliment to the king, to St George. It was Handel's local church as he lived only a stone's throw away in Brook Street, and he often played the organ there, particularly late in his career. The interior is very much as it must have been in Handel's day. Handel was closely involved in parish affairs and was a worshipper there for thirty-five years. The composer Thomas Roseingrave was organist from 1725 to 1737. The organ, completed in 1725, was built by Gerald Smith, nephew of 'Father' Smith. It has undergone several rebuilds since then. The present organ is by Harrison and Harrison, built inside the old case in 1972. This is another church in use for concerts and organ recitals as well as services, and is a well-known venue for society weddings. Today the church is home of the London Handel Festival.

St James's, Piccadilly
Piccadilly
Tube: Piccadilly Circus

Sir Christopher Wren was architect of St James's, which was consecrated in July 1684, the first rector being Dr Tenison, formerly the vicar of St Martin-in-the-Fields. The church was badly damaged by air raids in October 1940, when the rectory and vestry were destroyed and fire gutted the interior. The organ case and font were undamaged. The church was restored by 1954 and rededicated.

The organ had been built by Renatus Harris on commission from King James II in 1685 for the Catholic chapel in Whitehall Palace. It was subsequently given by Queen Mary to St James's in 1691 and installed by 'Father' Smith. Some of the original pipework remains after alterations in 1852, when a new chair case containing a choir organ was placed in the front of the Upper Gallery, and after the war damage of 1940. In 1954 the console was transferred to the Lower Gallery. The organ case is ornamented by figures carved by Grinling Gibbons. The funeral of the French composer François André Philidor was held here in August 1795. Leopold Stokowski was organist 1903–5. Today concerts are held in the church almost daily.

St John's, Smith Square
Smith Square
Tube: Westminster or St James's Park

St John's, Smith Square was designed in the baroque style by Thomas Archer (1668–1743) and built between 1713 and 1728. Archer had undertaken a Grand Tour and the building reflects those he had seen in Italy. It stands in a square of terraced houses and is embellished with columns, cornices and pediments, but inside is an elegant classic space, without stained glass, ideal as a concert venue.

The church sustained a direct hit on the night of 10 May 1941, in the same raid that destroyed the Queen's Hall and, like it, was gutted by fire. It stood open to the elements and was a wreck for the next twenty years or so, until the Friends of St John's was established in 1962 by Lady Parker of Waddington to raise money to restore the church to Archer's original design, for use as a concert hall. The rebuild started in 1965 and the first recital was given in October 1969 by Dame Joan Sutherland and Richard Bonynge.

The building was in use as a concert hall for over twenty years without an organ, though increasingly concert promoters found themselves having to bring instruments in for specific concerts. Eventually one was installed in 1993 (using the antique organ case built in 1734 by Jordan, Byfield and Bridges), built by Johannes Klais of Bonn and named 'The Sainsbury Organ' in recognition of that family's contribution to the appeal.

In October 2000 the Academy of Ancient Music became the church's period instrument orchestra in residence. The audience capacity is 600, with an additional 180 when the gallery is in use. There is a programme of lunchtime and daily evening concerts, though the church is usually not in regular use during August. Recording sessions are also held there during the daytime. The Footstool Restaurant in the Crypt is available for lunch and dinner roughly timed with concert hours. The crypt was not damaged during wartime bombing, so the eighteenth-century brickwork is still in evidence.

The Orchestra of St John's, Smith Square was founded in 1967 by John Lubbock as the Camden Chamber Orchestra, and invited to become the Orchestra of St John's in 1973. It soon acquired a high artistic profile, appearing for the first time in the Proms in 1976. The composer John Woolrich has long been associated with the orchestra. Through recent changes of name it became the Orchestra of St John's and then simply OSJ. It is now also the resident orchestra of the Blackheath Concert Halls.

St Martin-in-the-Fields
Trafalgar Square
Tube: Charing Cross or Leicester Square

The church is the fourth on this site and was built to a design by James Gibbs and completed in 1726. It is distinctive for its Corinthian columns supporting a pediment with tower and steeple. The current organ, built by J. W. Walker and Sons, was installed in 1990 and has 3,637 pipes. This is a church with a long musical history. Handel played here and the well-known chamber orchestra, the Academy of St Martin-in-the-Fields, was founded here in 1959. The church is regularly the location of live broadcast services. Free lunchtime concerts are frequently held, and also candlelit evening concerts aimed at a tourist audience.

St Paul's, Covent Garden
Covent Garden
Tube: Covent Garden or Charing Cross

Designed by Inigo Jones and completed in 1633, this is known as the actors' church. The theatrical connection began in the seventeenth century – the Theatre Royal

Drury Lane and the Royal Opera House are nearby. Today the Actors' Church Union has its offices here.

There are plaques in memory of many of the famous names in the performing arts world in the garden and on the walls, including Ivor Novello, Tamara Karsavina, Noël Coward, Constant Lambert, Gracie Fields and David Webster. Memorial services for famous actors and musicians are held from time to time. A typical example was that for Anthony Burgess, writer and composer, held on 16 June 1994. Among those baptised in St Paul's were W. S. Gilbert and the painter J. M. W. Turner. Thomas Arne is buried here and John Wesley preached at the church. The organ is by Henry Bevington, built in 1861, incorporating part of the case designed by the architect Thomas Hardwick during a large-scale restoration begun in 1788.

Westminster Abbey
Parliament Square
Tube: Westminster or St James's Park

The abbey was built in the eighth century, and rebuilt by Edward the Confessor and Henry III. The west towers were added by Sir Christopher Wren during his restoration from 1698 to 1723, though they were subsequently given their present appearance by Hawksmoor, completed in 1745. It has traditionally been the favoured venue for coronations, royal weddings and funerals.

There is a very long tradition of choir singing at the abbey, and boys probably joined with novices in singing masses and daily services from as early as 1170. The sixteenth-century foundations of Henry VIII and Elizabeth I funded the education of choirboys. The first Chorister School opened in 1848 in a room off the south cloister, and in 1891 a choir house was built in Little Smith Street. The present choir school, in Dean's Yard, opened in 1915. The school was evacuated to Christ's Hospital, near Horsham, in 1939 but disbanded a year later. In 1947 the choir reassembled under Sir William McKie and sang at the dedication of the Battle of Britain window in July 1947, and at the wedding of the then Princess Elizabeth with Philip Mountbatten that November. The choir also sang at the coronation in 1953 and at subsequent royal occasions, including royal weddings. The choir school now has thirty-eight boys aged 7–13.

Over the centuries the organs of Westminster Abbey have experienced many changes, additions and reconstructions. Soon after the Restoration in 1660 an organ was in use again

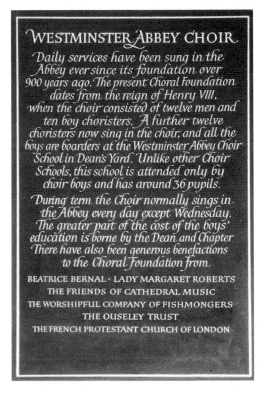

47   Summary of the Westminster Abbey Choir on the Cloister Wall.

WESTMINSTER ABBEY CHOIR

Daily services have been sung in the Abbey ever since its foundation over 900 years ago. The present Choral Foundation dates from the reign of Henry VIII, when the choir consisted of twelve men and ten boy choristers. A further twelve choristers now sing in the choir, and all the boys are boarders at the Westminster Abbey Choir School in Dean's Yard. Unlike other Choir Schools, this school is attended only by choir-boys and has around 36 pupils.

During term the Choir normally sings in the Abbey every day except Wednesday. The greater part of the cost of the boys' education is borne by the Dean and Chapter. There have also been generous benefactions to the Choral Foundation from

BEATRICE BERNAL · LADY MARGARET ROBERTS
THE FRIENDS OF CATHEDRAL MUSIC
THE WORSHIPFUL COMPANY OF FISHMONGERS
THE OUSELEY TRUST
THE FRENCH PROTESTANT CHURCH OF LONDON

Organists of Westminster Abbey	
1570–1574	Robert White
1585–1621	Edmund Hooper
1621–1623	James Parsons
1623–1625	Orlando Gibbons
1625–1644	Richard Portman
	[Commonwealth]
1661–1666	Christopher Gibbons
1666–1668	Albertus Bryne
1669–1679	John Blow
1679–1695	Henry Purcell
1695–1708	John Blow
1708–1727	William Croft
1727–1762	John Robinson
1762–1793	Benjamin Cooke
1793–1802	Samuel Arnold
1803–1814	Robert Cooke
1814–1819	George Ebenezer Williams
1819–1831	Thomas Greatorex
1831–1882	James Turle
1882–1918	Sir Frederick Bridge
1918–1927	Sir Sydney Nicholson
1928–1940	Sir Ernest Bullock
1941–1945	Osborne Peasgood (Acting Organist and organist for the Royal Wedding of November 1947)
1941–1963	Sir William McKie
1963–1981	Douglas Guest
1981–1987	Simon Preston
1988–1998	Martin Neary
1998–1999	Martin Baker (Acting Organist)
2000–	James O'Donnell

at services and probably included parts of the instrument played before the Commonwealth. It was rebuilt by Bernard Smith in 1694, and rebuilt again by Christopher Schrider (Shrider) in 1710. A new organ, also by Schrider, was in use from 1730. He had been given the previous organ as part payment and there has been much discussion as to where that organ had gone – Vauxhall Gardens and Barnsbury Chapel have been suggested, also Shoreham, near Sevenoaks in Kent. In 1884 the whole instrument was recast by Hill and Son, with a four-manual console. In the 1890s Hill made further alterations including the addition of a Celestial organ. In 1926 the Abbey organ-builders contract moved from Hill, Norman and Beard to Harrison. In 1928 Albert Schweitzer gave a recital at the Abbey and pronounced it the best organ on which he had performed for many years. However the organ committee found it so worn out that they feared it might break down during a service – these differing opinions might merely mean it was not in fashion at the time. The establishment of a rebuilding fund was given impetus by the death of George V in 1936 and the coronation of George VI the following year, and the organ was built just before the Second World War. The most recent rebuild was completed in 1987.

Occasional organs were also set up over the years – one under Purcell for the coronation of James II in 1685; King George II's coronation organ was by Schrider in 1727; Canterbury cathedral's organ, by Samuel Green, was set up for use at the Handel Commemoration in 1784 and then returned; in 1834 an organ by Gray was erected for a 'Royal Musical Festival'; and an organ by Hill and Davison was erected for the coronation of Queen Victoria in 1838.

The abbey is the last resting-place of many distinguished musicians and composers and contains numerous busts and memorials to others buried elsewhere. These are discussed in Chapter 4.

Westminster Cathedral
Victoria Street
Tube: Victoria or St James's Square

Originally the land on which the Roman Catholic cathedral stands was part of the marsh round Westminster, and after the Reformation the land was used as a maze,

Masters of Music Westminster Cathedral	
1901–1924	Richard Runciman Terry (Appointed Musical Director 1901, designated Organist and Director of the Cathedral Choir 1904)
1924–1929	Vernon Russell
1929–1934	Position lapsed; Lancelot Long, Head of Choir School
1934–1939	Fr Vernon Russell
1939–1941	Fr William Stacey Bainbridge
1940–1945	Choir School closed and evacuated for duration of the war
1941–1946	William Hyde
1946–1959	George Malcolm with Hyde as his assistant
1959–1961	Francis Cameron
1961–1964	Colin Mawby Acting Master
1964–1978	Colin Mawby Master of Cathedral Music (Revd D. Higgins Acting Master 1977)
1978–1979	Revd D. Higgins Acting Master
1979–1982	Stephen Cleobury
1982–1988	David Hill
1988–2000	James O'Donnell
2000–	Martin Baker

48   Postcard view of Westminster cathedral taken soon after it opened in 1904.

then a pleasure garden and for bull baiting. It was then sold for the construction of a prison and acquired on behalf of the church in 1884. The cathedral is in the neo-Byzantine style and has a fine campanile soaring some 274 feet with public access to its viewing platform. (Someone falls from it in the 1940 Hitchcock film *Foreign Correspondent*.) It is constructed in terracotta brick and Portland stone and was designed by architect John Bentley. The foundation stone was laid in 1895 and the fabric of the building finished eight years later. The interior, though incomplete, contains fine marble and mosaics; the fourteen Stations of the Cross are by Eric Gill. The first London performance of Elgar's *The Dream of Gerontius* was given here in 1903.

The choir was established at the instigation of Cardinal Herbert Vaughan, the founder of the cathedral, as one of his main priorities, appointing Richard Runciman Terry (who was knighted in 1922) as the first Musical Director, from

1904 Organist and Director of the Cathedral Choir. The celebrity of the choir was quickly established, influential with the leading non-Catholic composers of the day and instrumental in the revival of a huge literature of music, notably from the sixteen and seventeenth centuries. Holst and Vaughan Williams were materially influenced by Terry's discoveries, and composers including Howells, Britten, Berkeley and Mathias (and most recently Francis Greer and James MacMillan) have written music for the choir. The choir made recordings from a very early date, the first being in 1908. Here, despite a loss of momentum in the twenty years after Terry, a succession of pioneering choirmasters revived much of the English Catholic liturgical repertoire of the sixteenth century as well as encouraging the composers of the day to write for the choir.

Kensington/ Knightsbridge

Brompton Oratory
Brompton Road
Tube: South Kensington

Dark and baroque inside, though vast, the Oratory is fronted by a statue of Cardinal Newman, famous, among other things, for the poem that Elgar set in *The Dream of Gerontius*. This Roman Catholic church was built in the late 1870s to designs by Herbert Gribble and is Italianate in style with extravagant decorations and statuary and several side chapels. The choir of the London Oratory and the junior choir are renowned and award-winning. The organ was built by J. W. Walker and Sons and completed in 1954, having forty-five stops on three manuals and pedals. There are also a manual 16-stop organ (1975) and a 3-stop chamber organ (1979).

The Directors of Music in the late nineteenth century were composers, and though forgotten today Thomas Wingham had his Second and Fourth symphonies played by August Manns at the Crystal Palace in 1872 and 1883, while Wingham's pupil and successor at the Oratory after he died in 1893, A. Barclay Jones, wrote his Symphony in C minor in tribute to his teacher and heard it played at Crystal Palace in 1896.

Here, in a side chapel, Edward and Alice Elgar were married on 8 May 1889 without either's parents being present, and with a very small number of friends in attendance.

St Paul's, Knightsbridge
Wilton Place
Tube: Hyde Park Corner or Knightsbridge

This highly decorated Victorian church was the first in London to support the Oxford Movement, whose members tried to restore a 'sense of Catholic order and spirituality to the Established Church and to enrich its worship by the recovery of its ancient traditions'. This beautiful church is ornamented with an elaborate rood screen and reredos, and has a wooden gallery and cast iron pillars. Painted Stations of the Cross on three sides of the nave are by Gerald Mora and the tiled panels between them by Daniel Bell depict scenes from the life of Jesus. From time to time the BBC records programmes here and there are also evening concerts.

Christ Church, Spitalfields
Commercial Street, EC1
(nearest tube: Liverpool Street)

Out of the Centre

For many years this glorious Hawksmoor church, completed in 1729, has been in the process of restoration. Musically it is particularly associated with the City of London and Spitalfields festivals. The pristine grandeur of the refurbished church, finally opened in 2004, came as a shock to those who had long become familiar with attending performances there amid the dilapidation, the scaffolding and the on-going building work. Now, with its twenty-five-year £10m restoration completed, it stands proudly again as one of London's most atmospheric church acoustics. Any event there is worth the attention of visitors. The organ by Richard Bridge has yet to be restored.

St Anne's, Limehouse
Commercial Road
Docklands Light Railway: Limehouse

The church was designed by Nicholas Hawksmoor and consecrated in 1730. When it was built it would have been in open fields. The organ won the prize medal at the 1851 Exhibition at the Crystal Palace and was built by Gray and Davison. In consequence of a serious fire in 1850 the church was restored between 1852 and 1856, but was again damaged during the Blitz.

St Cyprian's, Glentworth Street
Clarence Gate Gardens, Glentworth Street
Tube: Baker Street or Marylebone

The church is opposite the flat where composer George Lloyd and his wife Nancy lived for the last twenty years or so of their lives. The ornate Victorian Gothic church is one of the early buildings of Ninian Comper. Built in the 1890s and completed in 1903 it exemplified his vision of 'English Perpendicular'. The main feeling is of height, light and space with richly ornate colourful or gilded fixtures and fittings, and a painted ceiling. It is extensively used for a very wide variety of concerts and musical events, and in 2003 became the regular location of the concerts presented by the British Music Information Centre.

St Mary Magdalene, Paddington
Westbourne Green
Tube: Warwick Avenue

The Anglo-Catholic Victorian church of St Mary Magdalene has a vital musical life, largely through the Saint Mary Magdalene Church Music Society. The church was made to look larger than it really is to fit on what was once a restricted site by the Grand Union Canal by giving the impression of an aisle on the north side which does not exist. The building by G. E. Street is grandly decorated, and the south aisle Lady Chapel is by Ninian Comper, who also designed the Gothic crypt in Victorian medieval. The Church Music Society started a tradition of performing a French requiem with full orchestra each All Soul's Day (2 November) in 1963, the Society under the Presidency of the French composer Maurice Duruflé, who had conducted the first British performance of his *Cum Jubilo Mass* at St Mary's in 1960. His widow succeeds him as President of the Society. The Requiems included in the on-going annual cycle, presented with full orchestra, now after a forty-year tradition are those by Fauré, Duruflé, Desenclos, Inghelbrecht, Guy-Ropartz, Alfred Bruneau and Saint-Saëns. On each occasion they are given their rightful place in the liturgical context of a Mass. The Church is also the occasional location of concerts and recording sessions.

Southwark Cathedral
London Bridge
Tube: London Bridge

This delightful Anglican cathedral on the south side of London Bridge, adjacent to the Borough market, and within walking distance of the Globe Theatre, has recently been refurbished with a new visitors' centre and refectory and makes an ideal point of quiet repose or lunch on any London trip. Visitors should note the memorial to actor Sam Wanamaker and the Globe Theatre, the one to Shakespeare and another to poet John Gower. The cathedral, with its fine organ, is rewarding not only for its services and many special events. An active concert programme takes place including choral and orchestral concerts and organ recitals.

In 1979 an evening choral and orchestral concert took place with a choir from Stoke-on-Trent, who were travelling down by coach. They arrived late, after the concert had started, and it was only then that it was discovered that the cathedral then had only one lavatory. An early interval had to be taken in order to present the choral works in comfort.

Ceremonial occasions

One of the best free London musical shows is the various activities of the capital's military bands, particularly at the Changing of the Guard at Buckingham Palace. (Daily April to June, otherwise every other day, web diary at changing-the-guard.com/schedule.htm). This is mainly undertaken by the five foot guards bands of the Household Division, but other bands appear from time to time. To maximise your enjoyment of the show find the band first on the parade ground of Wellington Barracks at Birdcage Walk (road access in Petty France, but view from Birdcage Walk) where they come out and play soon after 10.30 a.m. They then march, still playing, to the Palace, enter the forecourt and play during the ceremony around 11.30 a.m.

At Wellington Barracks we find the Grenadier, Coldstream and Scots guards; at Chelsea Barracks are the Welsh and Irish Guards; and at Knightsbridge Barracks the Blues and Royals (Household Cavalry) who alternate with the Life Guards.

For the Changing of the Queen's Life Guards at the Horse Guards in Whitehall, the soldiers are mounted. (Daily 11 a.m, Sundays 10 a.m.) Here every June is held Beating Retreat (two performances and two rehearsals) and the Queen's Birthday Parade on the nearest Saturday to 12 June, all for massed bands. The week before is the Colonel's Review, a similar event. Attendance at these if you want to sit in a stand is by ticket (which can be bought from the soldiers on duty the week of the event) but for the impecunious, rehearsals may be attended free of charge, or watched from nearby.

State occasions take place in Westminster Abbey or St Paul's cathedral. Coronations in Westminster Abbey; the funeral of Sir Winston Churchill, and earlier Queen Victoria's jubilee service were at St Paul's. Since Queen Victoria's jubilees in 1887 and 1897, and especially the coronation of King Edward VII in 1902, state celebrations of this sort have turned into festivals of new British music. Handel's *Zadok the Priest* has been sung at every coronation since its composition in 1727.

On major state occasions rehearsals are often held in front of Buckingham Palace around 4 a.m.

Cenotaph and Remembrance Day

The Cenotaph in Whitehall (tube: Westminster) has been the focus of Remembrance Day (11 November) since 1919, but it has never been an occasion for elaborate music, and although Elgar, for example, produced *With Proud Thanksgiving* for its unveiling, it was never sung there, hymns and military music being all that has been used. The Ceremony of Remembrance (each year on the nearest Sunday to 11 November) features massed bands and pipers playing before and after the service. The familiar music includes marches, patriotic music and music with regimental associations. In 2004 it included a band arrangement of Purcell's 'Dido's Lament'. *The Last Post* is sounded after the two minutes' silence at 11 a.m. and the subsequent veterans parade continues for the best part of an hour accompanied by continuous music from the bands.

3 • Conservatoires, Museums, Libraries, Portraits and Pictures

Conservatoires

During the second half of the nineteenth century the Leipzig Conservatoire, founded by Mendelssohn in 1843, achieved a high reputation across Europe, and British composers from Sullivan (1858–61) to Ethel Smyth (1877–8) and Delius (1886–8) studied there, though even by the time Smyth arrived the institution was on the wane. Aspiring British composers all looked to Germany for their musical education. Stanford studied with Kiel in Berlin, while towards the end of the century a group of British composers went to Frankfurt. The young Elgar was too poor to achieve his ambition of studying in Germany, which was probably his stylistic salvation, but his aspiration was typical of the period.

The need for a London-based institution of similar high standing was increasingly obvious throughout the century, both for the training of instrumentalists to feed the huge and ever-growing London market for music, for singers and for composers. In this the Royal Academy of Music, founded in 1822, was perceived to have failed, resulting in the establishment of the National Training School that effectively was the precursor of the Royal College of Music in 1883. This need was further demonstrated by the response to the Trinity College of Music and the Guildhall School of Music in the last quarter of the nineteenth century. The demand that was becoming apparent in the closing decades of the century was not only for professional musicians, but also for church organists and choirmasters, teachers and a growing constituency of trained amateurs, and it resulted in the formation of several London-based conservatoires and training schools, considered here alphabetically, as well as others that did not become established.

Barnard's Inn Hall: Gresham Chair of Music
Gresham College, Barnard's Inn Hall, Holborn, EC1
Tube: Chancery Lane

This is not a regular educational institution with a large enrolled student body. The Gresham Chair was founded as one of seven professorships established in 1596 to provide free adult education under the will of Sir Thomas Gresham at his house in Bishopsgate. It is the world's oldest chair of music. The first professor was John Bull who had to have special leave to lecture in English rather than Latin. The College

49 (facing page) The opening ceremony of the Royal Academy of Music premises in Marylebone Road, 22 June 1912. Most of the leading Academy names of the day can be seen on the platform including Corder (extreme right), Mackenzie (to the right of the podium) and Matthay (fourth from the left). To the right behind Mackenzie stands the celebrated pianist Oscar Beringer. The organist is Dr Henry W. Richards; to his left stands Benjamin Dale, the figure to his right is probably the violin professor Hans Wesserley. The female choir and harps are there to perform Corder's 50-part motet *Sing Unto God* for womens' choir, organ, harps, trumpets and drums. On the extreme left, Sir Hubert Parry, Director of the Royal College of Music can be seen by the steps to the platform. (Photograph by Alexander Corbett.)

was demolished in 1768, and the Corporation of London built a new college with a theatre and concert hall on the corner of Gresham Street and Basinghall Street, also now demolished. At first, chair-holders had to lecture twice a week, later only now and again. For a long time the Chair was only a notional entity but it is now located at Barnard's Inn Hall jointly run by the Mercer's Company and the City of London. Since 1991 lectures have been given at Barnard's Inn Hall, Holborn. Distinguished holders of the professorship of music included Sir Frederick Bridge, Sir Henry Walford Davies, Antony Hopkins and the pianist David Owen Norris. The current professor is Adrian Thomas.

Guildhall School of Music and Drama
Silk Street, Barbican, EC2
Tube: Barbican or Moorgate

Founded in 1880 under the control of the Corporation of London, the Guildhall School of Music and Drama was thus the first municipal musical conservatoire in the UK. Its first principal was Weist Hill, who was conductor of the successful Guildhall Orchestral and Choral Society. Largely attracting amateur musicians and with a preponderance of young women, the student body grew quickly from its opening roll of sixty-two part-time pupils to over 3,500 in January 1889. In 1887 it moved to a new building at Blackfriars which survives (John Carpenter Street adjoining the Thames). The life of the School in its new building was vividly evoked in an illustrated article in *The Graphic* for 12 January 1889. At this time it was primarily an institution for training amateurs, and aimed at a London catchment area – the nomination of an Alderman of the City of London was a requirement to be accepted as a student.

50 The Guildhall School of Music and Drama today.

Principals of the Guildhall School of Music and Drama	
1880–1891	T. H. Weist Hill
1891–1896	Sir Joseph Barnby
1896–1910	W. H. Cummings
1910–1938	Sir Landon Ronald
1938–1958	Edric Cundell
1958–1962	Gordon Thorne
1965–1977	Allen Percival
1978–1988	John Hosier
1988–2002	Ian Horsbrugh
2002–2003	Genesta McIntosh
2003–2004	Peter Derrick (acting principal)
2004–	Barry Ife

The building was variously extended and the objectives became more and more professional. In 1935 the School incorporated drama into its remit.

Here the composer Edmund Rubbra taught composition in the 1970s. In 1977 the School moved to modern purpose-built accommodation adjacent to the Barbican Concert Hall, which opened in 1982. It now offers training for the BMus and MMus degrees, courses in opera, voice and music therapy, and a postgraduate diploma in musical performance. The Guildhall School has a remarkable tradition of interesting revivals for its end-of-term staged opera productions in its in-house theatre, which are open to the public.

Celebrated alumni (all Gold Medal winners) include the cellist Jacqueline du Pré and a succession of acclaimed singers including Owen Brannigan, Benjamin Luxon, Bryn Terfel, Patricia Rozario and Susan Bickley.

London College of Music
Thames Valley University, South Ealing Road, Ealing, W5
Tube: Ealing Broadway

Founded in 1887, the London College of Music was long at 47 Great Marlborough Street, near to Schott's music publishers, occupying its distinctive building, which survives, until the mid-1990s. It offers full-time tuition in practical and theoretical subjects and professional diplomas, and has now moved to Ealing as part of Thames Valley University.

John McCabe tells the following story from when he was principal in the 1980s. Two senior student brass players had gigs in the West End on a Saturday evening and had permission to enter the building late at night to deposit their instruments. Having played until the small hours – and doubtless had a few drinks – they entered the building and met an elderly man with a moustache, wearing an old-fashioned tweed jacket, apparently the caretaker, who smiled amiably. They did not know him, but in retrospect they had the impression he seemed to be hovering a few inches above the floor. Then he vanished. They left in a hurry. On telling the story the following week, a longstanding member of staff identified him as the caretaker who had been killed in an air raid. 'Where you say he was standing used to be four inches higher – the floor was lowered when the building was renovated after the war.' The students wanted to have the 'ghost' exorcised, but he was never seen again and in due course the College moved from the building.

Principals of the London College of Music	
1887–1897	Alfred J. Caldicott
1913– ?1935	Frederick J. Karn
1944–1954	H. Bromley-Derry
1954–1964	Reginald Hunt
1964–1982	W. S. Lloyd-Webber
1982–1989	John McCabe
1989–1995	Bill Webb
1995–1996	Richard Roberts
1996–1998	Alistair Creamer
1999–2001	Patricia Thompson
2001–2005	Colin Lawson

We have been unable to trace any details for other years.

Morley College
61 Westminster Bridge Road, SE1
Tube: Lambeth North

At Waterloo, Morley College had its beginnings in 1885 with regular evening classes held in the Old Vic Theatre dressing rooms. These were the brainchild of Emma Cons, who had taken a lease on the theatre and arranged lectures, concerts and variety shows. In 1889 part of the building was given over to educational activities and named Morley College in honour of the support given by Samuel Morley, MP, temperance worker and textile manufacturer. By 1924 Morley College had moved to a building on its present site, with a new wing added in 1937. All but the new wing was destroyed by bombs in 1940, and it was not rebuilt until 1958.

Gustav Holst became the first musical director in 1907 and greatly increased the musical side of its activities, in 1909 giving a pioneering revival of extensive extracts from Purcell's *King Arthur*, and in 1911 at the Old Vic the first complete performance of the music from Purcell's *The Fairy Queen* for over two hundred years. Holst retired in 1924 and was succeeded by Arnold Goldsborough and Arnold Foster. In 1932 at Morley College a young Michael Tippett formed an orchestra of unemployed musicians.

Morley's most influential period came in the period immediately after the Second World War when Tippett, followed in 1952 by the composers Peter Racine Fricker (1952–65) and John Gardner made it a noted centre of the new music. It has always had a strong musical tradition, with connections with such institutions as the National Opera Studio and more recently the Centre for Young Musicians.

Several composers taught there, notably Michael Tippett, who became a focus for the new generation of post Second World War composers, and for the revival of composers such as Monteverdi in 1946, Morley forces giving a celebrated broadcast of the *Vespers of 1610* in 1947. Tippett and his Morley College singers left just one recorded example of their achievement, Tallis's forty-part motet *Spem in Alium* on HMV 78s. Today Morley College is an active centre of evening classes and adult education.

Royal Academy of Music
Marylebone Road, NW1
Tube: Baker Street or Regent's Park

Founded in 1822 by Lord Burghersh, himself a composer, the Academy opened in March 1823 with King George IV as patron and William Crotch as first principal. It was then in Tenterden Street, Hanover Square, and suffered from inadequate funding from the first. When it opened there were only twenty-one young boarders. It received its Royal Charter in June 1830, and was awarded a government grant under Gladstone's administrations, which was rescinded by Disraeli, who perceived it as not delivering the instrumentalists or composers needed by British music.

Arthur Sullivan was a student from 1856 to 1858. By 1880 the Academy had more than 340 pupils and launched a system of metropolitan examinations for teachers.

Principals in the nineteenth century were some of the leading British composers of the day, including Cipriani Potter for over twenty-five years, Sterndale Bennett for nine, Macfarren for twelve and Alexander Campbell Mackenzie for thirty-six years, an incumbency that continued until beyond the First World War. Yet curiously little of their music (see Part II) has survived.

However, the Academy faced renewed challenges when the Royal College of Music was opened in 1883. But, despite the RCM's successes teaching composition, almost immediately there appeared from the Academy a vibrant generation of composers headed by Bantock, Holbrooke and, soon after, Bax, Bowen, Dale, Montague

51 The Royal Academy of Music in Tenterden Street.

Phillips and Eric Coates, all pupils of Frederick Corder. This was also the time of a notable contribution of instrumental teaching, particularly under Tobias Matthay for piano, whose pupils included York Bowen, Myra Hess, Irene Scharrer and Harriet Cohen. Lionel Tertis became the focus for the discovery of the viola as a solo instrument, with a range of new concertos, sonatas and solos written for him by the composers who were students at the Academy in the early 1900s.

The Academy moved to its present home in the Marylebone Road in 1912, formally opened on 22 June. Today it offers BMus and MMus degrees and a Ph.D., initially with King's College, London and from 1999 as offered by the University of London, of which the Academy is a constituent college member. The Academy awards the DipRAM for outstanding recital performance. Public concerts (usually free) take place in the Duke's Hall, and opera is performed termly in the Sir Jack Lyons Theatre. A new gift shop has recently opened, selling items based on the Academy's collections of iconography, manuscripts and instruments, plus more general material. It is open from 12.30 to 6.30 p.m., Monday to Friday.

In 1984 the Academy launched a series of groundbreaking new music festivals that each year saw one of the world's leading composers in residence for performances of their music, starting with the Polish composer Witold Lutosławski in 1984 and following him with Tippett, Penderecki, Messiaen, Henze, Berio, Elliot Carter, Schnittke, Ligeti, Donatoni, Birtwistle, former Academy composers (Bennett, Maw and so forth), film musicians (including John Williams, Malcolm Arnold), Arvo Pärt, Kagel, Kurtág (the first festival in collaboration with the South Bank) and Berio (also in collaboration with the South Bank). Organised for twenty years by the composer Paul Patterson, he received a Leslie Boosey Award in 1996 in recognition of his achievement. Indeed the format was taken up by the South Bank and later by the BBC at the Barbican.

Paintings Hanging in Duke's Hall

William Crotch, aged 11 by Sir William Beechey, 1786
Lilian Eldée (1870–1904) by Archibald Stuart Wortley.
Sir Harrison Birtwistle (b. 1934) by Adam Birtwistle.
Phyllis Neilson-Terry (1892–1977) by Charles Buchel, 1909.
Prince Arthur, Duke of Connaught (1850–1942) by Louis Ginett after Philip de Laszlo (1939).
Samuel Wesley (1766–1837) by John Russell, RA, 1776.
Charles Wesley (1757–1834) by John Russell, RA.
William Crotch (1775–1847) when aged three by John Sanders, 1778.
Julia Neilson-Terry (1868–1957) in *The Dancing Girl* by the Hon John Collier, 1891.
Alfred Gibson (1849–1924) by Herbert Oliver, 1899.
Lord Burghersh (John Fane, 11th Earl of Westmorland) (1784–1859) by Julia Goodman, 1858.
Frederick Bowen Jewson (1823–1891) aged 9. Artist unknown, *c.* 1832.
Giulia Grisi (1811–1869) by François Bouchot, 1840.
Manuel Garcia, Jr (1805–1906) by Galinborough Anderson, 1919, after John Singer Sargent.
Sir Alexander Campbell Mackenzie (1847–1935) by René l'Hôpital, 1923.
Sir David Lumsden (b. 1928) by Jeff Stultiens, 1993.

Principals of the Royal Academy of Music

1823–1832	William Crotch
1832–1859	Cipriani Potter
1859–1866	Charles Lucas
1866–1875	Sir William Sterndale Bennett
1875–1887	Sir George A. Macfarren
1888–1924	Sir Alexander Campbell Mackenzie
1924–1936	Sir John B. McEwen
1936–1949	Sir Stanley Marchant
1949–1955	Sir Reginald Thatcher
1955–1968	Sir Thomas Armstrong
1968–1982	Sir Anthony Lewis
1982–1993	Sir David Lumsden
1993–1995	Lynn Harrell
1995–	Curtis Price

The Academy library at York Gate, Marylebone Road, owns extensive holdings of manuscript and printed music by former alumni including York Bowen, Mackenzie, Holbrooke and Bax. The library also holds Sir Henry Wood's collection of orchestral scores and parts, comprising his own bound run of his Queen's Hall programmes including the Proms. Other notable collections are the Angelina Goetz's score library, the R. J. S. Stevens collection of catches and glees and manuscripts of seventeenth- and eighteenth-century Italian operas and cantatas, collections of organ and church music, Otto Klemperer's library of scores and parts plus archives. In 2004, the Academy acquired the Yehudi Menuhin Archive, one of the most valuable and comprehensive collections ever assembled by an individual musician. The acquisition was made possible by a very generous and major grant of £1.2m from the Foyle Foundation. Donations have also been received from several individuals. An additional grant from the Foyle Foundation will also enable the Academy to conserve the archive and make it accessible to the widest possible audience. The archive, to be known as the Foyle Menuhin Archive, will be catalogued in detail, and parts of it will be digitised and made fully available to the public. Items from the archive will be displayed regularly in the Academy's free 'living museum' and research centre, the York Gate Collections.

The Academy's historical collections have been enormously enhanced by the acquisition of the McCann Collection – bequeathed by the agent Norman McCann – which in 2004 is still being gradually sorted and processed. All the pictures and significant documents will eventually be accessible via the Academy website.

York Gate Collections displays many fine items from the Academy's holdings. All the instruments, including a large collection of Cremonese stringed instruments, are painstakingly maintained in playing condition; those that are not on loan to students or professional musicians will be on display. Other exhibits include musical memorabilia and original manuscripts. The museum is an integral part of Academy life: regular events take place in the galleries, including performances and demonstrations on some of the instruments on display, and the collections will be used intensively by students for performance practice and other research.

Much of the Academy's historical collection of iconography, along with its renowned collection of stringed instruments, engravings, paintings, sculpture, historic photographs and selections of archive material, historic manuscripts, letters and printed music is available on a new website launched in September 2004, initially of 5,000 records, most with digital images (www.ram.ac.uk).

Significant paintings and sculptures are located round the building where they can be seen by visitors. The major sequence of these will be found in the Duke's Hall, the principal concert hall of the Academy.

The celebrated bronze bust of Sir Henry J. Wood (1869–1944) by Donald Gilbert, 1936, formerly at the Queen's Hall, is the central image on the hall's far wall, and is transported to the Royal Albert Hall for the Proms every year (see Chapter 4). There are regular concerts in the hall which are open to the public and where admission is often free. Publicity for future events will be found on the Academy website and in literature and diaries available from the Academy.

Other pictures and busts can be seen around the building, including the Victorian busts of famous composers rescued from the façade of the bombed Queen's Hall (in the foyer of the new David Josefowitz Recital Hall) and Henry Carr's painting of the Griller Quartet on loan to the Academy from Jean Harvey and hanging on a second floor corridor.

52   Donald Gilbert's bust of Sir Henry Wood on its Proms pedestal at the Royal Albert Hall, 2004.

Royal College of Music
Prince Consort Road, South Kensington, SW7
Tube: South Kensington

The Royal College of Music opened in 1883 in the former premises of the National Training School for Music (adjacent to the Royal Albert Hall), which had been launched in 1876 with Sir Arthur Sullivan as first principal. This building was later the home of the Royal College of Organists. Sullivan does not seem to have had a vision for musical education and he resigned in 1881, to be briefly succeeded by Stainer. The following year the School was replaced by the College, which took over the building and its assets. Its first Director was George Grove. The first board of professors included Jenny Lind, Parratt, Parry and Stanford. Just before the opening, Grove was knighted, together with Sullivan and George Macfarren (Principal of the Royal Academy).

The accommodation proved unsuited to its purpose and the College's present premises, designed by Sir Arthur Blomfield, were opened by the Prince of Wales (later King Edward VII) early in May 1894, with a brilliant state ceremony, a *coup de théâtre* that must have contributed significantly to the College's pre-eminent standing in Victorian musical circles. The building largely owed its existence to the gift of £45,000 by Samson Fox (1838–1903) of Leeds, and was assessed by *The Graphic* as 'one of the

Directors of the Royal College of Music	
1882–1894	Sir George Grove
1895–1918	Sir Hubert Parry
1918–1937	Sir Hugh Allen
1938–1952	Sir George Dyson
1953–1959	Sir Ernest Bullock
1960–1974	Sir Keith Falkner
1974–1984	Sir David Willcocks
1985–1993	Michael Gough Matthews
1993–2005	Dame Janet Ritterman
2005–	Colin Lawson

53   The Royal College of Music photographed in the summer of 2004.

54   *Truth* in its Christmas number for 1883, shows a band of aristocratic supporters of the Royal College of Music playing outside the Royal Academy. The future King Edward VII takes round his hat while a diminutive Sullivan stands to his right and in the doorway the blind Macfarren stands disdainfully.

handsomest and most commodious builds [*sic*] devoted to the study of the musical art in Europe.'

The College was notable from the first for awarding endowed scholarships on a national basis and in May 1883 there were fifty scholars and forty-two fee-paying students. A concert hall was opened in 1901, with an organ donated by the then Director, Sir Hubert Parry (rebuilt in 1958). In 1986 the 400-seat Britten Opera Theatre, designed by Sir Hugh Casson, was opened and has been the venue for many distinguished student productions and performances by visiting companies.

The College's reputation as the *alma mater* of most of the generation of British composers who came to prominence in the first half of the twentieth century derives from the longstanding influence of Sir Charles Villiers Stanford, who taught there from 1883 to 1923 and whose pupils they were. Much later Stanford's success was emulated by a more contemporary composition teacher. This was John Lambert who taught composition from 1963 until 1990, and whose pupils include Julian Anderson, Oliver Knussen, Mark-Anthony Turnage and Simon Bainbridge.

There was a period in the 1970s and '80s when, directed by Edwin Roxburgh, the College's Twentieth-Century Ensemble became celebrated for performing works by leading avant-garde composers such as Stockhausen and Elliott Carter, particularly where large forces were required, some of their performances being broadcast by the BBC.

The College now has around 520 undergraduate and postgraduate students and offers its own degrees and diplomas, including a doctorate in music. It has a notable wider role because of the internationally significant research collection held in its Library and Centre for Performance History, the latter the owner of the pre-eminent UK collection of concert programmes, now of increased significance owing to the rise of interest in nineteenth- and twentieth-century performance history.

The Royal College's collection of pictures is evident in paintings and busts exhibited throughout the building and especially in the Concert Hall, and their curation is undertaken by the Centre for Performance History. The large portrait of their benefactor Samuel Ernest Palmer by Sir Arthur Stockdale Cope faces the reception desk in the front hall. A handlist of portraits, busts and medallions is available from the College.

The Centre for Performance History also incorporates an internationally celebrated museum of instruments. This is normally open to the public on Wednesday afternoons in term time, or by arrangement. Lecture tours with demonstrations and concerts also take place. Catalogues and sets of postcards of important items in the collection have been published. There are around thirty keyboard, and a wide range of woodwind, brass and stringed instruments dating from the sixteenth century onwards. These include the South German clavicytherium (c. 1480), which is perhaps the earliest surviving stringed keyboard instrument, a spinet that once belonged to Handel and a clavichord owned by Haydn. There is also an ethnological section with instruments from Africa and Asia. The college publishes a catalogue in two volumes (see Bibliography).

The library includes a wide range of manuscript and printed music dating from the sixteenth to the twentieth centuries. Much of this reflects musical taste in London in the eighteenth and nineteenth centuries, with many works by English and Italian composers and, from the late nineteenth century onwards, by college alumni. There are also autographs of Haydn, Mozart, Schubert and Elgar, and the manuscript score of Dvořák's Eighth Symphony, used by the composer for its first run of performances in the UK. The Library subsumes the libraries of the Sacred Harmonic Society, the Concerts of Ancient Music and Sir George Grove and a part of the library of the Musical Union. Manuscripts and printed music from Novello and Co, the Nicanor Zabaleta harp music collection and the Cavendish Collection of library music from Boosey and Hawkes are more recent acquisitions. Sir George Grove's own annotated run of his Crystal Palace programmes was purchased at Sotheby's in 2000.

Paintings Hanging at the Royal College of Music

Sir Hugh Allen by Leonard Campbell Taylor, 1929.
Dennis Arundell by Hugh Buss, 1920.
Thomas Attwood, artist unknown, ca 1815.
Sir Adrian Boult by Kazunori Ishibashi, 1923.
William Boyce attrib. Mason Chamberlain, c. 1765–70.
Sir Ernest Bullock by John Ward, 1961.
Frédéric Chopin, artist unknown, c. 1848.
William Walter Cobbett, artist unknown, c. 1920.
Sir George Dyson by Anthony Devas, 1952.
Sir Edward Elgar by Talbot Hughes, 1905.
Sir Keith Falkner by Leonard Boden, 1974.
Carlo Broschi Farinelli by Bartolommeo Nazari, 1734.
Francesco Geminiani, artist unknown, c. 1735.
Sir George Grove by Charles Wellington Furse, 1895.
George Frederick Handel after Thomas Hudson, 1756.
Joseph Haydn by Thomas Hardy, 1791.
Sir George Henschel by Felix Moscheles, 1880.
Herbert Howells by Richard Walker, 1972.
Joseph Joachim by Eduard Julius Friedrich Bendemann, 1870.
Sir John Blackwood McEwen by Reginald Grenville Eves, 1937.
August Manns by John Pettie, 1892.
Michael Gough Matthews by Tim Rukavina, 1991.
Ignacy Jan Paderewski by Sir Edward Coley Burne-Jones, 1890.
Johann Peter Salomon by Thomas Hardy, c. 1791.
Albert Sammons by Alexander Akerbladh, 1950.
Sir Malcolm Sargent by Sir Gerald Kelly, 1948.
William Shield by Thomas Hardy, c. 1795.
Dame Ethel Smyth by Neville Lytton, 1936.
Sir Charles Villiers Stanford by Sir Hubert von Herkomer, 1882.
Sir Arthur Sullivan by F. Lynch after Sir John Everett Millais, 1888.
Sir Michael Tippett by Juliet Pannett, 1957.
Carl Maria von Weber by John Cawse, 1826.
Samuel Sebastian Wesley by William Keighley Briggs, 1849.
Ralph Vaughan Williams by Sir Gerald Kelly, 1952.

55   Adjacent to the Royal Albert Hall, this distinctive building was successively the National Training School, the Royal College of Music and the Royal College of Organists, the latter remaining for many years.

Royal College of Organists
Formerly adjacent to the Royal Albert Hall
Tube: South Kensington

Founded in Bloomsbury in 1864 as the College of Organists by Richard Limpus, organist of St Michael's Cornhill, the college was granted its royal charter in 1893. Exams leading to fellowship of the college were instituted in 1866, and a teaching department was established in the 1870s. It moved into the old Royal College of Music premises, beside the Royal Albert Hall, in 1904. The building is interestingly ornate and worth a visit. The college remained in Kensington Gore until 1991, when the administration moved to St Andrew's Church in Holborn. The college is now re-established in Birmingham.

Trinity College of Music
King Charles Court, Old Royal Naval College, Greenwich, SE10
Train: Cutty Sark (Docklands Light Railway); or by river bus to Greenwich Pier

Trinity College of Music was founded in 1872 as the Church Choral Society and College of Church Music, London by the Revd Henry George Bonavia Hunt who became the Warden of the college from 1872 to 1892 and later Professor of Musical History. Sir Frederick Gore Ouseley was president. It preceded that expansion in London conservatoires which took place some ten or more years later. Initial meetings were held at St Botolph's, Bishopsgate and teaching was in the evenings at the Central Foundation Schools of London, Cowper Street, EC2. It then moved to the Russell Institution. In 1875 the College was incorporated as Trinity College, London with two divisions: Academic and Choral. In 1876 the college moved to 61 Weymouth Street, W1, and teaching was then undertaken during the day. A theory of music examination was introduced in 1877. In 1880 the college moved to 13 Mandeville Place, W1, and in 1917 it expanded into the house next door (No. 11), formerly the home of Lillie Langtry. Here Trinity College of Music operated, three turnings along from the Wigmore Hall, for well over a century. The building remains, and includes internal memorial windows that could not be moved when the College went to Greenwich in 2001. These are of Chaucer, Shakespeare (dedicated to the memory of Bonavia Hunt), Purcell, John of Fornsete and Bantock. The former Bridge Memorial Library also has a window.

Once a recognised college of music in the University of London, Trinity is now co-located with the University of Greenwich on the site of the Royal Naval College, Greenwich. It was a pioneer of musical examinations from local centres throughout Great Britain and Ireland, and in due course across the Empire. The composer Sir Granville Bantock, while on a world examination tour for Trinity during the winter of 1938/9, completed his *Cyprian Goddess* Symphony in Fiji.

Trinity was also a notable pioneer of examined degrees in music, an initiative started as early as 1876 with London University and later Trinity funded the forward-looking King Edward VII Chair of Music there. By the College's Jubilee in 1922, there were weekly college concerts, chamber concerts, choral concerts in Steinway Hall, orchestral concerts at Queen's Hall and light opera performances in London theatres. The college continued to operate during the Second World War and today, continues to present an active programme of performances, lectures and opera productions, being responsible for many interesting operatic revivals, including the UK stage premiere of Berthold Goldschmidt's *Beatrice Cenci*.

The college holds many interesting paintings and artefacts. A permanent gallery on the two floors of practice rooms exhibits paintings on musical subjects by students at the Wimbledon School of Art. These have to be seen by appointment as they are not in a public area. There are various named rooms, for example in celebration of Meredith Davies, Philip Jones and John Hosier, some of which contain framed memorabilia. In the Principal's Office are portraits of William Croft by Kneller, two of Handel and of J. C. Bach. There is also a desk that once belonged to Bantock, with his name on it, and a Dolmetsch spinet. In the Peacock Room (a public room) are busts of Grieg and Charles Kennedy Scott and the Charles Dibdin memorial – a life-size figure of Dibdin. The college also owns a portrait of Sir Granville Bantock by Jean Jameson, three paintings by Sir Henry Wood and, in the Barbirolli Room, a portrait by Brian Denington (reproduced on page 199), his baton and photographs of the conductor. The library holds manuscripts of Lionel Tertis, Kaikhosru Shapurji Sorabji, Elgar's *The Black Knight*, much of Sir John Barbirolli's library, the Antonio de Almeida collection of orchestral full scores, and an extensive holding of Bantock printed scores. The Mander and Mitchenson Theatre Collection (which can be accessed by appointment, or by telephone) is an unparalleled collection of theatrical and musical images. The library is one of the London access points (with the Barbican Library) for Music Preserved's (formerly the Music Performance Research Centre) collection of historic live sound recordings.

Trinity acquired the Blackheath Halls (see Chapter 7) in July 2003. In October 2003 Trinity College of Music and Laban, the pre-eminent UK dance college, announced their forthcoming merger (in 2005) creating the first British conservatoire of music and dance, each institution intending to retain its individual character in premises only five minutes walk apart. Laban's new building at Deptford Creekside won the 2003 RIBA Stirling Prize and was described by Gerry Robinson, Chairman of the Arts Council of England as 'one of the marvels of the moment'.

The removal of Trinity to Greenwich was celebrated with panache on 18 October 2001 with a service of thanksgiving in Westminster Abbey before the whole establishment voyaged in formal procession down the River Thames from Westminster Pier, headed by *HMS Westminster*. Tower Bridge was opened for

Principals/Chairmen of Trinity College of Music	
1872–1905	Henry Bonavia Hunt
1908–1924	Sir Frederick Bridge
1924–1929	Joseph Cox Bridge
1929–1944	Stanley Roper (Roper was the first to be designated 'Principal')
1944–1965	Wilfrid Greenhouse Allt
1965–1979	Myers Foggin
1979–1988	Meredith Davies
1988–1994	Philip Jones
1994–	Gavin Henderson

them as they sailed through, and they were greeted at Greenwich with school children lining the bank, music playing and four skydivers trailing smoke landing on the Greenwich lawns.

Libraries and Museums

Barbican Music Library
Barbican Centre, EC2
Tube: Moorgate or Barbican

At the Barbican Centre, the Barbican Music Library is the second largest public music library in London. Unlike Westminster Music Library (incorporating Central Music Library) it also includes recordings, and is one of the largest recorded music collections in London that is available for loan to the public, covering classical, pop, jazz and film. It is also one of the locations for accessing Music Preserved, which is a growing reference resource, covering audio recordings of both recent performances from venues all over London, and historic performances, none of which are available commercially.

The library's holdings include scores, songbooks, operas and other choral music, solo and chamber works, and a notable collection of music by British composers of the late nineteenth and early twentieth centuries. There are also books about music and musicians, over seventy periodical titles, plus other titles that are no longer published, and a collection of journals published by societies specialising in particular composers or conductors. The library holds regular exhibitions on musical topics.

British Library
96 Euston Road, NW1
Tube: King's Cross and Euston

The British Library moved to the Euston Road from the British Museum in 2000. In addition to the Music Library, several departments of the library include collections of interest in the field of music, not all of them accessible in the same room. As the premier UK official deposit library, the holdings of printed music are very extensive, though not without the occasional lacuna where an item or publisher has not been deposited. Any initial search for printed music or books on music is best made via Copac (Copac.ac.uk) where the enquirer will find locations for other leading British libraries if the British Library does not hold an item. The four principal collections are the Department of Manuscripts, the Department of Printed Books, the Royal Music Library and the National Sound Archive.

In the Department of Manuscripts some early manuscripts can be found in the Cotton, Harley and Sloane collections and the Royal Library. Many manuscripts were received by gift or bequest, especially those by Samuel Wesley, seventeenth- and eighteenth-century vocal music, Beethoven, Mozart and Schubert. More modern autograph manuscripts include extensive holdings of William Baines, Bax,

Boughton, Havergal Brian, Dohnányi, Elgar, Grainger, Holst, Ireland, Smyth, Tippett and Vaughan Williams. The letters and papers of Warlock and Sir Henry Wood are deposited here, and there are manuscripts from Tippett and Sullivan, and the correspondence of the Royal Philharmonic Society.

A special collection of note in the Department of Printed Books is the Paul Hirsch Music Library containing printed music and literature and opera full scores. The library of Church House collection of hymn and psalm books, Sir John Barbirolli's conducting scores, and literature on music is also held in the Department.

The Royal Music Library should be noted for its collection of Purcell and Handel autographs.

The National Sound Archive was founded by Patrick Saul. It opened in 1955 as the British Institute of Recorded Sound at Russell Square, subsequently moving to dedicated premises in Exhibition Road, South Kensington, near the Royal Albert Hall and the Royal College of Music. It became part of the British Library in 1983 and moved with it to Euston Road. Among its seven main subject areas are classical music, international music, jazz and popular music. The archive contains over a million discs, 185,000 tapes and other recordings. There are copies of recordings issued in the UK, together with selected commercial discs from abroad, radio broadcasts and privately made recordings. Recordings may be listened to by appointment in the dedicated carrels in the Music Reading Room, and the catalogue (known as *Cadenza*) is accessible via the British Library website. The National Sound Archive Reference collection of books and journals (including *Radio Times*) is on open access in the Humanities 2 reading room and can often be a more convenient source than ordering an item in one of the other reading rooms.

British Music Information Centre
Lincoln House, 75 Westminster Bridge Road, SE1
Tube: Lambeth North

Long established at 10 Stratford Place, W1, the British Music Information Centre moved in May 2004. This library and information resource is primarily intended for promoting living British composers to performers, but it also hosts researchers into twentieth-century British classical music. A collection of scores and recordings is available to the public, with a catalogue of holdings and knowledgeable staff to help. The current catalogue can be searched via the Centre's website. Older material is now held off site.

Westminster Music Library, incorporating Central Music Library Ltd
160 Buckingham Palace Road, SW1
Tube: Victoria; or bus 11 stops outside

The first floor of Westminster Public Library's branch at Buckingham Palace Road houses Westminster Music Library, incorporating Central Music Library Ltd

(CML), with the Barbican, London's leading public music library. CML was established as a private library in 1947 and attracted various bequests, including the library of the celebrated music critic Edwin Evans, whose portrait in oils, painted in 1916 by Mary Eristoff, is also held. In 1947 the library was invited to deposit the collection in Westminster Public Libraries. Westminster's readers were to have free use of the collection, which would be added to regularly and supported by the income from a capital sum established for the purpose. CML was intended to be a genuinely 'national' asset, freely and equally at the disposal of all. The changing political and financial climate in local government has tended to emphasise its local role in Westminster. Nevertheless, by the unique nature of its holdings, it has a national standing. It is notable for its extensive coverage of scores from the early twentieth century, a bound run of Promenade Concert programmes and the extensive collection of press cuttings, once Edwin Evans's working library. Recent acquisitions may be searched on the Westminster Public Library website, but much of the older material in the Central Music Library collections can still be accessed only via the card catalogue in the library. The library does not hold recordings.

English Folk Dance and Song Society: Vaughan Williams Memorial Library

Cecil Sharp House, 2 Regent's Park Road, NW1
Tube: Camden Town and buses 274, C2

This was previously the Cecil Sharp Library, consisting of his personal collection bequeathed to the English Folk Dance Society in 1924. Cecil Sharp House opened in 1930 and was the library's first permanent home. Since then it has developed with the bequests of many other folklorists and collectors (notably Vaughan Williams, Lucy Broadwood, George Butterworth and Maud Karpeles among many others), the papers, notebooks and the field readings of Percy Grainger, Mike Yates and the BBC Folk Music Archive. The library is a dynamic and expert centre that is constantly growing, and as such is de facto the national English folk music and dance archive. It is now a multi-media library, open for reference to visitors, with a variety of collections such as press cuttings, prints, photographs, ephemera, videos, ciné film and more. The material mainly relates to British folk culture and the elements of this culture in North America and Ireland in particular. Non-members can use the library for reference or research but are charged a daily fee.

Fenton House
See Chapter 7

Foundling Museum
40 Brunswick Square, WC1
Tube: Russell Square

The Foundling Museum is a separate but closely linked body to the Thomas Coram Foundation, which has moved to an adjacent campus. Redeveloped in 2004 the building contains three restored rooms from the Foundling Hospital – the Court room (said to be one of the finest British Rococo interiors with its striking plaster-work ceiling by William Wilton), the Committee room and the Picture Gallery, with paintings from the collection on the walls. There is also a Handel study centre, with research facilities, and a library and a gallery displaying items from the Gerald Coke Handel Collection, including Handel's will, his conducting score of the Foundling Hospital Anthem with notes in his own hand, and a fair copy of the full score of *Messiah*. The art collection also includes a bust of Handel by Roubiliac and the original keyboard of the organ presented by Handel to the chapel.

The original Foundling Hospital was established as a refuge for abandoned children by Captain Thomas Coram, assisted by his friend William Hogarth, in 1739; the first children were admitted in 1741. Hogarth gave his own paintings for the walls of the new building, as did many other contemporary British artists. These attracted the art-loving public to view them, and it was probably the first public gallery providing exhibition space for artists.

Handel was closely associated with fundraising to help Coram to build a chapel for the Foundling Hospital and the first part of *Messiah* was given there. The Hospital stood in Brunswick Square from the eighteenth century to 1926 when it was demolished. The present building was the headquarters of the foundation, now housed next door, and was completed in 1937. Regular tours are offered: check times on www.foundlingmuseum.org.uk.

Guildhall Library
Aldermanbury, EC2
Tube: Moorgate and Mansion House

Guildhall Library is a major public reference library that specialises in the history of London, focusing on the City. The collection consists of three sections: printed books; manuscripts; and prints, maps and drawings. Material of musical interest can be found throughout. The library also holds the archives of the Worshipful Company of Musicians, a collection of glees and the Gresham collection of music of the seventeenth and eighteenth centuries.

The large collection of historical trade directories and reference books will be a prime source for everyone researching the history of the music and associated trades. It will also be a valuable source for all histories of London theatres.

The library catalogue can be searched via the Internet, but more specifically the *Collage* catalogue system is accessible via the internet (collage.cityof london.gov.uk/about) and gives access to some 25,000 prints, paintings and drawings, under 'Leisure', the relevant sections being music, theatres and pleasure gardens. It is notably strong in eighteenth- and early nineteenth-century prints of Vauxhall and other gardens and in modern drawings relating to the flute. The photograph collection is accessible only via manual sources.

Handel House Museum
25 Brook Street, W1
Tube: Bond Street

Handel lived here during most of his fame in London, from 1723 until he died in 1759. He was the first occupant of 25 Brook Street and the streets around were being newly developed when he first moved in. Many of his most celebrated works were written here. Handel was well-known and admired in London. He played the organ regularly in St George's Hanover Square, only a short walk away, and later at services at St Paul's cathedral.

The museum opened in November 2001 in the well-restored Brook Street house and was the first museum in London to be devoted to one composer. The exhibition covers four themes: Handel's London, Handel the man, rehearsal and performance, and composition. There are many oil paintings and prints of Handel and friends such as Thomas Arne and John Gay, and often someone will be heard playing in the music room. There is a programme of live music and events, and a 'Thursday live' concert series at 6 p.m. and 7 p.m. with recitals in the Rehearsal and Performance room.

Horniman Museum
See Chapter 7

Kneller Hall
For the Museum of Instruments at Kneller Hall, see Chapter 7

Royal Opera House Archives
Royal Opera House, Covent Garden, WC2
Tube: Covent Garden, Charing Cross, Leicester Square or Embankment

The Royal Opera House Archives, now re-housed, provide a major resource on the history of musical theatre in London since earliest times. Apart from portraits, photographs and ephemera of productions, a notable resource is the scrapbooks of press reports of productions.

Theatre Museum
Tavistock Street, Covent Garden, WC2 (public access from Russell Street)
Tube: Covent Garden

Situated almost next door to the Royal Opera House, Covent Garden, subtitled the 'National Museum for the Performing Arts' and set up by the Victoria and Albert Museum, this unique institution holds documents on the history of opera and ballet (including the costumes for Diaghilev's *Rite of Spring*) from 1700 onwards, and prints and portraits of composers and musicians. The permanent exhibition features models, costumes, paintings and posters and the effects of celebrated theatrical figures from the past. There is a changing range of temporary exhibitions. There are also recordings of performances. The library is accessible for research by appointment and regular tours are available during the day.

In November 2003 what was billed as 'the World's largest Picasso' – the drop curtain for the Ballets Russes' ballet *Le Train Bleu*, painted and signed by Picasso in 1924 – was unrolled for the first time in twenty years from the museum's archives to launch an appeal for £12 million to modernise and extend the museum.

*   *   *

Portraits and Pictures

Musical iconography will, incidentally, be found in the many galleries, libraries and institutions in London. Some of these have been discussed above. Musical images appear among the national galleries in central London, particularly at the National Portrait Gallery and its associated archive.

National Gallery
Trafalgar Square, WC2
Tube: Charing Cross or Leicester Square

Along with most representative art collections, musical images appear from time to time in the collection of the National Gallery. The Micro Gallery on the first floor of the Sainsbury Wing provides access to every painting in the collection and is very easy to use. Paintings can be accessed by artist, period, subject or genre. To find pictures on a musical theme, use the category 'Everyday Life: Making Music'. Images come up arranged chronologically and give details of title, artist and date. When an image is enlarged it appears accompanied by the commentary provided with the actual picture in the gallery. A card to print out the images costs £2. The Micro Gallery is open daily from 10 a.m. to 5.30 p.m. (8.30 p.m. on Wed) and no appointment is necessary. Details of the collection can also be accessed via the website www.nationalgallery.org.uk, which contains pictures of the permanent collection and long-term loans. These are illustrated and described in the collection online.

Notable musical images in the collection include two by Hendrick ter Brugghen, *The Concert* (1626) and *A Woman Playing a Theorbo to Two Men* (1667–8). An image of a concert 150 years earlier comes in Lorenzo Costa's *A Concert* of 1485–95. Celebrated musical details to be found in famous National Gallery pictures include Holbein the Younger's well-known painting *The Ambassadors* in which a superb image of a lute appears as a detail, a detail published by the Gallery as a postcard. A musical interest is also to be found in *Man and Woman Seated by a Virginal* and *A Woman Seated at a Table and a Man Tuning a Violin*, both by Gabriel Metsu.

National Portrait Gallery
St Martin's Place, WC2
Tube: Charing Cross or Leicester Square

Founded in December 1856, the gallery had no permanent home for forty years, moving from Great George Street to the Royal Horticultural Society building in Exhibition Road, and then the collection was sent on loan to Bethnal Green Museum. Finally in 1889 the government assigned a site in St Martin's Place and the new gallery (already too small) opened in April 1896. A large extension was built in 1933. The top floor galleries were refurbished in the late 1980s, followed by the entrance hall and staircase. New galleries were opened in November 1993. In 1996 the nineteenth- and twentieth-century galleries on the first floor were remodelled.

There is much material of interest to music lovers – as was seen in the exhibition 'Variations on a theme: 150 years of photographs of British composers', which was held in the spring of 1997, all of these exhibits are still available from the Gallery or its archives. It included photographs of Lutyens, Gerhard, Britten, Mackenzie and lighter composers such as Vivian Ellis, Ray Noble, Coward, Bart, Dankworth and the Beatles, as well as Panufnik, Goldschmidt, Maw, Goehr and Maconchy. Composers of an earlier age, such as Thomas Dunhill, Norman O'Neill and Armstrong Gibbs, also figured. Many musicians were portrayed in paintings and drawings, and there were also bronzes of Harriet Cohen, Sir Noël Coward, Cyril Scott, Roger Quilter, Herbert Howells, Sir Lennox Berkeley, Frederick Delius, Eric Fenby, Dame Ethel Smyth and the conductors Sir Henry Wood and Sir Adrian Boult.

The permanent collection is in chronological order, with the earliest material on the second floor and the most modern on the ground floor. Portraits of particular interest to the musical visitor will be found in the rooms devoted to the arts, for instance, Room 6, 'Science and the Arts in the C17th'; Room 12, 'The Arts in the later C18th'; and Room 28, 'Late Victorian Arts'.

On the second floor in Room 10, 'The Arts in the early C18th', is a large oil painting by Marcus Tuscher (1742) of the Shudi family, noted harpsichord makers who later founded the firm that became Broadwoods. Room 12 contains a very large portrait of the blind Handel, by Thomas Hudson, painted in 1756 for Charles Jennens, a friend who selected the words for *Messiah*. Nearby is an oil of Johann Christian Bach by Gainsborough (*c.* 1776) and one of the Sharp family, who were famous for organising fortnightly concerts on Sundays, painted by Zoffany in 1779–81.

Descending to the first floor, Room 24, 'Early Victorian Arts', has a portrait of singer Jenny Lind, an oil by Edouard Magnus, 1861. Room 28, 'Late Victorian Arts' displays fine portraits of W. S. Gilbert by Frank Holl and Sir Arthur Sullivan by Millais. Nearby is a painting of Adelina Patti by J. Sant. Room 29 has a bust of Elgar, and a bronze by Percival Hedley, modelled in 1905 but not cast until 1927. In Room 30 is a pencil drawing done in 1965 by Michael Ayrton and an etching of Hans Keller by Milein Cosman (his wife). Room 31 is a feast for music lovers, with a *c.* 1925 bronze of William Walton by Maurice Lambert, brother of Constant; a fine oil painting by Paule Vezelay in 1925 of Eugene Goossens and Richard Tauber in rehearsal; and a pen and ink drawing of Constant Lambert by Oriel Ross. There are also oil paintings of Constant Lambert in 1926 by Christopher Wood, Arthur Bliss by Mark Gertler (1932), Frederick Delius by Ernest Procter (painted on the occasion of the Delius festival in 1929), Harriet Cohen by Ronald Ossery Dunlop, *c.* 1930, Lord Berners painting a picture by Rex Whistler in 1929, and the well-known portrait of Gustav Holst in his soundproof composing room at St Paul's Girls' School by Millicent Woodforde (1910). This gallery is called 'The Armistice to the New Elizabethans'. At time of writing it also contained a display cabinet of mainly black and white photographs of singers, entitled '1950's hit parade'. Before moving down to the ground floor we come to the Balcony Gallery (Room 32) with a bronze of Ninette de Valois by F. C. McWilliam (1964) and a portrait in oils by Sam Walsh of Paul McCartney, 1964.

On the ground floor will be found a room devoted to 'Later C20th Arts'. Here are bronzes of Sir Thomas Beecham in 1937 by David Wynne and one of Ralph Vaughan Williams by Jacob Epstein (1950). Vaughan Williams also appears in a familiar oil painting by Sir Gerald Kelly, and other musical figures in the gallery include Kathleen Ferrier (an oil painting by Maurice Codner, 1946), Benjamin Britten and Peter Pears painted together by Kenneth Green in 1943, soon after their return from the USA, Noël Coward by Clemence Dane, and a striking portrait of William Walton by Michael Ayrton. The section on 'Britain since 1990' includes a portrait of Michael Tippett by Martin Rose in acrylic on canvas, painted in 1989, in which for many looking for a good likeness, the technique stands in the way of representation.

An added service is the IT Gallery on the mezzanine floor. It has 10 touch-screen browsers. Users can access the 15,000 portraits in the gallery plus some portraits in the archive and photographic collections. Composers, musicians and performers, both classical and popular, can be found under the Music subheading and, when the selected portrait is enlarged, users can search under Sitter, Artist, Portrait and Magnify (to pick up the smallest detail of the painting). Brief biographical details are provided. Images can be printed free in black and white, a payment is made for colour. No appointment is necessary. The gallery also has a search facility on CD-Rom of the primary collection, and the website can be accessed on www.npg.org.uk.

Royal Opera House Covent Garden
Bow Street, Covent Garden Piazza, WC2
Tube: Covent Garden, Charing Cross, Embankment or Leicester Square

The Royal Opera House has a generous selection of paintings, illustrations and busts on display – see Chapter 1.

Royal Philharmonic Society
10 Stratford Place, W1
Tube: Bond Street

The Royal Philharmonic Society is one of the world's longest-standing concert-giving organisations, founded in 1813. Unfortunately it no longer has a regular orchestral concert series. Concerts were first given in the Argyll Rooms, after twenty years in 1833 moving to the Hanover Square Rooms from where the Society later moved to St James's Hall in 1869 and to the Queen's Hall in 1894. Concerts transferred to the Royal Albert Hall after the Queen's Hall was destroyed in an air raid in 1941, and to the Royal Festival Hall after it opened in 1951. Regular concerts tailed off during the 1990s and stopped completely in 1999.

The prestigious library, including the manuscript of Beethoven's *Choral Symphony*, long on loan to the British Library, was purchased by that library as the outcome of a national appeal in 2002. The complete bound set of the printed programmes is still held at the Royal Philharmonic Society, but is not routinely available for reference. Another set is available to researchers at the British Library. The bust of Beethoven by Schaller (at present on loan to the British Library, but not sold to them with the rest of the collection) used to have pride of place on the platform during concerts.

The Society was given its Royal Charter in 1912 to commemorate its centenary. Sir Thomas Beecham became chairman during the First World War, and raised substantial funds, but in 1927 his plans to establish a permanent orchestra with the BBC failed and instead he founded the London Philharmonic Orchestra in 1932, which was hired by the Royal Philharmonic Society for several seasons. This led to the end of the Society's own orchestra. The Society continued to put on concerts throughout the Second World War and thereafter. Its name was used by agreement by the Royal Philharmonic Orchestra when Beecham formed that orchestra after the Second World War. The Society gave an ambitious series at the Royal Festival Hall for its 175th birthday in 1988. Its Gold Medal has long been one of the most prestigious of musical awards and the Society continues to bestow various honours and awards in music.

Royal Society of Musicians
10 Stratford Place, W1
Tube: Bond Street

The Royal Society of Musicians was established in 1738 to help musicians in reduced circumstances. It became one of Handel's favourite charities and he did much to support it, taking part in concerts and leaving the society a substantial amount of money in his will for the support of 'decay'd' musicians. Initially meeting in taverns, in 1808 the society took up its first permanent home at 11–13 Lisle Street, Leicester Fields (now Leicester Square), where it remained until 1931 when it moved to its present offices in Stratford Place.

The society owns many important portraits, including those of Handel, Corelli, Geminiani and Purcell. There is a copy of a Haydn portrait and others of singers Charles Edward Horn, John Sinclair and Marian Mackenzie. There are also portraits of Rossini, Sir George Smart, Sir William Sterndale Bennett, a pencil sketch of Weber, and many other pictures and mementoes. Busts of Haydn, Beethoven, Vaughan Williams and the conductor Alfred Mellon stand in the basement of the building. Viewing is strictly by appointment.

Tate Britain
Millbank, SW1
Tube: Pimlico

Like the National Gallery, Tate Britain has a number of pictures that have musical subjects, though many of the more modern ones are less representational than those of an earlier generation. The two most celebrated paintings in the collection with a musical theme are probably Augustus John's well-known portrait of the cellist Guilhermina Suggia (1923) and Richard Jack's 1912 *Rehearsal with Nikisch*, one of the very few images to show the inside of the Queen's Hall in colour. Other musical paintings include Turner's *Musicians* (1827) and Edward Francis Burney's *Amateurs of Tye-Wig Music ('Musicians of the Old School')* (c. 1820), the artist's reworking in oils of a series of watercolours intended to satirise the battle between modern and ancient taste.

Pictures in the Tate can be researched on the web. An online database of 50,000 works covers all four sites. These can be accessed on www.tate.org.uk. Under 'General collections' users can search by subject or artist and can browse or go for a specific topic. Under 'Leisure and pastimes' is found 'Music and Entertainment', or users can go straight to 'Composers' or 'Musicians'. Details of the holdings appear and then the images selected can be accessed, with details of sitter, artist, provenance and description. There are also computer points in the gallery for visitors to use, or they can get help via the information desks.

Victoria and Albert Museum
Corner of Exhibition Road and Brompton Road (entrances in both), SW1
Tube: South Kensington

The Victoria and Albert Museum is of musical interest both for its collection of instruments and for musical materials in its library, although theatre material is held at the Theatre Museum in Covent Garden, a branch of the Victoria and Albert Museum.

The musical instrument collection of the historian Carl Engel was acquired by the museum in 1882. It forms the nucleus of the museum's collection, which can be seen in a dedicated gallery on the first floor. Only some fifteen per cent of the holdings can be displayed at any time. These are beautifully presented and include virginals, lutes, viols, baroque oboes, guitars, harpsichords and french horns. Nearly all are by well-known makers such as a tenor viol made by Henry Jaye, a baroque flute by Peter Bressau, and a harpsichord by Pascal Taskin. One notable exhibit is Queen Elizabeth I's virginals, probably made in Venice in the late sixteenth century. Interesting, too, to see the baryton, that now forgotten instrument much favoured by Haydn's employer Prince Nicholas Esterhazy, for which Haydn wrote more than a hundred pieces. The museum also holds some 350 musical instruments from South Asia that are not on display.

Concerts used to be given at the museum, prestigious occasions including the first London performance of Malcolm Arnold's Guitar Concerto on 6 March 1960. Lunchtime chamber music Proms are still given in the Lecture Theatre during the Proms seasons.

Guides to the collection include a booklet, a recording of the instruments and colour slides.

Worshipful Company of Musicians
74–75 Watling Street, EC4
Tube: Mansion House

The Worshipful Company was originally the Fellowship of Minstrels, which received ordinances in 1350 and was incorporated as a guild in 1500. With the charter of James I it took its present name, was granted the privileges and influence enjoyed by other livery companies, and was given control over music-making in and within three miles of London (except for Westminster and Southwark). It lost influence under charters of successive kings (Charles I, Charles II and James II) and began to admit businessmen, but interest was revived with the election of William Chappell in 1870 and more musicians were admitted. More recently its objective has been to promote all aspects of music, mainly by awarding prizes and scholarships. Awards are made to singers, composers, organ students and students at music schools and military schools, a notable activity in 2003 being prizes, scholarships and awards to young jazz musicians. Livery numbers are about 150.

HERE RESTS OUR BELOVED
LORENZO BARBIROLLI
1864 - 1928
R · I · P
WHO WAS JOINED IN ETERNAL REST
BY OUR DARLING MÉMÉ
ON 2ND OCTOBER 1963
AGED 91

AND BY THEIR DISTINGUISHED SON
JOHN
KNIGHT AND COMPANION OF HONOUR
BORN IN LONDON DECEMBER 2nd 1899
DIED IN LONDON JULY 29th 1970
MAY HE REST IN PEACE

DENNIS BRAIN
born MAY 17 1921
died SEPTEMBER 1 1957

My call transforms
The hall to autumn
tinted grove

LEOPOLD
STOKOWSKI
18 APRIL 1882 – 13 SEPTEMBER 197

Music is the Voice of the All

BALFE
THE COMPOSER
BORN
MAY 15TH 1808
DIED
OCTOBER 20TH 1870

ALSO LINA ROSA

SIR JOSEPH BARNBY

WILLIAM SHIELD
MUSICIAN AND COMPOSER
BORN MARCH 5TH 1748
DIED JANUARY 25TH 1829

JOHANN PETER ·
SALOMON
MUSICIAN
BORN 1745   DIED 1815
HE BROUGHT
HAYDN TO ENGLAND IN
1791 AND 1794

MUZIO CLEMENTI
CALLED
THE FATHER OF THE PIANOFORTE
HIS FAME AS A MUSICIAN
AND COMPOSER
ACKNOWLEDGED THROUGHOUT EUROPE
PROCURED HIM THE HONOUR
OF A PUBLIC INTERMENT
IN THIS CLOISTER
BORN AT ROME 1752
DIED AT EVESHAM 1832

IN MEMORY OF
THOMAS ARNE
MUSICIAN AND PARISHIONER
1710 – 1778
BAPTIZED IN THIS CHURCH
BURIED IN THIS CHURCHYARD

"RULE BRITANNIA"

LET US PRAISE FAMOUS MEN... SUCH AS
FOUND OUT MUSICAL TUNES
ECCLUS. XLIV 1.5

4 • Graves and Memorials

Before the 1830s, burials usually took place in churchyards, but the growth in London's population meant that these graveyards became polluted and dangerously overflowing with coffins and corpses. In reaction to this appalling situation, the General Cemetery Company was founded around 1831 with an eye to the example of the immense Père Lachaise cemetery in Paris. In 1832 the first joint stock company in London – Kensal Green – was established, and thereafter six others: Abney Park, Brompton, Highgate, Nunhead, Tower Hamlets and West Norwood. Kensal Green led the garden cemetery movement, which is referred to by Betjeman in his introduction to a booklet on Highgate Cemetery: 'cemeteries in big cities in Britain were generously laid out in the eighteenth-century tradition of landscape gardens', and indeed now they represent oases of peace in the bustling metropolis.

Later, municipal cemeteries were established, as were cemeteries associated with particular religions such as St Mary's Roman Catholic Cemetery at Kensal Green, the Jewish Cemetery at Golders Green and the one-time Dissenters' graveyard at Bunhill Fields. Another solution to the escalating problem of space was cremation, and the Cremation Society was founded in 1874 with a plot at Woking Cemetery for a crematorium. Golders Green opened in 1902, arguably the foremost and best-known crematorium in the world.

In the following pages some of the London cemeteries and churches where musicians and composers were laid to rest or commemorated are discussed, but even when the location is known it is not always an easy task to find particular graves, especially those from the nineteenth century. Many graves are now overgrown and hard to trace. Some, however, are in cemeteries with helpful staff and adequate documentation to point out relevant sites. Sometimes graves are plotted on a map or are even listed on computer, as at the Roman Catholic Cemetery at Kensal Green. A useful website is www.findagrave.com. Researchers can search worldwide by name, location, date, claim to fame. Obituaries and descriptions of graves are provided.

Graves

56 (facing page)   Montage of gravestones and memorials: Sir John Barbirolli (St Mary's Roman Catholic Cemetery, Kensal Green: his ashes are buried in his parent's grave), Dennis Brain (Hampstead Cemetery: the words on the gravestone are by Paul Hindemith), Leopold Stokowski (St Marylebone Cemetery, East Finchley), Michael Balfe (Kensal Green Cemetery), Charles Barritt (while the organist Charles Herbert Barritt lies in obscurity in Hampstead Cemetery, he is remembered for his striking 1929 memorial, a white marble miniature organ, with music resting on the stand and a bench in front), Sir Joseph Barnby (West Norwood Cemetery), William Shield and Johann Peter Salomon (flagstone in the Westminster Abbey cloisters), Muzio Clementi (adjoining Shield and Salomon in Westminster Abbey) and Thomas Arne (Memorial tablet on the wall of St Paul's Church, Covent Garden).

Brompton Cemetery
Entrances from Lillie Road near West Brompton tube or Fulham Road, Fulham Broadway, SW10

Brompton lies peacefully behind brick walls, a sheltered green area isolated from the bustle and lorries of the Old Brompton Road where it meets Lillie Road. It is easily reached from West Brompton tube station (District line). Turn right out of the station and the main entrance is a few yards down on the right.

The cemetery was opened in 1840 and has a wide central avenue stretching to the Fulham Road, with chapel and office about three-quarters of the way down. Among musical people buried here are Richard Tauber, the celebrated tenor. His grave is on the left-hand side of the main avenue, less than a third of the way down. It consists of a slab with an inscription reading 'Richard Tauber, born in Linz 1891 died in London 1948'. Each year on his birthday, 16 May, the grave is adorned with flowers and sometimes messages from admirers. Further down are the graves of Alfred Mellon and Lionel Monckton. The graves of J. B. Cramer and John Ella and the ashes of Constant Lambert are also buried here.

Bunhill Fields
City Road, EC1
Managed by the Corporation of London
Tube and Train: Old Street – leave by exit 4, walk down City Road a short distance and Bunhill Fields is on the right opposite Wesley's Chapel

Originally a Dissenters' burial ground of four acres, not a churchyard, it has been disused since 1853. The stones are very weathered, and in many cases it is impossible to decipher the inscriptions, but it is a grassy sanctuary and the noise of City Road is muted here. The cemetery was improved in the 1860s and again a century later. Part of the area is now gardens, and locked gates protect the graves, but there is a caretaker who can open the gates and aid visitors. A useful illustrated booklet about the cemetery is available from the caretaker. Buried here are John Bunyan, William Blake and Daniel Defoe. It is also the last resting-place of the hymnodist Isaac Watts ('When I survey the wondrous cross', 'Jesus shall reign where'ere the sun', 'O God our help in ages past' and numerous others) and also of Susanna Wesley, mother of nineteen children, the most eminent of whom were John and Charles Wesley. John is buried in his own chapel across City Road.

Golders Green Crematorium
Hoop Lane, NW11
Tube: Golders Green is about ten minutes walk away; or buses along the Finchley Road stop very near Hoop Lane

Golders Green Crematorium was opened in 1902 by the London Cremation Company and is set in twelve acres. The grounds are framed by a long red brick cloister covered with commemorative tablets, chapels of various sizes, columbaria and a Chapel of Memory. Musicians who have been cremated here are almost too numerous to list and many figure on the wall tablets and are remembered by rose bushes or wooden benches. Among them are Sir John Barbirolli (though his ashes have been removed, as have some others), Sir Arthur Bliss, the music publisher William Boosey, Eric Coates, Harriet Cohen, Harold Darke, Eric Fogg, Benjamin Frankel, Sir Edward German, W. S. Gilbert, Berthold Goldschmidt, Sir Charles Groves, Dame Myra Hess, Gustav Holst, William Lloyd Webber, Benno Moiseiwitsch, Norman O'Neill, musicologist Christopher Palmer, Sir Landon Ronald, Sir Charles Villiers Stanford and Ralph Vaughan Williams. On the light music side are Larry Adler, Lionel Bart, Ray Ellington, Vivian Ellis, Max Jaffa, Albert Ketèlbey, Ivor Novello, Ronnie Scott and Victor Sylvester (father and son). Most recently remembered by the authors was the cremation of broadcaster and record reviewer Michael Oliver, on 8 September 2002.

Hampstead Cemetery
Fortune Green Road, West Hampstead, NW6
Tube: West Hamptead; or bus 385 passes the gate

Buried here are musicians Leonard Brain, the oboist, and his more famous brother, horn player Dennis Brain. Leonard's grave has the familiar lines from *Samson Agonistes*:

> Nothing is here for tears, nothing to wail
> Or knock the breast; no weakness, no contempt,
> Dispraise or blame; nothing but well and fair,
> And what may quiet us in a death so noble.

Dennis's has words attributed to Paul Hindemith, actually an English gloss on lines from the 'Declamation' section of Hindemith's horn concerto:

> My call transforms
> The hall to Autumn
>   tinted groves
> What is into what
> Has been.

Both graves may be found by turning right at the chapel then to the right far path. Leonard is fourth in, two along, then another musician – Norman McPhail Blair (Maurice Elwin) – and Dennis Brain. The grave of Sir George Macfarren, composer and one-time principal of the Royal Academy of Music, can be found by turning left at the chapel, then right and following a winding path for 100 yards. He is buried on the right, immediately behind Joseph Haydn Parry, composer of operettas such as *Cigarette* and *Miami*. Also here is the family grave of Fred Gaisberg of HMV recording studios. A sight not to be missed is the memorial to organist Charles Barritt, a white marble church organ sculpted with intricate detail, even to the music on the stand (illustrated at the beginning of this chapter, p. 114).

Highgate Cemetery

Swains Lane, N6

Tube: Archway – ten minutes walk up Highgate Hill to Waterlow Park on the left, follow plan in park and take the exit next to the cemetery gates; buses 143, 210 and 271 pass the park entrance

There is an entrance fee for the Eastern Cemetery, and the Western Cemetery is accessible only by guided tour, for which there is also a fee. Tours take place at noon, 2 p.m. and 4 p.m. on weekdays and on the hour from 11 a.m. until 4 p.m. at the weekend. The East Cemetery opens at 10 a.m. (11 a.m. at weekends) and closes at 5 p.m. (4 p.m in winter).

Highgate Cemetery was opened in 1839 and is now privately owned. It is on thirty-seven acres of land and is still in use for burials. Of musical interest are the memorial tablet to 'John Matt late of the Royal Opera House, died 23/5/1910 aged 66 in London' which is on the colonnade inside the entrance to the West Cemetery; Maria Dulcken (1811–1850), piano teacher to the young Queen Victoria (though her grave is not seen on the tour); and the tomb of Carl Rosa (1842–1889, founder of the opera company that bore his name). Others commemorated here are the contralto Charlotte Sainton-Dolby (1821–1895), distinguished organ builder Henry Willis and Anna Mahler, daughter of Gustav. The East Cemetery is the last resting place of Shura Cherkassky (1911–1995); the cabaret artiste 'Hutch' (Leslie A. Hutchinson, 1900–1969); William Henry Monk (1823–1889), composer of church music but noted chiefly for the hymn 'Abide With Me'; organist and composer Sir George Thalben-Ball (1896–1987), organist at the Temple Church; and H. Thornton, pianist and entertainer of the troops in the First World War – his monument is a piano. There are guides and maps to both East and West cemeteries and a list of the more eminent people buried here.

Jewish Cemetery, Golders Green

Hoop Lane, NW11

Directions as for Golders Green Crematorium above

The cemetery was founded in 1895 and is on the left up Hoop Lane, facing the crematorium. The office is on the left of the gateway and the caretaker can look up any particular grave. No photography is allowed. Notable musicians' graves include that of the cellist Jacqueline du Pré, which is at the edge of the pathway on the left. The grave is also on the left and is conspicuous for its gold lettering on blue-grey marble which reads 'Jacqueline du Pré beloved wife of Daniel Barenboim 26-1-1945 – 19-10-1987'. Further along on the right is the small weathered tombstone of Sir Frederic Hymen Cowen, composer and conductor of various orchestras including the Hallé. This is ornamented with leaves on each side and the inscription reads 'In loving memory of Frederic Hymen Cowen, KT, Mus Doc Cantab, Edin. Born Kingston Jamaica Jan 29 1852, died in London Oct 6 1935'.

Kensal Green (All Souls Cemetery)
Harrow Road, W10
Tube: Kensal Green, then turn left out of the station and immediately right into
Harrow Road. The entrance to the cemetery and crematorium and
St Mary's Roman Catholic Cemetery (see below) is on the left

This is one of the largest London cemeteries, spreading over fifty-six acres and managed by the General Cemetery Company. It was the first of the large joint-stock cemeteries round London. It was opened in 1833 with two chapels, one for Dissenters, the other Anglican. This is a difficult cemetery to find one's way around, mainly owing to its size. There is a plan of grave sites and a very helpful guide to 'persons of note commemorated at . . . Kensal Green' published by the friends of the cemetery, which gives grave numbers and sites as well as a brief description and drawing of the grave. Musicians and composers buried here, or whose ashes are here, include Michael Balfe, Sir Julius Benedict, William Chappell (publisher), George Grossmith, John Hullah (singer and teacher), Cipriani Potter and Sir Landon Ronald. Balfe, composer of numerous operas, including *The Bohemian Girl*, lies in a grave south-east of the Circle, crowned by a pink granite obelisk.

St Marylebone
East Finchley, N2, at the junction of East End Road and the North Circular Road
Tube: East Finchley is twenty minutes walk away; or buses 143 and 611 pass the gate

Founded in 1854, this is a very peaceful and well laid out cemetery and everything is easily accessible by car within the grounds. Music lovers will be most interested in the grave of the conductor Leopold Stokowski. This lies where the East Avenue crosses Rosemary Avenue. A hedge is at the corner and Stokowski's grave two markers down. It has a grey mottled granite stone with the motto 'Music is the Voice of the All' (see p. 114). Also buried here is Sir Henry Bishop.

St Mary's Roman Catholic Cemetery
Turn right once inside the main gateway to Kensal Green Cemetery , W10
(see above for directions)

Buried here are the ashes of the conductor Sir John Barbirolli, the composer Baron Frédéric d'Erlanger, and the Victorian pianist, organist and composer Thomas Wingham, director of music at the Brompton Oratory. Walk up the long drive past the chapel on the right and the Superintendent's Office beyond. The office will provide a map and details of site and marker numbers. Barbirolli's grave (no. 251NE) is on the left in the further extension straight ahead. It is located eleven rows in from the path and is in white marble with a scroll. His ashes (he was cremated at Golders Green) are buried with those of his parents. Baron d'Erlanger's family grave (no. 818) is located past the chapel and on the right path opposite a mausoleum inscribed FROSI. The inscription reads: 'Sacred to the memory of Marguerite Matilda Slidell born 1842 – died 1927 widow of Baron Frédéric Emile d'Erlanger. Robin Fer d'Erlanger born 24.1.86 died 13.10.1934. Baron Frédéric A d'Erlanger born 29.5.1868 died 23.4.1943'. The tomb is a raised concrete tablet surmounted by a cross. Thomas Wingham lies nine graves in, on the third row of the left-hand corner at the bottom of the loop.

Wesley Memorial Garden
Marylebone High Street, W1
Tube: Baker Street

Walk down Marylebone High Street and very soon, after leaving Marylebone Road, you will see on your right a school with a blue plaque on the wall saying that Leopold Stokowski was a pupil here. Adjacent is the Wesley Memorial Garden, a small garden created in 1951 on the site of the old Parish Church that was demolished in 1949 after being bomb-damaged. The eye is drawn at once to a stone obelisk marking the graves of Charles Wesley and his son Samuel, 'eminent musical composer and organist'. Charles was the brother of John Wesley, founder of Methodism, and Samuel the father of Samuel Sebastian Wesley. Sarah, wife of Charles, is also commemorated. (John Wesley is buried at the Chapel in City Road that bears his name.) Stephen Storace, composer, also lies here. A planning proposal for Marylebone School to build an underground arts and sports centre under its playground, which would entail disinterring many graves including that of Charles Wesley, had not matured at the time of writing.

West Norwood Cemetery (South Metropolitan Cemetery)
Norwood High Street, SE27
Opposite the stately pillared St Luke's Church
Train: West Norwood

One of the large joint stock companies around London, founded in 1837, it is enclosed in tall ornamental gates designed by Sir William Tite, designer of the Royal Exchange and Brookwood Cemetery. The grounds spread gently up a hill and cover thirty-nine acres. Many people with musical associations are buried here. Near the entrance and just before the path divides lies Sir Joseph Barnby, composer, conductor of the Royal Choral Society for twenty-four years and one time principal of the Guildhall School of Music. His grave is surmounted by a large cross and is found just behind a domed mausoleum to Alfred Longsdon. Also buried here are Sir August Manns, conductor of Crystal Palace concerts for nearly fifty years; Richard Limpus, organist of St Michael's Cornhill and founder of the Royal College of Organists; and James Turle, one-time organist and master of the choristers at Westminster Abbey.

Other than the statues of Handel by Roubiliac in Westminster Abbey and the Victoria and Albert Museum, there are comparatively few public statues to composers other than those displayed within buildings such as the Royal Festival Hall, Royal Albert Hall and the conservatoires.

There is a large statue of composer Michael Balfe in the stalls foyer at the Theatre Royal, Drury Lane. Nearby in the main foyer there is a seated bronze of Noël Coward by Angela Conner.

Sir W. S. Gilbert has a medallion set in the south wall of Victoria Embankment, near Hungerford Bridge. It shows his left profile with puppets from the operas at each side and the figures of Comedy and Tragedy and a simple inscription to 'W. S. Gilbert/Playwright and poet/His foe was folly/& his weapon wit.' It was designed by Sir George Frampton in 1915.

The memorial to Sir Arthur Sullivan is in Embankment Gardens near the Adelphi. It consists of a bust of Sullivan with a nymph weeping below, its erection funded by public subscription. The inscription is from *The Yeomen of the Guard*:

> Is Life a boon?
> If so, it must befall
> That Death, whene'er he call,
> Must call too soon.

Designed by Sir William Goscombe John, it was unveiled in 1903.

A modern stylised statue commemorating Henry Purcell is on the green just off Victoria Street near the Westminster City Council building, and on the corner of Broadway. It consists of a bust of Purcell's head under an exuberant periwig of flowers. The pedestal reads 'The Flowering of the English Baroque/A memorial to Henry Purcell/by the sculptor/Glynn Williams/unveiled by/HRH The Princess Margaret/Countess of Snowdon/on the tercentenary of the death of the Composer/22 November 1995'.

A John Wesley memorial in the form of a page from his journal is on the wall of Nettleton Court next to the Museum of London. It marks the spot of the founder of Methodism's conversion in 1738.

Royal Albert Hall
Kensington Gore, SW7
Tube: South Kensington or High Street Kensington

Extensive rebuilding and refurbishment took place at the Royal Albert Hall from 2000 to 2003. As a consequence many familiar paintings and statues have been moved and at the time of writing their future permanent location is not known. Entering by the main entrance facing Kensington Gardens, on the stairs is a portrait of Sir Henry Wood by Flora Lyon and one of Sir Malcolm Sargent by John Gilroy. There is a bust of Sargent by William Timlyn on the window ledge.

Statues and memorials

57 Statue of Noël Coward by Angela Conner in the front lobby of the Theatre Royal, Drury Lane

During the summer Promenade Concert seasons a bust of Sir Henry Wood is brought from the Royal Academy of Music and placed in the hall in front of the organ. At other times of the year it can be seen in the Duke's Hall at the Academy. In the foyer is the well-known portrait of Delius by Ernest Procter, and a bust of Joseph Barnby is at the time of writing in the office.

Albert Memorial
Kensington Gardens, SW7
Tube: High Street Kensington or South Kensington

On the frieze of the newly renovated Memorial are figures of artists sculpted by Henry Hugh Armstead. These include musicians. On the south side, facing the Albert Hall, are Gibbons, Lawes, Purcell and Tallis. On the east side are Arne, Bishop and Boyce. The musicians depicted are not exclusively British, and others shown on the memorial are Auber, J. S. Bach, Beethoven, Carissimi, Gluck, Grétry, Handel, Haydn, Josquin des Prez, Lulli [*sic*], Méhul, Mendelssohn, Mozart, Palestrina, Rameau, Rossini and Weber.

58   Some of the composers represented by Henry Hugh Armstead on the Albert Memorial: J. S. Bach, Gluck, Handel, Mozart, Mendelssohn, Haydn (sitting), Weber, Beethoven, Tallis, Gibbons, Lawes and Purcell.

Royal Festival Hall
South Bank Centre, Belvedere Road, SE1
Tube: Waterloo or Embankment

During the writing of this book the busts of musicians, including some of the most familiar images of musicians from the second half of the twentieth century, all once on display in the public areas of the Royal Festival Hall have been removed and are presently stored in the basement, where they are accessible only by appointment. The closure of the hall for refurbishment over the period 2005–7 means they will not be seen again until the reconstruction programme has been completed.

Statues once familiar in the Royal Festival Hall included sculpted busts of musicians and composers. In the main entrance area Sir Adrian Boult (William Redgrave) and Sir Robert Mayer (Epstein) were on the stairs between levels 4 and 5. Sir Thomas Beecham (D. Wynne) and Ralph Vaughan Williams (D. McFall) were on level 5. Beethoven (J. Schaller) was on level 6. Other statues included Epstein's bust of Otto Klemperer and C. Wheeler's of Yehudi Menuhin.

St Paul's Cathedral
St Paul's Churchyard, EC4
Tube: St Paul's or walk up Ludgate Hill from Blackfriars

In the Crypt can be seen the graves or memorials of many distinguished organists and musicians associated with St Paul's. Sir John Goss, organist, has a splendid marble memorial on the wall which boasts a bas-relief of the choir and underneath several staves of music. Round the corner is a memorial to Maria Hackett, who fought for improvements in the treatment, feeding and education of the boy choristers in the early 1800s. Nearby is a stone tablet to Ivor Novello with a profile of his head. There is a splendid copper gravestone for Sir Arthur Sullivan and next to him a mosaic tablet in honour of Sir Hubert Parry. The tomb of William Boyce is near Parry and on the same stone is commemorated organist Dr Maurice Greene, who was reinterred here in 1888.

Three tablets side by side in the Crypt are in honour of organists Sir George Martin, Sir John Dykes Bower and Jonathan Battishill. Stanley Marchant, organist and one-time principal of the Royal College of Music, is also remembered, as are Charles Macpherson and Sir John Stainer. The grave of Thomas Attwood lies by the Wellington monument, and Jeremiah Clarke is also buried here.

Victoria and Albert Museum
Corner of Exhibition and Brompton Roads, SW7
Tube: South Kensington

One of the Roubiliac statues of Handel is displayed here. It stood first in Vauxhall Gardens, was later acquired by Novello's and by the Victoria and Albert Museum in 1964 when Novello left their Wardour Street showrooms. A second statue of Handel by Roubiliac is in Westminster Abbey, and a bust by him was seen at the Queen's Gallery, Buckingham Palace, in 2004, and is usually located at Windsor (see p. 186).

Westminster Abbey
Broad Sanctuary, Parliament Square, SW1
Tube: Westminster or St James's Park

Many famous musicians are buried or commemorated in the Abbey, some with memorials as well as gravestones. Those buried here include Samuel Arnold, John Banister, Thomas Baltzar, Thomas Blagrove, John Blow, Muzio Clementi, Benjamin Cooke, Robert Cooke, William Croft, Thomas Sanders Dupuis, Bernard Gates, Christopher Gibbons, Thomas Greatorex, Douglas Guest, George Frideric Handel, William Heather, Edmund Hooper, Herbert Howells, Pelham Humfrey, Henry Lawes, Sir William McKie, John Parsons, Osborne Peasgood, Henry Purcell, John Robinson, Johann Peter Salomon, William Shield, Sir Charles Villiers Stanford,

William Sterndale Bennett, Ralph Vaughan Williams, George Williams and John Wilson.

Other musicians commemorated here include Michael Balfe, Sir Adrian Boult, Sir Frederick Bridge, Benjamin Britten, Charles Burney, Sir Edward Elgar, Orlando Gibbons, Jenny Lind, Sir Sydney Nicholson, James Turle and Sir William Walton.

Finding the various locations described below can be at first sight confusing but there are usually helpful vergers on hand to direct you. Beginning at the nave, with the entrance behind you, walk to the left and forward to a gate to the Musicians' or North Aisle, passing on the way the stone commemorating Sir William Herschel, composer and astronomer. First within the gate is the stone in memory of Sir Edward Elgar (who is buried at Little Malvern). This was unveiled on 1 June 1972. Move on to tablets covering the ashes of Ralph Vaughan Williams and Herbert Howells. Next comes the gravestone to Sir Charles Villiers Stanford, hailed as 'A Great Musician' and the gravestone of Sir William Sterndale Bennett. Note the stone commemorating Benjamin Britten (buried at Aldeburgh). Above is a stained glass window and a stone celebrating James Turle, organist of the Abbey.

William Croft, organist of the Chapel Royal and the Abbey, has two memorials, a gravestone and a white marble monument with a relief of an organ on the base. Also with two memorials is Henry Purcell – the gravestone is shared with his wife Frances – note the words (in Latin) '. . . Immortals, welcome an illustrious guest, Your gain, our loss . . .' Nearby is a white marble wall-tablet to Purcell, with a flaming urn at the top, a grotesque mask and heraldic shield below. The inscription reads: 'Here lies Henry Purcell Esq/Who left this life/And is gone to that blessed place/Where only his harmony/Can be exceeded'. Adjoining Purcell's grave is that of Dr Samuel Arnold, organist and composer.

On the wall to the right is an oval medallion with a profile bust to Michael Balfe – to the left memorials to William Croft (as mentioned above), to Charles Burney (buried at Royal Hospital, Chelsea) and to John Blow. On the floor below is a black tablet in memory of Adrian Cedric Boult, conductor, next to a tablet for Sir William Walton. On the right is a memorial to Orlando Gibbons which takes the form of a black marble bust.

The South Transept is popularly known as 'Poet's Corner' and contains numerous memorials to poets and authors, including on the floor a large stone to the poets of the First World War, and memorials to Auden, Byron, Lewis Carroll, George Eliot, T. S. Eliot, Henry James, D. H. Lawrence, Edward Lear and Lord Tennyson, among others. However, it is also the home of a marble monument to Jenny Lind-Goldschmidt, with a portrait medallion and the inscription: 'I know that my Redeemer liveth'. Nearby is what is probably the memorial everyone asks to see, to arguably the best-known composer who lies in the Abbey – Handel. It takes the form of a standing white marble life-size figure leaning on its left elbow, by Roubiliac, dating from 1759. On

Some memorial services held at Westminster Abbey since 1946	
1946	Hugh Percy Allen (Director of the Royal College of Music)
1988	Sir Frederick Ashton
1961	Sir Thomas Beecham (Commemoration in Music)
1975	Sir Arthur Bliss
1977	Benjamin Britten (Memorial stone here)
1991	Dame Margot Fonteyn
1988	Leon Goossens
1986	Dame Anna Neagle
1986	Sir Peter Pears
1967	Sir Malcolm Sargent
1991	Dame Eva Turner
1983	Sir William Walton (Memorial stone here)

the left is an organ and above right an angel playing a harp. On the right is a group of musical instruments and the score of *Messiah* open at: 'I know that my Redeemer liveth'. Handel is buried beneath a gravestone in front of this statue; the brass lettering reads: 'George Frederic Handel. Born 23 February 1684 died 14 April 1759' and it bears a coat of arms at the top.

The South aisle contains a memorial stone to Noël Coward. The stone is of Belgian black marble with letters laid in a white marble mastic and was unveiled on 28 March 1984 by the Queen Mother. The inscription reads: 'Noël Coward/Playwright. Actor/composer/16 December 1899/26 March 1973/Buried in Jamaica/ "A Talent to Amuse"'. Nearby is a memorial to broadcaster Richard Dimbleby, and further down the aisle one commemorating the Methodist brothers John and Charles Wesley.

Walking out into the cloisters, the South Cloister contains the gravestone of William Shield and Johann Peter Salomon adjoining Clementi. Dean Ireland apparently refused to let a tablet be erected for Shield in 1829. Shield was buried there at the request of George IV and the choirs of the Chapel Royal and St Paul's cathedral attended. Salomon's inscription was only added in 1938. Laid down in 1876, the inscription reads: 'Muzio Clementi/called/the father of the pianoforte/his fame as a musician/and composer/acknowledged throughout Europe/provided him the honour/of a public interment/in this cloister/Born at Rome 1752/died at Evesham 1832.' (See p. 114.)

The Little Cloister contains the gravestone of John Wilson, in the east walk between the door to 3 Little Cloister and the door to St Catherine's Chapel.

The West Cloister commemorates many organists of the Abbey, including Sir Frederick Bridge, Osborne Harold Peasgood, Sir Sydney Nicholson, founder and director of the Royal School of Church Music, Sir William McKie, Thomas Greatorex and Douglas Guest.

Some London cemeteries where musicians and composers are buried or were cremated

Brompton
J. B. Cramer
John Ella
Constant Lambert (ashes)
Albert Mellon
Lionel Monckton
Richard Tauber

Bunhill Fields
Joseph Hart
Isaac Watts
Susanna Wesley

Golders Green Crematorium
Larry Adler
Lionel Bart
Sir Arthur Bliss
William Boosey
Eric Coates
Harriet Cohen
Harold Darke
Ray Ellington
Vivian Ellis
Kathleen Ferrier
Eric Fogg
Benjamin Frankel
Sir Edward German
W. S. Gilbert
Berthold Goldschmidt
Sir Charles Groves
Dame Myra Hess
Gustav Holst
Max Jaffa
Albert Ketèlbey
William Lloyd Webber
Benno Moiseiwitsch
Ivor Novello
Michael Oliver
Norman O'Neill
Christopher Palmer
Sir Landon Ronald
Ronnie Scott
Sir Charles Villiers Stanford
Victor Sylvester (father and son)
Ralph Vaughan Williams

Hampstead
Charles Barritt

Norman McPhail Blair
Dennis Brain
Leonard Brain
Fred Gaisberg
Sir George Macfarren
Joseph Haydn Parry

Highgate East
Shura Cherkassky
'Hutch'(Leslie A. Hutchinson)
William Henry Monk
Sir George Thalben-Ball
Harry Thornton

Highgate West
Maria Louise Dulcken
Carl Rosa
Charlotte Sainton-Dolby
Henry Willis

Jewish Cemetery Golders Green
Sir Frederic Cowen
Jacqueline du Pré

Kensal Green
Michael Balfe
Sir Julius Benedict
William Chappell
George Grossmith
John Hullah
Cipriani Potter
Sir Landon Ronald

St Mary Roman Catholic Cemetery Kensal Green
Sir John Barbirolli (ashes)
Baron Frédéric d'Erlanger
Thomas Wingham

St Marylebone
Sir Henry Bishop
Leopold Stokowski

West Norwood
Sir Joseph Barnby
Richard Limpus
Sir August Manns
James Turle

5 • BBC, Orchestras and Music Publishers

The British Broadcasting Corporation was founded as the British Broadcasting Company in 1922 and made a significant contribution to music from the first. It must be regarded as the single most important British musical institution of the twentieth century. It first operated from 2 Savoy Hill, a building that still stands (plaque; tube: Temple) and moved to the newly built Broadcasting House (tube: Oxford Circus), in Upper Regent Street in 1932. There it was located adjacent to Queen's Hall, opposite the Langham Hotel, and was a five-minute walk from most music publishers, instrument suppliers and smaller halls. It became the focus for London music-making until the war and the destruction of Queen's Hall. During 2003 a substantial programme of refurbishment and development was underway, and Broadcasting House was still swathed in colourful plastic sheeting when this book was completed in 2004.

Broadcasting House was designed with a concert hall, where many important performances took place in the 1930s but which proved too small and later became the Radio Theatre. The BBC soon developed the Maida Vale studios (tube: Warwick Avenue – see p. 165) which became the home of the BBC Symphony Orchestra and where invited audiences may still hear free concerts both during selected recording sessions and live transmissions; probably the best musical bargain in London. Later the BBC acquired other buildings, including the Hippodrome at Golders Green, the Æolian Hall (no longer BBC) and a range of premises for television leading to the construction of the Television Centre at White City.

Though initially seen as a threat by many in the musical profession, the BBC soon established itself as the largest market for music and musicians in the country. In 1927 the BBC took over the Proms, at Queen's Hall until the bombing, and from 1941 at the Royal Albert Hall. In 1941 and 1942 the Proms were run independently by Keith Douglas. Today the Proms at the Royal Albert Hall have been developed into an enormous summer festival in which many of the world's most celebrated orchestras and performers are showcased.

The BBC has many orchestras, though fewer now than in their heyday. Today there are only two BBC orchestras operating from London, the flagship BBC Symphony Orchestra and the smaller BBC Concert Orchestra. Both appear frequently at public concerts and at BBC recording sessions and invitation concerts. The Concert

59 (facing page)   The BBC Concert Orchestra conducted by Gavin Sutherland, recording at the Maida Vale Studio 1, 2003.

60   Broadcasting House and the spire of All Souls, Langham Place from the coffee shop at the St George's Hotel.

BBC Directors of Music/Controller Radio 3	
1924–1930	Percy Pitt
1930–1942	Adrian Boult*
1942–1944	Arthur Bliss*
1944–1946	Victor Hely-Hutchinson
1946–1948	Kenneth Wright (acting)
1948–1950	Steuart Wilson*
1950–1952	Herbert Murrill
1952–1959	Richard Howgill
1959–1972	William Glock*
1972–1985	Robert Ponsonby
1985–1992	John Drummond
1992–1998	Nicholas Kenyon
1998–	Roger Wright

* Were later knighted

Orchestra underpins the popular *Friday Night is Music Night* series on Radio 2, where audience attendance is encouraged and free.

BBC choirs are among the best in London and include the BBC Singers, a choir of young professionals that has helped launch the careers of many now leading artists, and the BBC Symphony Chorus (formerly Choral Society), a large top-line amateur choir, entry to which is by auditions that are held regularly. Membership gives singers music-making with big names at top halls.

The BBC libraries, in particular its once internationally famous music library, are now much diminished, and not as available to the musical public as they once were, while the BBC Sound Archives are accessible to outsiders only through the National Sound Archive at the British Library. The BBC Written Archives are available to all researchers by appointment, but are located outside London, at Caversham near Reading. Dates of current BBC performances and free concerts can be accessed through the Radio 3 website or the individual websites of the constituent performing groups.

In 2003 the BBC started work on a new flagship building in White City. To be called The Music Box, it is scheduled to open in 2007, and intended to house both the BBC's London orchestras in one custom-built space. In January 2004 the winning architect was announced as Foreign Office Architects. The facilities will supersede Maida Vale and the Golders Green Hippodrome and will include two studios for live performances and recordings with an audience capacity of up to six hundred. New works have been commissioned to mark the occasion.

*   *   *

Orchestras   The growth of permanent orchestras in London during the twentieth century was one of the most remarkable musical developments in a city long over-provided with musical activity, but without a history of permanent orchestras. This has meant that London has an unprecedented number of fine orchestras that during the peak days of orchestral recording (say from 1970 to 1990) made it the recording capital of the world and underpinned the availability of an enormous number of top-line freelance artists, making it still the place to set up recording projects. Various reports on orchestral provision in London have underlined the excess that is not reflected in any other city in the world. In addition to the major names discussed below there is a large number of other ensembles, chamber orchestras, period instrument groups and ad hoc orchestras, as well as the orchestras of the Royal Opera and English National Opera that are not discussed here, and other orchestras that have come and gone over the years.

All the following orchestras appear regularly in concerts in London, the London Symphony Orchestra at the Barbican, the others at the Royal Festival Hall and elsewhere. Visitors wanting to hear them should get the orchestras' annual concerts schedule or check the appropriate web site.

BBC Concert Orchestra
Room G152, BBC White City, 201 Wood Lane, W12

The orchestra originated with the earlier Opera Orchestra conducted by Stanford Robinson, and dates from 1952 when it was established to bridge the gap between variety and the symphonic repertoire, with a particular remit to perform lighter works when 'light music' was a notable strand of BBC music programming. The first conductors were successively Gilbert Vinter and Charles Mackerras, but it was probably put on the map by Vilém Tauský in the 1960s. The present conductor is Barry Wordsworth, though a wide range of visiting conductors work with the orchestra, especially on commercial recordings. The Concert Orchestra has developed a large following for its light music programmes, but also appears whenever recordings are required of otherwise unavailable music for BBC programmes, and as such gets through a large and varied repertoire. Its biggest following is for the weekly *Friday Night is Music Night*.

BBC Symphony Orchestra
BBC Maida Vale Studios, Delaware Road, W9

The BBC Symphony Orchestra was founded in 1930, with the intention of making it one of the world's premier orchestras, an ambition in which, at least in its first decade, it succeeded. Sir Adrian Boult was closely associated with the setting up of the orchestra and became conductor from its inception in 1930/31 to his formal retirement in 1950. Also in the early 1930s he became Director of Music at the BBC, a post he held until 1942. The orchestra has always performed and broadcast public concerts, often of unusual and contemporary repertory. It hosted a festival of new British music in 1934 and concert performances of countless British premieres. Celebrated in the 1930s for its appearances with Toscanini, many of whose performances have survived onto CD, guest conductors included all the leading names of the day such as Koussevitzky, Walter and Weingartner, as well as composers Webern, Milhaud, Schoenberg and Stravinsky. The orchestra attracted and retained fine players because it offered full-time year-round contracts, though it allowed no deputising. It continued playing through the Second World War, first from Bristol and then for most of the duration from Bedford, and was a major force at the Proms, by then at the Royal Albert Hall. After the war many players left to work freelance or join new orchestras.

After Boult's retirement in 1950, Sir Malcolm Sargent became Chief Conductor. More of a showman but with narrower stylistic sympathies, he was possibly the right man for the time. He was succeeded by Rudolf Schwartz (1957–62) whose tenure was not always recognised as successful at the time. His successor was Antal Dorati (1962–3). Curiously, while Dorati secured fine performances, players of the time remember the band as hating him, one calling him 'Mr Karate' to his face. The succession of Colin Davis (1967–71), Pierre Boulez (1971–5), Rudolf Kempe (1975–6) and Gennadi Rozhdestvensky (1978–81) gave the BBC Orchestra a high profile with some superb performances of repertoire not played by the other London orchestras. The long service of Sir John Pritchard (1982–1991) and Sir Andrew Davis (1989–2000) created a two-decade artistic plateau, Davis in particularly being noted for his championship and eloquent readings of the early twentieth-century repertoire of British choral and orchestral music. The orchestra was subsequently conducted by Leonard Slatkin, who, particularly at the outset, explored more American repertoire than his predecessors and also presided over the last night of the Proms in 2001, soon after the horror of the terrorist outrages in New York and Washington on September 11th, finding a personal response to the occasion which was entirely appropriate. Slatkin's stewardship of the orchestra ended when he conducted the Last Night of the Proms on 11 September 2004. At the time of writing his successor has not been announced.

The BBC Symphony Orchestra, free as commentators have remarked 'from the tyranny of the box office', has introduced more first performances and British first performances in their London concerts, in broadcasts and at the Proms, than the other London orchestras, including works commissioned by the BBC. Often these were conducted by their composers. Many of these performances have re-surfaced on CD, as surviving archive recordings and BBC transcription discs have been given wider circulation. World premieres by the BBC Symphony Orchestra have included Delius's: *A Song of Summer* (1932) and *Idyll* (1933); Vaughan Williams's Piano Concerto (1933), Fourth Symphony (1935) and Sixth Symphony (1948); Frank Bridge's *Oration* (1936); Kodály's *Te Deum* (1936); Hindemith's *Symphonic Dances* (1937); Britten's Piano Concerto (1938); Tippett's *Vision of St Augustine* (1966); Boulez's *Doubles* (1965) and *Rituel* (1975); and an enormous number of British works of the day. UK premieres of the latest works by leading composers have ranged from Berg and Webern to Berio and Elliott Carter.

The BBC's commitment to new music has made the BBC Symphony Orchestra one of the most expert in the world in dealing with demanding new scores, though in the 1960s and '70s many of the older players were unsympathetic to William

Glock's vision of being at the musical cutting edge. It is a matter of historical comment that in the 1970s the orchestra boasted certain orchestral players who occasionally misbehaved in modern music. There were a number of unpublicised scandals, still remembered in the profession, when composers as varied as Lutosławski, Penderecki and Peter Maxwell Davies were given a rough time by certain players unsympathetic to modern music. Those players met their match in Pierre Boulez though, when that conductor's discriminating ear quickly enabled him to establish the game, and meeting the perpetrators, eye to eye, remarked 'I think we understand each other now', and superb professionals that they were they were able to deliver what he required.

The orchestra later adopted the Barbican for its London public concerts and instituted special themed weekends from the 1990s, that for John Cage and American music taking place in January 2004, when one BBC announcer referred to the Barbican as the orchestra's 'spiritual home'.

City of London Sinfonia
11 Drum Street, E1

This chamber orchestra was founded in 1971 by conductor Richard Hickox and took its present name in 1979. It does not appear in London as frequently as the major London orchestras, but is well known as a recording orchestra under Hickox, with over a hundred CDs to its name. Notable recordings have been those of Britten operas *A Midsummer Night's Dream*, *Peter Grimes* and *Albert Herring*, *Grimes* winning a Grammy Award. In London the orchestra appears regularly at the Barbican, particularly in themed series, of which that devoted to Britten and Shostakovich in the 2000/1 season was outstanding. There is an active education and community programme and it has been associated with the Hospital for Sick Children, Great Ormond Street. The orchestra has had a long association with the composers John Rutter and Sir John Tavener, giving the world premiere of Tavener's *The Apocalypse* at the Proms in 1994 and *Fall and Resurrection* at St Paul's in 2000.

London Philharmonic Orchestra
4th Floor, 89 Albert Embankment, SE1

Founded in 1932 by Sir Thomas Beecham, the orchestra and its backers, who included among their number Robert Mayer and Samuel Courtauld, secured a leading position in London's musical life. In addition to appearing at concerts bearing the names of Mayer and Courtauld it performed for the Royal Philharmonic Society, whose annual series of concerts occupied an important place in the calendar. The orchestra's first concert on 7 October 1932, which was given by the Society, has been regarded as a significant milestone in London concert life for the standard of performance achieved.

The orchestra also gave a regular series of Sunday afternoon concerts. It appeared at Covent Garden for the summer seasons of International Opera and accompanied the dancers of the Ballets Russes de Monte Carlo. It was engaged by the Royal Choral Society, whose concerts, with those of the Robert Mayer Children's Concerts and the Courtauld-Sargent Concerts saw the young Malcolm Sargent play a prominent part in their activities, and it undertook annual provincial tours, appearing at festivals in places such as Leeds, Norwich and Sheffield. While remaining very much Beecham's orchestra, many distinguished conductors appeared with it, among them Sir Adrian Boult, Wilhelm Furtwangler, Felix Weingartner, Bruno Walter and Sir Henry Wood. It became the first choice for the leading conductors and soloists of the day who were recording at Abbey Road, including Elgar, Weingartner, Koussevitzky, Cortot, Heifetz, Kreisler and Schnabel.

When Beecham went to the USA in 1940, the orchestra became a self-governing organisation. Facing financial disaster it spent the war touring the length and breadth of the country. The film *Battle for Music* (1944) in which members of the orchestra appear, if slightly stiltedly, documents its fight for survival after the outbreak of war in 1939, and how it triumphantly overcame the problems. From 1945 onwards it performed under many distinguished visitors, including Ernest Ansermet, Erich Kleiber, Charles Munch, Victor de Sabata and Bruno Walter, before appointing Eduard van Beinum as Principal Conductor from the beginning of 1949. If also made two recordings with Ernest Bloch conducting his own music. Sir Adrian Boult took over in the autumn of the following year, after retiring from the BBC. (When Beecham returned after the war he founded yet another orchestra, the Royal Philharmonic, in 1946.)

The history of the orchestra during the second half of the twentieth century has mirrored the history of other orchestras in that period, consisting of alternate periods of feast and famine, often reflecting the introduction, take-up and over-exploitation of successive recorded formats. The partnership with Sir Adrian Boult led to the orchestra being specially associated with that conductor's remarkable Indian summer, during which he recorded, in London, largely at Kingsway Hall or Abbey Road, much of the major British repertoire by Elgar, Vaughan Williams and their contemporaries. Although many of these recordings were made for EMI, the label that pioneered the partnership of Boult and the orchestra was the small British label Lyrita, whose founder Richard Itter specialised in revivals of British music, and which provided much work for the orchestra at a difficult time. There was a particularly warm atmosphere among all involved on many of those occasions.

Despite financial difficulties during the 1950s it is worth noting the pioneering Festival Hall series of concerts, 'Music of A Century' – the century in question being the twentieth – which ran from 1956–7 to 1960–61. At a time of considerable ignorance and hostility to such repertoire, these concerts were in advance of their time, anticipating similar series by other London orchestras by over a decade. For example, Constantin Silvestri gave a concert pairing works by Rawsthorne and Britten with Stravinsky's Symphony in Three Movements and Bartók's Concerto for

Orchestra, neither then the iconic scores they are now. The last concert of the series was even more uncompromising. William Steinberg from Pittsburgh, Principal Conductor from the autumn 1958 to spring 1960, directed performances of Hindemith's then new *Pittsburgh* Symphony, Stravinsky's *Threni*, and, with the Johnny Dankworth Orchestra, Liebermann's *Concerto for Jazz Band and Symphony Orchestra* and the world premiere of the Dankworth/Seiber *Improvisations for Jazz Band and Symphony Orchestra*, thought a 'wow' at the time by one's school friends.

In the summer of 1964 the orchestra performed for the first time at Glyndebourne, a partnership that continues to this day, the orchestra earning as much praise for its skill in the opera house as for its performances on the concert platform.

The appointment of Bernard Haitink as Principal Conductor, from the autumn of 1967, ushered in a particularly fruitful period for the orchestra, during which, in addition to many fine London concerts, it earned plaudits for its work overseas. In 1956 it had been the first western orchestra to visit Russia; now it broke fresh ground by performing in China and making other tours, including a remarkably successful visit to the USA as part of that nation's bi-centennial celebrations.

Responding to the establishment of the London Symphony Orchestra as the resident orchestra at the Barbican, the London Philharmonic Orchestra became, from the autumn of 1992, resident orchestra at the Royal Festival Hall, a residency that is today shared with the Philharmonia.

From the outset the orchestra has worked with an enormous range of conductors. In its more recent history Bernard Haitink, Sir Georg Solti and Klaus Tennstedt have been associated with some of its greatest triumphs, with all three leaving a substantial discography. Kurt Masur was appointed Principal Conductor in 2000.

As the twenty-first century takes shape the range of work undertaken by the orchestra is wider than ever. Its work on the concert platform, which is far from being confined to the standard orchestral repertoire, today includes new commissions, an annual series spotlighting a contemporary composer, and the accompaniment, conducted by Carl Davis, to the enormously successful 'Silver Screen Classics' as well as family concerts and performances for schools. In the opera house the relationship with Glyndebourne, which continues to prosper, has been added to by a partnership with Opera Rara, embracing studio recording and concert performance. Most recently the orchestra has undertaken the sound track for *The Lord of the Rings*, from which the composer, Howard Shore, has constructed an independent concert piece that has played to enthusiastic audiences in both the Festival Hall and the Albert Hall.

London Sinfonietta
Dominion House, 101 Southwark Street, SE1
Tube: London Bridge

The London Sinfonietta, founded in 1968 by David Atherton and Nicholas Snowman, appears at the Queen Elizabeth Hall. It is one of the world's leading

61   The London Sinfonietta conducted by David Robertson at the Proms, Royal Albert Hall, 13 August 2004. After Bright Sheng's *The Songs and Dances of Tears* featuring Chinese instruments the soloists acknowledge the applause: Wu Man (pipa), Joel Fan (piano), Yo-Yo Ma (cello) and Wu Tong (shen).

modern music ensembles, and under its music director Oliver Knussen, its concerts may require a very small or a very large ensemble, though generally tending to be of chamber music size. (At the 2004 Proms they presented Messiaen's enormous *Turangalîla*.) With a remarkable record of commissions and first performances and first British performances, it has also featured a 'New to London' series introducing new music by leading composers. The Sinfonietta has also been associated with major festivals of the music of the leading composers of the twentieth century, while its annual 'State of the Nation' series features emerging British composers.

London Symphony Orchestra
Barbican Centre, EC2; and St Luke's, 161 Old Street, EC1
Tube: Barbican or Moorgate; and Old Street

There were orchestras in London before today's London Symphony Orchestra that used that title, the billing was used for a pick-up orchestra, for example, by George Henschel's concerts at St James's Hall in the mid-1890s.

The London Symphony Orchestra we know today was founded in 1904 as a consequence of Henry Wood's move that year to end the deputy system in the Queen's Hall Orchestra. The players who walked out founded their own self-governing orchestra, which gave its first concert on 9 June 1904. One of the horn section became Managing Director and remained until after the First World War. They began with a concert conducted by Hans Richter, and soon by Nikisch, Steinbach, Colonne, Henschel, Arbós, Safonov, Młynarski, Koussevitsky, Mengelberg, in fact all the leading conductors of the day. Richter was principal conductor until 1911. The orchestra's celebrated association with Elgar also dates from its first ten years, and it gave the first London performance of Elgar's First Symphony in 1908. Elgar became Principal Conductor for the 1911–12 season, and was followed by Nikisch, who took the orchestra to the USA on tour. A new generation of British conductors began to emerge, including Beecham, Goossens and Boult. In the 1920s visiting conductors included Albert Coates, Damrosch, Koussevitzky and Mengelberg, the latter becoming Principal Conductor in 1930–31, followed by Sir Hamilton Harty.

Up to the late 1940s, until the Philharmonia Orchestra came on the scene, the London Symphony Orchestra was also the best-known British film music orchestra, at first under the name the 'London Film Symphony Orchestra', in which guise they appeared on the radio in 1938 conducted by Muir Mathieson in six concerts of film music, including Bliss's *Things to Come*. During the war their soundtracks were recorded at Denham.

In 1946 The Crown Film Unit commissioned Benjamin Britten to write a score for their film *Instruments of the orchestra* in which the orchestra was conducted by Sir Malcolm Sargent. The music, *Variations and Fugue on a Theme of Purcell*, now known as *Young Person's Guide to the Orchestra*, is now a popular repertoire work. As both the film and the soundtrack have been reissued for a modern audience by

Beulah it is fairly easy to assess the orchestra immediately after the war, where their presentation is a useful archetypal portrait of the largely male orchestras of the day. They recorded it at Wembley Town Hall and the film was shot as the music was played back at the Pinewood Studios.

The leader from 1912 to 1936, W. H. Reed – Elgar's 'Billy' Reed – became chairman in 1935 and reorganised the orchestra. In 1945 it became a 'non-profit-distributing company' under the presidency of William Walton.

The early 1950s were notable for the appointment of Josef Krips as conductor and for their recordings for Decca with Anthony Collins of the Sibelius symphonies, in their day pre-eminent readings. The Sibelius marks for today's CD collectors the end of the old orchestra, for in 1955 all the leading names resigned in protest to force the hand of their board, who had fired the first clarinet when, with an extraordinary sense of déjà vu, he had sent a deputy to play at a concert. However, the management took the opportunity to replace all of them with a new team of very talented young players, thus establishing the basis of the orchestra's future stature.

In the late 1960s and early '70s the orchestra acquired a reputation for arrogance, and one can remember at certain recording sessions the brass, in particular, gave one conductor such a hard time that the leader had to call them to order. It difficult to understand how, on such occasions, internationally famous wind players could be recording with a cigarette on the go during the session, rested on the corner of the music stand between takes. Yet such was the standing of the orchestra that in 1973 they were the first British orchestra to be invited to Salzburg for the festival.

The succession of conductors from the 1960s was remarkable, starting with the octogenarian Pierre Monteux (1961–4), István Kertész (1965–8) and then by the eleven year laureateship of André Previn (1968–79), who succeeded not only in a milestone series of recordings, including the complete symphonies of Vaughan Williams, but also in presenting the orchestra to the widest audience on BBC television. Subsequently Claudio Abbado (1979–88), Michael Tilson Thomas (1988–95) and Sir Colin Davis (since 1995), successively strikingly different musical personalities, have maintained the orchestra's reputation at a very high level.

Two legendary conductors need a separate mention. First Leonard Bernstein, whose personal involvement in the 1986 Bernstein Festival is a notable pinnacle of the orchestra's history. Bernstein's recordings with the orchestra have not only included his own opera *Candide*, but also celebrated performances of Mahler's second and eighth symphonies, Stravinsky's *Symphony of Psalms* and Verdi's *Requiem* from a packed Royal Albert Hall in 1970. Second Leopold Stokowski, who conducted the orchestra in 1912, but was not invited back until 1960. For his sixtieth anniversary concert in 1972 with the orchestra he repeated his programme from 1912 at first at the Royal Festival Hall, but then again by public demand at the much larger Royal Albert Hall.

Since the 1980s the orchestra has been in residence at the Barbican, where it appears regularly, and in 2003 it opened its new rehearsal rooms and performing arts centre at St Luke's, Old Street, which is available to the public. Most of the London orchestras do not have facilities where the public can routinely be welcomed, but the London Symphony Orchestra have inaugurated St Luke's, a restored Hawksmoor church, not only as a rehearsal hall, but as the home of its community and music education programme. It offers free lunchtime concerts, community events and Balinese gamelan sessions. This location is also available for hire for non-orchestra events and recordings.

The orchestra's Centenary Concert took place at the Barbican on 9 June 2004 and consisted of a wide conspectus of leading soloists in excerpts and short pieces conducted by more than half a dozen leading conductors associated with it. The launching of the orchestra's own CD label, LSO Live, dominated by Colin Davis's unsurpassed Berlioz series, has reached an international audience and preserves an archive of live performances from which its achievement at the beginning of a new century can be assessed by generations to come. A centennial history in recordings is on Andante AN4100.

Philharmonia Orchestra
1st Floor, 125 High Holborn, WC1V

The Philharmonia is different from the other London orchestras in that it was established first as a recording orchestra. Founded by Walter Legge of EMI records in 1945, it was intended from the outset to be of outstanding quality. It looked largely to the wartime RAF orchestra from which were selected some of the leading players of the day as they were demobbed. After a few recordings made in the summer of 1945 the orchestra gave a public concert at the Kingsway Hall, in which Sir Thomas Beecham conducted an all-Mozart programme and received very favourable reviews.

The orchestra was quickly established as the leading London orchestra and appeared at the Edinburgh Festival, making recordings and notably playing film music (Bax: *Oliver Twist* and Walton: *Hamlet*). When Richard Strauss came to London in 1947 the only concert that he conducted in its entirety was with the Philharmonia at the Albert Hall. The Philharmonia became associated with the leading conductors of the age, Klemperer, Karajan, Furtwängler, Kubelík, Böhm and Igor Markevich. It was effectively Walter Legge's orchestra and reflected his concept of excellence both in playing and repertoire. In 1952 this promotion as a great orchestra was confirmed when it completed a successful European tour, appeared with Toscanini at the Royal Festival Hall and recorded *Tristan* with Fürtwangler and Kirsten Flagstad, one of the great landmark recordings. Later Legge was instrumental in making the Philharmonia synonymous with Klemperer and EMI, through his recordings, particularly of Beethoven.

In 1964 Legge announced the 'suspension' of the orchestra in what was a personal protest at musical conditions in the UK, arguing that it was impossible for the orchestra to maintain the standards it had set itself. Whatever Legge's real objective, the players did not accept the demise of their orchestra and it reformed as the New Philharmonia and operated thus until 1977, when it was able to revert to the former name, which, colloquially, most music lovers had never ceased to use. Klemperer's last years are associated with the orchestra, and his Festival Hall concerts attracted packed houses, with queues outside on the night hoping for 'returns'. The writer remembers Klemperer's Mahler Second, where the aged conductor was helped on the platform, sat slumped on a high stool throughout, the tiny baton barely moving, and after a blazing 'Aufersteh'n, ja aufersteh'n' the tumultuous applause really seemed to signal the end of an era.

All the London orchestras have had recurrent financial crises, and in the early 1970s the New Philharmonia found itself in a seriously adverse position, needing to spend considerable sums to attract leading conductors, particularly Lorin Maazel, and making substantial losses even on successful major initiatives, such as Mahler's Eighth Symphony at the Royal Albert Hall. In 1972 there were discussions on a possible merger of the New Philharmonia with another London orchestra, probably the London Philharmonic, which did not mature.

In 1975 Gavin Henderson, still in his twenties, became General Manager (much later he became Principal of Trinity College of Music) and presided over bringing new blood into the orchestra. The orchestra's association with the leading conductors of the day at this time included Maazel, Muti, Jésus López-Cobos, Ashkenazy, Kurt Sanderling and the first appearance of a very young Simon Rattle. Muti would be Musical Director from 1973 to 1982. Henderson was also the king-pin in organising, in co-operation with the GLC and the BBC, a Havergal Brian centenary festival at Alexandra Palace (see p. 171) and the Albert Hall. When Gwydion Brooke, the long-standing first bassoon, retired in 1979, the orchestra marked the occasion by programming, at the Festival Hall, the overture to his father, Joseph Holbrooke's opera *Dylan*, which 'Gwyd' as everyone called him had championed for a lifetime. From the late 1970s until the launch of CD in 1983 the number of recording sessions steadily fell, only reviving when the new CD format created a new market and a new – if shortlived – pricing structure for recorded music. Yet in 1979 they recorded William Alwyn's opera *Miss Julie* for Lyrita and in 1980 the orchestra recorded no fewer than five major operas.

Subsequent conductors associated with the orchestra included Ashkenazy, Principal Guest Conductor from 1982, and Giuseppe Sinopoli, who although little known in the UK in 1983 succeeded Muti. Other high-profile events at the time included an Elgar cycle – a bold move then before such cycles had become regular features for all the London orchestras – and the appearance of Bernard Haitink in Elgar's First Symphony in 1984 before he recorded it.

The Philharmonia became resident orchestra at the Royal Festival Hall in 1995 and maintains a widely diversified artistic programme focused not only in London. Claiming to be the world's most recorded orchestra (though all the London orchestras have substantial recorded histories and have made similar assertions) its

Principal Conductor in 2004, Christoph von Dohnányi, is joined by many of the leading conductors of the day for its innovative programming of new music, with seasons devoted to György Ligeti and the Finnish composer Magnus Lindberg. In a vivid high-profile Channel 4 television series, *Philharmonic*, the orchestra's day-to-day life and problems were ruthlessly exposed, underlining the essentially hard life of the British rank and file orchestral player today.

Royal Philharmonic Orchestra
16 Clerkenwell Green, EC1

The Royal Philharmonic Orchestra was formed in 1946 by Sir Thomas Beecham, who kept control until his death in 1961. Formed with the intention of being unsurpassed in the UK, it gave its first concert at the Davis Theatre, Croydon, and came into immediate competition with the Philharmonia, which had been founded with the same intention, and with which in the earliest days it shared some players. In 1950 it was the first British orchestra to tour the USA since the London Symphony Orchestra's tour before the First World War.

The name came from the Royal Philharmonic Society, which received royalties from the orchestra's recordings with Beecham. The orchestra played not only for concerts and operas directed by Sir Thomas, but it also appeared in the Powell-Pressburger film *The Red Shoes*, where it recorded Brian Easdale's newly composed ballet sequence before the film was shot. The orchestra did not perform at the Royal Festival Hall, which Beecham disliked and was very rude about when it first opened. Its home for many years after it was first formed was at the Odeon Cinema, Swiss Cottage.

Beecham's death in 1961 left the orchestra's future in jeopardy both financially and organisationally. There was a particular issue concerning the name 'Royal Philharmonic' which the Royal Philharmonic Society wished to rescind while the Festival Hall was unwilling to take the orchestra's bookings, and there was no history of public funding for the orchestra, such as was enjoyed by the other London orchestras, immediately precipitating discussions of whether a fourth London orchestra was desirable. In 1963 the orchestra also lost its long-standing association with the Glyndebourne Opera. It responded later that year with a very successful tour of the USA with Sir Malcolm Sargent, playing fifty-seven concerts in sixty-three days.

Beecham was followed by Rudolf Kempe, who had been named as Associate Conductor at Beecham's request in 1960 and was principal conductor from 1961 to 1975, for most of that time also being artistic director. Such was the regard in which he was held he was made 'Conductor for Life', which was tragically all too brief for he died in 1976.

In the 1960s the orchestra gradually achieved stability, achieving the authority to use the designation 'Royal' in its own right and in 1967 it began to appear at the Royal Festival Hall.

The pattern of a charismatic figure who remained associated with the orchestra for long periods even after their formal appointment as Chief or Principal Conductor ended, was repeated with Antal Dorati (Chief Conductor 1975–8; Conductor Laureate 1978–88) and Walter Weller (Principal Conductor 1980–85; Principal Guest Conductor 1985–9). André Previn (Music Director 1985–8; Principal Conductor 1988–92) came to the orchestra with the experience of his earlier long association with the London Symphony Orchestra. Previn was followed by the Russian conductor Yuri Temirkanov, who had long been Principal Guest Conductor and became Principal Conductor in 1992. Meantime Vladimir Ashkenazy had been Music Director for seven years (1987–94), being succeeded by Daniele Gatti, appointed Music Director in 1996 and still in post in 2004. When Ashkenazy returned to Russia for the first time in twenty-six years in November 1989 he conducted the RPO.

Continuity has also been reinforced by long-serving Guest and Associate Conductors, notably Sir Charles Groves (Associate Conductor 1967–92), Yehudi Menuhin (President/Associate Conductor from 1981 to his death in 1999) and Vernon Handley, Associate Conductor since 1993. With Handley the orchestra received a Gramophone Award in 1989 for their recording of Robert Simpson's austere Ninth Symphony. One particularly notable series of theirs has been Handley's recorded cycle of Sir Granville Bantock's orchestral music for Hyperion, which at regular intervals over a ten-year span has so far encompassed six volumes and has rehabilitated the critical evaluation of Bantock as a composer.

The orchestra has also maintained a longstanding formal relationship with the composer Sir Peter Maxwell Davies, both as an Associate Conductor and Associate Composer. The orchestra visited Orkney to give the first performance of his Violin Concerto, written for its fortieth anniversary, with Isaac Stern and André Previn, in June 1986, and returned for the twentieth St Magnus Festival in 1996 when it gave the premiere of his Sixth Symphony in the Phoenix Cinema, Kirkwall.

The orchestra's strategy to cope with the turbulent orchestral scene in the early twenty-first century has been to diversify, playing a wide touring programme, enjoying residencies outside London, notably at Nottingham's Royal Concert Hall, and by establishing a London home at the Royal Albert Hall in 1995. The orchestra has also developed a special association with Classic FM, the commercial classical radio station. During the 1980s the orchestra was able to build a substantial financial surplus by various popular activities. After the success of its *Hooked on Classics* CD it developed a large catalogue of budget price CDs of popular classics on its own Tring International label. A Gala concert at the Albert Hall starring Pavarotti was an enormous success. The orchestra appeared on a wide variety of commercial occasions (some thought them too commercial) often providing music with a beat. Summer seasons at the South Bank complex provided direct competition to the Proms at the Albert Hall for several years.

In 2004 the orchestra announced the opening of its Cadogan Hall, developed in a former church located at Sloane Terrace just off Sloane Square, to become its base and rehearsal hall with the intention of presenting orchestral concerts there.

The orchestra's van bears the motto 'Britain's National Orchestra', a claim that has raised some criticism. Viewed historically, it is piquant to remember that the RPO office is at 16 Clerkenwell Green, only a short walk from the site of the 'musical small coals man' Thomas Britton's pioneering concerts in his loft three hundred years before.

*   *   *

Music publishers (See also Walk 1)

To anyone who first came to know the London music-publishing scene in the early 1960s or before, it now seems a halcyon period. In those days most of the music publishers were within a few hundred yards of each other on two or three blocks in central London, either side of Oxford Street, and east of Regent Street. In the morning one could see the collectors for the music shops going round the trade counters with their orders, and it could all be done in an hour or two. The trade counters were run by the most formidable staff; they were seemingly formally unqualified, but they had an amazing fund of knowledge that their employers never seemed to recognise. You could go into a particular trade counter and ask for any piece of music and be directed to wherever it was available. Similarly, when one wanted to read an article in a back issue of *The Musical Times* one did not go into a library, or photocopy it – there were no easily accessible photocopiers – but to Novello's magnificent and imposing sales room in Wardour Street where sales staff could provide a mint copy of an issue from, say, 1919, at the original cover price of four pence.

The first crash came when Chappell's was burned down in 1964. Fortunately very few works were completely lost, though among those that were was the Sullivan Cello Concerto. Within two years two of those major publishers, Novello and Stainer and Bell, had moved from long-standing premises, and all those works that had been in stock and in print for years – Parry Symphonies for eighteen shillings, for example – were not passed on to libraries or the secondhand trade; it would seem they were destroyed. Many copies of printed full scores were thrown out. Works that one had assumed were easily available just disappeared overnight. And so it went on, and the whole of the music publishing industry gradually moved out of central London and appeared to destroy part of the British musical heritage as they went. The losses were largely of Victorian music, a part of the heritage that at the time was thought to have had its day. Yet, in fact, this was the very repertoire that would almost immediately start to be explored by a new generation. Subsequently there came a round of take-overs and further closures that had the effect of making even more music unavailable, and also reduced the extent to which the music of living composers was published by the main houses, as celebrated composers had their retainers cancelled and their once readily available music declared out of print.

Augener
18 Great Marlborough Street, W1

This English music publisher began in Brighton in 1860. From 1873 to 1937 they were sole agent for Peters Edition, and from 1871 to 1960 they published the *Monthly Musical Record*. George Augener's (1830–1915) family home at 5 The Cedars, Clapham Common (still there, see p. 245), became a focus for musical life in the late nineteenth century where he entertained a succession of leading composers and artists of the day. In 1898 they acquired the trade name and goodwill of Robert Cocks and amalgamated both firms as Augener Ltd in 1904. The firm was bought by Willy Strecker in 1910 and via him reverted to Schotts in 1913. However, Schott's forfeited ownership at the start of the First World War, and Augener became independent again. They were long established at 18 Great Marlborough Street almost opposite Schott.

For many years Augener were de facto the leading publisher of the day, as far as amateur performers were concerned, because their enormous catalogue contained inexpensive editions of most of the standard piano classics. In 1960 Augener acquired Joseph Weeks and the following year Joseph Williams. In 1962 they were themselves bought by Galaxy Music Corporation and became part of Galliard, the name Augener disappearing. Augener's long-standing premises in Great Marlborough Street stood empty and derelict for a long time before the whole block was redeveloped and all trace of such shops disappeared. In 1972 Galliard was absorbed by Stainer and Bell.

Augener were also well-known for their fine engraving and printing at their music printing factory at 287 Acton Lane, Park Royal, NW10. This has long gone, but one of the present authors can remember the works still operational there, craftsmen working on traditional engraving with punches, as late as 1964.

Boosey and Hawkes
295 Upper Regent Street, W1
Tube: Oxford Circus

The firm had its beginnings in a bookshop founded by Thomas Boosé in the late eighteenth century and was known as Boosey and Sons from 1819. A separate music section was established in 1816 under Thomas's son – another Thomas. They began as importers of foreign music but later published Bellini, Donizetti, Hummel, Rossini and Verdi.

From 1851 the firm manufactured wind instruments and from 1868 brass. In the late nineteenth century, they concentrated on the ballad and at the end of the nineteenth century educational music. Boosey's promoted the London Ballad Concerts from 1867 at St James's Hall and later the Queen's Hall – one of the better-known works being Sullivan's *The Lost Chord*. In the late nineteenth century Boosey published Stanford, including several of his operas, and, for the 1897 Birmingham Festival issued Stanford's specially commissioned *Requiem* in full score and parts as well as the vocal score, though the work was not quite the success they had been expecting.

However, they tempted Elgar away from Novello while he was feeling aggrieved with them, and thus acquired the *Pomp and Circumstance* marches. In 1930 the firm amalgamated with Hawkes and Son and became Boosey and Hawkes. Through this they acquired brass and military band music and copyrights or agencies for composers such as Bartók, Mahler, Prokofiev, Strauss and Stravinsky. They started the magazine *Tempo* in 1939. During the war Universal Edition of Vienna operated under their auspices. Boosey and Hawkes probably became best-known to a slightly later generation as the publisher of Benjamin Britten, before he fell out with them and became part of the move to launch the new publisher Faber Music. As a publisher, Boosey had been established at 295 Regent Street continuously from 1874.

Breitkopf and Härtel
54 Great Marlborough Street, W1

The long-standing Leipzig music publisher and engraver opened a London retail outlet at 151 Oxford Street in 1890, transferring to 54 Great Marlborough Street in 1892, where they were managed by Otto Kling, two doors along from Schott's. This lasted until the firm was closed by the exigencies of the First World War in 1916. Over twenty years of activity they had taken a vigorous and high profile role in publishing British music, especially that of the emerging school of younger composers including Delius, Vaughan Williams and Bantock and providing high quality and competitive engraving and printing services from their Leipzig workshops that underpinned the entire British music publishing industry. Kling was successful in developing a wide circle of musical contacts and was a personal friend of Bantock. The Breitkopf imprint was regarded by many British composers as the first choice for publication, giving them an international distribution and a superb standard of production. This extensive and symbiotic relationship collapsed almost overnight on the outbreak of war in August 1914. After the war Breitkopf and Härtel's editions were distributed in the UK by the British and Continental Music Agencies, and later many works (manuscript scores and parts) were destroyed by the Allied bombing of Leipzig in the Second World War.

Chappell and Co.
50 New Bond Street, W1
Tube: Bond Street

The music publishers, concert agents and piano manufacturers were founded in 1810 by Johann Baptist Cramer (pianist and composer), Francis Latour and Samuel Chappell. They published educational music, sold pianos, promoted concerts and played a large part in founding the Philharmonic Society. The business was sold to Chappell in about 1830 and his successor was William Chappell, who founded the Music Antiquarian Society in 1840, which held its meetings at Chappell's premises.

The manufacture of pianos began in the 1840s and the Monday and Saturday popular concerts started in 1858 in St James's Hall, directed by Samuel Chappell. Artists appearing at this venue included Joachim, Patti, Clara Schumann and Santley. An association with Gilbert and Sullivan began in the 1870s and Thomas Chappell financed the Comedy Opera Company, which staged some of their operas before D'Oyley Carte came on the scene. Towards the end of the nineteenth century Chappell's was in decline and William Boosey of Boosey and Hawkes was appointed in 1894 to run a concert series; the firm's fortunes improved and Boosey was made Managing Director in 1902. In May 1909 Chappell developed the piano business at 50 Bond Street with a refit, inviting 'their friends and clients to afternoon tea . . . the new suite

62   Selling pianos and music to a discerning and aspirational audience – the opening of Chappell's refitted showroom in 1909.

of pianoforte showrooms have been designed by Mr Walter Crane in the style of Queen Anne.' The premises went through to St George Street with a splendid board room. The Queen's Hall was later leased by Chappell's, who ran the Promenade concerts there from 1915 to 1926.

As well as issuing classical music, Chappell became the leading publisher for show business. The firm was bought by Louis Dreyfus in 1929, whose brother Max ran Chappell Inc in New York and had given him European rights to the American shows of the day with their enormous popular following. On the demise of Murdoch and Murdoch, subsequent to wartime bombing, in 1943 Chappell's acquired Murdoch's 'serious' list, which included most of the music of Sir Arnold Bax. In 1964 the destruction of Chappell's Bond Street showroom by a disastrous fire, not only rendered all of Bax's music out of print but also resulted in the loss of Sullivan's early Cello concerto, still in manuscript, of which only a cello part survived. After Louis's death Philips (later PolyGram) acquired Chappell's in 1968 and shifted the emphasis more to pop music. In 1969 Chappell was bought again and in 1987 was taken over by Warner Communications and became Warner-Chappell (with offices in Hammersmith). Kemble Pianos bought the New Bond Street premises, which are still called 'Chappell of Bond Street'.

J. and W. Chester
11 Great Marlborough Street, W1

Chester Music was founded in 1860 by John and William Chester of Brighton. At the beginning of the First World War the firm, in Brighton, was bought by

Otto Kling of Switzerland, former London manager of Breitkopf and Härtel, who acquired the former hire library of Breitkopf for Chester. He moved the company to London, where he was eventually succeeded by his son Harry Kling. When first established they responded to wartime conditions and specialised in British and non-German continental music, particularly Russian, French and Spanish, and held the agencies for Jürgenson, Belaieff and Bessel. In the early 1920s Chester were materially involved in supplying the core collection of the BBC orchestral library.

The longstanding Managing Director was R. D. Gibson, who in a recorded interview with Lewis Foreman in 1977, shortly after his retirement, described how, through an introduction, his father obtained for him a six-month trial – he described it as being more like an apprenticeship – his father subsequently investing in the firm and thus putting Gibson on the board, who later succeeded Harry Kling as Managing Director in 1936.

Gibson believed that there must be a personal friendship and contact between composer and publisher, and a confidence in each other, as he put it 'so one is not trying to outdo the other'. Thus Francis Poulenc was one of the young composers Chester published early on, before he had established relations with his subsequent French publishers, and later Chester also published his late instrumental works. Other composers Chester were particularly associated with in the 1920s were de Falla and Stravinsky. Later came British composers Lennox Berkeley, Antony Hopkins, Lord Berners and Eugene Goossens, perhaps then better known as a conductor. In the late 1950s Chester merged with Wilhelm Hansen of Denmark. In 1960 Chester issued an album to mark the centenary of the original founding of the firm which consisted of the facsimile reproduction of piano works specially written for the occasion and dedicated to Douglas Gibson, by Berkeley, Goossens, Ireland, Malipiero and Poulenc.

In 1968 they moved to Eagle Court, EC1, and joined the Music Sales Group in 1988. This group includes Schirmer and Novello. The Chester Archives, including fabulous manuscripts by Rachmaninov and Stravinsky, were sold at Sotheby's after the move from Eagle Court. The firm is now, with Novello, in Frith Street, Soho, while the hire library is at Bury St Edmunds.

J. B. Cramer and Co. Ltd
23 Garrick Street, WC2
Tube: Leicester Square

The imprint of Cramer is one of very long standing in London, first appearing as Cramer, Addison and Beale, piano manufacturers, in 1824 at 201 Regent Street. The firm successively became Cramer, Beale and Chappell; Cramer, Beale and Wood; Cramer and Co.; and Cramer, Wood and Co. before its present form, established in 1895. Although at a variety of addresses it was to be found at 201 Regent Street and adjacent properties for much of the nineteenth century.

Francesco Berger remarked that 'Cramer's afterwards passed into the hands of George Wood, an enterprising Scotchman, who, besides publishing music, manufactured pianos, dabbled in operatic speculations, and started a musical paper with the title 'The Orchestra' . . . Addison left Cramer's and joined Hollier and Lucas in establishing another first-class music publishing firm a little further down on the other side of Regent Street.' This was Addison, Hollier and Lucas, who published most of the operas by Balfe, Wallace, Macfarren and Benedict produced by the Pyne and Harrison management. This partnership lasted from 1856 to 1863 at 210 Regent Street, and later at 11 Little Marlborough Street. Lucas was principal of the nearby Royal Academy of Music and had an active playing career as organist and cellist.

In the mid-nineteenth century Cramer acquired much popular music with illustrated engraved title pages from Jullien, whose retail premises were in the nearby shop at 214 Regent Street, when he went out of business in 1858. For much of the twentieth century the company was at 139 New Bond Street, but its present address at 23 Garrick Street has no shop front, and the business is now as much concerned with library supply as music publishing.

J. Curwen and Sons
29 Maiden Lane, WC2

This family of music publishers and music educationists started in the 1840s with John Curwen championing a system of tonic sol-fa training in music for children. He published material on the system and devoted his time to the tonic sol-fa movement and to his publishing business, set up in 1863. The firm published church music as well as educational music at this time. John's son (also John), was trained as a musician and took over the firm after his father's death in 1880. He expanded the list to include choral music and light opera. His nephew became head of the firm in 1919 and enlarged its range to orchestral music, publishing Holst, Vaughan Williams, Bantock and Ethel Smyth, among others. This included Holst's *The Planets* and Vaughan Williams's opera *Hugh The Drover*.

In 1969 Curwen collapsed and the firm was bought by Crowell, Collier and Macmillan. The dissolution of the catalogue was an awful lesson for some of the more minor British composers involved, for when in 1971 Curwen's London office closed, many of their manuscript scores were lost. The former Curwen catalogue was split, some passing to Faber Music, some to the publisher Kenneth Roberton. A few manuscript items were selected by the British Library, but the bulk remained in the basement at 29 Maiden Lane. These were taken to Kenneth Roberton's premises at Wendover, Bucks, but were eventually claimed by Crowell's then Curwen offices in the Strand. Eventually Curwen was bought by Schirmer and the archive, in some 120 cartons, was held in a London warehouse for some time before being shipped to New York, and ultimately destroyed.

Faber Music Ltd
3 Queen Square, WC1
Tube: Russell Square

When Benjamin Britten parted from Boosey and Hawkes in 1964, Faber Music was set-up under the aegis of Faber and Faber to publish his music. Various works were taken over from the redundant Curwen catalogue, including music by Holst and Vaughan Williams. The publisher has tended to specialise in leading younger British composers, including Thomas Adès, Oliver Knussen and George Benjamin. Faber covers concert works by Paul McCartney, and has also published all the early chamber works of Vaughan Williams which the Vaughan Williams's Estate decided to publish at the beginning of the twenty-first century after nearly a century's ban. Among a wide-ranging catalogue Faber also produced their elegant published score of Deryck Cooke's version of Mahler's Tenth Symphony.

Novello and Co.
8–9 Frith Street, W1
Tube: Tottenham Court Road

Novello the music publisher originated with Vincent Novello, who, besides publishing, was an organist, choirmaster, conductor and composer. He was a member of the Philharmonic Society from the outset in 1813 and often conducted concerts from the keyboard. In 1811 he brought out a *Collection of Sacred Music,* in 1816 he issued *The Fitzwilliam Music* and then an edition of Purcell's sacred music. His eldest son, J. Alfred Novello, established the business and opened premises in Soho in 1829. To tie in with the growth of interest in choral music, the firm issued popular choral works, including vocal scores of Handel oratorios. *The Musical Times and Singing Class Circular* was founded in 1844 and each octavo issue contained one or two choral pieces, a practice that led to Novello's octavo editions. Alfred established his own printing office in 1847.

Novello also published books on music. In 1857 under Alfred's successor, Henry Littleton, the firm expanded further and began to publish modern anthems and hymn books, secular music, oratorios and operatic vocal scores. Novello's also promoted concerts and published choral works for festivals. In 1896 it became a limited company. Its interests broadened to include school music.

Novello moved to their once-familiar premises at 160 Wardour Street in 1906, survived the Blitz, and remained there until 1964. (See Walk 1.)

Novello have long been known for their octavo vocal scores with their familiar brown and maroon covers. Among British composers associated with the publisher were Elgar, Parry, Stanford, Mackenzie, Goss, Coleridge-Taylor and later Bantock, Bliss and Holst. Contemporary composers include Joubert, McCabe and Musgrave. Novello started issuing printed orchestral full scores of the British music they published in the late nineteenth century, and between 1890 and 1910 published superb editions, many of them engraved and printed in Germany, not only of Elgar, but also

63   Novello's Wardour Street showroom, one of London's most distinctive musical landmarks for over half a century, at its opening in 1906.

of Parry, Stanford, Cowen, Sullivan and other now forgotten composers of the day who they clearly thought were worth the investment. These included Macfarren, Benedict, Barnett, Frederic Cliffe, Sir George Henschel and Arthur Hervey.

During the twentieth century Novello maintained a large-scale and active publishing programme, very much continuing the tradition established in earlier years. In 1970 they became part of the Granada Group. In 1988 the company was taken over by Filmtrax and in 1993 by Music Sales. *The Musical Times* moved from Novello's in 1988 after 144 years continuous publication. The bulk of the Novello archives went to the British Library in the late 1980s, but some were later auctioned. These included not only a large number of manuscripts and letters by Elgar, Sullivan and others, but also file copies of nineteenth-century orchestral full scores which, sold as a job lot, were purchased by the dealer John May, who issued a sale catalogue devoted to them.

Oxford University Press
44 Conduit Street, W1

The Press's music activities no longer operate from London. Initially at Amen House, Warwick Square, EC4, after relocation to Oxford during the war they returned to premises at 44 Conduit Street until 1983. The Music Department was started in 1923, when Humphrey Milford appointed Hubert Foss, then only twenty-four, to establish it. There had been some earlier interest in music and books on music, which might be said to have started with the publication of the *Oxford History of Music* in 1901–5, and *Demeter*, a masque with music by Hadow and words by Robert Bridges. There was also later *The Oxford Song Book*. Foss developed the music publishing side with sheet music, 'Oxford Choral Songs and Oxford Church Music', and by purchasing the Anglo-French Music Company in 1925. Widely used standard texts were soon established, among music probably the best-known being the *Oxford Book of Carols* which has remained familiar ever since it first appeared. Among books *The Oxford Companion to Music*, edited by Percy Scholes (now revised by Alison Latham), is probably the most ubiquitous. The early growth was phenomenal, and the separate music division established under Foss undertook a publishing programme of an average two thousand works annually (much of which was educational) during the first ten years. The emphasis was on contemporary English music by composers such as Lambert, Vaughan Williams, Walton and Warlock. They had Benjamin Britten but let him get away. Talking about Foss, E. J. Dent wrote 'The modern English school could never have made headway without Hubert's understanding encouragement and practical help'. The press also published other anthologies besides the *Oxford Book of Carols* as well as new editions of Old English music. It still publishes contemporary British composers (Rutter, Mathias, Hoddinott and more recently Michael Berkeley, Anthony Powers and John Buller), choral, organ and educational music.

The press embraced the preparation of new performing editions of standard works, publishing the full score of David Lloyd-Jones's edition of Musorgsky's opera *Boris Godunov* in 1974 and Mozart's *Requiem*, edited by Richard Maunder, in 1987. In 1998 they started on a full-scale scholarly edition of the music of Sir William Walton with the Symphony in B minor edited by David Lloyd-Jones.

Books on music separated from the Music Department after the war, and after being published from Oxford for many years, at the end of the twentieth century moved to New York.

W. Paxton and Co.
36–8 Dean Street, W1.

Founded in the mid-1850s at 408 Oxford Street, later at 95, the music publisher Paxton moved to 36–8 Dean Street in 1942, where it remained until the catalogue was bought by Novello in 1971. For many years it was run by the brothers Leslie and Cyril Neil, the latter a great friend of the composer Sir Granville Bantock, many of whose late shorter works he commissioned to help the old composer keep the wolf from the door. Paxton was also known for its extensive library of mood music recordings, largely on 78s with their distinctive pink and blue labels, which included works by Bantock, Dunhill and Holbrooke. The recordings did not survive the closure of the Dean Street shop after the change of ownership, though a few of those by Bantock, now out of copyright, have been reissued on CD by Dutton Laboratories. In the 1920s Paxton's became known for typesetting and printing, the substantial vocal score of John Foulds's *A World Requiem* being processed in just eighteen days when it was taken up for the Festival of Remembrance in the Royal Albert Hall.

Playford

John Playford (1623–1687) and his son Henry Playford (1657–1709) were London's best-known music publishers in the second half of the seventeenth century, the regard of the leading composers of the day celebrated in Nahum Tate's 'Pastoral Elegy' on the death of John, which was set by Purcell ('Gentle shepherds, you that know/ The charms of tuneful breath') and published in 1687. Playford made bequests to both Purcell and John Blow in his will, underlining his regard for them. Playford was long associated with his shop at the Temple Church and later also at his house/shop in Arundel Street.

John Playford's *The English Dancing Master*, later *The Dancing Master*, and *A Musical Banquet* appeared as early as 1651, at the beginning of the Commonwealth, and remained available in various editions until well into the eighteenth century. Playford's *Introduction to the Skill of Music* was the volume that Pepys took with him down the Thames to Greenwich, from where he walked to Woolwich while reading it. Indeed, to judge from his diary, Pepys was constantly popping into Playford's shop and acquiring the latest publications, doubtless reflecting the lifestyle of those of his status at the time. Playford was succeeded by his son, but though none of their premises survive, today's location of the Temple Church in the

Inner Temple would probably not be completely unfamiliar to him. What does survive are the books he printed, copies of which are held in major libraries including the British Library.

Ricordi
271 Regent Street, W1

The London branch of the celebrated Italian publisher Ricordi was established in 1875 and became a UK limited company in 1887. Ricordi's were successively at 263, 283 and 271 Regent Street, the latter from 1925 to 1969. From 1970 they were represented from a part-time office at Chesham, Buckinghamshire, and in 1995 the parent company merged with BMG Ariola.

For many years after the Second World War until the closure of the London office the operas, notably of Verdi and Puccini, but also of lesser operatic composers of the period, were promoted by Arthur Owen from 271 Regent Street. His office was the constant port of call of a wide variety of musicians seeking advice and ideas from Ricordi's catalogue. It was supported from Milan by an archive that had not suffered the ravages of the war visited on many German houses, and where one could regularly meet artists as varied as international opera stars and the conductors of the London fringe looking for revivals.

Schott and Co.
48 Great Marlborough Street, W1
Tube: Oxford Circus

The prestigious German music publisher, founded in Mainz in 1770, operated in London from 89 St James Street from 1838 moving to 159 Regent Street between 1852 and 1908. Elgar must have known the Regent Street Offices from the 1870s when he purchased violin music for his own lessons, and in 1884 he sold them the copyright for what was effectively his Op. 1, the *Romance in E*, for a shilling and twenty free copies. In 1889 Elgar, the newly married struggling and impecunious young composer, also sold them the printed copyright of *Salut d'Amour*, which would be one of his bestsellers, outright for two guineas. Fortunately he did not relinquish performing and mechanical copyrights.

64   Schott's shop front at 48 Great Marlborough Street.

Another British composer who went to Schotts looking for a European market was the young Cyril Scott, though many of his hopes were dashed by the First World War, which made his published scores unobtainable. Schotts moved to 48 Great Marlborough Street in 1909 and are still there. In 1910 the manager Willy Strecker took over the London company Augener, but both firms were expropriated during the First World War and Schott's forfeited the ownership of Augener, who for many years had retail premises almost opposite at 18 Great Marlborough Street. In 1924 Schott became a limited company and expanded in the 1960s with new premises in Kent.

The London branch of Schott continued to operate during the Second World War, and its ambivalent position is clear from the German-language edition of Tippett's *A Child of Our Time* (*Ein Kind unserer Zeit*) printed by Schott in London in 1944 but, despite this, also bearing a Schott, Mainz imprint. The final revision of Tippett's unknown early Symphony in B-flat was destroyed when Schott's headquarters in Mainz was bombed during the war.

Schott established themselves with a wide musical public after the war with their extensive series of performing editions of recorder music, edited by Walter Bergman, largely of eighteenth-century music but also including some newly written titles. Tippett formed a lifelong relationship with Schotts, who published all his music, and they were also of operational assistance in promoting the revival of Percy Grainger, many of whose works they also publish.

The London office now constitutes a retail showroom, shared with Universal Edition. The firm has been known as Schott Musik International since 1995.

Stainer and Bell Ltd
PO Box 110, Victoria House, 23 Gruneisen Road, Finchley, N3

The music publisher Stainer and Bell was founded in 1907 as an outlet for British music. It published the later works of Stanford, Holst, Vaughan Williams, Bantock and Boughton. In 1917 the Carnegie United Kingdom Trust's Publication Scheme was launched to produce the works of British composers of the day, and the Trust appointed Stainer and Bell to publish the Carnegie Collection, which they did in superb examples of music engraving, between 1918 and 1928, when the scheme closed. The Trust invited composers to submit scores, and the substantial numbers of works considered by their panel resulted in them issuing many of what are now regarded as the iconic British works of the time. The Trust also funded the cost of sending these on approval to likely performers and purchasers. There were other similar series such as that of Tudor church music, and in 1951 it started to issue the *Musica Britannica* series for the Royal Musical Association, and since 1963 the *Early English Church Music* series. In February 1971 Stainer and Bell became a partner with Galliard Ltd, buying it in 1972 and subsequently removing from central London.

United Music Publishers Ltd
42 Rivington Street, EC2

Established in 1932 with the purpose of promoting French music in the UK, United Music Publishers described itself on its letterhead as 'Centre de la Musique Française'. It operated at first from 11 Sutton Street, W1, but long from 1 Montague Street, WC1. Here Felix Aprahamian worked as adviser in the years immediately after the war promoting French music in London and hosting Poulenc, Messiaen and their contemporaries.

Universal Edition (London)
48 Great Marlborough Street, W1
Tube: Oxford Circus

Universal Edition was founded in Vienna in 1901 and, under the influence of Emil Hertzka, soon became the leading publisher of the new music. Composers published including Mahler, Korngold, Schreker, Zemlinsky, Bartók and the Second Vienna School. The London Office was opened by Alfred Kalmus in 1936, and during the war while the parent company's activities were muted, operated there under the auspices of Boosey and Hawkes until 1951. Among the early substantial UK publications were the full scores of Edmund Rubbra's Symphonies Nos 1 and 3, and his *Sinfonia Concertante* for piano and orchestra, though Rubbra did not remain with Universal. Avant garde British composers on their later list include Harrison Birtwistle, David Bedford, Simon Holt, Dominic Muldowney and Michael Finnissy. The year the London office celebrated its fiftieth anniversary, Birtwistle's *The Mask of Orpheus* received its acclaimed London premiere.

At first at 23 Berners Street, Universal Editions was long at 2–3 Fareham Street, W1, off Dean Street, and now shares a showroom with Schott at 48 Great Marlborough Street.

John Walsh

The two John Walshes, father and son, dominated London music printing and publishing after John Playford. The first John Walsh (1665–1736) adopted engraving as his preferred method of origination, pioneering the use of punches, and publishing engraved music on an unprecedented scale. He shared an imprint with John Hare in the 1690s, his work at the time stating 'and likewise to be had at Mr Hare's shop'. Both Walshes were styled 'instrument maker to his Majesty' and the father published a long-standing periodical *The Monthly Mask of Vocal Music*, by which the latest theatre songs were disseminated, which continued from October 1702 to September 1727.

No trace of their long-standing premises remain, which were at the sign of the Harp and Hobby in Catherine Street 'near Somerset House' in the Strand. Walsh is probably most famously associated with Handel, whose regular publisher he became in 1730, notably with John Walsh junior (1709–1766). It has been estimated that the music of Handel constituted about half the younger Walsh's total output.

*   *   *

The major London auction houses hold regular music sales, sometimes as dedicated sales, at other times in more general sales.

Auction houses

Bonhams
101 Bond Street, W1
Tube: Bond Street

Founded in 1793 and, since the merger in 2001 with Phillips, the third largest auction house in the world, Bonhams has thirty-eight regional offices in the UK, including fifteen regional salerooms, a main saleroom at 101 Bond Street and headquarters in Knightsbridge. They are particularly known for sales of pianos, other musical instruments, books, maps, scores and pictures.

Christie's
85 Old Brompton Road, SW7; and King Street, St James's, SW1
Tube: Knightsbridge; and Piccadilly Circus or Green Park

Founded in 1766 by James Christie in Pall Mall, Christie's now has offices throughout the UK and abroad. They have long offered music manuscripts as part of general sales (although there was a sale devoted solely to music in June 1992). Increasing their involvement in the field, in 2003 they launched a new regular Music Sale, the first of this series taking place on 3 December 2003. This will now take place annually. Information and catalogues are available on the Christie's website, www.christies.com. The two highest-value music scores sold at Christie's in the last few years were both by Mozart: the first, on 6 June 2001, lot 37, was the autograph of the piano duet in G major (K. 357/500a), which made £355,750 (including premium), at the time the highest price at auction for a single piece by Mozart. The highlight of the sale on 3 December 2003 was also a Mozart manuscript, the autograph score for the song 'Als Luise die Briefe ihres ungetreuen Liebhabers verbrannte' (K. 520), which made £251,650 (including premium). This sale also included a dazzling collection of 31 letters by Mendelssohn (lot 33).

Christie's may well also be the leaders in musical instrument sales, which take place at their South Kensington rooms (as well as in New York). Christie's claim they hold the record for the highest price paid for any musical instrument at auction when they sold the Stradivarius violin 'The Kreutzer' for £947,500 in South Kensington in April 1998. Stringed instruments predominate at Christie's, but sales also include guitars, wind and keyboard instruments up to 1820.

Phillips
101 Bond Street, W1
Tube: Bond Street

Founded in 1796, Phillips were best known for sales of fine musical instruments which took place fairly frequently and included violins, violas, cellos and bows, as well as some printed music and music manuscripts. They merged with Bonhams in 2001 and continue trading under the Bonhams name.

Puttick and Simpson
47 Leicester Square, WC2

In the nineteenth century auction houses tended to act as clearing houses for valuable copyright material of the moment, including printing plates of popular songs and operas, and also for the dispersal of the copyrights of bankrupt and closed publishers. Puttick and Simpson in Leicester Square were celebrated as the leading experts in the field. For example, when the publishing firm of Thomas d'Almaine dissolved on d'Almaine's death in 1866 the entire holdings of plates and copyrights were sold at auction, the song 'Kathleen Mavourneen' realising £532. When the publisher Robert Addison's copyrights were sold in 1869, Costa's 1855 Birmingham festival oratorio *Eli* went for £1,462. This was still an active practice at the end of the nineteenth century, Scott Gatty's *True Till Death*, formerly published by Patey and Willis of 44 Great Marlborough Street, fetching £640. Puttick and Simpson were incorporated in Phillips early in the twentieth century.

65 Typical Puttick and Simpson advertisement, this example dating from 1895.

Sotheby's
34–5 New Bond Street, W1
Tube: Bond Street

Sotheby's is best known for sales of paintings by famous artists which go for fabulous sums. However they have regular sales of music, of musical manuscripts and of musical instruments, schedules of which are announced on the internet and in the national press. Their showrooms in Bond Street and elsewhere in London are therefore worth keeping on one's itinerary as musical sales tend to have a wide spread of material, with estimates at levels that ordinary mortals can afford, and with regular viewings available to those interested.

Samuel Baker held the first sale under his name in 1744. When he died in 1778 his estate was divided between his partner and his nephew, John Sotheby, and for the next eighty years the family dominated the firm, extending its role to prints and later to all areas of fine and decorative arts. In 1917 it moved to larger premises in Bond Street. Now there are offices worldwide, particularly in New York, and Sotheby's has broken new ground with auctions on the internet.

As well as many important manuscripts by the most celebrated composers of the past, recent years have seen the emergence of a variety of major twentieth-century music manuscripts, such as certain works of Igor Stravinsky, of a remarkable correspondence between Dimitri Shostakovich and Tanya Glivenko (6 December 1991) and another correspondence between Shostakovich and Elena Konstantinovskaya (26 May 1994). Catalogues for Sotheby's twice-yearly music sales in May and December can now be viewed on the web.

6 • Recording Session London

During the twentieth century, at several turning points in the developing technical history of the recording industry, companies have found themselves faced with having to find recording studios without the time or resources to build them specially. The existence of a variety of concert halls, churches and other convenient venues have allowed the London-based recording industry to find a ready-made infrastructure at times of change in its development, and none more so than in the last quarter of the twentieth century.

In the days of acoustic recording, before 1925, it was necessary to have a small and specialised room to be used as a studio. The singer sang into the bell of a horn that focused the sound waves via a membrane onto a disc of soft wax. Although singers with piano accompaniment could be recorded with mobile apparatus, orchestras needed such studios, into which the players were very tightly packed. The producer Joe Batten tells us that the recording studio for the Edison Bell acoustic recording of Elgar's *The Dream of Gerontius*, into which was crammed an orchestra of twenty-four with the organ part played by a bass concertina, a 'choir' of just eight singers, and the three soloists and conductor, measured thirty feet by eight.

The original office and studios of The Gramophone Company, arguably the world's first recording studio, was at 31 Maiden Lane, and although it does not survive, the original portico is still intact, though the stone doorstep on which so many famous musicians arrived was removed in a 2002 rebuild. Inside, though not accessible to visitors, a BBC feature in 2004 revealed that the basement room that formerly acted as the recording studio, also survives. Here Gaisberg made his first recordings. In Rules' Restaurant (still very much in business) nearby in Maiden Lane, he found singer Miss Syria Lamonte working behind the bar who became the company's first solo artist. Later, HMV built their studio at Hayes, opened immediately before the First World War. It was probably the best-known of studios, but all manner of temporary accommodation must have been used by the many companies that flourished before electrical recording became the norm in 1925–6. The other notable early studio, operational before 1900, and visited by many leading singers and instrumentalists of the day who had been persuaded to record, was at the offices of the Gramophone and Typewriter Company at 21 City Road. However, it is probable that the home of Edison's agent in the UK, Colonel G. E. Gouraud at 'Little Menlow' at Sydenham, near Crystal Palace, was also used for some of the ear-

66 Recording in the cramped space of the Gramophone Company's studio at City Road, on 16 December 1907. The soprano Tetrazzini is conducted by Percy Pitt. Fred Gaisberg can be seen in the centre below Pitt's music.

liest recordings, and after dinner he recorded on cylinder the voice of Sullivan, which survives.

Nearly eighty labels appeared in the UK before the First World War when, after some initial panic that the war would destroy the market for records, the demand grew, stimulated by the wartime popularity of portable gramophones, which with war-related releases gave the acoustic gramophone a new lease of life.

Electrical recording became a technical possibility in 1925, using the Western Electric System, and electrical recordings began to appear during 1926, quickly rendering the older methods redundant. While the new recording technology allowed orchestras to be put on disc in a much more realistic way, it also meant they had to play in a big space. Once it became a requirement to have a large and natural acoustic in which to make recordings it was necessary to find halls suitable for the purpose. The then principal record companies quickly contracted the leading halls of the day, not only for their own use but also to exclude the competition. Thus HMV recorded in Queen's Hall until their own custom-built Abbey Road Studios were ready in 1931.

Until the late 1940s all recordings for commercial release were cut onto discs of wax that were then processed, and pressings made from metal masters. This meant that editing was not possible. With the advent of tape, recording was freed from the constraints of the back-up of a large industrial installation, and editing of recordings became possible. Tape recording was developed in Germany and brought to practical use for broadcasting during the war. After the war this Magnetophon Sound Recording and Reproduction System was the subject of a British Intelligence Objectives Sub-committee report that effectively disseminated it to the recording industry and it was developed, notably by EMI in the UK for studio use at Abbey Road. The use of tape for recording was possibly the most important development in breaking the former de facto monopoly of the major recording companies during the second half of the twentieth century.

Many halls were used for recording, but of those existing halls that were pressed into use Central Hall, Westminster; Kingsway Hall (now redeveloped as a hotel); Queen's Hall (destroyed in 1941); and the Royal Albert Hall are of particular note. Even the Crystal Palace (burned down in 1936) was used to record a performance of *Messiah* in 1926 by Columbia, who had been beaten by HMV to Queen's Hall. Not only did they use these halls for recording sessions, but between the wars the occasional live event was also recorded at all of them, usually via a telephone line to head office or by HMV's mobile van.

Looking through the surviving recording ledgers for Columbia (at the excellent EMI Archives at Dawley Road, Hayes, now closed to the public) one finds that Columbia at one time or another recorded in London at their own studios in Petty France, Westminster, and also at the Portman Rooms, Baker Street; the Shepherd's Bush Pavilion; St George's Chapel, Windsor; the Tivoli Theatre; St George's church, Hanover Square; Central Hall, Westminster; the Regal Cinema, Marble Arch; and the Theatre Royal Drury Lane. After the amalgamation with HMV in 1931 they had access to the new Abbey Road Studios.

It has long proved difficult to determine exactly where the Columbia Studios in Petty France actually were. Thanks to some brilliant detective work in the Westminster Rate Books by Philip Stuart it seems probable that the hall was in the concert hall of the London Soldiers Home in Buckingham Gate, about fifty yards from the end of Petty France, then called York Road. The Portman Rooms saw some legendary artists in 1929 including Bruno Walter conducting *Tales from the Vienna Woods*, Glazunov conducting his suite *Les Saisons* (on 10 June and 14 July), and Fanny Davies playing piano music by Schumann (20–22 June).

Smaller ensembles and all manner of popular groups needed a more modest acoustic. HMV's activities at Queen's Hall were given flexibility by the Small Queen's Hall, the recital room above the main hall, where they recorded jazz and popular music as well as songs and smaller orchestral works. Here Elgar set down his music for small orchestra in the late 1920s, and John McCormack recorded songs. Columbia used Central Hall, Westminster, for many of their most prestigious orchestral recordings in the late 1920s. It was there that Beecham, with Heddle Nash and BBC forces, recorded Gounod's *Faust* on 3, 8 and 9 April 1929.

Kingsway Hall, the celebrated Methodist hall (half-way down Kingsway), was probably first used for organ recordings, examples of distinguished organists who recorded there including Widor (in 1926), Herbert Dawson (in 1926) and Reginald Goss Custard (in 1927). HMV had various orchestral sessions, notably some of the early recordings conducted by Barbirolli. These would have been linked by GPO landlines to HMV's studio at Queen's Hall, and later to Abbey Road. In the late 1930s there was a sudden growth in recordings at Kingsway Hall, possibly the first being in 1937, when Efrem Kurtz conducted extracts from *Coppélia* and the waltz from *Swan Lake* on 19 July 1937 for Columbia. The hall was not used frequently in this way at that time, but in July 1938 we find Columbia there again with the London Philharmonic Orchestra and Dorati in *Swan Lake* excerpts and two months later Efrem Kurtz and the same orchestra doing *Gaîté Parisienne*. The hall was used on 2 December 1938 by the BBC Chorus and Leslie Woodgate to record Arnold Bax's *a capella* tour-de-force *Mater Ora Filium*. They started using the hall for recordings with Sir Thomas Beecham and the orchestra and many recordings were made extending into the early months of the war. In February the distinguished German conductor Felix Weingartner was there with the orchestra in a repertoire of Brahms, Mozart, Liszt and Beethoven.

Immediately after the war the lack of Queen's Hall, destroyed by enemy bombing in 1941, was strongly felt. Consequently Decca probably made its first ffrr (full frequency range recording) orchestral recordings in 1944 in Kingsway Hall, a celebrated Tchaikovsky Fifth Symphony with the National Symphony Orchestra conducted by Sydney Beer with Dennis Brain as first horn, and in October 1945 Columbia were back, with the soprano Isobel Baillie, with Constant Lambert conducting and with Arthur Grumiaux and Gerald Moore in Mozart's Violin Sonata (K. 454).

Use of the hall by both EMI and Decca grew. In March 1948 Furtwängler record-ed Brahms's Second Symphony at the Kingsway Hall, and Beecham recorded some

---

Recording venues

Kingsway Hall, Kingsway, London – used by HMV from the late 1920s and by Columbia after the merger of HMV & Columbia. Used by Decca from 1944, also by the PolyGram Group until the hall's closure in 1984.

Portman Rooms, Baker Street – used by Columbia in the late 1920s (now demolished).

Queen's Hall – used by HMV (later EMI) during the late 1920s and 1930s. Destroyed 1941.

Central Hall, Westminster – used by Columbia from 1926 until 1933, and by EMI in 1946.

Chenil Galleries (actually New Chenil Galleries) in the King's Road, next to Chelsea Town Hall, in 1925 replacing an earlier gallery built in 1905. The hall seated about 250 people.

Fyvie Hall, Regent Street Polytechnic – used by Columbia during the late 1920s.

Embassy Theatre, Swiss Cottage – used by HMV in late 1920s and early 1930s.

Scala Theatre, Charlotte Street – used by Columbia during late 1920s (now demolished).

Wigmore Hall, Wigmore Street – used by Columbia during late 1920s, and by various companies for ad hoc recordings since.

St Augustine's Church, Kilburn Park Road, Kilburn (1884) – used mainly by EMI/CfP from 1959 onwards. Also Cala. BBC Proms occasionally.

The Gramophone Co. Studios, Hayes – HMV: until late 1920s.

Edison Bell Studios, Glengall Road, Peckham – until late 1920s.

Carlton Rooms, Maida Vale – used by Decca and Argo during 1950s.

Walthamstow Town Hall – used by Decca, RCA, Lyrita, Westminster, Everest among others from 1946 onwards, and is still in use today.

Friends' Meeting House, Euston Road – used by EMI in 1945.

Conway Hall, Red Lion Square (1929) – used by various smaller companies.

Columbia Studios, Petty France, Victoria – used after the First War, but after the merger of HMV and Columbia in 1931, and the building of the Abbey Road Studios, the old Columbia studios became obsolete and they were closed in 1932.

Decca Recording Studios, 165 Broadhurst Gardens, NW6 – sold after PolyGram merger in 1980s. Renamed Lilian Baylis House, the rehearsal rooms for English National Opera.

CTS Studios, Bayswater – opened in mid 1950s for mainly pop work, but used by L'Oiseau-Lyre in 1964. Closed in 1975 and moved to Wembley. Closed again 2002 and moved to the Watford Colosseum.

Hollymont Studios, Hampstead Hill – used by Argo prior to 1957.

Levy Sound Studios, 732 New Bond Street, W1 – from the 1930s to the 1960s were a freelance indepen-dent recording studio and also offered off-air recording facilities in the 1930s before they were widely available elsewhere.

Olympic Studios, 117 Church Road, Barnes, SW13 – originally built as Byfield Hall in 1906. Later a the-atre. Opened as studio in 1952. Used by various companies mainly for pop. CBS/Sony used in 1960s by sessions with John Williams and Boulez (Webern series). Later bought by Virgin and eventually passed to EMI.

Parlophone Recording Studios, Carlton Hill, NW8 – probably opened in the early 1920s, closed 18 March 1933 when recording was transferred to Abbey Road. Artists who recorded there included Richard Tauber, Ronald Frankau and Elsie and Doris Waters.

Royal Albert Hall – used by various companies for large scale recording and for organ recordings. Many public performances, particularly from the Proms were later issued on CD.

Barking Assembly Rooms – used by various companies from the late 1960s onwards including CBS/Sony, CfP, Unicorn.

Brent (formerly Wembley) Town Hall, Forty Lane – completed 1940. Used by EMI, Mercury, Philips, L'Oiseau-Lyre until 1980s.

Dominion Cinema, Southall – experimental EMI session on 27 March 1962 excerpts from Verdi.

Bishopsgate Institute – vanguard in 1967, Philips in 1971, miscellaneous sessions.

Pye Studios, Great Cumberland Place – used 1960s–1970s

St John's Smith Square, SW1 – many companies from late 1960s onwards

Hornsey Town Hall – very occasionally by EMI in 1956–7.

of his best-known performances with the Royal Philharmonic Orchestra. Here three separate cycles of Vaughan Williams's symphonies were recorded over thirty years, by Sir Adrian Boult, André Previn and Leonard Slatkin, and the legendary *Tristan* with Flagstad and Furtwängler and Silvestri's recording of Enescu's *Romanian Rhapsody No. 1* with the Vienna Philharmonic Orchestra also took place. The Kingsway Hall came into its own more and more over the next thirty years, when it was used by all the major record companies, and where, because of its gallery, it was suitable for creating all kinds of spatial effects when stereo recording was introduced around 1960. Bernard Herrmann's recording of *The Planets* was begun there until the excessive fortissimo demanded by the conductor in 'Mars' actually caused plaster to be dislodged from the ceiling and the sessions were moved elsewhere. All of RCA's *Classic Film Score* series were recorded there.

The Kingsway Hall was always grubby and a little threadbare, and the Methodist Minister, the Revd Donald Soper (later Lord Soper) did little to co-operate with companies hiring the hall. Yet, despite the audible rumble of trains passing beneath, and the traffic outside, it was thought by many to be the finest acoustic in London, and certainly the custom-built Festival Hall across the River Thames lay silent for much of the day because its acoustic was unsuitable for recording, other than organ recitals, and its administration not attuned to the developing freelance world of recording. At the Kingsway Hall the producer John Culshaw and the Decca team came to record Britten's *War Requiem* with the composer soon after its amazing reception at the 1962 Coventry Festival. This was the session at which the Russian soprano Galina Vishnevskaya, the producer John Culshaw tells us, 'lay on the floor of the vestry and shrieked at the top of her voice', as she felt she was being belittled in being asked to sing from the gallery of the hall – making full use of the special effects possible in the hall's acoustic – while the two male soloists were in the main hall below. Kingsway Hall was used for one sequence in the film *The Magic Bow*.

In the early days the record companies also founded their own studios, often in derelict warehouses or run-down commercial premises. These included the Edison Bell Studios in Glengall Road, Peckham, which continued until Edison Bell went out of business in the late 1920s. The Columbia Studios in Petty France, Victoria, already mentioned, were used after the First World War, but after the merger of HMV and Columbia in 1929 and the building of the Abbey Road Studios the old Columbia studios became obsolete and they were closed in 1932, though the two labels preserved their separate identities and were fiercely secretive in maintaining their respective schedules in the same building.

Another, smaller, hall used from time to time was Conway Hall, Red Lion Square. This is still used for regular concerts on Sunday evenings (see Chapter 1). Usually the place for instrumental and chamber recordings, it was the location for James Galway's recording of the Mozart flute concerti in December 1984 and July 1985 (RCA RL 87861).

Some examples of Royal Albert Hall Concerts issued on CD	
15 Sept. 1964:	Vaughan Williams: Symphony No. 8 (BBC Symphony Orchestra/ Stokowski) BBC Radio Classics 15656 9131–2
14 May 1974:	Brahms: Symphony No 4 etc (New Philharmonia Orchestra/ Stokowski) BBC Radio Classics BBC RD 9107
20 July 1981:	Mahler: *Das Klagende Lied* (Soloists/BBC choirs/ BBC Symphony Orchestra/ Rozhdestvensky) BBC Radio Classics BBC 15656 9141–2
25 June 1987:	'Let All the World' RSCM 60th anniversary concert Argo 421 418–22H
5 Aug. 1988:	Busoni: Piano Concerto (BBC Singers/BBC Symphony Orchestra/Elder/Peter Donohoe) EMI CDC7 49996–2
27 Aug. 1991:	Bruckner: Symphony No 7 (Philharmonia Orchestra/Welser-Möst) EMI CDC7 54434–2
10 Sept. 2001:	Vaughan Williams: *A Sea Symphony* Joan Rodgers (sop) Simon Keenlyside (bar) Choruses/BBC SO/ Slatkin BBC MM244 (Cover-mounted CD with *BBC Music Magazine*, Aug 2004)
31 July 1994:	Ethel Smyth: *The Wreckers* (Soloists/Huddersfield Choral Society/BBC Philharmonia Orchestra/Orchestra de la Martinez) Conifer 75605 51250 2
8 May 1995:	Pavarotti 60th birthday concert Decca448–701–2DH2

The emergence of Decca as a serious competitor to EMI in the 1930s and after the war meant they needed their own studio. The Decca Recording Studios, in Broadhurst Gardens, Hampstead, had been built as 'Falcon Works' in 1884. Converted by a predecessor of Decca, Crystalate, as studios in 1933, they were purchased by Decca in 1937, but were sold after Decca merged with PolyGram in the 1980s. The dimensions were relatively small and Decca also used Hampstead Town Hall. After Decca was taken over, the studios were renamed Lilian Baylis House, and they became the rehearsal rooms for English National Opera, and continue thus in 2004.

It is interesting to remember that when, on 9 and 10 December 1935, Decca made its pioneering recording of the then new Symphony in B minor by the young William Walton with the London Symphony Orchestra conducted by Sir Hamilton Harty, it was at Thames Street, in an old warehouse high above Cannon Street Station (since demolished) in the City. The weather 'was cruelly cold', remembered one player who was there, while Boyd Neel who found himself recording there on other occasions remembered 'one reached it through a graveyard, and up many flights of narrow rickety stairs'. Other ad hoc studios used by Decca at this date included the Chenil Galleries, Chelsea, where notably 'arty' and county audiences supported concerts, and where Vaughan Williams attended to supervise the Boyd Neel String Orchestra recording his *Fantasia on a Theme of Thomas Tallis* on 29 January 1936. Generally in the 1930s the Chenil Galleries were used to record dance records.

The Second World War generated a wide following for serious music, and on the London musical scene there was a need for studios as well as for concert halls. Recordings had been made from the Royal Albert Hall since the inception of electrical recording, possibly the first to survive being extracts from a public performance of *The Dream of Gerontius* conducted by Elgar on 26 February 1927. After the war Furtwängler recorded Beethoven's Second Symphony there on 3 October 1948, and in 1971 Leonard Bernstein recorded Verdi's *Requiem* with a starry solo line-up (CBS CD 77231).

Many notable public concerts given in the Royal Albert Hall that were not intended as recording sessions were recorded and have been subsequently issued on commercial LPs and CDs, giving a vivid portrait of the performing life of the hall over the years since the Second World War.

Not least among the recordings from the Royal Albert Hall have been recitals on the organ, one of the principal reasons for which recording sessions are held in the hall. These are discussed in the section on organ recordings below.

The Royal Opera House Covent Garden
Tube: Covent Garden, Charing Cross, Leicester Square or Embankment

Covent Garden has been used as a concert hall from time to time in the past, but not often as a recording studio. Nevertheless over the years many live performances from Covent Garden have appeared on commercially issued discs, starting with the Melba Farewell Concerts in 1926, and the most significant of these from before the war were issued in an historical album by EMI. The Melba Farewell Concert recordings, including the speeches by Lord Stanley and Melba herself, appeared on LP in an EMI boxed set (RLS 742) and on CD on Eklipse Records (EKRCD4). Perhaps the most celebrated off-air recordings from Covent Garden are those of productions starring Maria Callas in the 1950s. Covent Garden recordings have also been issued from off-air acetate discs, particularly Beecham's Wagner from the late 1930s. In 1968 Decca issued an 'Anniversary Album' of extracts of postwar performances at Covent Garden (boxed set of 2 LPs (MET 392–3)). This includes a variety of performances otherwise not recorded such as Peter Pears as Pandarus in Walton's *Troilus and Cressida*, Forbes Robertson as Claggart in *Billy Budd* and Amy Shuard as Elektra in Strauss's opera.

English National Opera at the London Coliseum
Tube: Leicester Square and Charing Cross

The English National Opera at the London Coliseum has been the source of a number of live performances issued on LP or CD, notably Reginald Goodall's performances of Wagner's *Ring* with Rita Hunter and Alberto Remedios, Mark Elder's of Verdi's *Otello* and *Rigoletto* and Sir Charles Mackerras of Donizetti's *Mary Stuart*. Many of these have subsequently been issued on video – now DVD – including Britten's *Gloriana* conducted by Mark Elder. (See Ken Wlaschin's *Encyclopedia of Opera on Screen* for full listing.)

Abbey Road Studios
3 Abbey Road
Tube: St John's Wood

The EMI studios at Abbey Road have become synonymous with an international audience for their association with The Beatles, particularly remembered for their celebrated record sleeve showing the Fab Four on the pedestrian crossing in Abbey Road almost outside. In fact the studios are historically far more celebrated for their ties with the leading composers and artists in the 1930s, and in the early days being particularly associated with Elgar, who recorded *Pomp and Circumstance* No. 1 with the London Symphony Orchestra at the opening ceremony on 12 November 1931, before an audience that included George Bernard Shaw and Sir Landon Ronald. The link with Elgar is celebrated by a plaque on the front wall.

The house at 3 Abbey Road was originally built in the 1830s as a fashionable mansion set in a 250-foot garden. After a couple of changes of ownership it was converted into flats during the First World War and became associated with Maundy Gregory, who achieved notoriety for arranging the sale of honours. In 1929 the premises were purchased by The Gramophone Company Ltd and converted into offices and three large studios – the world's first dedicated recording studios were built on what had been the garden.

Throughout the 78 rpm era and into the early days of LP (which HMV did not adopt until 1952, two years after it was introduced by Decca) recording at Abbey Road was dominated by classical artists and classical repertoire, and the story of the studios is the story of such celebrated artists as Elgar, Yehudi Menuhin, Artur Schnabel, Sir Thomas Beecham (who lived one minute away in Grove End Road; plaque) and Sir Malcolm Sargent. In the 1930s the popular music of the day began to be recorded there, by such band leaders as Joe Loss and Geraldo. Well-known singers included Gracie Fields and Max Miller, while international names like Paul Robeson, Fred Astaire, Noël Coward, Fats Waller and Glen Miller and the Band of the Army Air Force all worked there.

In the 1930s Abbey Road was also known for its Compton cinema organ in Studio One which was used to record popular artists like Reginald Dixon. After the war the organ was removed. During the 1930s occasional public concerts were recorded at Abbey Road via landline from halls such as the Queen's Hall.

By the time of compact disc in 1983 a large number of independent commercial recording studios had sprung up, aimed at the growing pop music industry, and pioneered a wide variety of new techniques. There had also been a huge expansion of film music recordings. Generally these facilities were not used for major classical recordings and hence are beyond the scope of this chapter, but as far as the EMI studios are concerned they changed from being an in-house facility providing a service to one company, to being an autonomous financially independent business. It resulted in the studios being developed and updated for every new requirement, especially multi-media, and its subsequent marketing as the world's best-known recording studio.

The latest generation of artists who have recorded at the studios, a number of them over many years, include such household names as Placido Domingo, Dame Kiri Te Kanawa and Sir Simon Rattle. A major development was the Gheorghiu and Alagna recording of *Tosca,* which was recorded and filmed in the studios for issue on CD and DVD.

Almost uniquely, because of its Beatles associations, Abbey Road is set up to field approaches from enthusiasts and tourists, and tourists going to there via St John's Wood tube station (four or five hundred yards away) should note the Abbey Road Café adjacent to the entrance to the tube station which sells official Abbey Road merchandise and memorabilia concentrating on The Beatles. The Abbey Road studios have been in various documentaries about pop stars, were the subject of a television documentary in the 1990s and also appear as a location in the film *The Magic Bow.*

The Independent Record Companies

Deconsecrated churches have also played a significant part in London's post-war musical life, especially St John's, Smith Square, which, bombed during the war, was rebuilt and brought back into use as one of London's best-loved smaller concert halls. It also has an active role during the daytime as a favourite recording venue, with a distinctive acoustic, for smaller forces. South of the river, the Henry Wood Hall occupies the glorious and imposing eighteenth-century building of the former Trinity Church, located in Trinity Church Square off Trinity Street, SE1. As well as a dedicated recording studio, it is also the headquarters offices for the London Philharmonic Orchestra, whose library is located in the Crypt. Alongside is the similar library of the Royal Philharmonic Orchestra. On the stairs to the gallery hangs Nathan Hendel's portrait of Sir Henry Wood. There is normally no access to the casual caller, though on rare occasions there have been BBC performances there before invited audiences, and if one occurs, readers are urged to take advantage of the opportunity.

The rise of independent record labels in the 1970s and '80s meant that a whole infrastructure of freelance suppliers grew up, including halls, engineers and producers. Various town halls round London became favoured by many record companies, the two most used being Walthamstow Assembly Rooms and Watford Town Hall (later known as the Colosseum, the latter going bankrupt in the summer of 2004 when the hall reverted to its former name). Watford was greatly favoured by Richard Itter of the Lyrita label, and had an acoustic almost as highly regarded in its day as the Kingsway Hall. It has achieved more recent celebrity as the location for the recording sessions for Howard Shore's music for the films *The Lord of the Rings*, done there because of the large forces involved, including chorus. Generally it is the independent labels that in 2004 are still systematically recording in these places, the freelance infrastructure that had enjoyed such a success in the 1980s and '90s being much reduced.

But the most effective hidden resource turned out to be various churches round London that have been favoured not only for their acoustic but for their easy availability, informality and comparatively low cost. Examples of churches used include All Saints' Church, East Finchley, a favourite location for Dutton Laboratories with their on-going series of chamber music by British composers in their Epoch series. Dutton also record at the Rosslyn Hill Chapel, Hampstead; St Silas the Martyr, NW5 and St Augustine's, Kilburn, though in the latter traffic noise, the bane of London recording locations, is increasingly evident.

Among the independent recording companies Hyperion have a long tradition of recording in churches around London and elsewhere. Their Schubert and

67   Recording session at St Giles, Cripplegate.

Schumann song series were made at All Saints, Durham Road. Other halls include St Michael's, Highgate; the Rosslyn Hill Chapel, Hampstead; All Hallows, Gospel Oak in North London; and St Paul's, New Southgate, further out (a ten-minute walk from Arnos Grove tube). St Jude's on the Hill, the church at the centre of Hampstead Garden Suburb, is used by both Hyperion and Chandos for orchestral recordings and illustrates the problems of working with such limited facilities for the players, especially in winter. In May 1995 it was the location for Harry Christophers's recording with The Sixteen of Handel's *Esther* in the original 1718 version. (Now on Regis RRC 2025.)

Other churches include St Giles, Cripplegate, which has been used for the largest forces, including the Rita Hunter recording of *Götterdämmerung* Act 3 scenes 2 and 3 (Chandos CHAN 8534). Raymond Leppard's English Chamber Choir recording of Handel's *Messiah* was recorded there in 1976 (Erato/WEA 2292-45447-2) and Brahms's First Piano Concerto with Barry Douglas and the London Symphony Orchestra conducted by Skrowaczewski (RCA). This is also a church where live performances are given, the Koch Schwann recording of Britten's *Curlew River* being taken from such a concert, given on 25 February 1993. This can be a rather cavernous acoustic, the studio recordings showing how this can be controlled by microphone placings, whereas the occasion of commercially recording a live performance finds its actual characteristics more closely reflected in the issued sound.

Another church that has been widely used for recordings is All Saints Church, Tooting, where again the reverberation is considerable but the sound that can be obtained in the control room is spacious but warm. The only down side here is the junior school next door, where playtime can be noisy. At the end of the Chandos recording of Bax's Third Symphony with the London Philharmonic Orchestra and Bryden Thomson, the childrens' playground noise can momentarily be heard in the few seconds' ambience after the music has faded, if one turns up the volume at the end.

Film Recordings

The film industry had a succession of facilities just outside London. The Rank Organisation had its own studios (Anvil) at Denham, where the music for two of the *Star Wars* movies was recorded (*The Empire Strikes Back* was at Abbey Road), but these were bulldozed when Rank went to the wall. Crown Films had a scoring stage at Beaconsfield where the music director was Eric Rogers (of the *Carry On* films fame), but that is now the National Film and Television School. In the 1950s, even Ealing Studios at Ealing Broadway were used and Borehamwood also had a scoring stage. The BBC used its own TV studios at Lime Grove, Shepherd's Bush, now transferred to nearby White City. The CTS studios remained at Wembley where the music for most of the *James Bond* films was recorded, along with *Batman* and many other major films. With the redevelopment of Wembley Stadium, CTS later removed to Watford Colosseum where major films continue to be 'scored'. Another municipal hall, the Barking Assembly Rooms, was a favourite location for the film music composer and conductor Bernard Herrmann ('Benny' to all), and his opera *Wuthering Heights*, fully subsidised by its composer, was recorded there.

Organs

The major religious buildings of various denominations in London, the large number of churches, not only in the City and in central London but also in the enormous area of greater London, all have organs and many have been recorded. The major concert halls also have organs and have been used for various recording sessions. A comprehensive list would make a book-length study (see p. 77).

BBC

The BBC Studios at Maida Vale, with its curious low-level construction that betrays the pre-First World War origin of the building as a roller-skating rink, is the home of the BBC Symphony Orchestra. Here during the season the BBC will often host live performances in front of an invited audience with free tickets. (For tickets currently on offer check the BBC website at www.bbc.co.uk/whatson/tickets). Yet BBC recording sessions (and also live broadcasts) are held at varying locations, and these frequently feature unusual or rarely heard repertoire given by top-line performers.

Maida Vale was originally 'The Maida Vale [Roller] Skating Palace and Club'. With a lease from 1909, it opened in 1910 but was wound up in 1912. The building is 131 feet wide and 494 feet long with one main studio (MV1) and six others, increasingly smaller. On the wall of MV3 is a plaque remembering that Bing Crosby made his last recording there in 1977. Although already in use, the premises were secured by the BBC in August 1937, but were not finally purchased from the Church Commissioners until 1971.

BBC broadcasts also take place from the regular concert halls in London, notably the Barbican, the Royal Festival Hall, the Wigmore Hall and at St John's, Smith Square at lunchtimes. St Paul's Church Knightsbridge, St Giles Cripplegate and other City churches are also used, particularly for choral and quasi-liturgical repertoire. The BBC now has a permanent installation at the Barbican. The Henry Wood

68   The Bing Crosby memorial plaque in Studio 3 at Maida Vale.

69   A recording session at Henry Wood Hall: Martyn Brabbins conducts members of the Nash Ensemble in Bliss's 'Storm' from his music for *The Tempest*.

Hall at Borough is a regular recording studio and is normally not available to the public, but is occasionally used by the BBC for invitation concerts, and since 2003 has been used thus for *Friday Night is Music Night* with an invited audience.

The Golders Green Hippodrome is a traditional theatre adjacent to Golders Green tube and bus station which first opened in 1913. The first outside broadcast, of *Die Fledemaus* Act II, came from there on 29 November 1930, with Heddle Nash and Marjorie Parry, conducted by John Barbirolli. In 1943, when owned by the theatre impresario Prince Littler, it was used to source forces programmes for the BBC. There were also occasional concerts by the London Symphony Orchestra which started in 1940. For example on 25 February 1940 Sir Henry Wood presented such a programme, which included Solomon in Beethoven's Second Piano Concerto. Other wartime concerts included the Beecham Sunday Concerts in January 1940. Early in 1968 it was hired by the BBC from Marfield Theatre Enterprises Ltd for a period of twenty-four months, and in 1970 the BBC acquired the freehold. Since 1972 it has been a BBC studio and is the home of the BBC Concert Orchestra. It was temporarily out of use after a large block of plaster fell out of the ceiling without warning in 2000, but it was refurbished and reopened as a state-of-the-art facility in September 2001.

BBC recording venues in central London come and go. One more recent one is the Mermaid Theatre, Puddle Dock (adjacent to Blackfriars tube station) which though closed as a regular theatre has become a home of *Friday Night is Music Night*.

The BBC has announced it is developing a new music recording centre in a state-of-the-art building now in progress at White City (see p. 128).

*   *   *

Historical CD Compilations Celebrating Specific Halls

A number of CD anthologies have been issued of 78 recordings made in halls that are no longer extant.

Barbican Hall

Most of the 'LSO Live' recordings, largely conducted by Colin Davis and issued by the orchestra itself and available from them, are of performances recorded in the hall from 2000 onwards.

Concert Hall, Broadcasting House

The Concert Hall in Broadcasting House was comparatively small, but was used for the performance of many large-scale scores in the 1930s, especially for late-night invitation concerts of modern music, which were then broadcast live. The hall was not used for music after the war, and later became the Radio Theatre. Most of these 1930s broadcasts do not survive, but the UK premiere of Berg's Violin Concerto, the second performance anywhere, conducted by Webern on 1 May 1936 does. It was recorded only because the soloist, Louis Krasner, had a commercial studio record it for him off air. These acetates were eventually dubbed by Richard C. Burns of Packburn Electronics Inc., and issued on CD by Murray Khouri on the Testament label in 1991. Berg: Violin Concerto (UK premiere) Louis Krasner (vln)/BBCSO/ Webern. Recording of broadcast of 1 May 1936 (Testament SBT 1004).

Crystal Palace

Recordings were made at Crystal Palace during the electrical era (that is from 1926 onward) until the building burned down in November 1936. Among the first of these were choral extracts from a live performance of Handel's *Messiah*. This was the last of the celebrated Handel Festivals, with massed performers conducted by Sir Henry Wood, and took place in June 1926, our only recorded evidence of what those occasions were actually like. Later, music played at the National Brass Band Festivals in the 1930s was recorded. There were also items from specific events such as the Festival of English Church Music in July 1933 and nonconformist and Salvation Army recordings. In 1928 an orchestra of four thousand child violinists was recorded. Sadly there is no recording of the organ as such, but it occasionally appears distantly, notably in *Messiah*. Those re-issued on CD include *Live at the Crystal Palace* – sixteen tracks recorded between 1926 and 1934 including brass bands, the Festival of English Music and the National Union of School Orchestras (Beulah 1PD1); Crystal Palace Champions – band recordings from 1928 to 1936, including music by Ireland, Elgar, Bliss, Meyerbeer, Holst, Bath, Iles and Handel (Beulah 1PD2); and Sir George Grove and the Crystal Palace – an anthology of historical vocal recordings of singers who sang in the Crystal Palace, plus the complete takes of *Messiah* from the 1926 Handel Festival and the voice of the composer George Lloyd reminiscing about the hall (Symposium 1251).

Queen's Hall

Queens Hall was used as a recording studio from the advent of electrical recording in 1925. Recordings of public concerts survive from the 1930s (see p. 42).

A Salute to Henry Wood – includes an archive recording of a Promenade Concert from the Queen's Hall on 8 September 1936, including *Rosamunde* (Schubert);

Sinfonia Concertante K. 364 (Mozart); 'L'amerò, sarò costante' (*Il Re Pastore*, Mozart); *Exsultate, jubilate* (Mozart) (Symposium 1150).

Historic Organs (Queen's Hall Organ) – tracks played by Reginald Goss Custard, J. Arthur Meale, Albert Schweitzer and Marcel Dupré (Beulah 1PD5).

Ionisation – an anthology of historic off-air recordings from 1927 to 1945, including *God Save the King* from Toscanini's concert in the Queen's Hall, 19 May 1938, with an extended passage of audience ambience in the hall and Beethoven's Eighth Symphony conducted by Sir Henry Wood (3 January 1936) (Symposium 1253).

Many other recordings survive from the 1930s by artists as celebrated as Toscanini, Beecham, Szigeti and Mengelberg (see list in Chapter 1).

Royal Albert Hall

BBC Proms Centenary, 1895–1995, BBC Radio Classics (DMCD98, two discs) – recordings taken from public performances in the Royal Albert Hall, London during the Henry Wood Promenade Concerts between 1954 and 1983. Also available as a limited edition containing an additional CD featuring some of the Last Night speeches introduced by Sir John Drummond (BOXD98SE).

Royal Opera House, Covent Garden

Attempts were made to record live performances in the Royal Opera House from 1926, notably the Melba Farewell Concerts.

Royal Opera House Covent Garden. Historic Recordings of Actual Performances. EMI boxed set three LPs RLS 742. (Includes recordings made in the house in June 1926, June and July 1928 and May 1936.) The Melba recordings are also on CD. (For this and Decca's 'Anniversary Album', see p. 161.)

Sadler's Wells

The Stars of The Old Vic and Sadler's Wells (EMI RLS 707, three LPs) – an anthology of commercial recordings, including some previously unissued, prefaced by a recording of the voice of Lilian Baylis recalling her life's work. Similar material was issued by Dutton on a series of five CDs of 'Stars of English Opera'.

Westminster Abbey

Notable state occasions in Westminster Abbey have been issued commercially (HMV/EMI), including extracts from the coronation of King George VI in 1937, only on 78s, and the coronation of HM Queen Elizabeth II, which has appeared on CD (EMI 7243 5 66582 2 6). Such recordings give a clear impression of the acoustic and ambience, and of the organ.

Wigmore Hall

Wigmore Hall Centenary Celebrations – recordings of songs and chamber music broadcast from the Wigmore Hall from 1951 to 2000 by major artists of the day. *BBC Music Magazine* Vol. 9 No. 10 (June 2001) issued this CD (which includes interactive CD-ROM capability with background material on the Wigmore Hall), and it is available with that back issue.

The BBC have also issued some of their Lunchtime Concerts from the Wigmore Hall, for example, Haydn, Beethoven and Wolf sung by Sir Thomas Allen (baritone) with Malcolm Martineau (piano) from 5 April 1999 on BBCW 1004–2.

Possibly the first recording from the Wigmore Hall was for the Columbia Graphophone Company, when the Australian baritone Harold Williams recorded 'Gainst the Power' from Gounod's *Faust* with the BBC Chorus and orchestra, perhaps the first ever recording of a BBC chorus (PLS-2). It was part of a promotion pack for Columbia's new 'Viva-tonal' electrical system launched at a lunch at the Connaught Rooms on 16 September 1926. (For Wood's speech see p. 312.)

BBC Legends

The BBC Legends series of historical BBC broadcasts issued by IMG Artists, retrieved from the BBC and private archives, includes recordings made in all the principal London halls from the 1930s, among them Queen's Hall, the Royal Albert Hall and the Royal Festival Hall.

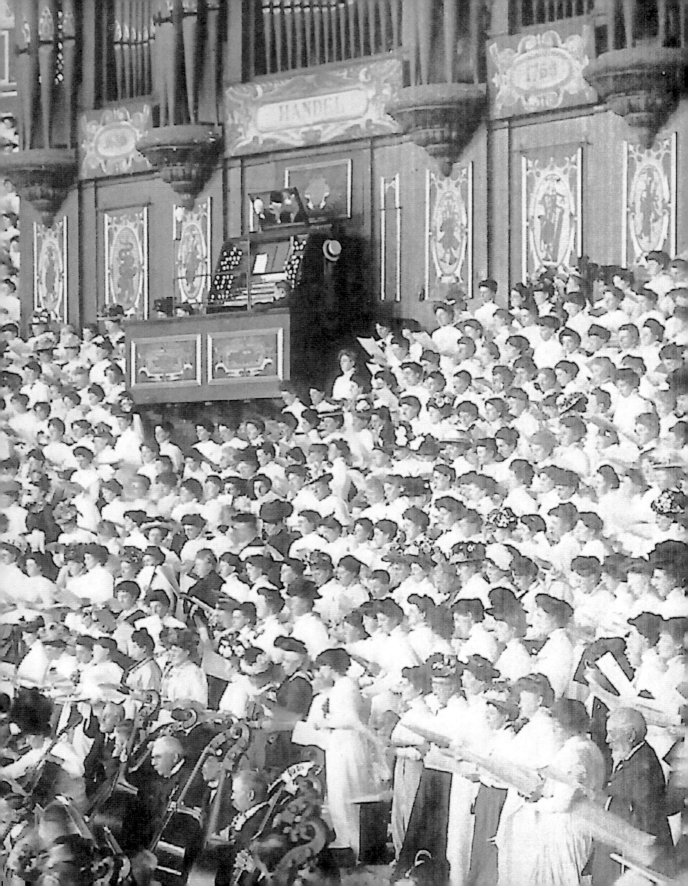

7 • Out of the Centre: some places of interest in the suburbs and environs of London

Alexandra Palace

Wood Green, N22
Tube: Wood Green, then W3 bus or free shuttle available on show days;
train to Alexandra Palace station from King's Cross, Finsbury Park
or Moorgate, then shuttle or W3 bus

North

'Ally Pally' opened in 1873 and was famed for its magnificent Willis organ. Shockingly, Alexandra Palace was destroyed by fire very soon after the opening and the original organ lost. It reopened in June 1875 with a concert hall, theatre and large hall, but was not as popular as Crystal Palace. The Alexandra Palace Choral Society was directed from its inception in 1873 by Weist Hill, later Director of the Guildhall School of Music. Its programmes included revivals of Handel's *Esther* and *Susanna*, with a choir of three hundred voices. During the First World War it became a barracks and then it was used to house German prisoners of war. In 1936 it became the main London BBC broadcasting station after Crystal Palace was destroyed and hosted the world's first television transmitter (Marconi-EMI). In May 1937 it successfully transmitted the coronation of George VI. The service was closed down during the Second World War.

In the 1970s the BBC occasionally used Alexandra Palace for broadcasting works for huge forces. A typical example was the series of four programmes of works by Havergal Brian in which Brian's large-scale forces were shared with music by Richard Strauss, Berlioz and Beethoven. One of these was Brian's *Das Siegeslied*, his fourth symphony, a massive setting of Psalm 68. This started early on a Sunday evening and was announced as a free concert. For an unusual programme it was amazing how large an audience assembled, something upon which the critics remarked. It was also an occasion on which some acoustic oddities were noticed in the hall, notably a transient phenomenon sounding like a 'poof' reflected from the ceiling every time the tuba played, an effect not picked up by the microphones. Inevitably in so reverberant an acoustic, then some five seconds, such vast forces sounded thrilling from the front of the audience but very muddy from the back. It clearly was not a hall for regular concert use. In 1980 much of the building was again destroyed by fire, but nevertheless it was rebuilt once more and is now used as a venue for exhibitions and conferences, funfairs, banquets and special events.

70 The Handel choir and orchestra at a Handel Festival at Crystal Palace.

The palace is set in 196 acres of parkland and has been restored to its previous splendour. It can clearly be seen from all main-line trains running north out of King's Cross/St Pancras, where it appears on the left, high on a hill a few minutes up the line.

Fenton House
Windmill Hill, Hampstead, NW3
Tube: Hampstead

This late seventeenth-century house belongs to the National Trust. On display is the Benton Fletcher Collection of early keyboard instruments, most of which are in working order and available for harpsichordists and early music ensembles to play. A Hans Ruckers harpsichord of 1612 is reputed to have belonged to Handel, who left it to his amanuensis J. C. Smith, who then bequeathed it to George III. It is now on loan to Fenton House from the Royal Collection. A manuscript final page of a Mendelssohn *Capriccio* for piano, from 1829, is also displayed. Demonstration tours are given by the Keeper, and auditions to play the instruments can be arranged; would-be players should apply in writing one month in advance to the Keeper of Instruments. During the winter months the house is open only at weekends.

Kenwood House
Hampstead Lane, NW3
Tube: Hampstead or Highgate, then walk or take bus 210. For all concerts a free shuttle bus runs from Golders Green and East Finchley tube stations

Kenwood was built in the early seventeenth century and underwent extensive rebuilding over the eighteenth and nineteenth centuries. It was bought by Lord Iveagh of the Guinness family in the 1920s and opened to the public. In 1929 an Act was passed to safeguard the house, grounds and art collection. Open-air concerts with fireworks are held in the grounds from late June to September with the orchestra playing on the far side of the lake from the audience. Kenwood is open from 10 a.m. to 4 p.m. except for Wednesdays and Fridays, when it opens at (10.30 a.m.). Admission to the grounds is free but by ticket for concerts.

Round House
Chalk Farm Road, NW1
Tube: Chalk Farm

The Round House, a former railway engine shed dating from 1847, is striking for its industrial appearance and unique ambience. It flourished as an idiosyncratic concert hall and theatre from 1966 to 1983, first coming to attention as a venue for pioneering pop concerts in the mid 1960s, associated with the Rolling Stones, Pink Floyd and Jimi Hendrix. It was extensively used by the BBC for modern music and was favoured by Pierre Boulez for avant garde concerts, which he introduced in person. The hall was used during the Proms seasons from 1971 to 1982 for two or three concerts of such music each year. In 1981 the New London Consort were there with their Prom programme of 'Dufay and his contemporaries'. It was also used for electronic music, works by composers such as Justin Connolly (*Tetramorph*) and David Rowland (*Dreamtime*) being given there. The last Prom at the Round House was on 1 August 1982, when Peter Eötvös and the London Sinfonietta gave music by Boulez, Ligeti and Kurtág. After the building had lain empty for a decade and a half, the Roundhouse Trust was formed in 1998 to restore it to arts use.

Crystal Palace   South

Crystal Palace Parade, SE26
Train to Crystal Palace from Victoria

Originally built in Hyde Park for the Great Exhibition of 1851, the Crystal Palace was re-erected in Sydenham in 1854, and greatly enlarged. It was destroyed in a spectacular fire on the evening of 30 November 1936. (One end of the building, including the library, had already been devastated by fire on 30 December 1866. It was not rebuilt.) The site remains as a park, athletics track and TV transmission mast and a museum is located nearby.

The Crystal Palace, with its celebrated series of Saturday Concerts, provided London's principal orchestral concert series other than the Philharmonic Society's series during the second half of the nineteenth century, directed by August Manns, who was knighted for his services to music. Manns was originally employed as a bandsman, copyist and sub-conductor, and thus was at first expected to wear uniform. Subsequently reappointed, he remained Musical Director from 1855 to 1901. Manns and his concerts thus played a significant role in developing the London audience for music and in expanding the repertoire. This concert series saw the first British performances of most of the late nineteenth-century repertoire later deemed as iconic, as well as a wide range of the new British music of the day, and played a significant role in the emergence of many of the British composers considered important at the turn of the century.

The concerts began on 20 October 1855, but there was then no special room for music within Crystal Palace, nor provision for a full orchestra. The early concerts were held in various locations in the building and the direc-

71 Crystal Palace as seen from the road, postcard postmarked 11 June 1906.

Crystal Palace Parade, Upper Norwood.

tors, prompted by their secretary George Grove, must have quickly realised that they had inadvertently tapped a considerable potential public demand. The Concert Room was finally completed in 1859 within the Crystal Palace building. A similar history underlines the formation of a viable orchestra, which at first consisted of about thirty-four players, selected – with the exception of four specially engaged strings from London – entirely from the members of the Crystal Palace Company's Band (at that time a wind band of sixty-four players). With these forces, Manns notes that 'the first attempt at Symphony was made at the sixth concert, on Saturday, the 1st of December, 1855, when the two middle movements of Beethoven's Seventh Symphony were performed in the North Transept'. This attempt seems to have been successful, for Beethoven's Second, Fourth and Eighth and Mendelssohn's 'Scotch' symphonies are to be found in the programmes of the next four Saturdays, and Schumann's Fourth and Schubert's Ninth had received their Crystal Palace christening before the end of the First Series had been reached in April 1856.

The concerts became celebrated not only for their repertoire but also as a notable platform on the concert itinerary of soloists across Europe. Manns was delighted to point out that 'amongst the frequent applications for the loan of scores and parts of various unusual works which have from time to time been performed at the Crystal Palace Saturday Concerts, is one from Vienna itself – for *one of Schubert's MS Symphonies* – a strange fact, upon which all who have co-operated in the establishment and healthy development of these Concerts – i.e. the directors, executants, critics, and audience – and more particularly Sir George Grove may look with special gratification'. When Manns retired he received many letters of congratulations. That from Frederick Corder summarised his achievement as far as British composers were concerned: 'for how many years were you the sole champion and helper of the young English composers . . . with only a scanty meed of approval from the press and a half support of the fickle public'.

In 1895 there appeared a catalogue of the works played at the Crystal Palace during Manns's forty years of Saturday Concerts, showing he had given a total of 1,550 works by 300 composers of whom 104 were British. The concerts continued for another five years, but with the rise of Queen's Hall in central London, and increasing provision of orchestral concerts elsewhere in the capital, patrons were less and less willing to make the journey to Sydenham. In fact, not unlike CD manufacturers a century later, the Crystal Palace was a victim of an unprecedented glut in concert-giving.

The Crystal Palace also saw the development of the Triennial Handel Festivals from 1857 to 1926, in which enormous numbers of performers put on Handel's oratorios to vast audiences. These were started in 1857 and became triennial from 1859; they were for many years conducted by Sir Michael Costa until he was succeeded by Manns in 1883. The Handel Organ by Gray and Davison was the largest in the UK. With such enormous numbers of people present, the various sections reached a size unimaginable today; in 1859 there were 3,120 in the choir, including an amazing 810 tenors, and the orchestra totalled 501, while over four days the audience came to

81,319. A notable feature of Victorian choirs was a huge number of male altos, there being 418 in 1859, which fell to 73 in 1900. The logistics of delivering so large a gathering by train, feeding them and providing sanitary facilities when the programmes were inordinately long were a triumph of Victorian organisation. By the end of the century the numbers attending, though still large, had been in decline for a decade. The last festival was in 1926 and there survives a commercial recording of five choruses from *Messiah* made in the hall, one of the earliest electrical recordings, giving a feeling for the atmosphere and sound of the occasion (see p. 167).

The composer George Lloyd, who lived nearby, described the Crystal Palace in an interview with Lewis Foreman:

> When I was a student . . . I would pick up the bus just opposite the Crystal Palace. It was an enormous building, it was several hundred yards long . . . it was so vast you would not see any one particular [part] . . . there were palm trees . . . you were not conscious of this great dome above you. In the centre of the whole thing they had this organ, the organ had been there ever since the Crystal Palace was brought to Norwood [and] was not the organ they had in Hyde Park which was a very modest sized one . . . they had a new organ and it was the biggest organ I have ever seen, it made the Albert Hall organ sound like a baroque! It was absolutely gigantic the sound that was produced. We used to go sometimes for boxing matches . . . and between times they used to turn on their organist and you had this tremendous sound coming at you . . . They had a concert hall *inside* the whole thing – that was a big hall . . . For ordinary concerts they had them in this concert hall but they used the main body of the building, where the organ was, that was where they had their Handel Festivals. They used to have an orchestra of about seven hundred. My father [a flautist] went in for it one time [presumably at the 1926 and last Festival conducted by Sir Henry Wood] and there were seven firsts and ten seconds, there were about twenty-five flute players, and Henry Wood did everything with a megaphone.

Around 1881 a faculty of music was attached to the Crystal Palace School of Art, Science and Literature's Ladies' division. Its teachers included Manns, Prout, Stainer and Sir Frederick Bridge. Over a few years the faculty expanded to include, as well as instrumental classes, violin, cello, ensemble, composition and orchestration. It also put on its own concerts and recitals.

The Crystal Palace Society has issued a video of historical film clips shot at Crystal Palace, and although much of it concerns sports and football, it includes

---

Some first Crystal Palace performances of major works (mainly first London performances)

Berlioz: *Grande Messe des Morts* 26 May 1883

Brahms: Piano Concerto No. 1, 9 March 1872; Symphony No. 1, 31 March 1877; *Alto Rhapsody*, 9 February 1878; Symphony No. 2, 5 October 1878; Violin Concerto, 22 February 1879; Piano Concerto No. 2, 14 October 1882; Symphony No. 3, 18 October 1884; Symphony No. 4, 9 March 1889; *Variations on a Theme by Haydn*, 7 March 1874

Bruch: Violin Concerto in G, 19 February 1870

Chopin: Piano Concerto No. 1, 31 March 1866; Piano Concerto No. 2, 15 April 1871

Dvořák: Symphony No. 9, 20 October 1894

Glinka: Overture *Russlan and Ludmilla*, 4 July 1874

Grieg: Piano Concerto, 18 April 1874; *Peer Gynt* Suite No. 1, 23 February 1889

Liszt: Piano Concerto in E-flat, 27 January 1872; Piano Concerto No. 2, 21 November 1874

Saint-Saëns: Piano Concerto No. 2, 15 March 1879

Schubert: Symphony No. 9, 5 April 1856

Schumann: Piano Concerto, 5 March 1864

Tchaikovsky: Piano Concerto in B-flat minor, 11 March 1876; *Pathetique Symphony*, 27 October 1894

Wagner: *Tannhäuser* Overture, 2 May 1857; Prelude to *Lohengrin*, 16 April 1870; *Rienzi* Overture, 12 October 1872; Overture *The Flying Dutchman*, 12 October 1875; Prelude to *Tristan und Isolde*, 13 November 1886

sufficient shots of the structure to give a good feeling for the size of the building. It includes sequences from the feature film *Listen to the Band,* telling a story of a band competing in the National Brass Band Competition.

Norwood and Sydenham
Easiest to access by car; otherwise train to Sydenham or West Norwood

Before the Crystal Palace was built at Sydenham, Norwood with its elevated position south of London was within easy reach of the metropolis even before the introduction of the railways. It was a desirable and cultivated district, whose semi-rural character and connecting railway to London was later vividly recorded in the impressionist paintings of Camille Pissaro. Here lived an active community of well-off artistic people. Perhaps grandest of the dwellings was Westwood House, the home of Henry Littleton, owner of the publisher Novello.

South of the Crystal Palace site is Beulah Hill where from 1821 to 1834 lived Thomas Attwood. Attwood's house was called 'Roselawn' and was demolished in the 1960s, the site redeveloped at the end of Founders Gardens and Hermitage Gardens. Only on a fine spring day is it now possible to get anything like the country house feeling he must have enjoyed. The young Felix Mendelssohn stayed with Attwood in 1829 and 1832, writing part of his opera *Son and Stranger* (*Die Heimkehr aus der Fremde*) and completing his Capriccio in E minor.

With the rise of Crystal Palace as a major musical centre many musical figures resided nearby, none more important at the time than the conductor August Manns, who lived at 'Gleadale', Harold Road, Norwood, moving at the end of his life, in the summer of 1901, to White Lodge, on nearby Beulah Hill.

North of the Crystal Palace grounds runs Sydenham Road where at 208 for forty years lived Sir George Grove. His house does not survive, but a Lewisham Council plaque records the site. A little nearer Crystal Palace off the same road would have been the short-lived mansion of Henry Littleton, the sole proprietor of the publisher Novello and Co. since 1866. This was Westwood House which the architect John Loughborough Pearson built for Littleton in the manner of a red brick French château, complete with gables and turrets, terraces and ornamental gardens and an avenue carriage drive with ornamental lodge. Littleton purchased the site in 1874, and the building was opened with performances in the 60 feet by 30 feet music room in the summer of 1881. Here Littleton entertained Dvořák, Liszt and other celebrated musicians visiting London. But when Littleton died in May 1888, the house immediately went into decline and was sold at auction in 1899 to the National Union of Teachers Orphanage and became institutionalised. It survived to 1952 when it was finally demolished and the Sheenewood Estate built over the site, which was on the south side of Westwood Hill, near Sydenham station, leading up to Crystal Palace.

Among more humble musical households in the district was that of Havergal Brian at 10a Lunham Road, Upper Norwood, SE19, less than half a mile from the

Crystal Palace. His previous address had been 1 Jasper Road, even nearer to the Palace. Brian wrote how 'on the night of the disaster I stood only a few hundred yards from the Palace looking out of my window: and then, what seemed only a beautiful glow in autumn, burst into flames and I realised that the Palace was burning. In what seemed a few moments the centre transept crashed and in my dismay I thought that all that Manns had done was vanquished . . .'

Samuel Coleridge-Taylor lived for two years, soon after his marriage, further south of Crystal Palace at 30 Dagnall Park, South Norwood, SE25, near Selhurst station. The couple had been married at nearby Holy Trinity Church, South Norwood, on 30 December 1899, the marriage celebrated at the time he was writing *Hiawatha's Wedding Feast*, soon to become his best-known work.

Blackheath Concert Halls
Blackheath Vale, SE3
Tube: New Cross or New Cross Gate then bus 53; train to Blackheath from Victoria

A succession of makeshift halls rose and fell in Blackheath in the mid-nineteenth century until in the 1870s a roller-skating rink was built in Blackheath Grove, which doubled as a concert hall for the next twenty years. But enthusiasm for large-scale choral works and the popularity of the Royal Albert Hall and the Crystal Palace led to the launch of a fund to erect a purpose-built hall.

A group of local artists and musicians founded a new hall, conservatoire and art school that was opened on 26 October 1895; the first public performance was Gilbert and Sullivan's *HMS Pinafore*. The concert hall became the main venue for operas, plays and large-scale concerts. It was also used for lectures, meetings, discussions and dances until 1939 (with a break from 1915 to 1920, when it was requisitioned by the Royal Army Pay Corps). Musicians performing there were singers such as Clara Butt, and pianists including Myra Hess, Wilhelm Backhaus and Mark Hambourg. Composers were Coleridge-Taylor, Percy Grainger and Edward German among others. Use of the main hall for large choral and orchestral works diminished in the years after the First World War, and it was used more by amateur groups. It was closed in 1939 and offered to the Ministry of Works, remaining government property until 1976. The Blackheath Concert Hall Company was wound up in 1978 and demolition of the building proposed. To prevent this, it was purchased by the Blackheath Preservation Trust and leased to the National Centre for Orchestral Studies in 1980. A new charity – the Blackheath Halls – was created with the aim of restoring and reopening the building for public performances. After over £450,000 was raised and restoration carried out, the Concert Halls reopened in December 1985.

Since 1986 the Concert Halls have been used for concerts of all types of music, as venues for meetings, dances, films and much else, including hosting the Greenwich Festival. The halls are also increasingly popular for large-scale recording sessions. Notable examples of CDs recorded there include Hyperion's recording of Parry's short oratorio *Job* (1997) and the Chandos recording of John Veale's Violin Concerto (2001).

In 2003 the lease was acquired by Trinity College of Music for a nominal sum, making the halls part of the teaching infrastructure of the college and making them available for student concerts and rehearsals. The halls are still open for commercial bookings including concerts, recordings and wine-tasting. The Blackheath Conservatoire will remain and operate independently. The halls closed temporarily in the summer of 2004 for refurbishment.

Greenwich Palace
Old Royal Naval College, Greenwich, SE10
Dockland Light Railway to Cutty Sark, or river bus to Greenwich Pier

The Palace of Greenwich on the south side of the Thames in Greenwich Park was reputedly the favourite residence of the Tudor monarchs, and was connected by river to the Palaces of Whitehall and Hampton Court. Anne Boleyn gave birth here to the future Queen Elizabeth I and James I gave the palace to his Queen, Anne of Denmark, for whom Inigo Jones designed the Queen's House. During the Commonwealth (1650–60) the palace was run down and turned into a biscuit factory. The original building fell into disrepair and was then demolished. On the restoration of the monarchy Charles II decided on a new building. This survived through the first half of the eighteenth century to become the Royal Naval Hospital, and was eventually occupied as the Royal Naval College in 1873. In 2001 it was taken over by the newly formed University of Greenwich, and Trinity College of Music soon adopted one building.

The most notable composer to work at Greenwich Palace was Alfonso Ferrabosco (*c.* 1575–1628), who was born and lived most of his life there, and was buried at Greenwich. He was the eldest but illegitimate son of the Bolognese composer Alfonso Ferrabosco who was at the English court between 1562 and 1578. The son enjoyed wide musical influence, writing music for viols and songs for court masques, and was a prominent string player at court. Trinity College of Music is now established at the Old Royal Naval College at Greenwich

St Alfege Church
Greenwich High Road, SE10
Dockland Light Railway to Cutty Sark, or river bus to Greenwich Pier

This was Thomas Tallis's church, though the original building was destroyed in a gale in 1710. The present church by Hawksmoor was damaged in the bombing in 1941, and restored in 1953. A Tallis commemorative evensong is sung as near as possible to his anniversary on 23 November. Tallis's organ is here, now in a glass case. In 1953 a stained glass panel was placed at the west end of the south wall and shows Tallis writing. A replica of an original brass monument is at the east end of the south aisle, and was erected in 1935. Its wording is as follows:

Enterred here doth ly a worthy Wight
Who for a long Tyme in Musick bore the Bell:
His Name to shew was Thomas Tallys hyght.
In honest vertuous Lyff he dyd excell.
He serv'd long Tyme in Chappell with grete prayse.
Fower Sovereygnes Reygnes (a Thing not often seen)
I mean King Henry and Prynce Edward's Dayes.
Quene Mary, and Elizabeth our Quene.
He maryed was, though Children he had none,
And lyv'd in Love full thre and thirty Yeres.
Wyth loyal Spouse, whos Name yclyipt was Jone.
Who here entomb'd him Company now bears.
As he dyd lyve, so also did he dy.
In myld and quyet Sort (O! happy Man)
To God ful oft for Mercy did he cry.
Wherefore he lyves, let Death do what he can.

72   The Tallis Window at St Alfege, Greenwich.

Horniman Museum
London Road, Forest Hill, SE23
Train to Forest Hill from Charing Cross or London Bridge

Celebrated for its varied collections, the Horniman includes one of western musical instruments, in particular the Dolmetsch Collection. A new musical instrument library opened in autumn 2002, purpose-built for the collection, which consists of instruments from many different cultures. In the newly constructed gallery an enormous glass wall case presents a remarkable survey, in families of almost every instrument. There is a concertina display – an instrument created and made in London. Another is on the science of musical instrument making – drums, stringed instruments and wind. The archives include Adam Carse's papers and Neil Wayne's concertina archive.

In 2004 the museum acquired the historic archives and instrument collection of Boosey and Hawkes. Founded by David James Blaikley in the late nineteenth century, it includes over three hundred historic musical instruments, mostly brass and woodwind, including those made by Boosey and Hawkes and their subsidiaries and predecessors. It also features many instruments by other makers that illustrate important English and continental developments in design and manufacture. The paper archives include a century of production records from Distin, Boosey and Co. and Boosey and Hawkes, Rudall Carte and Besson and Co. All materials are currently housed at the Museum's Study Collection Centre in Greenwich, accessible by appointment. The archives will ultimately move to the Museum's library and some of the instruments will be displayed.

Eynsford, Kent
Train from Victoria to Eynsford

Eynsford was the location for the celebrated musical ménage of Peter Warlock (Philip Heseltine) and E. J. Moeran between 1925 and 1928. Their cottage is in the main street and has a plaque recording their residence. They took the lease over from Hubert Foss, founder of the Oxford University Press music department. Here Heseltine and Moeran had a succession of musical friends to stay, including Arnold Bax, who wrote his *Romantic Overture* there. Bax was also preparing the manuscript of his tone poem *In the Faery Hills* for publication, Heseltine noting Bax's deletions in his own copy. Here Bax met various young musical friends for the first time, including the composers Constant Lambert and Patrick Hadley. This was an atmosphere of riotous weekends focused on the Five Bells public house, where Heseltine introduced Bax to the poem *Walsinghame*, attributed to Sir Walter Raleigh, which Bax immediately set for baritone, chorus and orchestra. He dedicated it to Heseltine who promptly responded with *Sorrow's Lullaby*, a setting of Thomas Lovell Beddoes's poem for soprano and baritone accompanied by string quartet.

73   The house shared from 1925 to 1928 by Peter Warlock and E. J. Moeran at Eynsford, Kent.

The station is at the extreme south-east end of the village. Turn right onto the main road (Station Road) and walk through the village for about half a mile. The Five Bells pub is beyond the church on the right, and diagonally opposite, next to the Baptist church, is the cottage. For the flavour of the Warlock years at Eynsford see the painter Nina Hamnett's autobiography *Is She a Lady?*

East/East End

People's Palace
Mile End Road, Stepney, E1
Tube: Mile End

The People's Palace was effectively intended as a recreation and education centre for the poor of East London. Among those whose initiative founded it was the father of sometime MP John Profumo. The foundation stone was laid by Queen Alexandra when Princess of Wales. It was opened by Queen Victoria in 1887. Burnt down in 1931, it was rebuilt, opening in December that year. During the Second World War it was used by the BBC, and in the 1940s was a notable concert hall, the location of many BBC broadcast symphony concerts, its use necessary because of the destruction of the Queen's Hall in 1941. It is now part of Queen Mary College, University of London.

Theatre Royal, Stratford East
Gerry Raffles Square, Stratford, E15
Tube: Stratford

The Theatre Royal, Stratford East was built in 1884, opening on 17 December with Bulwer Lytton's *Richelieu*. In 1953, a dilapidated palace of varieties in bad repair, it was rented by Joan Littlewood and Gerry Raffles, and taken over by Joan Littlewood's company Theatre Workshop. They restored its fortunes with pioneering plays, some of which transferred to London's West End. Two renowned hit musical shows were Lionel Bart's *Fings Ain't What They Used to Be* (1959), and Joan Littlewood's last production, *Oh! What a Lovely War* (1963). The Angel Lane area, the location of the theatre, has been redeveloped since then, the redevelopment incorporating the theatre.

Whitechapel Bell Foundry
34 Whitechapel Road, E1
Tube: Aldgate East or Whitechapel

The Whitechapel Bell Foundry has been claimed to be the oldest manufacturing company in Britain, founded in 1570. The present building dates from 1670 and was originally a coaching inn. The company manufactures bells and their fittings. After so long a history the foundry has cast some of the world's most celebrated bells, including the original Liberty Bell, Big Ben and the present bells of St Mary le Bow and Clement Danes and Washington Cathedral in Washington, D.C. The foundry also casts handbells, and the twentieth-century tradition of handbell ringing in the USA was founded on Whitechapel handbells. The foundry has a museum and gift shop and runs tours, though these need to be pre-booked (this can be done via email: tours@whitechapelbellfoundry.co.uk).

Lyric Theatre, Hammersmith   West
King Street, W6
Tube: Hammersmith

Designed by the celebrated Victorian theatre architect Frank Matcham, the Lyric opened in 1895. Typical of its date, it was an elaborate gilded edifice, but small, with only five hundred seats, and by 1918 the theatre had fallen on hard times when it was purchased by Nigel Playfair. In that year Playfair was persuaded to produce a one-act play for a charity matinée, and, as told by Martin Lee-Browne:

> Needing some scenery, he was told that he might find it in an old blood-and-thunder theatre at Hammersmith; when he went there he discovered that not only was it semi-derelict inside but that it was in serious financial difficulties and for sale. Literally on an impulse, he made an offer which was accepted, and within a fortnight he and a temporary backer became the building's new owners. He

then persuaded [the novelist Arnold] Bennett and an accountant called Alistair Taylor to join him; Bennett found enough people to form a syndicate to finance the venture, with the three of them as its Directors – and they ran the theatre extremely successfully (at least in artistic terms) until Playfair's death in 1934. Playfair became a great authority on the eighteenth-century English theatre, and developed into one of the most interesting producers of his day.

The Lyric Theatre, Hammersmith became celebrated as the home in the 1920s of *The Beggar's Opera*, with the music newly arranged by Frederic Austin. John Gay's (1695–1732) ballad opera with music written and arranged by Dr J. C. Pepusch had first been seen in 1728 and had enjoyed innumerable revivals in the eighteenth and early nineteenth centuries (and of course in our own day with versions by Bliss and Britten). With designs by Claud Lovat Fraser (who died in 1921) it ran from 6 June 1920 until 23 December 1923, a record-breaking 1,463 performances. Later Austin and Playfair produced Gay's sequel, *Polly*, with the text largely reconstructed by Clifford Bax; but although it ran for twelve weeks it was not a success on the scale of its predecessor.

While *The Beggar's Opera* ran, occasionally other events would take place on a Sunday, notably Arthur Bliss's series of chamber orchestral concerts, mainly of modern music, on Sunday evenings. These included the first professional production of Gustav Holst's chamber opera *Savitri* on 23 June 1921.

The Music Director of the Lyric for nine years from 1923 was Alfred Reynolds, who arranged or wrote various scores for the theatre. These included eighteenth-century scores such as Linley's *The Duenna* (1924), Dibdin's *Lionel and Clarissa* (1925) and Arne's *Love in a Village* (1928). Reynolds not only arranged eighteenth-century scores but also inserted original songs by himself whenever he felt the need. Later there was a revue, *Riverside Nights*, the one-acter *The Fountain of Youth* (1931) and a full-length light opera, *Derby Day*, with words by A. P. Herbert in 1932. The influence of Herbert, one of the best-known British writers of his day, was considerable, and in 1931 Playfair had produced Thomas Dunhill's light operatic setting of his *Tantivy Towers*. This charmingly lyrical confection was so successful it transferred to London's West End, where it ran for some six months in 1931, confirmed for a later audience by Chris de Souza's 1982 production for the John Lewis Partnership Opera Company. In satirising the then contemporary arty Chelsea circles with the country hunting set, he presents a Wodehousian love-match between art and county. The finale to act II, based on the tune 'D'ye ken John Peel', is brilliantly amusing, when it might, in less skilful hands, have been just embarrassing.

Playfair died in 1934. Later musical highlights at the Lyric included a 1951 Britten season by the English Opera Group and productions by Robert LePage and the ENO Company. It was also the home of revue in the 1940s and '50s, but was closed down in 1966 with overwhelming financial problems and, like so many other fine London buildings in the '50s and '60s, an age of unprecedented architectural vandalism, was earmarked for demolition. However, with public support the original

74   Claude Lovat Fraser's postcard advertising *The Beggar's Opera* at the Lyric Theatre, Hammersmith.

plasterwork was moved to a new theatre in a modern building in King Street and the theatre reopened in 1979. It nearly closed again in 1994 but was rescued and survives on a varied programme of innovative productions, including opera.

Barnes
Train to Barnes from Waterloo; or bus from Hammersmith Broadway

Barnes is associated with composers Holst, Howells and Bliss. Composer Gustav Holst lived at 10 The Terrace (Terrace Gardens), from 1908 to 1913, and the house has a plaque placed there by the Barnes Music Club at the time of their mounting local performances of two of Holst's operas in 1963. The plaque was unveiled by Herbert Howells. Holst moved to 10 Luxemburg Gardens, Brook Green, Hammersmith, near to St Paul's Girls' School, where he taught. Both the birthplace and childhood home of Sir Arthur Bliss – Hawthornden, Queen's Ride, Barnes Common – and the home of Herbert Howells – Redmarley, Station Road, Barnes Common – were destroyed in a bombing raid in September 1940.

The Musical Museum
368 High Street, Brentford
Tube: Gunnersbury; or buses 65, 237 or 267 from South Ealing

This museum in a disused church is primarily focused on player and automatic pianos, organs and miniature and cinema pianos, and musical boxes. It includes the last surviving self-playing Wurlitzer cinema organ. Non-keyboard instruments include a Phonoliszt Violina, a mechanical violin playing three instruments at once, and a Mills Violino-Virtuoso, which combines automatic violin and piano. Supporting the pianolas and player pianos is an extensive collection of piano rolls. In the summer of 2003 the museum was closed for development, scheduled to reopen in a new building nearby in 2005.

Eton College
Train to Windsor and Eton Riverside from Waterloo, then on foot across the bridge over the River Thames from Windsor

Eton College and College Chapel date from the fifteenth century, and important musical archives include the Eton Choirbook, the unique source of some of the most impressive early Tudor composers of church music. This is music to be heard in a big space, including that of John Browne, Richard Davy and William Cornysh. Music preserved in the Eton Choirbook, though intended for use at Eton, can be linked with the Chapel Royal. This music has been conspicuously recorded by Harry Christophers and The Sixteen. Seeing the vaulted ceiling of the chapel and hearing the choir singing there one begins to understand how music such as

Browne's *Stabat Mater* gives a glorious musical parallel to the Perpendicular in English cathedral architecture. Recorded by the Sixteen, Richard Davy's *O Domine caeli*, is a wide-spanning and intricate work lasting around fifteen minutes that fully embodies location and source. Here the composer seems to contrast the resonant vibrant sound of the *tutti* acclamations with the soaring flights in the solos.

Across the road is School Hall, the concert hall opened in 1891 with the first performance of Parry's tuneful fifteen-minute choral work *Eton*, setting words by Swinburne evocative of both Eton and the nearby River Thames in a section 'Still the reaches of the river'. This hall was refurbished in 2001 and is still used for concerts by local choral societies. For many years it was the regular location of the Broadheath Singers' annual concerts at which Robert Tucker revived forgotten choral repertoire by early twentieth-century British composers.

Eton has produced more than its fair share of significant names in the musical world. A variety of composers have been educated at Eton College, from Walter Lambe in the fifteenth century and Thomas Arne in the eighteenth. Among others, we might note Joah Bates, associate of Handel and conductor of the Handel Festival in 1784 in which the nineteenth-century tradition of Handel played by vast assemblies of performers was born. During the mid-nineteenth century appeared Sir Hubert Parry, and in the twentieth George Butterworth, killed in the First World War; Philip Heseltine, known to all music lovers as 'Peter Warlock'; and Lord Berners (Gerald Tyrrwhit), eccentric, composer and diplomat. (Liking to keep a first-class compartment to himself when travelling by train, Berners would don a masquerade mask and lean out of the train window beckoning to travellers who might have been inclined to join him, effectively causing them to change their minds.) Other twentieth-century musical old Etonians include John Christie, of Glyndebourne fame; E. J. Dent, Cambridge academic and champion of both Mozart and modern music; Donald Francis Tovey, pianist, composer and professor of music at Edinburgh; composers Thomas F. Dunhill and Roger Quilter; and jazz trumpeter and well-known radio personality Humphrey Lyttelton.

Kneller Hall: The Royal Military School of Music
Kneller Road
Tube to Hounslow or train to Twickenham from Waterloo

75   The Museum of instruments at Kneller Hall.

Situated adjacent to the famous Twickenham Rugby Ground, Kneller Hall is the headquarters of the Corps of Army Music, founded in 1994. It is only open to the general public on 'Open House' weekends held in late September each year and for summer open-air concerts in the bandstand known locally as 'The Rock'. It is a Grade II listed building and was designed by Wren for the portrait painter Sir Godfrey Kneller. Since 1857 it has been the home of the British Army's School of Music and contains a bandstand, practice rooms, chapel and museum. The museum, notable for its rich collection of old instruments, also has photographs of past directors, posters and sheet music.

Windsor, Berkshire
Train to Windsor and Eton Riverside from Waterloo

Musical interest in Windsor is focused on the castle, which dominates the town. St George's chapel was founded by Edward III in 1348 and the present building dates from 1475. The first master of the choristers was appointed in the 1360s. In view of its long history, and the standing of the holder, the post of organist and master of the choristers has had notable incumbents, some of them holding the post for many years. Holding the post astride the Tudor period, John Merbecke, organist from 1531 to 1585, possibly saw some of the most turbulent religious years in British history. During the reign of Mary he was found with a copy of John Calvin's works, and he and three others, including members of his choir, were condemned to burn at the stake. Although he was reprieved, his associates were not so lucky. Merbecke's Tudor house can still be found in The Cloisters, the courtyard beyond the north wall of the chapel. Memorials for subsequent holders of the post, Nathaniel Giles and William Child, are also in the chapel. Child's gravestone, now very worn, is inscribed: 'Here lyes the body of Will. Child, Dr of Musick, one of the organists of the Chapple at Whitehall and of His Majesty's Free Chappel at Windsor 65 years. He was born in Bristol and dyed here the 23rd of March 1697 in the 91st year of his age. He paved the body of the Quire.'

There are other musical memorials, but possibly the next well-known name is that of Sir George Elvey, who became organist of St George's Chapel in 1835 when only nineteen, beating S. S. Wesley to the appointment. Elvey had previously won the Gresham Prize with an anthem (*Bow downe thine ear*) when Wesley's *The Wilderness* arrived too late to be considered. Elvey, like many other incumbents of his post, was long-serving, remaining for forty-seven years. As well as a celebrated writer of hymn tunes he improved the organ, the choir and its repertoire. He is buried outside to the west of the Chapel, and in the Rutland Chapel there is a window and a brass memorial. After Elvey came Sir Walter Parratt, who retained the post from 1882 to 1924, combining it with his professorship of the organ at the Royal College of Music; he thus taught many of the big names of the British organ world for the next fifty years.

After Parratt there were three short-lived appointments, first E. H. Fellowes, well-known for his work editing and publishing Tudor church music. He was followed by Sir Henry Walford Davies, appointed in 1927. Pupil of Parratt, Walford Davies shared his master's enthusiasm for the organ builder Frederick Rothwell, whom he commissioned to divide the organ case, by which change he made visible the internal panorama and the wonderful fan-vaulting. Walford Davies resigned the post after only five years when he was offered a series of radio talks by the BBC which became hugely popular. Davies's successor was Charles Hylton Stewart, who is forgotten today as he died soon after taking up the appointment. The tradition of retaining the post for an extensive period was renewed by Sir William Harris, composer and organist, who remained in it for twenty-eight years and was succeeded in 1961 by Sidney Campbell. In 1974 the organist and choirmaster was Christopher Robinson, described by some commentators as one of the finest trainers of boys' voices but who made his long-standing reputation with his recordings with the choir of St John's College, Cambridge. The current organist is Timothy Byram-Wigfield.

The Waterloo Chamber, which is the main banqueting-room and ballroom of the castle, was the location for the many Royal command performances before Queen Victoria. Among the paintings hanging in the state apartments of Windsor Castle is Gainsborough's portrait of the oboist J. C. Fischer and in the Queen's Presence Chamber will be found a bust of Handel by Roubiliac, who also sculpted the celebrated memorial to Handel in Westminster Abbey. The Archives and Chapter Library of the chapel are within the Lower Ward, the Vicar's Hall Undercroft, while the Royal Archives are also largely at Windsor. Both contain musical material and are accessible by prior appointment.

On 20 November 1992 the north-east corner of the castle, including the St George's Hall, was seriously damaged by fire and its restoration, including the re-casting of five huge chandeliers from the surviving example, employed many traditional craftsmen.

North West

St Lawrence Whitchurch, Little Stanmore
Whitchurch Lane, Edgware
Tube: Canons Park

The church has strong musical associations with Handel as it was the parish church on the estate of James Brydges, later first Duke of Chandos and benefactor of Handel from 1717 to 1721. The original church was demolished, save for the medieval tower, and rebuilt to designs by John James in 1715. The interior was ornamented by fine artists and is full of interest – rows of box pews in light oak lead the eye to the canvases by Belluci on either side of the altar. Baroque monochrome frescoes depicting Faith, Hope and Charity, Matthew, Mark, Luke and John, and Saints Peter and Paul ornament the side walls, and the oak carvings are attributed to Grinling Gibbons. The vaulted roof of the nave is divided into eight panels showing some of Christ's miracles and was painted by Louis Laguerre. At the west end is the Duke's gallery, the ceiling of which is adorned with a copy of Raphael's *Transfiguration* and from where the occupant has an almost theatrical view of the proceedings below.

While he lived on the estate Handel wrote the *Chandos* anthems and *Te Deum*, the oratorio *Esther* and *Acis and Galatea*. Behind the altar in its original position at the east end of the church is the organ so often played by Handel when composer in residence. It was built by Gerard Smith in about 1717 with six stops only and is still in its wooden case, with carvings by Grinling Gibbons. However, it has been enlarged and improved several times (1847, 1877, 1913 and 1949). The most recent restoration has been carried out by Goetze and Gwynn, still in the same style and with pedals added and reversed black and white keys. The keyboard used by Handel is now preserved in a glass case next to the mausoleum. The organ is available for sound recording and the church with its Germanic baroque interior for film or TV use. The pictures, stained glass windows and fittings from the house were sold in 1747 and can be seen at St Michael's Church, Great Witley, Worcestershire.

Grim's Dyke
Old Redding, Harrow Weald, Harrow
Tube: Stanmore or Harrow-on-the-Hill and then by taxi; or train to
Headstone Lane from Euston and a long walk

The country mansion built by Norman Shaw in 1870–72 and owned by W. S. Gilbert as his country home from 1890 to 1911 is now a hotel. The house and grounds have been restored to their former neo-Elizabethan magnificence. Here Gilbert wrote *Utopia Ltd* and *The Grand Duke*. Gilbert drowned in the lake he had built there while trying to save a local girl, Ruby Preece, who had come to swim and got into difficulties. The house was acquired in 1937 by Middlesex County Council and the LCC and they leased it to the North Western Regional Hospital Board until 1963.

During the war it was a centre for secret operations, and Eisenhower and Churchill are reputed to have been seen there. It was later used as a film and TV location, including episodes of *The Saint* and *Jason King*, and horror films starring Vincent Price and Boris Karloff among others. In 1970 it opened as a hotel and country club and is now known as the Grim's Dyke Hotel and is a favoured location for weddings and conferences. It has developed its Gilbert and Sullivan association with special events, costumed operettas, dinners, open air performances and matinee cream teas and guided tours. The lake in which Gilbert drowned is still there, though in 2003 was very overgrown and choked with rushes.

76   Grim's Dyke, Harrow Weald, and plaque (above).

We should also note Gilbert's memorial at All Saint's Church, Harrow Weald, with bas relief by Bertram Mackenna showing Gilbert's profile flanked by marble statuettes of Justice and Comedy. Under his name and dates is a quotation from Proverbs: 'The tongue of the just is as choice silver'. His ashes were buried at St John the Evangelist, Stanmore, after his cremation at Golder's Green on 2 June 1911.

St George's, Headstone
Pinner View, Harrow
Tube: Harrow-on-the-Hill or North Harrow, both a long walk from St George's;
buses 183, 350 and H10 pass the top of Pinner View

St George's parish was formed in 1906 and a temporary building dedicated in 1907 which seated only 300. An organ fund was started that year and a performance of Stainer's *The Crucifixion* given on Good Friday 1908 with a second-hand pipe organ installed by Frederick Rothwell. The foundation stone for the new church designed by John Samuel Alder was laid on 22 October 1910. It was consecrated a year later and is in the Gothic tradition. The three-manual organ was built in 1915 at a cost of £1,500 by Rothwell, who was a friend of Henry Walford Davies. The Rothwell organ is important for his patented stop-key control system, whereby stop-keys placed above each manual replaced the conventional stop knobs on either side of the console. It was first heard at a service of dedication with a recital by Sydney Toms, organist of St James's Church Piccadilly, in September 1915. Walford Davies frequently played the organ here. It is the largest organ built as new by Rothwell, one of the few still working, and it has recently been restored and awarded a Historic Organ certificate by the British Institute of Organ Studies. The restored Rothwell organ, played by Roger Fisher, can be heard on Dutton Epoch CDLX 7108.

Delius's home in Watford during the First World War
The Dower House, Mill Lane, Watford
Tube or main line to Watford Junction, then half-hour walk or bus 500 from
Watford town centre

The composer Frederick Delius and his wife, Jelka, arrived in London from their home in France in November 1914, to all intents and purposes refugees. Delius had earlier visited London, but only occasionally, and initially they were put up by Thomas Beecham – not yet Sir Thomas – at his London home, The Cottage, at Hobart Place. But Beecham, clearly envisaging theirs would be a longer stay, looked round for accommodation for them. We do not quite know how he came to take a short lease on Grove Mill House – now The Dower House – Mill Lane, Watford, but Delius and Jelka were installed there in December 1914 probably at Beecham's expense.

Grove Mill Lane was a noted beauty spot in Watford in the early years of the century, the subject of many picture postcards. Today the lane runs off the Hempstead Road shortly before the roundabout leading to the M25 (exit 19). Once one has turned into it, in springtime at least, it bears a striking likeness to its representation nearly ninety years ago. We have a good idea of the outlook and general ambience when Delius was there, for the Mill is located on the river Gade where it divides, one stream forming the mill race. The house is surrounded by the river and at the foot of the garden where the two strands reunite it is wide enough (although much narrower) to have startling resonances of the tree-fringed bank of the Loing at Grez.

Although after they left Watford the Deliuses were not complimentary about it, Beecham's choice of a country location – even in winter – seems to have stimulated Delius's imagination, for during his six months living there Delius was working consistently and several major works were completed or progressed, while others dated during the Watford months were clearly conceived and completed at Grove Mill House. On 3 December, in Manchester, he heard May and Beatrice Harrison play the Brahms Double Concerto, and in the light of their success with it, Delius promised them a double concerto from him. Returning to Watford, the concerto was composed and thus constitutes the most significant piece of music ever written in Watford.

Owned in the 1960s by the television chef Fanny Craddock, Grove Mill House was known in the nineteenth century as an appendage to the estate of Lord

Clarendon, whose stately home The Grove was above Grove Mill Lane in what were once extensive grounds, now a luxury hotel, golf course and spa. In Delius's day the garden was probably rather neglected but Maria Earl in her book *Pot Pourri from a Surrey Garden* remembers how it appeared to her in the mid-nineteenth century as 'a beautiful wild, old-fashioned garden . . . An ever-flowing mill-stream ran all round the garden; and the hedges of China-roses, Sweetbriar, Honeysuckle, and white Hawthorne tucked their toes into the soft mud, and throve year after year.'

The Grand Union Canal runs very near by and does an L-bend to pass the house and adjacent mill. From the garden, it appears to encircle it at a higher level, and so the shape of barges and those travelling on them can be seen. Very much 'boatmen on the river' with all manner of Delian resonances of 'travellers we apassing by' (from his opera *A Village Romeo and Juliet*). Seen as shadows through mist with distantly echoing voices, they must be haunting indeed.

77   Grove Mill House (now The Dower House), Watford, where Delius spent the winter of 1914/15 and wrote the Double Concerto.

Hubert Foss's House   Rickmansworth

Nightingale Corner (now Butler House), Nightingale Road, Rickmansworth
Tube: Rickmansworth

In 1929 Muriel Wood, wife of the conductor Sir Henry Wood, wrote a note of welcome to a new neighbour: 'My dear Mrs Foss – A note seems a silly sort of way to welcome you to the neighbourhood, but I can't think of any other as your garden is sure to be full of flowers, so let me just say that we hope you will be as happy at Nightingale Corner as we have been at Appletree Farm and that we shall see you more often than one sees one's neighbours.' At this time Hubert Foss, the founder of the Oxford University Press music department, had moved to Nightingale Corner, Rickmansworth, the corner house (recently renamed Butler House) where Nightingale Road turns through 90 degrees to cross the railway, and so the garden (unfortunately being built on in 2004) backed on to the line. In fact the house had been built about 1899 and was originally called Bowlands but the Fosses changed it.

Here the Fosses entertained musical friends and contacts. Mrs Foss, the soprano Dora Stevens, invited the leading musicians of the day to Nightingale Corner. Particular visitors including the critic Edwin Evans, the conductor Leslie Heward, and composers Bax, Britten, Lambert, Moeran, Vaughan Williams and Foss's protégé the young William Walton. Dora Foss particularly remembered Walton:

> We loved Willie's visits. We spent hours listening to his playing of what ever the current composition was – *Belshazzar's Feast*, the Symphony, etc., and Hubert

78 Edwin Evans, Leslie Heward and William Walton with the singer Dora Stevens (Mrs Foss) and Hubert Foss in the garden at Nightingale Corner, Rickmansworth, c. 1931.

discussed, advised and encouraged him . . . We sat long over meals while Willie regaled us with current gossip and comments on friends and foes alike. How we laughed! He was quite anxious to further a very superficial acquaintance with Arnold Bax so we invited them both to dine with us quietly without any other guests . . . Arnold left by the last train and Willie stayed on with us for a day or two.

Victoria Hotel (now Long Island Exchange)
Opposite Rickmansworth Station, Rickmansworth

The composer Arnold Bax, after a long affair with the pianist Harriet Cohen during the First World War, left his wife and children at Beaconsfield at the beginning of March 1918. Initially he put up at The Crown at Amersham (see p. 192) and then travelled three stops down the Metropolitan line to Rickmansworth where he wrote to his brother Clifford on 6 March from the Victoria Hotel (in those days without the road between, just a walk across the grass from the station). Bax stayed for several weeks at the hotel, from where in March and April 1918 he conducted a vivid but repetitive correspondence with his lady-love, whose health was far from good. It is not known for certain if he wrote any music while he was staying there, but a cello and piano piece called *Folk-Tale*, completed on 3 April, is a likely candidate, as is at least part of the First String Quartet, which had its first performance in June 1918.

Bax was not the only musician to be based at the Victoria Hotel, for Keith Douglas, who was a resident there, ran the Promenade Concerts from there for two years during the war. The outbreak of the Second World War had been a disaster for the musical profession throughout the country, the BBC cancelling all activities for several weeks before it was realised that music would be an essential morale-builder during the war. This had included the Proms, which were halted at the beginning of September 1939, and, owing to indecision on the part of BBC management, were in trouble. As a consequence the promotion of the Proms was taken over for two years during the war (1940 and 1941) by the Royal Philharmonic Society, and in effect they were personally promoted and financially guaranteed by Douglas, who was then its chairman. We are grateful to Felix Aprahamian for discussing with us his memories of visiting Douglas at Rickmansworth on Proms business when he represented the London Philharmonic Orchestra during the war.

Chorleywood (Chorley Wood)
Appletree Farm, Dog Kennel Lane, Chorleywood
Tube to Chorleywood then walk across Chorleywood Common

Possibly the most significant champion of British music in the first three decades of the twentieth century was the conductor Sir Henry Wood. One has only to travel a mile or so up the Chorleywood Road from Rickmansworth, or one stop on the Metropolitan line, to find oneself at another once-vibrant musical centre. Here many of the leading musicians of the day visited Wood at his country home, Appletree Farm on Chorleywood Common. Wood entertained composers as varied as Janáček, Bloch, Hindemith and Kodály, as well as many British composers and performers. The latter included Bantock, Havergal Brian, Ethel Smyth, Arnold Bax and Harriet Cohen. In the barn Sir Henry indulged his hobby of carpentry and painted in oils, his painting of Chorleywood Common now hanging in the Royal Academy of Music.

His younger daughter Avril remembered that:

He had turned one of the small barns into a very well-equipped carpenter's shop and he would spend hours there, standing in his shirt sleeves and often singing loudly to himself in a rather raucous voice – sawing away at huge railway sleepers for a staircase he was making to reach an upper gallery in the big barn which he had turned into a very fine music room. He had had a parquet floor put in and he himself made a vast window to the barn and this was the scene of large parties which my parents gave throughout the summer, and to which came, I suppose, in the course of the years almost every famous musician of the day.

Dora Foss remembered how she took Walton to meet Wood. 'It was while Willie was staying with us that he first met Sir Henry Wood. We took him up to the Woods' at Appletree Farm House one Sunday and it was on that occasion that Hindemith was there too. We walked round and round the garden together'.

It is told how having an internationally famous conductor living in the district gave the Rickmansworth post office some problems as a constant succession of telegrams were delivered the three miles by messenger boys on bicycles – one of whom when interviewed in 1990 by the late Arthur Jacobs remembered Wood 'Always in a grey suit with a big floppy bow tie painting in the garden or hammer in hand repairing fences – He often gave me a sixpenny tip and sometimes apples – Lady Wood never gave a tip.' Sir Henry Wood remained at Chorleywood until the mid-1930s, only leaving as a consequence of the break-up of his second marriage.

Amersham
Tube: Amersham

Two stops up the Metropolitan line from Chorleywood is Amersham. In the early autumn of 1916 Arnold Bax was then in the heady first months of his love-affair with the pianist Harriet Cohen. Married since 1911 Bax had two young children and was living at Beaconsfield, and during the First World War he wrote the gorgeous orchestral tone poems with which he would make his reputation when three of them, *The Garden of Fand*, *November Woods* and *Tintagel*, were performed after the war. It was *November Woods* that reflected autobiographical and personal concerns in images of the stormy Buckinghamshire countryside.

Bax had fallen for Harriet in 1915 when she was nineteen and he thirty-one. By 1916 they were meeting secretly, one of their favourite rendezvous being Amersham, Bax cycling from Beaconsfield, Harriet travelling by Metropolitan line from London. It must have been on such an occasion that they met one stormy late October day in 1916, and hastening down Rectory Hill from the station they passed the church and made for The Crown, as Bax described in 'Amersham', a poem written by him at the time:

79   Inside the barn at Appletree Farm, Chorleywood. Painting by Sir Henry Wood.

> Then in the drowsy town the inn of dreams
> Shut out awhile October's sky of dread;
> Drugged in the wood-reek, under the black beams,
> Nestled against my arm her little head

Bax's orchestral tone poem *November Woods* is important for its unspoken autobiographical programme. Here the composer's indecision between domestic responsibilities and romantic passion were sublimated in music that evoked the conflict in terms of stormy nature. The exact location of the real November Woods – if they are not just a figment of Bax's imagination – is unknown, and it could be any patch of woodland between Amersham and Beaconsfield. Having driven back and forth along the route, trying to take account of the changing landscape of trees, however, it seems likely it is the wood below the station and Dr Challenors Boys School on Rectory Hill and Station Road, on the way down to Amersham old town from the station.

Part II

Composers and Musicians in London

London has long been a demanding and active musical centre. At first the musical vitality, at least in so far as it has come down to us, revolved around the court and the church. We might consider the development of the modern period of musical life to have started with the return of Charles II in 1660, and since the earliest years of the eighteenth century London has been a voracious musical market where a wide variety of continental musicians have found a ready audience, some as visiting virtuosi and others settling here for many years and building up a long-lasting market for their skills. A variety of composers and other leading musicians, visitors as well as British, are surveyed here in alphabetical order.

Isaac Albéniz (1860–1909)

From 1889 to 1894 the Spanish composer Albéniz primarily worked and lived in London. Having established himself, his wife and family arrived in the summer of 1891 and they lived at 16 Michael's Grove (now 16 Egerton Terrace) off the Brompton Road, where they remained until 1894. For some of this time the Spanish violinist Enrique Arbós lived at the same address.

Albéniz first performed at a piano recital at Prince's Hall, 191 Piccadilly on 13 June 1889. (The building, which dates from 1881–3, still survives and is easily recognised from its superscription 'Royal Institute of Painters in Watercolours'.) During the summer of 1889 he played on several occasions, at 19 Harley Street, for the Royal Amateur Orchestral Society, at the short-lived Lyric Club in Coventry Street, at the Crystal Palace, and on 22 August he deputised for the celebrated Ukrainian pianist Vladimir de Pachmann in a Promenade concert at Her Majesty's Theatre. He was so successful he appeared again at Her Majesty's on 2 September. In December he played piano transcriptions from *The Ring* at a Conversazione of the Wagner Society held at the Prince's Hall.

Between January and June 1891 Albéniz had ten concerts at St James's Hall, in one of which he accompanied Arbós in a violin and piano transcription of the Mendelssohn concerto. The critic Herman Klein was a close friend of Albéniz and remembered him as a 'charming Chopin-player', and highlighted his 'warm, lovable nature, his frank, gracious manners and sunny disposition'.

80 (facing page)   The Grosvenor Gallery, 17 April 1886. The reception of the 'Abbé' Liszt by the British musical hierarchy. Liszt shakes hands with Joachim as the composer William Shakespeare looks on. Also depicted are Sullivan, Manns, Chappell, Sir Frederick Leighton and Antoinette Stirling. In the background Walter Bache, who arranged the visit.

In London Albéniz came into the orbit of Henry Lowenfeld, financier and theatrical entrepreneur, and the wealthy banker Francis Money-Coutts. In exchange for a regular salary and his house Albéniz assigned all rights in his music for ten years to Lowenfeld, and he undertook to set Money-Coutts's lyrics and libretti, a process that resulted in the operas *Henry Clifford*, *Pepita Jiménez* and *Merlin*. He would have visited Money-Coutts, with whom a friendly relationship developed, at his London flat at 26 Walsingham House in Piccadilly, the site later redeveloped as the Ritz Hotel.

In 1890 Albéniz performed twice at St James's Hall, in programmes in which he tried to promote contemporary Spanish music and where, on 21 November, he introduced his own 'light and delicate' *Concerto Fantastique*. On 8 June 1890 he also played at the Steinway Hall.

For the latter part of Albeniz's time in London he wrote popular theatre music, under his agreement with Lowenfeld. His first score was a substantial new finale for an English version of Lecocq's comic opera *Le Coeur et la Main*, now called *Incognita*. This ran for 101 performances in the late autumn of 1892 at the new Lyric Theatre. This was almost immediately followed at the Lyric by Albéniz's own comic opera *The Magic Opal* (dedicated to Henry Lowenfeld's wife), which ran for two months and soon reappeared in an amended version at the Prince of Wales's Theatre with Albéniz conducting for a further six weeks.

Albéniz's final work for the London stage, also at the Prince of Wales, consisted of eight new numbers for the English version of Millöcker's operetta *Der Arme Jonathan* (*Poor Jonathan*) which was a flop and closed after only two weeks.

Albéniz, probably under pressure from his French wife, left London for Paris in the summer of 1894, but still visited London, for Herman Klein writes of an 'interesting lunch' in 1895 at which Money-Coutts entertained Albéniz and others.

Thomas Arne (1710–1778)

Thomas Arne was the paramount London composer of music for the theatre for several decades in the mid-eighteenth century, with stage masques and incidental music. *Comus*, *Alfred* and *The Judgement of Paris* were all celebrated extended scores, *Alfred* being the music in which 'Rule Britannia' first appeared. He was also one of the leading composers of opera, and the pastoral comedy *Thomas and Sally* (which is reputed to have been the first use of the clarinet in an opera in England) was seen at Covent Garden in 1761, while the three-act opera *Artaxerxes*, first staged at Covent Garden in 1762 has received a modern recording. He was a founder-member of the Royal Society of Musicians in 1738. Arne was house composer at the Theatre Royal, Drury Lane for several years and also composed songs for Vauxhall Gardens in the 1730s and '40s. A plaque records his residence in King Street, near Covent Garden. He died at his home in Bow Street and is buried at St Paul's, Covent Garden. (See p. 114.)

Thomas Attwood (1765–1838)

Organist and composer, Attwood started as a chorister at the Chapel Royal, where he was later organist from 1836 to 1838. For several years in the 1780s he lived in Naples and Vienna, ostensibly studying music, and he was a pupil of Mozart – his corrected exercises with Mozart survive. In 1787 he was appointed assistant organist at St George the Martyr, Queen Square, and in 1796 he became an organist at St Paul's cathedral. The same year he was appointed composer to the Chapel Royal. In the 1790s he developed a role as music teacher to royalty. He wrote a quantity of church music, glees and songs, and was a founder member of the Philharmonic Society in 1813.

From 1821–34 he lived at a house on Beulah Hill, Norwood called 'Roselawn', then a pleasingly semi-rural elevated position and before the coming of the railway enjoying the advantages of the country with the proximity to London. The site is now occupied by much more recently built houses, and the area has lost much of its exclusivity. Attwood became friendly with Mendelssohn, who stayed with him in 1829 and 1834. During the first of these visits, while he was convalescing from a fall from a carriage, Mendelssohn wrote appreciatively: 'This is Norwood . . . famous for its good air'. He later dedicated *Three Preludes and Fugues for the Organ* (Op. 37) to Attwood. Attwood conducted the world premiere of *Fingal's Cave* in 1832, and admired Mendelssohn's virtuosic performances at the St Paul's organ. Attwood wrote some three dozen scores, largely for the London stage between 1792 and 1825, in some of which he incorporates music by his teacher, Mozart. These include entertainments, musical farces and pantomimes, Attwood's contributions being songs, many of which were published. His church music is probably now better remembered and includes *I was glad*, written for the coronation of King George IV, but later superseded by Parry's setting, and *O Lord, Grant the King a Long Life*, a coronation anthem for William IV. His more extended church music includes a variety of treble solos reflecting his lyrical gift. He later lived and died at 17 Cheyne Walk, Chelsea and is buried beneath the organ in St Paul's cathedral.

Johann Christian Bach (1735–1782)

The youngest son of J. S. Bach, J. C. Bach was born in Leipzig in 1735 and has become known as 'the London Bach' as a result of his residence in London for the last twenty years of his life. He was established in London by the great success of his opera *Orione* in 1762, and found the burgeoning music publishing trade an active source both of income and reputation. In 1764 he shared lodgings with Carl Friedrich Abel and they established their subscription concerts, variously at Spring Gardens, Carlisle House in Soho Square in 1765 and again in 1774, and from 1768–74 at Almack's Assembly Rooms in King Street. J. C. Bach was London agent for Zumpe's newly invented square piano and wrote various keyboard concertos that may have been intended for it, notably the Op. 7 set in 1770. In 1775 the Bach–Abel concerts took place at the Hanover Square Rooms. The Rooms were built by

Giovanni Andrea Gallini, and Bach and Abel had a financial stake at the inception. The concerts continued under their joint management until 1781 but did not make money. Bach lived in London from 1762 to 1772, with lodgings in Soho, Mayfair, Richmond and Paddington, and in the next decade made trips to Mannheim and Paris. He was appointed music master to the Queen. He also composed several operatic works for the King's Theatre and songs for Vauxhall Gardens. He died in London on 1 January 1782 and is buried in St Pancras churchyard. An unattributed portrait, said to have come from the collection of Bernard MacGeorge of Glasgow, hangs in the Principal's office at Trinity College of Music at Greenwich.

Michael Balfe (1808–1870)

81   Statue of Balfe by Leo A. Malempré in the inner lobby of the Theatre Royal, Drury Lane. It was first exhibited at the Royal Academy in 1874.

Balfe was a towering figure on the mid-nineteenth-century London stage, and his opera *The Bohemian Girl* was probably the most popular English opera of the second half of the nineteenth century. The songs and arias from it were widely performed in all manner of arrangements. Born in Dublin, he was both opera singer and composer, and first visited London in 1823, leaving in 1825. He returned in 1833, and later was a producer at Drury Lane (his statue by Leo A. Malempré, now stands in the inner foyer). He sang in opera there and at the Lyceum and also had operas performed at the Italian Opera at the Lyceum 1857–8 and at Her Majesty's. Balfe's operas first seen in London include: *The Siege of Rochelle* (Drury Lane, 1835), *The Maid of Artois* (Drury Lane, 1836), *Catherine Grey* (Drury Lane, 1837), *Joan of Arc* (1837), *Diadeste, or The Veiled Lady* (1838), *Falstaff* (1838), *Keolanthe, or The Unearthly Bride* (1841), *The Bohemian Girl* (1843), *The Daughter of St Mark* (1844), *The Enchantress* (1845), *The Bondman* (1846), *The Devil's In It* (1847), *The Maid of Honour* (1847), *The Sicilian Bride* (1852), *The Rose of Castile* (1857), *Satanella, or The Power of Love* (1858) and *Bianca, or The Bravo's Bride* (1860).

In 1846 Balfe was appointed conductor of the London Italian Opera at Her Majesty's Theatre. Wilhelm Ganz remembers Balfe vividly in his autobiography: 'Balfe composed a new opera every season for the Pyne and Harrison English Opera Season at the Lyceum or Covent Garden Theatres . . . I believe he got a thousand pounds each from Messrs Boosey & Co., but he generally spent his money pretty freely . . . and he was about the only operatic composer I ever saw riding about on horseback'. Balfe is buried at Kensal Green cemetery and (as Ganz remembered) Balfe's wife 'did everything she could to keep his memory green and had a tablet erected to him in Westminster Abbey'. Between 1861 and 1865 he lived at 12 Seymour Street, W1 (plaque).

Sir John Barbirolli (1899–1970)

The son of a poor Catholic Italian family, Giovanni Battista Barbirolli was born in rooms over a bakery in Southampton Row, Holborn (where there is now a plaque). The family moved while he was a baby to 37 Drury Lane. As a child he attended St

Clement Danes School, then in Houghton Street, and he showed musical talent from an early age. He was a student at Trinity College of Music 1910–12 as a cellist (where Brian Denington's modern portrait of Barbirolli the conductor in action hangs in the Barbirolli Room), and he transferred to the Royal Academy of Music during 1912–16, soon after it had moved to Marylebone Road. As early as 1911 he recorded *Oh Star of Eve* and *Broken Melody* for Edison Bell at 21 City Road, playing a cello nearly twice his height, a fact seized on by the record company's publicity.

In 1913 he was living at 46 Marchmont Street, near Russell Square. Barbirolli became the youngest player in the Queen's Hall Orchestra in 1916, and gave his first professional recital at the Æolian Hall the following year, on 13 June 1917, when he played Debussy's then still new Cello Sonata from memory. In 1918 Barbirolli had to enlist. Fortunately the army provided him with the opportunity to conduct when a voluntary

82   Sir John Barbirolli, painting by Brian Denington hanging in the Barbirolli Room at Trinity College of Music.

orchestra was formed. On being demobilised he embarked on a freelance musical career and played the cello in the orchestra at the first performance of Elgar's Cello Concerto in October 1919. On 21 January 1921 he appeared as soloist with the Bournemouth Municipal Orchestra at a very early performance of Elgar's master-piece. Barbirolli gradually emerged as a conductor and on 14 December 1925 he appeared at Wigmore Hall in a special concert intended to promote the music of Bernard van Dieren, Barbirolli's task being to conduct a scene from van Dieren's comic opera *The Tailor,* which resulted in some very favourable notices and an invi-tation from Frederic Austin to conduct for the British National Opera Company on tour. Soon he was beginning to be booked for recordings. On 12 December 1927, Beecham was unable to appear at Queen's Hall and Barbirolli deputised and scored a triumph. Thirty-five years later Colin Davis would come to prominence in a sim-ilar way. Barbirolli went to New York to become conductor of the New York Philharmonic-Symphony in succession to Toscanini in 1936 – a sensation in the UK at the time for a conductor whose career was barely ten years old.

Barbirolli's first marriage in 1932 had proved unsuccessful and his second marriage, to Evelyn Rothwell, the oboist, took place on 5 July 1939. They held their wed-ding breakfast at Pagani's in Great Portland Street, in their King Edward VII room. Lady Barbirolli remembers it still for its personal service, compact scale and for the drawings made by patrons on the walls. Both the restaurant and the Holborn Registry Office where they were married were destroyed in the bombing that soon followed.

Barbirolli returned to Manchester in 1943 as conductor of the Hallé Orchestra, which he found in desperate straits, and built it to international celebrity. He contrived to appear frequently in London, however, a typical occasion being when he brought Nielsen's Fourth Symphony, the *Inextinguishable*, to the Festival Hall on 27 September 1963. On that occasion people constantly came in late during the first item, a Haydn symphony, and after the first movement Barbirolli turned round, thrust his great talon of a thumb under his lapel and glowered at the audience, the new-comers scurrying to their seats like naughty children. On other occasions he was asked to present the prizes at his old school, by then St Clement Danes Holborn Estate Grammar School in Du Cane Road, Hammersmith, W6 (the building was demolished in 2004), where on the platform he struck a diminutive figure beside the burly sixth formers to whom he was handing books. He died at 45 Huntsworth Mews, NW1. He was cremated and his ashes were buried in his parents' grave at the Roman Catholic cemetery in Kensal Green. A ginko tree was planted in Tavistock Square in his memory in 2004.

Sir Joseph Barnby (1838–1896)

It is now difficult to conceive of the stature of Barnby in his day, as composer, conductor and organist. He became a student at the Royal Academy of Music in 1854 and entered for the first Mendelssohn Scholarship in 1856, but was defeated by Arthur Sullivan. He established his career as an organist, from 1863 to 1871 at St Andrew's, Wells Street, and from 1871 to 1886 at St Anne's, Wardour Street, Soho. In 1871 he was responsible for the first British church performance of the *St Matthew Passion* in Westminster Abbey. In 1875 he became director of music at Eton College (until 1892). His ubiquity may have derived from his role as musical adviser to Novello's from 1861, and Novello established Barnby's Choir, which performed oratorio concerts from 1869 to 1872 when it amalgamated with another choir and became the Royal Choral Society. Barnby also conducted daily concerts in the Royal Albert Hall, and the Novello Concerts that were established three years after the opening of the hall consisted of a concert every evening of the week during the winter season. Different categories of concert took place on different nights, including a Wagner night (conducted by Edward Dannreuther), a popular night and a classical night (conducted by Barnby). There was also a regular English night where composers such as Sullivan, Macfarren, Sterndale Bennett, W. G. Cusins and J. F. Barnett could be regularly heard. From 1870 Barnby directed concerts of the London Music Society which gave Dvořák's *Stabat Mater* in 1883 – its English premiere. In 1884 he gave the English premiere of Wagner's *Parsifal*. Among his compositions were an oratorio *Rebekah* and the well-known song 'Sweet and Low', as well as many hymns. He became principal of the Guildhall School of Music in 1892. He lived at 9 St George's Square and is buried at West Norwood Cemetery in a grave surmounted by a cross inscribed: 'Erected in affectionate remembrance by members of the Royal Choral Society of whom he was for twenty four years the conductor'.

Béla Bartók (1881–1945)

The young Bartók first came to England in 1904 at the invitation of Hans Richter, but appeared in Manchester rather than London, where Richter conducted Bartók's Straussian tone poem *Kossuth*, and Bartók himself appeared as pianist in the same concert. Bartók travelled via London and after his Manchester engagements spent six days in London at the home of Mrs Oliverson, a wealthy patron of the arts. In the following year he returned to England and while his appearance was again with the Hallé in Manchester, he visited London hoping to elicit future invitations to appear, which in fact were not accomplished.

Bartók began to be heard in London as a composer in 1914 when the pianist Franz Liebich played two minor piano pieces – the *Two Elegies* at the Æolian Hall on 11 March 1914, and on 11 May that year Henry Wood, surprisingly, considering the comparatively small size of the hall, included the *Two Portraits* for violin and orchestra in a concert there. Bartók was down to be featured in the 1914 Proms at Queen's Hall, but was at first omitted owing to his then status as an enemy alien. However, the Suite No. 1 was actually performed, on 1 September, and Henry Wood recalled that at the rehearsal the horn-player Alfred E. Brain objected on grounds of modernity. Bartók does not figure again on the London scene until after the war.

In the 1920s he was widely regarded as a musical bogeyman, culminating in the celebrated front cover article of *The Radio Times* in 1927: 'Is Bartok Mad or Are We?' by Percy Scholes. Immediately after the war Bartók had various champions among the younger British composers, such as Philip Heseltine (Peter Warlock) and Arthur Bliss; the latter, being well-off, was able to mount performances of chamber music. However, at this stage Bartók's latest works were unheard. He returned to England in 1922, arriving on 10 March, and his letters are written 'c/o Jelly d'Arányi at 18 Elm Park Gardens, SW10'. In fact he did not stay with the d'Arányis but with Duncan and Freda Wilson at 7 Sydney Place, SW7 (plaque). Wilson was a civil servant and later ended his career as Sir Duncan and HM Chief Inspector of Factories.

Bartók had appeared at various private concerts and receptions in London and had undertaken an engagement in Aberystwyth before he came to his London concert, which was at the Æolian Hall on 24 March. He had already received wide press coverage – indeed he was 'news' in a way that he seems not to have expected – and the concert received wide critical attention. Bartók and d'Arányi had already given the first performance of his First Violin Sonata in a private concert on 14 March at the official Residence of the Hungarian chargé d'affaires, 18 Hyde Park Terrace, which had, in fact, been widely reported. When it now appeared in a concert that also included Bartók playing his Suite Op. 14 and Improvisations Op. 20 as well as some earlier piano miniatures and with Grace Crawford singing four of the *Eight*

Hungarian Folksongs, the critics found considerable difficulty in coming to grips with Bartók's style. Ernest Newman, in the *Manchester Guardian*, also put his finger on what would be an ongoing problem for Bartók in selling himself to his audience:

> He is a striking example of the composer who counts for a good deal with the cognoscenti but is almost wholly unknown to the general public. After seeing him I can understand why his fame is not greater than it is. He is evidently completely lacking in that art of self-advertisement without which even the loftiest genius cannot get very far today. He is altogether too modest. His platform manners are not the sort to make an impression on any audience. He comes on and goes off almost apologetically . . . he is a capable pianist but not a virtuoso; here, again, he fails to capture the imagination of the ordinary audience.

Bartók remained in London for several days, attending concerts and musical events, including a party given by Marconi. On 30 March he gave a concert in Liverpool and, returning to London, played in a private party at the home of the Wilsons before leaving London for Paris with the d'Arányis on 3 April.

Bartók had succeeded in placing himself securely on the map as a significant modern composer, and had generated much press coverage, possibly more important then in promoting him than it would be now. Bartók would return on several occasions, and looked increasingly to the BBC for his engagements. London was then becoming regarded throughout Europe as an important centre for new music, and Bartók's appearances played a significant if intermittent role in this.

Bartók returned in May 1923, yet it was not to be a tour by a big name artist from one prestigious centre to another, but a succession of minor engagements pieced together by his friends from anywhere who would offer a fee. It thus included a variety of schools and local concerts outside London. One performance he did secure in London was at George Woodhouse's Piano School at 9 Wigmore Street, when the *Daily Telegraph* noted 'No audience ever spent an evening less full of thrills . . . he plays in a precise and yet unaffected manner'. The climax of the visit was his appearance at a concert promoted by the newly formed International Society for Contemporary Music at the instigation of E. J. Dent on 7 May when Bartók and d'Arányi played both his Violin Sonatas, the second then new. In November he returned and appeared at the Æolian Hall in a recital with Jelly d'Arányi, where they played Bartók's Second Violin Sonata and gave several private concerts in London.

Bartók did not return for several years – 1926 was the year of the General Strike, while in the first part of 1927 an arranged BBC date, his first, was cancelled when Bartók was too ill to travel. However, in October 1927 Bartók was able to accept a BBC offer of two concerts to include him playing the UK premiere of his new First Piano Concerto on 10 October. This was in an all-Bartók programme consisting of the concerto surrounded by more approachable music, the *Two Portraits*, Op. 5 and the *Dance Suite* of 1923. Bartók's first two piano concertos remained 'difficult' works for most people until the 1960s. After this performance it is not surprising that there was a lot of adverse comment about Bartók from music lovers throughout the country, to such an extent that the BBC in its weekly listings journal *The Radio Times* ran the cover article dealing with the problem in its issue for 9 December 1927.

Other performances of Bartók's music were beginning to be heard, and, for example, when the Budapest Philharmonic Orchestra played at Queen's Hall on 18 June 1928 conducted by no less a figure than the composer Dohnányi, their programme included Bartók's *Deux Images*.

When Bartók returned on 4 March 1929 the BBC (or rather Bartók's champion at the BBC, Edward Clark) decided to mount a campaign to promote him, and Bartók appeared with the violinist Zoltán Székely, who a decade later would give the premiere of Bartók's (Second) Violin Concerto. The Third String Quartet was given its first broadcast performance on 12 February 1929 by the Vienna (Kolisch) Quartet and a week later it appeared at Wigmore Hall played by the Waldbauer Quartet, who had given the public premieres of Bartók's two earlier quartets. The Hungarian Quartet gave the first broadcast performance of the new Fourth Quartet on 22 February. The *Sunday Times* articulated what was probably most of the audience's reaction at that time: 'I could enjoy only the Scherzo, with its strange fancies and its flying forms and shadows. The bulk of the remainder was, to me, little more than a series of ugly noises'.

During much of the interwar period the BBC ran a series of Contemporary Music Concerts that were broadcast from various London venues. One was the Arts Theatre Club in Great Newport Street, Soho, from where on 4 March a succession of Bartók performances was rounded out by Bartók and Székely appearing in this BBC series playing the two recently composed Violin Rhapsodies and his Piano Sonata. Only the first half of the concert was broadcast and the Sonata was left to the second half, when Bartók is reported as twice having a memory lapse. *The Observer's* critic (probably Eric Blom) did not like Bartók's piano tone but felt that Székely believed in the music, noting 'Béla Bartók laid his compositions before us with the utmost clarity and a secure rhythmical sense, but with an ugly tone; music may be as strongly accentuated as it likes, but that is no reason for forcing the piano beyond what it can give.'

In 1930 Bartók made three visits to London and during the first of these, on 7 January 1930, with the violinist Joseph Szigeti he recorded *Hungarian Folk Tunes* (1926) on two sides for Columbia. In subsequent years he was in London for BBC broadcasts of major new works. In 1932 it was *The Miraculous Mandarin*, on 8 November 1933 the Second Piano Concerto, and on 25 May 1934 the Concerto was repeated in the same concert in which Aylmer Buesst conducted the *Cantata Profana*. This was broadcast from the new Concert Hall at Broadcasting House and highlights what must have been a problem for the assessment of some of these noisier modern premieres for it was a notably small hall.

Bartók did not then return to London until January 1936 when on the 7th at Queen's Hall he again played his First Piano Concerto, which now had a better reception. The BBC made a point of programming more Bartók at this time. On 9 February 1937 he was invited to London by the English branch of the ISCM for a concert at Cowdray Hall in which he played selections from *Mikrokosmos*. Zoltán Székely was also there and joined Bartók in his First Violin Sonata and Second Violin Rhapsody. On this visit to London Bartók made his only recording at the Abbey Road Studios when for Columbia he recorded just two of the *Mikrokosmos* – 124 'Staccato' and 146 'Ostinato'.

In June 1938 Bartók was featured in the London ISCM Festival with the *Sonata for Two Pianos and Percussion* for which he and his wife Ditta played the two pianos. For this the Bartóks stayed with the wealthy Meighar-Lovetts in Cadogan Square, Chelsea. The programme at Queen's Hall on 20 June in which Bartók appeared was the usual indigestible survey common to such festivals, but is also noteworthy for the appearance of Benjamin Britten's *Variations on a Theme of Frank Bridge.* That same afternoon Bartók had appeared at Boosey and Hawkes's showroom in Upper Regent Street where at an informal concert he had played fifteen pieces from *Mikrokosmos*. While in London the Bartóks attended various concerts associated with the festival. They did not come to London again. A statue of Bartók by Imre Varga was unveiled outside South Kensington tube station in October 2004, at the junction of Onslow Square and Old Brompton Road.

Sir Arnold Bax (1883–1953)

Bax was born in Streatham at 'Heath Villa', Angles Road, since renamed as 13 Pendennis Road, SW16. There is a plaque on the house today. Later his parents moved to various local addresses before settling at Ivy Bank, a large Hampstead mansion standing in nearly four acres where Haverstock Hill becomes Rosslyn Hill. (The lower boundary of the site was at Ornan Road on the left-hand side of the main road going up the hill, and continued to Belsize Lane.) That house was demolished in 1911 and the area completely developed. For Bax it was home, and its disposition and location made it of considerable importance in his development until he married at the age of twenty-seven. Bax moved to 19 Chester Terrace, Regent's Park and his parents to 7 Cavendish Square (or 'Cav' as Arnold and his brother referred to it), then one of the largest residential buildings in that part of central London. At the end of the war Bax took rooms at 155 Fellows Road, Swiss Cottage, a road of once grand Victorian villas (demolished in 1968), where he remained until 1939. Here he sketched most of his mature output between the wars, though generally he took the short scores to Ireland and later Scotland to set them out in full score.

Bax's music between the wars is associated with the halls in central London where it was first heard, the symphonies at Queen's Hall and the chamber music at the Æolian and Wigmore halls, and with his publishers Murdoch and Murdoch at

23 Princes Street, Oxford Circus, and later at 463 Oxford Street. Murdoch's was bombed during the war and was then taken over by Chappell & Co in 1943. The Queen's Hall was destroyed in 1941 and the Æolian Hall refitted as BBC studios. Bax's world of concerts and first performances through which he had come to prominence was no more. On the outbreak of war, he went to live in Sussex and died in Ireland.

Sir Thomas Beecham (1879–1961)

Beecham, thanks to funding by his father, quickly became one of the principal forces for change in London music before the First World War, and he remained one of the most outstanding, if idiosyncratic, musical characters on the London scene between the wars, and the architect of music-making of the highest quality. Launched with the New Symphony Orchestra at the Bechstein (now Wigmore) Hall in 1906, he soon moved to Queen's Hall and as well as many popular works that he would later refer to as 'lollipops', he also programmed new music by Holbrooke, W. H. Bell, Bantock, Bax and Delius, the latter to be associated with him throughout his career. In 1910 the Beecham Opera Company at Covent Garden scandalised audiences with Strauss's *Elektra*, and also included Delius's *A Village Romeo and Juliet* and Ethel Smyth's *The Wreckers*. Moving to His Majesty's Theatre he explored Offenbach's *The Tales of Hoffmann* and gave stage productions of Mozart's *Il Seraglio*, *The Marriage of Figaro* and *Così Fan Tutte* that revolutionised the reception of Mozart among London audiences. He lived a peripatetic life, and many of his letters are written from hotels. From 1910 to 1914 he lived at 32 (now 121 Upper) Hamilton Terrace and in 1914 at The Cottage, 8a Hobart Place. From 1916 to 1919 he was at the Albany, off Piccadilly. He later lived at 31 Grove End Road, St John's Wood, NW8 (plaque) and finally moved to 21 Harley House, Marylebone.

One Beecham initiative that was not sustained, though pioneering in its day, was his wind band of fifty-two players. On 19 October 1912 the *Daily Telegraph* reported: 'Sir Thomas Beecham's new wind band will make its inaugural official appearance at the Alhambra tomorrow evening, including the heckelphone, the bass oboe, the sarrusophone, the saxophone, celesta, basset horn, and bass trumpet. It is claimed for the newly formed band that already it is "far ahead of any combination of wind instruments in this country"'. Elsewhere it was referred to as the City of London Civic Band.

He founded the Beecham Symphony Orchestra, leader Albert Sammons, and gave the first concert in 1909. He ran Covent Garden opera seasons under his own name in 1910, and became principal conductor in 1932. He founded the London Philharmonic Orchestra in 1932 and the Royal Philharmonic Orchestra in 1946. His response to failing to secure control of existing orchestras, notably at the BBC in the 1930s and at Covent Garden after the war, was to establish a new one. Many of his recordings were made at HMV's Abbey Road Studios, where he had a long-standing reputation of being late for sessions, although living across the street.

There are many humorous stories about Sir Thomas Beecham, or 'Tommy' as everyone called him behind his back. The story one would most like to emulate took place on a hot summer's day. Beecham was walking up Regent Street from Piccadilly Circus to the BBC. Finding the heat unbearable he took off his jacket, hailed a taxi, threw the jacket on the back seat of the cab, and said 'follow me, my man' and continued his walk in the sun unencumbered.

Vincenzo Bellini (1801–1835)

The Sicilian-born composer Bellini came to London only once, but he was so celebrated a name for the London productions of his operas, he deserves mention. In London he lived at 3 Old Burlington Street, W1, from April to August 1833, and was lauded in society circles though he spoke no English. He saw a performance of *La Cenerentola* at the King's Theatre and the world premiere of Mendelssohn's *Italian Symphony* conducted by the composer at the Hanover Square Rooms in May 1833. The vogue for Italian opera that dominated London operatic life for a good deal of the nineteenth century owes much to the music of Bellini, notably *La Sonnambula*, which was widely played, and as a result of its being taken up in English by the celebrated soprano Malibran, the principal arias became well-known to a large public. As well as *La Sonnambula* at Drury Lane Bellini's operatic triumphs included *Norma, Il Pirata* and *I Capuleti ed I Montecchi* at the King's Theatre. Both Patti and

Albani first appeared in England as Amina. *I Puritani* was produced in London in 1835 with a brilliant cast as a vehicle for the celebrated soprano Madame Giuliana Grisi. Bellini was only thirty-three when he died, just two years after leaving England.

Sir Julius Benedict (1804–1885)

Though born in Stuttgart, the conductor and composer Julius Benedict moved to London from Naples when he was thirty. He settled in London in 1835 and in 1836 became musical director of the Opera Buffa at the Lyceum. In 1838 he produced his opera *The Gypsy's Warning* at the Theatre Royal, Drury Lane where he became orchestral director while Balfe's most popular operas were being performed. In 1848 he conducted *Elijah* with Jenny Lind in Exeter Hall and subsequently went to the USA with her on tour as her musical director. He returned to London in 1852 and was conductor at Her Majesty's Theatre and Drury Lane. He was also made conductor of the Harmonic Union. In 1862 his opera *The Lily of Killarney* was seen at Covent Garden and was a great success, becoming known, with Balfe's *Bohemian Girl* and Wallace's *Maritana*, as 'The English Ring'. He wrote oratorios for Norwich and Birmingham and also produced orchestral works, including two piano concertos and a Symphony in G minor (1873). While his vocal music is Italianate, the symphony contains distinct reminiscences of his teacher Weber. His parties and salons in his later years were celebrated for their lavish hospitality. He lived at 2 Manchester Square, W1 (plaque) from 1845–85 and is buried at Kensal Green.

Arthur Benjamin (1893–1960)

Although he was born in Australia, and spent periods abroad, Arthur Benjamin was a familiar figure in London music for many years. He first came to London to study composition with Stanford at the Royal College of Music in 1913, and he was also a talented pianist, on 10 July 1914 giving the first performance of his friend Herbert Howells's large-scale First Piano Concerto at Queen's Hall. On the outbreak of war in August 1914 he enlisted, at first in the army, but later the air corps. He was shot down and for a time was a prisoner of war. After the war he returned to Australia but reappeared in London in 1921, as a pianist, on one occasion in 1926 giving three concertos (Mozart K. 488, Rachmaninov's Third and Beethoven's Fourth) in the same concert. Less than three weeks later he gave the premiere of Bliss's piano suite *Masks* at the 'Concert Spirituel' at the Faculty of Arts Gallery, 10 Upper John Street, Golden Square on 2 February 1926. In 1924 he won a Carnegie Award for the publication of his *Pastoral Fantasy* for string quartet.

He became a professor at the Royal College of Music in 1926, in which capacity he was later the teacher of Benjamin Britten. An examiner for the Associated Board he toured Australia, Canada and the West Indies, in the latter writing his well-known *Jamaican Rumba*, which took his name round the world. Of his two lyrical and amusing one-act comic operas, *The Devil Take Her* (1931) and *Prima Donna* (1933), the former was produced at the Royal College of Music immediately it was written, while the latter had to wait until 1949 to be heard.

Benjamin was one of the ill-fated 'winners' of the Arts Council's abortive opera competition for the Festival of Britain in 1951. The Arts Council had launched a competition that had four 'winners', but none could be guaranteed a production, especially when it was revealed only one was UK-born, Alan Bush, and he was a celebrated Communist. Benjamin's opera was his vivid and dramatic version of Dickens's *A Tale of Two Cities*, which was eventually produced at Sadler's Wells in 1957, and was also seen on BBC television and later heard in a BBC Radio Three production.

In 1935 he wrote his *Romantic Fantasy*, a double concerto for violin, viola and orchestra. This used a motif from Bax's tone poem *In the Faery Hills*, and was first played at Queen's Hall by the violinist Eda Kersey (whose premature death in July 1944 was a great shock) and the violist Bernard Shore with the London Symphony Orchestra conducted by the composer. Later Eda Kersey was noted for her premiere and early performances of Bax's Violin Concerto, first heard in 1943.

Benjamin wrote *The Storm Clouds Cantata* that appears in the Royal Albert Hall scene at the end of Hitchcock's film *The Man Who Knew Too Much* in both its 1934 version and the 1956 re-make. This was followed by two other pioneering scores for the cinema, Alexander Korda's production of *The Scarlet Pimpernel* (1934) and the first British technicolour film *Wings of the Morning* in 1937. Benjamin lived in Vancouver during the Second World War but returned to London when it ended. Between the wars he lived at 66 Carlton Hill, St John's Wood, NW8 and after the Second World War at 3 Gloucester Gate Mews, NW1.

Sir William Sterndale Bennett (1816–1875)

William Sterndale Bennett became recognised at an early age as a significant new talent in British music, both as a composer and pianist. He started playing his own piano concertos when still in his teens. Sterndale Bennett was a student at the Royal Academy of Music and became Principal from 1866 to 1875. His tragedy was that for most of his life he allowed administrative and organisational work to overshadow his composition, and so except for a burst of creativity towards the end, notably in the late Symphony in G minor, all his music was written when he was young. Stylistically much of this is the art of the 1830s, not that of the 1860s. His friendship with Mendelssohn began when he played one of his own piano concertos at an Academy concert in the Hanover Square Rooms and Mendelssohn was in the audience (1833). He later met and became friends with Robert Schumann, who hailed him a genius. He was organist at St Anne's Chapel, Wandsworth, 1834–5, and became conductor director of the Philharmonic Society 1842–8 and 1856–66. He founded the Bach Society in 1849. There is a plaque at 38 Queensborough Terrace, W2 and in the 1870s he lived at 66 St John's Wood Road, now gone, and is buried in Westminster Abbey.

Hector Berlioz (1803–1869)

Although Berlioz's music did not have an early success in London – the first London performance of the overture *Benvenuto Cellini* at the Philharmonic Society on 16 March 1841 had been postponed from the previous season on account of its difficulty and it was reported as 'a massacre' – he achieved a quite special personal rapport when he arrived in London. Berlioz came to London five times as a conductor between 1847 and 1855 and was warmly received, the *Illustrated London News* remarking (12 February 1848) 'Berlioz is universally liked and respected'.

Berlioz's London concerts were a revelation to his audience for his performance standards, for his role as conductor and for his own music. In the summer of 1848 his concerts took place at the time of revolutionary activity across Europe. Consequently many refugees were in London and thus many high-calibre musicians took part who would otherwise probably not have been present.

Berlioz first arrived in London on 4 November 1847 and remained for over eight months, staying with the conductor and impresario Jullien at 76 Harley Street. Berlioz had been contracted as Musical Director of Jullien's Grand English Opera for six years, including four concerts of his own in the first year. However Jullien's enterprises were financially insecure, and he became insolvent, Berlioz producing only two of his concerts. Berlioz eventually moved to 26 Osnaburgh Street, Regent's Park (since demolished) in May 1848 when Jullien's creditors called. Berlioz left London on 13 July. His first concert, of his own music, was given under the patronage of Prince Albert at Drury Lane, on 7 February 1848, and 'all the musical celebrities of this metropolis, amateurs as well as artists, were assembled . . . it was the first time that the works of Berlioz . . . were performed before an English public, as we do not reckon a poor attempt to give some of his overtures at Philharmonic Concerts . . . as worthy of any notice . . . Berlioz conducted the concert with the greatest energy and precision.' His second concert, at the Hanover Square Rooms, on 29 June 1848 was the particular occasion when many refugees from European revolutions took part.

Berlioz's visits to London

4 November 1847–13 July 1848
9 May 1851–28 July 1851
4 March 1852–15 June 1852
14 May 1853–9 July 1853
8 June 1855–7 July 1855

Berlioz returned during the summer of the Great Exhibition in 1851, arriving on 9 May. On this occasion he had official duties as French representative on the international jury on musical instruments at the Great Exhibition. He stayed at 27 Queen Anne Street, Cavendish Square later moving to 58 Queen Square, WC1 (plaque). He left on 28 July arriving back in Paris on 6 August.

MUSIC.

M. BERLIOZ'S GRAND CONCERT.

Under the patronage of Prince Albert, Hector Berlioz, the celebrated French composer, gave a Concert at Drury Lane Theatre, on Monday night, at which all the musical celebrities of this metropolis, amateurs as well as artists, were assembled. This gathering was of great interest, for it was the first time that the works of Berlioz, which in France, Belgium, Germany, and Russia, have been heard with so much enthusiasm, were performed before an English public, as we do not reckon a poor attempt to give some of his overtures at Philharmonic Concerts, with bigotry, ignorance, and prejudice arrayed against him, as worthy of any notice. We have experienced little satisfaction at M. Jullien's wild management of operatic matters at Drury Lane; but many offences and mistakes may be overlooked charitably, for having enabled the *dilettanti* of this country to judge for themselves in respect to Berlioz's compositions. Our opinions of his genius have been before made known. For years familiar with his works, on the continent, we have conscientiously struggled to proclaim everywhere our unbounded admiration; and when we listened to the bursts of enthusiasm which broke forth last Monday night, we never felt more gratified than at this honest exhibition of sound judgment and pure taste. It was a proof to us of the decided advance of musical knowledge in our audiences. We had, we must confess, our misgivings; for the selection was by no means judicious, considering the miscellaneous character of a theatrical audience. It would have been more expedient to have commenced with the lyrical drama of "Faust," than many movements he has introduced frankly from his symphonies. The "Romeo and Juliet Symphony," for instance, in which there is a scherzo—the "Queen Mab Movement"—than which we know nothing in Beethoven to excel in point of fancy, imagination, poetic feeling, and elegant instrumentation.

A choral and instrumental phalanx of nearly 250 performers was assembled on this interesting occasion, occupying the stage and a portion of the orchestra and pit. The first part opened with the overture to the "Carnival of Rome," a composition full of vivacity and spirit; it was applauded, but it did not take the audience so strongly as we had thought—the novel employment of the wind instruments, and fantastic phrases for the stringed ones, evidently exciting surprise. The romance "The Young Breton Herdsman," sung by Miss Miran, produced no effect; to write frankly, it was not well sung, and even if it were well executed, we doubt its merit as a melody. Then came the "Harold in Italy" Symphony. We have been so accustomed to hear the "March of Pilgrims" rapturously encored, that we were much disappointed at the frigidity of the auditory; but at the end of this first part, Berlioz had not yet captivated his hearers. His peculiarities—we will also add his eccentricities—his orchestral novelties were not sufficiently understood. There is a delicious alto movement, which runs through this symphony, which was very skilfully played by Hill; but whether the instrument he played upon was defective in tone, or that he was not quite imbued with the poetic feeling necessary for the interpretation—this alto part did not come out as we have heard it in Paris, from the late tenor player, Urhan. The alto is Harold in his wanderings; it is the under-current of his feelings, whilst the Pilgrims pour forth their prayer, and the Brigands revel in their orgies—one of the most fearful musical pictures, if we may use the term, ever presented by any musician. The singular style, the novel phraseology, the vast design, the curious admixture of the instruments—evidently exacted another hearing for a verdict.

Part the second had a wonderful influence on public judgment. We no longer trembled for the poet-musician; his triumph was complete. The wondrous dramatic power and grandeur of conception manifested in the gleanings from Berlioz's lyric drama of "Faust," electrified the house. His copiousness of ideas, his mastery over all the resources of orchestration, his fanciful imaginings, were here clearly recognised. The hilarity and joyousness of the dance of peasants, the gigantic conception of the Hungarian march, with its soul-stirring climax, brought down thunders of applause, and the march was encored. Neither Mr. Sims Reeves, Mr. Gregg, nor Mr. Weiss, seemed to be masters of their parts. The two songs of the "Flea" and the "Rat," were quite a mistake on the part of the singers. The dance of sylphs was demanded a second time; the fairy music of Weber, in "Oberon," and that of Mendelssohn in the "Midsummer Night's Dream," are gems in instrumentation; to these must be added the imaginings of Berlioz. The house rang with the cheering, and the second part terminated with the double chorus of soldiers, in six-eight time, and the students in two-four, amidst a perfect *furore*, the composer being called for by band and audience.

The scena so admirably sung by Madame Dorus Gras, from the opera of "Benvenuto Cellini," opening the third part, was chiefly a vocal exercise. The broken and plaintive cries on one side, of the souls in purgatory, whilst the orchestra is exhausted in every form of accompaniment, formed one of the most exquisite streams of lamentation we have ever heard. As in Paris, the wail for the dead appeared to penetrate the heart's core. As for the finale for the Triumphal Symphony, it is positively astounding. The recitative played on the alto trombone, by Koenig, is a most touching strain of musical eloquence; the bassoon glides in with marvellous effect; and then, as the brass instruments come in gradually, the interest becomes more intense, and finally superb combinations of harmony break on the ear, until the whole attains an overwhelming climax. The applause was vehement, and the composer again called for.

Berlioz conducted the concert with the greatest energy and precision; there were few hitches, and but one of any moment, arising from the misapprehension of the Chorus Master.

84   The *Illustrated London News* reports one of Berlioz's successes in the issue of 12 February 1848.

In 1852 he returned to conduct six concerts for the New Philharmonic Society at Exeter Hall, the first on 14 March, the second on 14 April. This was the occasion of his London performances of Beethoven's Choral Symphony that appeared at the fourth and sixth concerts on 12 May and 9 June, for the first of which Berlioz demanded six rehearsals. The violinist William Ganz remembered that 'the first concert proved a veritable triumph for him, and it was generally admitted that no such orchestral performance had ever before been heard in England. The hall was crammed, and the audience was absolutely carried away and cheered him to the echo.' If London was impressed with Berlioz, he was impressed with the standard of performance he obtained, writing 'I shall really miss my magnificent orchestra and the chorus. What beautiful women's voices! I wish you could have heard Beethoven's Choral Symphony which we gave for the second time last Wednesday. Truly, the combined forces in the huge concert room of Exeter Hall were wonderfully impressive'. He left later in June 1852 and six months after was dismissive of Paris music-making, in comparison, writing, in a letter dated 26 December 1852 'As for making music myself in Paris that's something that won't happen again. I am content with London where I have good friends and a splendid orchestra and an admirable audience . . .'

He returned to London on 14 May 1853 and again stayed at 17 Old Cavendish Street. At a concert at the Philharmonic Society in Hanover Square *Harold in Italy*, which they had done before, was played in preference to a more demanding programme that Berlioz had suggested, owing to lack of rehearsal time. This visit to London was to present his opera *Benvenuto Cellini* at Covent Garden, which he did on 25 June 1853, but the performance was targeted by rabid supporters of Italian opera who wrecked it by cat-calls and audience intervention. This soured Berlioz's favourable impression of London, and he left almost immediately.

Berlioz returned to London for the last time in the summer of 1855, when his visit coincided with that of

Wagner. In fact if Henry Wylde had not refused to release him from his contract to conduct his New Philharmonic Society, it seems probable that Berlioz would have appeared with the Philharmonic Society rather than Wagner.

Berlioz arrived on 8 June 1855 and stayed at 13 Margaret Street, Portland Place. He had a successful concert at Exeter Hall, and on 22 June he visited Crystal Palace at Sydenham and was offered the new post of conductor of the Saturday Concerts there. His refusal allowed August Manns to be appointed; Manns would remain for the rest of the nineteenth century and be one of the most significant and long-lasting influences on the history of British music and music in England. Berlioz encountered Wagner during June, Wagner reporting to Minna he had got to know Berlioz 'very well, and I am delighted to be able to say that we are now the best of friends. He is really an amiable – but very unhappy man.' Berlioz and his wife attended Wagner's concert at Exeter Hall on 25 June and they drove back to Wagner's lodgings and 'remained together over a bowl of champagne punch, until 3 o'clock in the morning'. Berlioz left London for the last time on 7 July.

85   Berlioz as depicted in the *Illustrated London News*.

Sir Arthur Bliss (1891–1975)

Arthur Bliss was born at 'Hawthornden', Queen's Ride, Barnes, London, but the family moved after his mother died to 21 Holland Park, Bayswater, where Bliss lived for twenty-seven years with his father and brothers. After Cambridge he studied at the Royal College of Music with Stanford and saw active service in the First World War when his brother Kennard was killed. Bliss later dedicated his memorial 'symphony' *Morning Heroes* 'To the memory of my brother FRANCIS KENNARD BLISS and all other comrades killed in battle.' Bliss was gassed and wounded and returning from the war repudiated his earlier music and he espoused the new in art.

In 1923 the Bliss family moved to the USA, Bliss's father settling in California. It was here Bliss met his future wife Trudy Hoffman, and after their marriage in 1925 the couple returned to London and rented a flat in Redcliffe Square, then moved in 1929 to East Heath Lodge, 1 East Heath Road, where they lived until 1939. They were caught by the outbreak of war while on holiday in the USA and stayed in Berkeley, California until Bliss was invited back by Kenneth Wright (Director of Overseas Music at the BBC) in 1941. After arriving at Liverpool he initially stayed two years with old neighbours in Hampstead until the family was reunited in 1943 and lived briefly in a flat at 22 Harcourt House, 19 Cavendish Square before moving to Somerset. He also had a London home at 15 Cottesmore Gardens, W8 from 1948 to the 1950s. He lived from 1955 for the rest of his life at 8 The Lane – a fine spacious house that architecturally had been the last word in fashion in the 1930s in St John's Wood. Because of the way it stands on its plot, the front door seems to be on the side, and indeed one enters into a long narrow passage connecting the large drawing room and stairs to the kitchen. The house is no longer owned by the Bliss family, and for a time was the home of the television personality Esther Rantzen. Bliss's memorial service was in Westminster Abbey.

John Blow (1649–1708)

The composer Blow was the teacher of Henry Purcell, both preceding and succeeding him in the role of organist at Westminster Abbey. His musical career developed with the return of King Charles II in 1660 when the demand for music in church and court suddenly increased. He started as a chorister and later became organist and gentleman of the Chapel Royal and organist at Westminster Abbey. He was almoner and Master of the Choristers at St Paul's cathedral from 1687 to 1693 and also organist from 1687 to 1703. In 1683 he played the Father Smith organ to demonstrate its abilities at the competition to choose the best organ for the Temple Church. He resigned his appointment as organist at the Abbey (which he had taken up in 1668) in favour of his pupil Purcell in 1679. When Purcell died, Blow resumed the post until his own death. His *An Ode, on the Death of Mr Henry Purcell* (*'Mark how the lark and linnet sing'*) setting Dryden's effusive memorial poem was published the year after Purcell's passing, and must have been truly affecting for Purcell's contemporaries. Its final section is a poignant account of Purcell's reception in Heaven:

> The Heav'nly Quire, who heard his Notes from high,
> Let down the State of Musick from the Sky;
> They handed him along,
> And all the way He taught, and all the way they Sung.
>
> Ye brethren of the Lyre, and tunefull Voice
> Lament his lott; but at your own rejoyce,
> Now live secure and linger out your days,
> The Gods are pleas'd alone with Purcell's Layes,
> Nor know to mend their Choice.

Although Blow's flow of new works diminished after 1700, he supplied three anthems for the coronation of Queen Anne in 1702. He is buried in the north aisle of Westminster Abbey, near Purcell. His monument in the Abbey bears the epitaph 'His own Musical Compositions (Especially his Church Musick) are a far nobler Monument to his Memory, than any can be rais'd for Him'.

Nadia Boulanger (1887–1979)

The French teacher, organist and conductor Nadia Boulanger first appeared in London in November 1936, broadcasting five short programmes of French music ancient and modern (15–20 November), including music by her sister Lili Boulanger (*Renouveau*) and two Poulenc premieres, *Bell et Ressemblante* and

Litanies à la Vierge Noire. She also appeared at the French Embassy on 20 November and on the 24th she appeared at Queen's Hall, when she conducted the London Symphony Orchestra, the augmented Oriana Madrigal Society and her own vocal group in a programme consisting of Fauré's then little-known *Requiem*, Schütz's *Resurrection* and her pupil Lennox Berkeley's *Dithyrambe and Hymn*, under the patronage of the French Ambassador.

She returned in 1937 to record (on 11, 13 and 17 February) her celebrated performances of Monteverdi madrigals with HMV and in October again had a group of short BBC broadcasts, this time featuring extracts from French operas (8, 9, 10, 12 October). On 10 November she was interviewed on television from the Hotel Splendide at 105 Piccadilly, the building much later the headquarters of the Arts Council.

The format was followed again in November 1938 when the composers featured included Vivaldi, Carissimi and Monteverdi as well as her pupils. An invited audience for the latter concert included Lennox Berkeley, Hubert Foss, Kennedy Scott, Lord Berners and Priaulx Rainier.

Boulanger came again in 1946, appearing not only at Wigmore Hall but on the radio, and from then until 1950 the BBC keenly championed regular visits in which the format and repertoire adopted before the war was repeated and developed. In 1946 she remarked to George (later Sir George) Barnes, the first Controller of the Third Programme, that she would like to meet T. S. Eliot and thus found herself invited to dinner at the Oriental Club at 18 Hanover Square on 27 February 1947.

For these visits Boulanger at first stayed at 37 Vere Gardens, W8, and from 1948 at 27 Cumberland Terrace. In September she enquired about purchasing bagpipes and was directed to Henry Starck at 12 Kentish Town Road, NW1. She broadcast the Fauré *Requiem* in February 1947, and again on 27 February and 1 March 1949. In these programmes she enjoyed a growing relationship with the Boyd Neel Orchestra, also appearing with them at the Wigmore Hall on 27 May 1948.

In 1949 she expanded her BBC repertoire, in February appearing with Jean Françaix and the Philharmonia Orchestra in a programme of Françaix's music and Françaix's 'highly cultured, neat, warm and sensitive' playing of Mozart's Piano Concerto K. 271. There was also another performance of the Fauré *Requiem* in February 1949. Later in the year Bach and Stravinsky were coupled in programmes featuring the then little-known Brandenburg Concertos with leading British soloists of the day.

Boulanger's warm relationship with the BBC and her regular appearances suffered a hiccup in 1950 after she cancelled a booking to present a public rehearsal-lecture on Bach's Cantata 150, when the performance was switched to Birmingham, the work was announced to be sung in English and she did not get the rehearsal time she had asked for. Questions were subsequently asked as to whether existing BBC conductors might not be as effective in the repertoire she had been assigned.

Boulanger came again in 1953 and 1954, both times featuring works by Stravinsky and giving the occasional talk or interview, something she did on various occasions over the next twenty years. Later visits did not always focus on London – in 1960 it was the Bath Festival, in 1962 Wells cathedral and in 1968 the BBC Mozart Piano Competition at Cardiff. In the year of her 75th birthday, 1962, not only did she have a Festival Hall concert (with the English Chamber Orchestra) featuring Bach, Stravinsky's Violin Concerto and the Fauré *Requiem*, but she also appeared in *Monitor* on BBC television, giving a master class with RCM students.

In the minds of many British music lovers Boulanger was synonymous with the Fauré *Requiem*, and in October 1968 she returned to prerecord the work with the BBC Symphony Orchestra at the Fairfield Halls, Croydon in a programme that also included music by her sister Lili Boulanger, then almost completely unknown – performances that have resurfaced on CD on BBC Legends (BBCL 4026–2).

Sir Adrian Boult (1889–1983)

The conductor and BBC Director of Music in the 1930s was educated at Westminster School (adjacent to Westminster Abbey). Supported by a well-off family he was able to serve a long apprenticeship as a conductor, significantly attending Nikisch's rehearsals in Leipzig which remained a lifelong inspiration, and later working as a Professor at the Royal College of Music in the early 1920s. He was appointed conductor of the City of Birmingham Orchestra from October 1924 and founded the BBC Symphony Orchestra in 1930, conducting it for the next twenty years. For more than ten years he doubled as BBC Director of Music. His retirement was enforced by the BBC in 1950 as he had reached the normal age of retirement. This was handled remarkably clumsily and impersonally by a BBC that did not realise the then Director of Music, Steuart Wilson, had been the first husband of Boult's wife. Boult's sense of hurt would be long-lasting, but he became conductor of the London Philharmonic Orchestra 1950–57, and was also active at the Proms. He had been simultaneously BBC Music Director from 1930 to 1941 and chief conductor thereafter.

There was a brief barren period in the late 1950s when the conductor may well have felt his career was over, before his glorious Indian summer developed. EMI did much to build up Boult's recorded repertoire, including major recordings of Elgar, Vaughan Williams, Holst and Parry. But it was Richard Itter, the owner of the specialist label Lyrita Recorded Edition, who had him record a wide range of British music including not only Finzi, Bax and Parry but also a variety of living composers such as Malcolm Williamson, whose Organ Concerto, written in honour of Sir Adrian, and which he had previously conducted at the Proms, he recorded in 1975.

Boult liked to maintain an image of dignified urbanity to which the formidable protective duo of his wife and his secretary, Gwen Beckett, applied themselves with much energy. Nevertheless Boult had a remarkable temper – it is said he once pushed a piano off the platform while in a rage. At Lyrita's 1972 recording session of Bax orchestral tone poems at the Walthamstow Assembly Rooms, with the London Philharmonic Orchestra, Boult noticed that the timpanist was 'palming' a cigarette and having a crafty puff whenever the opportunity arose. One could see Boult getting more and more irritated, as his left hand nervously stroked his moustache, becoming faster and faster, until he suddenly shouted 'Mr X, I can't think why you persist smoking those damned things!' The player stubbed it out on the floor – 'Sorry Sir Adrian!' During these recording sessions Sir Adrian, a teetotaller, would have a glass of milk brought out for him at the break. There was no love lost on either side between Beecham and Boult, the former on one occasion remarking when Sir Adrian was expected, 'Awfully strong smell of Horlicks!'

His London flat at 41 Avenue Close, Primrose Hill, NW8 was damaged in the war in September 1940 when his library of beautifully bound full scores was destroyed. Later from 1966 to 1977, he lived at 78 Marlborough Mansions, Cannon Hill, NW6 (plaque), then at nearby 68 Compayne Gardens, NW6. During his later years he recorded widely and left a significant legacy of recordings, particularly of British music of the earlier twentieth century. Boult was very down to earth in many ways. When Nicholas Kenyon was commissioned to write his history of the BBC Symphony Orchestra, his first step was to write to Sir Adrian among others, hoping to hear back in a month or two. He tells how early the very next morning the phone rang. 'My name's Boult – you wrote to me. I hope you realise I'm very old; we better start immediately!' Kenyon was duly round at Boult's flat within twenty-four hours, and Boult survived long enough to write the foreword to the book. Boult moved to a nursing home in West Hampstead in 1982. His body was left to medical research and he has a memorial in Westminster Abbey.

William Boyce (1711–1779)

The composer was born in Maiden Lane (now Skinner's Lane, EC4). The family then lived at Joiners' Hall from 1723 to 1752 and Boyce lived at Quality Court from 1752 to 1763/4 and from 1764–79 at 79 Kensington Gore. He was a pupil of Maurice Greene, who became his mentor and friend, and was appointed organist at St Michael's, Cornhill and the Chapel Royal at St James's. He was a founder member of the Royal Society of Musicians. He is buried at St Paul's cathedral.

Frank Bridge (1879–1941)

For many years Bridge was best remembered as the teacher of Benjamin Britten, but since the foundation of the Frank Bridge Trust (now the Bridge Bequest) in the 1970s at the instigation of John Bishop, and the championship of Britten from the late 1960s, his work has been recognised as having a significant place in the British music of his times, and it is now widely played and recorded. He lived at 50 Elm

Park Mansions in Chelsea, but on marriage moved to 23 Foster Road in Chiswick and later to 4 Bedford Gardens, W8 (plaque). Generally Bridge is associated with Friston near Eastbourne where he spent the years of his maturity.

Benjamin Britten, Lord Britten (1913–1976)

Britten, the composer, is not generally associated with London, coming from Lowestoft and spending most of his life at or near Aldeburgh, Suffolk. However, particularly in his late teens and early twenties, he was part of the active 1930s London musical scene. He was a private pupil of Frank Bridge and of John Ireland at the Royal College of Music. Consequently he lived at various London addresses: 1933–5, 173 Cromwell Road; 1935–7 (plaque), Flat 2, West Cottage Road, West End Green; January–October 1937, 559 Finchley Road; and October 1937, 38 Upper Park Road, NW3, where he had a London pied-à-terre. Pears and Britten shared their first home together at 43 Nevern Square, SW5 during 1938, though Britten spent much time in Suffolk. Britten and Pears left England in April 1939 but returned in April 1942 and then lived at 104a Cheyne Walk, SW10 from 1942–3 and from 1943–6 were at 45a St John's Wood High Street, NW8. Subsequently based at Aldeburgh, from 1970 they also had a pied-à-terre address at 8 Halliford Street, N1.

Many of Britten's earliest performances, in 1932 and 1933, took place at the Mercury Theatre, where the Ballet Club found a platform for the Macnaghten–Lemare concerts. In November and December 1934 his name first appears as composer at Wigmore Hall, where his piano suite *Holiday Diary* appeared, as *New Studies*, on 30 November, and on 17 December when three movements of his Suite Op. 6 for violin and piano were played, both with Betty Humby as pianist.

Britten started work for the GPO Film Unit in the spring of 1935 and became the unit's only salaried composer, completing some twenty-seven films for them. He alternated between the company's offices at 21 Soho Square and the studios in Blackheath where the recordings were made. This 'dilapidated building at the end of Bennett Park' close to Blackheath Village survives as flats. Here he produced music for such well-known short documentaries as *Night Mail*, the whole genre given classic status by his now familiar music (with Auden's words). Britten started working on this in February 1935 and recorded the soundtrack on 15 January 1936 at Blackheath. His other similar films included *The King's Stamp* (1935), *Coal Face* (1936) and *Men of the Alps* (1936), while the last was *6d Telegram* (1939).

Britten had only three premieres at Queen's Hall. Sir Henry Wood gave the first concert performance of three of the *Soirées Musicales* during the 1937 Proms, and Wood also conducted Britten's Piano Concerto, in which the composer made his only appearance at Queen's Hall as a pianist, on 18 August 1938. Britten's farewell to Queen's Hall came when the Festival of Music for the People was held there in April 1939. Soon after the performance, of his *Ballad of Heroes,* on 5 April, Britten and Pears left London for Liverpool to sail to Canada. The one final Britten premiere at Queen's

Hall was on 6 April 1941 when Basil Cameron conducted the first UK performance of his Violin Concerto. Four nights later the hall was destroyed by the Luftwaffe.

During the thirty years of Britten's ascendancy, while the focus of much of his musical activity was Aldeburgh and the Aldeburgh Festival, he enjoyed many prestigious premieres and performances in London. Indeed the celebrity of Britten could be said to have started at Sadler's Wells theatre where *Peter Grimes* had its first performance on 7 June 1945. The Royal Festival Hall, Wigmore Hall and Covent Garden Opera House all saw many Britten first and subsequent performances, and he often appeared accompanying Pears, notably at Wigmore Hall and at BBC broadcast concerts at their Maida Vale studio. The first London performance of the *War Requiem* was at Westminster Abbey, on a night of an impenetrable fog, so bad that crossing Broad Sanctuary to the entrance necessitated literally feeling one's way. Nevertheless the Queen Mother duly arrived and the Abbey was packed.

After Britten died in 1976 there were many memorial concerts. Later, the Peter Pears Memorial Concert was given on 3 April 1987 at Friends House in the Euston Road, including the world premiere of Britten's discarded setting from the *Serenade* of 1943 – Tennyson's *Now Sleeps the Crimson Petal*.

Thomas Britton (1644–1714)

For over thirty-five years starting in 1678 the earliest concert series in London took place in the converted loft of Thomas Britton's house in Jerusalem Passage, EC1, off Aylesbury Street, though as a result of war damage, where Britton lived has been rebuilt since his day (now Britton Street, Clerkenwell, EC1). A plaque records 'here stood the house of Thomas Britton 1644–1714 the musical coalman'. Britton was buried at St James's church, Clerkenwell, itself also rebuilt in 1792. Although Britton's occupation was the humble one of a street hawker of charcoal his weekly concerts took place over his shop and were regularly patronised by the leading musicians of the day, including Pepusch and Handel. Britton died in 1714, it is said as a consequence of the shock caused by a practical joker.

Anton Bruckner (1824–1896)

Bruckner came to London as an organist. He stayed on his one visit in the summer of 1871 in Seyd's Guesthouse, which was on the site of the present City Gate House, 39–45 Finsbury Square, EC2 (plaque). He came to represent Austria in a concert to inaugurate the new organ at the Royal Albert Hall. This was the occasion of the London International Exhibition when participating countries were invited to send an organist to play on the new organ. France sent Saint-Saëns and Bruckner had been chosen after a competition. Bruckner played on 2 August and was so successful he subsequently gave five concerts at Crystal Palace, Sydenham. These were so well supported he subsequently played four more. Before the German National

Fête at Crystal Palace he played to an estimated 70,000 people. While he was in London Bruckner sketched the finale of his Second Symphony, which he started on 10 August. He left at the end of August and never returned.

Charles Burney (1726–1814)

Burney is remembered as a musical historian, celebrated for his accounts of musical tours in Europe, which were parodied at the time. He started out as a musical apprentice for seven years and lived firstly in Arne's house in 1744, then with Fulke Greville, who purchased his apprenticeship in 1748. He was organist at St Dionis, Fenchurch Street from 1748 and was also known as a harpsichordist. In the 1750s he moved to King's Lynn and returned to London in 1760. In 1773 he was organist at the Oxford Chapel (St Peter's, Vere Street). He then moved to a house that had once belonged to Isaac Newton in St Martin Street, Leicester Fields (now Square). In the 1770s and '80s he compiled his celebrated history of music in four volumes, and in 1784 he wrote an account of the Handel Commemoration that took place that year. He was organist at the Royal Hospital Chelsea, where he is buried. There is a memorial to him in Westminster Abbey.

Ferruccio Busoni (1866–1924)

The pianist-composer Busoni was born at Empoli, though brought up in Trieste, and died in Berlin. In a cosmopolitan life as one of the musical giants of his age, in the pursuit of extensive concert tours he visited London many times. In 1889 the twenty-three-year-old pianist was proposed for a visit to London by Theodore Steinway, who unfortunately died before the visit could take place. Busoni's actual first visit came in 1897, and considering he was unknown he launched himself in grand manner with a series of six recitals at St James's Hall starting on 28 October. In London he seems to have found a city that he liked from the start, and he returned twice in 1898, in June and December. In June 1899 he played the Tchaikovsky B-flat minor concerto for possibly the only time. In London in June 1900, on the 28th he attended Paderewski's performance of Cowen's *Concertstücke* in B-flat for piano and orchestra at Queen's Hall, but was dismissive about Cowen's music, which he found derivative.

Busoni appeared for the Philharmonic Society several times, first on 10 May 1900 when he played the Liszt Concerto in A. Preceding him on the programme was Elgar conducting Clara Butt in an early complete performance of *Sea Pictures*. He reappeared on 27 March 1901 with Liszt's E-flat concerto. Such was Busoni's stature in London, when the Bechstein (later Wigmore) Hall opened on 31 May 1901, it was with a recital by Ysaÿe and Busoni, and he played Beethoven's Piano Sonata in E-flat Op. 109 and ended with Brahms's *Paganini Variations*. He reappeared regularly at the Bechstein Hall during the pre-war period.

On 15 March 1905, in the first Philharmonic programme for that year, he played two concerti – Saint-Saëns's in F and Liszt's *Totentanz*. Busoni was by now a leading name to London audience and thus, when a pianist was required to play with a concert of celebrities, he was asked to appear. In June 1906 he appeared at the Royal Albert Hall in a celebration of the soprano Adelina Patti, then aged sixty-three. On the same bill was Patti's contemporary, Santley, then seventy-two, and a very mixed supporting programme. The autumn of 1908 saw him on an English provincial tour that ended in London. On 11 December 1908 at a Philharmonic Society Concert he played the Liszt Concerto in A again as well as Franck's *Prélude, Chorale and Fugue*. At this concert, between Busoni's appearances, Delius conducted (badly) the first performance of his *In a Summer Garden*.

Busoni was in London in March 1912, when on 21 March he played Liszt's *Totentanz* as well as two Liszt piano solos. This was in a curiously planned orchestral concert in which the cellist Casals also appeared and played an unaccompanied Bach cello suite. On 30 January 1913 Busoni performed Liszt's E-flat concerto at the Philharmonic Society concert at Queen's Hall. It was substituted at the rehearsal on the previous day when Frederick Stock's orchestration of Busoni's *Fantasia Contrapuntistica*, which he had never heard, turned out to require amendments and corrections that it was suggested could not be made in the orchestral parts in time.

While Busoni's music did not make a big impact in the UK during his lifetime, the public generally regarding him as a performer, many of his works were played in London, probably starting with the Second Violin Sonata played by Adolf Brodsky in February 1902 and followed by the First Violin Sonata played by Johann Kruse and Busoni's pupil Egon Petri at St James's Hall on 28 November 1903; but Busoni was present at neither. He did appear at Queen's Hall in his massive Piano Concerto with choral finale, in which Mark Hambourg was soloist with the New Symphony Orchestra and Busoni conducting on 8 June 1910. In the same programme Busoni and Hambourg appeared on two pianos in Liszt's rarely played *Concerto Pathétique*. Almost exactly two years later at Queen's Hall on 5 June 1912 Busoni conducted the first English performance of his *Berceuse Élégiaque*.

Busoni was based in Zurich from October 1915. He was back in London in September 1919 and conducted his new *Sarabande and Cortège* at Queen's Hall. While in London in 1919 he found himself in Columbia's recording studios at Petty France, where he waxed at least eight sides of Chopin, Liszt and Bach in his own arrangements. At Queen's Hall, with the London Symphony Orchestra, Busoni introduced two new works on 22 June 1920. These were the orchestral suite from his opera *Die Brautwahl* and the *Indian Fantasy*, Op. 44, in which Busoni appeared as piano soloist under the baton of Julius Harrison. In this concert he also conducted Liszt's *A Faust Symphony*.

Busoni was still appearing at Wigmore Hall and on 19 February 1921 he included his new three movement Toccata in his Wigmore recital. Presumably on the same trip soon afterwards his *Rondo Arlecchino*, Op. 46, was heard at Queen's Hall (14

March 1921) under Busoni's baton. Busoni's last visit to the UK came in 1922, when on 18 February he joined his pupil Egon Petri in playing his *Fantasia Contrapuntistica* in the version for two pianos at Wigmore Hall.

Dame Clara Butt (1873–1936)

The celebrated contralto Clara Butt made her debut in 1892 at the Royal Albert Hall, where she reappeared regularly for many years. She had won a scholarship to the Royal College of Music in 1889 and for her debut at the Royal Albert Hall on 7 December 1892 she sang the role of Ursula in Sullivan's dramatic cantata *The Golden Legend*, then an audience favourite. Elgar wrote *Sea Pictures* for her. After the premiere at Norwich in October 1899 he appeared with her at the piano in London in four of them. Soon afterwards repeated with orchestra. At six foot two Butt must have been a striking figure, and in *Sea Pictures*, aged twenty-seven, appeared in a stunning uncorsetted dress. She married the baritone Kennerly Rumford in 1900. The two promoted themselves by circulating the largest number of picture postcard photographs of any artist, including in due course herself with her children. They toured the empire with programmes of ballads and songs.

During the First World War she promoted a week of performances of Elgar's *The Dream of Gerontius* recording four extracts conducted by Sir Henry Wood, reminding us of her connection with the role of the Angel, though she was most associated by a popular audience with Elgar's *Land of Hope and Glory*. She lived at 7 Harley Road, NW3 from 1901 to 1929 (plaque), and was made DBE in 1920, probably in gratitude for her immense amount of work for war charities during 1914–18.

William Byrd (1543–1623)

Born in London to an apparently fairly well-off family, Byrd was probably a chorister in the Chapel Royal when his brothers were choristers at St Paul's. A pupil of Tallis, Byrd's first musical post seems to have been at Lincoln where he established himself as a composer. Becoming a Gentleman of the Chapel Royal in 1572 he returned to London where he shared the post of organist with Tallis. Byrd, a Catholic in a Protestant state, moved in aristocratic circles that had Catholic sympathies, a persuasion that coloured his later church music. Despite Byrd's religious beliefs he and Tallis received a licence from Queen Elizabeth for the right to print music in 1575 (and also a monopoly of lined manuscript paper), and in the first year produced a set of *Cantiones Sacrae* dedicated to the Queen.

From the late 1570s the climate for Catholics became much less tolerant, with laws compelling attendance at Church of England services, but Byrd still managed to write for Catholic services, notably Latin motets, sung domestically in patrician Catholic households. However, probably owing to his Royal patronage, Byrd seems to have successfully steered a diplomatic route through this religious minefield. While employed in London and in court circles, Byrd lived in Harlington,

Middlesex (now very near Heathrow Airport but then and until the 1940s a country village), and he moved to Essex in 1593, when he found a Catholic family at Ingatestone Hall, Essex where he could write his greatest works. The Hall, a gabled Tudor house, survives and still owns a virginal that may have been played by Byrd. He is commemorated at St Sepulchre's church, Holborn Viaduct, EC1.

Frédéric Chopin (1810–1849)

When Chopin came to London in 1848, with the sole objective of making money, he was in the last stages of his life and was far from well. He arrived in England on 20 April, and gave his first concert performance in London at 99 Eaton Place on 23 June 1848. He played at another concert on 7 July in Lord Falmouth's House in St James's Square. In May he had played before Queen Victoria at a christening, but did not make a strong impression on her. He lived first at 10 Bentinck Street, off Cavendish Square, and then in a flat at 48 Dover Street (from the end of April to summer 1848), which had room to accommodate three pianos sent to him by different manufacturers — Broadwood, Erard and Pleyel. At the end of October he was at 4 St James's Place. It bears a plaque that reads: 'From this house, in 1848, Frederic Chopin 1810–1849 went to Guildhall to give his last public performance'. Wilhelm Kuhe described the occasion in his *Musical Recollections*: '. . . an audience of 140 or 150 persons . . . His figure was attenuated to such as a degree that he looked almost transparent . . . No sooner, however, did his supple fingers begin to sweep the keyboard, than it was evident that a revelation of refined and poetic playing awaited us. His wondrous touch, the perfect finish of his execution, I can only suggest.' That was on 16 November 1848. Chopin stayed in St James's Place for only three weeks before leaving for Paris, and he died less than a year later.

Muzio Clementi (1752–1832)

The Italian-born composer and pianist Clementi lived in London for nearly sixty years and was a notable entrepreneur known not only as a keyboard player but as piano manufacturer and dealer, music publisher, impresario and composer. He was apprenticed as a musician to Peter Beckford, a minor landowner of the day, for seven years in the 1760s, on his country estate at Steepleton Iwerne, Dorset. In 1774 Clementi moved to London and gradually established himself, working as keyboard conductor at the King's Theatre, Haymarket, and as the composer of six Sonatas, Op. 2, and other works that became well-known. Away on a continental tour during the early 1780s, Clementi returned to England in 1783 and appeared regularly as piano or harpsichord soloist at the Hanover Square Rooms. In London Clementi enjoyed celebrity as a performer, often in his own works, and as one of the leading (and most expensive) teachers of the day. To study with him set a seal on a career, and his London pupils included J. B. Cramer, Johann Nepomuk Hummel, Meyerbeer and John Field. Thus he accepted the twelve- (said to be ten-) year-old

John Field as a pupil at the enormous apprenticeship premium of 100 guineas. Field's principal role was to demonstrate Clementi pianos to likely customers and from time to time to appear on a public platform as Clementi's pupil, Haydn noting him with approval as early as 1794.

One of Clementi's best-known works is the massive *Gradus ad Parnassum* studies for piano. Clementi's keyboard music was widely published in his day. He was also the composer of symphonies, not all of which have survived, but in the 1790s the appearance of Haydn in London eclipsed Clementi's success and he turned to music publishing and piano building. Clementi was joint owner with the Collard brothers of the celebrated piano firm. Clementi's piano workshop was long at Cheapside in the City but was also established at 195 Tottenham Court Road from 1806, Clementi living nearby at 29 Alfred Place, though neither building survives. For most of the first decade of the nineteenth century Clementi lived abroad, promoting his pianos and seeking new music for publication, and acquiring rights to some of Beethoven's music. Clementi, ever the opportunist, taking his cue from the demands of the Beethoven piano concerti newly arriving in England, published in 1810 Beethoven's 'Grand Concerto for the pianoforte' adding to the title page 'as newly constructed by Clementi & Co with additional keys up to F'.

He was one of the directors of the Philharmonic Society at its inception in 1813, and appeared at the piano (effectively the conductor) alternating with his pupil J. B. Cramer during the first season. Symphonies by Clementi appeared in the Fourth and Seventh Concerts. Clementi composed another symphony for the Philharmonic in 1816, but, although he produced new symphonies between 1819 and 1823, as a composer he was gradually eclipsed by Beethoven, as he had been twenty years before by Haydn. In the early 1820s he lived at 128 Kensington Church Street and William Horsley is reported to have bought the lease of 1 High Row, Kensington Gravel Pits (later Notting Hill) from Clementi.

In the mid-1820s Clementi lived at rural Elstree, near London. Moscheles would visit Clementi, finding him to be 'one of the most vigorous old fellows of seventy that I ever saw. In the early morning we watch him from our window running about the garden bareheaded, reckless of the morning dew. He is too lively ever to think of rest. At table he laughs and talks incessantly. He has a sharp temper, too, which we set down to the hot blood of his Italian nature. He plays on the piano now but rarely, and gives out that he has a stiff hand, the result of falling out of a sledge when he was in Russia, but there is a suspicion that his unwillingness is caused by his inability to follow the great progress the Bravura style has made since his time. His wife, an amiable Englishwoman, is a great contrast to him . . .'. Clementi asked Moscheles to play for him, and 'the latter would choose one of his host's Sonatas, while Clementi, listening with a complacent smile, his hands behind his back, his short, thick-set figure swinging to and fro, would call out at intervals, "Bravo". When the last note was over, he would tap Moscheles in a friendly way upon the shoulder, and warmly congratulate him on his performance.' Clementi retired in 1830 and moved away from London. He died in 1832 and his funeral was at a packed

Westminster Abbey on 29 March. The inscription on his grave in Westminster Abbey declares that he was 'the father of the pianoforte'.

Eric Coates (1886–1957)

In his autobiography Eric Coates describes how he came to London as a student at the Royal Academy of Music, then in Tenterden Street, off Hanover Square, the year before Oxford Circus tube station opened, and found digs with a family friend over a haberdashery store in Kilburn High Road. He vividly describes the journey in a 'rickety old horse-bus, bumping uncomfortably over the cobbles'. Coates became synonymous with light music during the first half of the twentieth century. As well as a composer he was also a viola player when young and a student of Lionel Tertis. He remembered his first meeting with the principal of the Royal Academy of Music, Sir Alexander Mackenzie, who soon told him that 'Harpists, singers and modern music were his abomination'.

Coates joined the Beecham Symphony Orchestra for five months, and later played with the Queen's Hall Orchestra and was principal viola for seven years. He lived in West Hampstead, St John's Wood, near Queen's Hall and in Hampstead Garden Suburb (at 7 Willifield Way, NW11 – plaque), and then moved to a flat in Baker Street. He composed several works associated with London (see Part III) and he also made a considerable reputation for popular ballads of which he wrote many very big-selling numbers.

Coates enjoyed a long and rewarding career based on the London music industry, becoming celebrated for his short orchestral works which, being a suitable duration for 78rpm discs, found a wide audience as recordings and later on the BBC, where many were used as theme music, probably the most celebrated being 'In Town Tonight'. Even in the days of acoustic records (up to 1925) some eighteen movements from nine works were widely recorded at the London studios of labels such as HMV, Columbia, Vocalion and Edison Bell. Some of these were conducted by the composer. Coates was a founder member and one-time director of the Performing Right Society, and he died in 1957 at 2 Mansfield Street, W1, where he lived from 1953 to 1957.

Samuel Coleridge-Taylor (1875–1912)

Born in Holborn, Coleridge-Taylor's father was of West African origin, but his mother remarried and the family moved to Croydon when he was young. He was always based in south London. He studied at the Royal College of Music where he was a favourite student of Stanford. Among the many stories concerning Stanford and his pupils is told the occasion, in 1896, when Coleridge-Taylor was proudly showing his professor his new Symphony in A minor. Stanford inadvertently spilled his tea on it and, as its young composer looked on in horror, remarked 'Good lord me b'hoy, it's a symphony in T!'

Coleridge-Taylor was already composing when he first went to the Royal College of Music and at the age of sixteen Novello published his anthem *In Thee, O Lord*. The next year there came another four anthems. Coleridge-Taylor first came to wider notice with his orchestral *Ballade in A minor* in 1898 written for the Three Choirs Festival at the instigation of Elgar, and a great success at Crystal Palace on 4 November that year. A week later his cantata *Hiawatha's Wedding Feast* had a huge success when Stanford conducted the first performance at the Royal College of Music. It literally went round the world, but Coleridge-Taylor sold the copyright to his publisher for £15 and although in its first fifteen years it sold over 140,000 copies and was sung by almost every choral society in the country he made nothing more from it. A succession of works followed, both commissions for choral works, including two sequels to *Hiawatha's Wedding Feast*, and orchestral works, and he developed a considerable reputation as a composer of light music and violin encores. He also conducted for the Handel Society from 1904 to 1912.

He later became a Professor at the Trinity College of Music in 1903, at the Guildhall School of Music in 1910 and at the Crystal Palace School of Music. At one time he lived at 30 Dagnall Park, South Norwood, SE25 (plaque) and at 10 Upper Grove in South Norwood. He is buried at Bandon Hill Cemetery, Croydon.

Frederick Corder (1852–1932)

Frederick Corder's life was focused on the Royal Academy of Music, largely at Tenterden Street but also at Marylebone Road after it moved in 1912. He studied at the Royal Academy of Music from 1873 to 1875, and was Professor of Composition there from 1888. He was thus Stanford's (at the Royal College of Music) direct opposite number, and the teacher of several generations of successful composers from Bantock and Holbrooke to York Bowen, Benjamin Dale and Arnold Bax. Many of the later popular light music composers, including Eric Coates and Montague Phillips, were his pupils in the early 1900s.

He became well known, with his wife, for rather stilted English translations of Wagner's operas. His music includes the opera *Nordisa,* in its day frequently performed by the Carl Rosa Opera Company, and one of the few operas demanding an avalanche on stage. Later Corder was unable to accept the new music and published an article 'On the Cult of the Wrong Note' in the first volume of the journal *The Musical Quarterly* in 1915. During his career at the Academy he lived at 13 Albion Road, Hampstead, NW3, and the young Bax was a frequent player at nearby tennis courts with Corder's son Paul, also a student composer at the Academy.

Sir Michael Costa (1808–1884)

Michael Costa was born in Naples. After studying in Italy and establishing an early reputation as a composer, he arrived in Birmingham in 1830, ostensibly to conduct a cantata. In the event he ended up singing the tenor solo, and subsequently came to London as orchestral pianist at the King's Theatre. He composed music for the ballet *Kenilworth* the following year, and in 1832 he became director of music. Thereafter he wrote other ballets, operas and oratorios. In 1846 he resigned, taking several members of the orchestra with him, and founded the new Italian Opera at Covent Garden.

He quickly built a major reputation as a pioneering conductor, establishing the use of the baton and setting new standards of performance. This was not only at the opera, and he became director for the Philharmonic Society concerts, and in 1848 took over the direction of the Sacred Harmonic Society (1848–82) at Exeter Hall and as their conductor directed the Handel Festivals at Crystal Palace from 1857 to 1880. He conducted the Philharmonic Society seasons until Wagner arrived as guest conductor for the 1855 season, and was at Covent Garden till 1868, when he returned to Her Majesty's Theatre. He was its musical director from 1871 to 1881 when it merged with the Covent Garden Company. He was knighted in 1869 and in 1871 he was appointed director of music of Her Majesty's Opera.

86   Charles Lyall's cartoon of Costa (seated) and Gounod rehearsing *The Redemption*.

Costa lived at 7 and later 59 Eccleston Square. He was a fervent apostle of high pitch, that now discredited and contentious nineteenth-century practice that Manns reversed at Crystal Palace as soon as he took over, and Henry Wood also rejected at the Promenade Concerts at Queen's Hall as a condition of his funding by Dr George Cathcart. Francesco Berger, in old age, remembered Costa at Eccleston Square: 'He was never married, but lived with his bachelor brother, Raffaello, in a fine house in Eccleston Square, where on Sunday mornings he received his friends in the polyglot costume of an elaborate dressing gown, *no trousers*, but with pants tucked into riding-boots!' Costa is buried at Kensal Green.

Sir Frederic Hymen Cowen (1852–1935)

Few musicians have experienced a more complete eclipse than that suffered by Sir Frederic Hymen Cowen after the First World War. In his day he was a celebrated composer, conductor and pianist. But apart from a few pieces of light music and some songs, his music was to all intents and purposes passé by 1920. He had been born in Kingston, Jamaica, but came to England when young. He was fortunate that his father, Frederic Augustus Cowen, had been treasurer to E. T. Smith and James Mapleson, the celebrated opera impresario, and afterwards Mapleson and Gye at Drury Lane. At the age of eight he produced an opera that was performed privately and his father's employer, the Earl of Dudley, funded him to study with Sir Julius Benedict. He made his debut as a pianist at the age of eleven and then studied in Leipzig and Berlin.

In London when only nineteen his first Piano Concerto and his First Symphony were performed at St James's Hall in December 1869. A choral work that would retain its currency throughout the nineteenth century, *The Rose Maiden*, was successfully produced when he was eighteen. Parental contacts came in useful again, and in 1871 he was appointed by Colonel Mapleson as pianist and accompanist to the Italian Opera, and he produced another symphony, which he was commissioned to write by the Liverpool Philharmonic Society, and an overture for the Norwich Festival. In 1873 he visited Italy, with a view to the composition of an opera that eventually became his light opera *Pauline*, produced at the Lyceum Theatre by Carl Rosa in November 1876. His *Scandinavian* Symphony was first performed at the close of 1880 and became one of the first British symphonies to have a wide following across Europe. It was played under Richter in Vienna and at Stuttgart. Many other works followed, and he succeeded Sir Arthur Sullivan as conductor of the Philharmonic Concerts, holding the post until 1892. He was re-appointed in 1900 and remained in the post till 1907.

In 1888 he applied for the post of Director of the Royal College of Music, but fortunately withdrew leaving the field open for Parry, on receiving the offer to act as conductor of the concerts at the Melbourne Centennial Exhibition in Australia at the then unprecedented fee of £5,000, an offer he accepted. Back in England in 1889 he composed the now largely forgotten cantata *St. John's Eve*, which was produced at the Crystal Palace the same year. His opera *Thorgrim* was written for and produced by the Carl Rosa Company in 1890, and a successor *Signa* was commissioned for the Royal English Opera House, to follow Sullivan's *Ivanhoe*, to which it bears a striking likeness in terms of treatment, but it was not performed there because *Ivanhoe* came off earlier than he expected and it was not ready in time. It was subsequently first produced in Milan in 1893 and, after revision, at Covent Garden the next year, and was the subject of a command performance before Queen Victoria at Windsor. A final opera, *Harold*, the libretto of which was written by Sir Edward Malet (the British Ambassador in Berlin), was also produced at Covent Garden in 1895.

In 1903 Cowen took over from Manns as conductor of the Handel Festival at Crystal Palace. A stream of compositions followed, all successfully produced at the time, and a revival of the 1897 scena *The Dream of Endymion* for tenor (soprano) and orchestra in 2002 hinted that if the music can be found, Cowen's distinctive lyrical music may yet attract an appreciative audience, perhaps on CD. Cowen's address was 73 Hamilton Terrace, Hampstead, in 1915, subsequently 54 Hamilton Terrace, later 79 St John's Wood Court, NW8. He spent his last years at 105 Maida Vale, W9, from where he conducted a vigorous campaign with the BBC to regain his former celebrity. He was unsuccessful, though two last works, *The Magic Goblet* and the *Miniature Variations,* were performed thanks to assiduous lobbying of the BBC. He is buried at the Jewish Cemetery, Golders Green.

Johann Baptist Cramer (1771–1858)

The composer, pianist and publisher J. B. Cramer arrived in London aged three. He made his debut as a pianist in 1781, when still a child, and gave many concerts thereafter. In the 1790s he challenged the supremacy of long-established pianists in London concert life as a soloist not only in professional concerts but also in the salons. He was a co-founder of the Philharmonic Society in 1813 and appointed to the Board of the Royal Academy of Music in 1822. His music publishing career started in 1805 with Cramer and Keys, and another venture began with Samuel Chappell in 1810. In 1824 the firm of Cramer, Addison and Beale was founded, later known as J. B. Cramer and Co. Ltd, which still exists. He lived in Kensington and is buried in Brompton Cemetery. Moscheles first encountered Cramer, in London, in 1821, later writing:

> His interpretations of Mozart and his own sweet Mozart-like compositions, are like breathings 'from the sweet south' . . . [he] is exceedingly intellectual and entertaining; he has a sharp satirical vein, and spares neither his own nor his neighbour's foibles . . . He is one of the most inveterate snuff-takers. Good housekeepers maintain that after every visit of the great master, the floor must be cleansed of the snuff he has spilt, while I, as a pianoforte player, cannot forgive him for disfiguring his aristocratic, long, thin fingers, with their beautifully shaped nails, by the use of it, and often clogging the action of the keys. Those thin, well shaped fingers are best suited for legato playing; they glide along imperceptibly from one key to the other, and whenever possible, avoid octave as well as staccato passages. Cramer sings on the piano in such a manner that he almost transforms a Mozart andante into a vocal piece, but I must resent the liberty he takes in introducing his own and frequently trivial embellishments.

In his later years he lived in Munich and Paris but returned to London and near the end of his life played a duet with Liszt, who was visiting the city.

Benjamin J. Dale (1885–1943)

With York Bowen and Arnold Bax, Benjamin James Dale was another brilliant composition student at the Royal Academy of Music under Corder in 1900, and a talented pianist, though he did not play in public. His orchestral overture *Horatius* was performed at the Portman Rooms, Baker Street on 10 May 1900 when he was still only fourteen. A prolific composer while a student, he was also an excellent young organist, and produced organ music. His huge student Piano Sonata in D minor of 1905 won the first prize in pianist Mark Hambourg's composition competition in 1906. It was quickly taken up by his fellow students York Bowen and Myra Hess. His teacher, Corder, was so impressed with the Sonata that it became the stimulus for the formation of the Society of British Composers as a mechanism for securing publication in what became the Avison Edition.

Caught while on holiday in Bayreuth in August 1914, Dale was interned at the civilian prison camp on Ruhleben Racecourse near Berlin during the First World War. Appointed a professor of harmony at the Academy in 1919, he became Warden of the Royal Academy of Music in 1936. After the war, administration seemed to take all his energies and he finished only two substantial further scores, the Violin

Sonata of 1922, and the half-hour orchestral tone poem *The Flowing Tide*. He worked on the latter for twenty years, tragically dying during the rehearsal for the first performance in 1944. For his last ten years Dale was one of the three professional representatives on the BBC's music panel, in which capacity he read (and often rejected) a wide variety of new works submitted by the composers of the day. Dale lived at 17c Abbey Road, St John's Wood, NW8 not far from the celebrated HMV recording studios.

Edward Dannreuther (1844–1905)

The pianist, teacher and writer Edward Dannreuther spent his youth in the USA and came to London in 1863 to perform at Crystal Palace. He returned and in 1867 with others formed the Working Men's Society, which had concerts performed at its meetings. He married in 1871 and took British citizenship. In 1872 he founded the London Wagner Society and conducted two of its concert series in 1873–4. Wagner and Cosima stayed with him at 12 Orme Square, Bayswater, during the 1877 Wagner Festival. He wrote and lectured extensively on Wagner and his music.

As a virtuoso pianist Dannreuther gave the British premiere of Tchaikovsky's Piano Concerto in B-flat minor and also introduced the piano concerto that he had commissioned from his pupil Hubert Parry. Dannreuther held a celebrated series of private concerts at his home, of music by, among others, Brahms, Parry, Stanford and Strauss, as well as his own songs. In 1895 he became professor of piano at the Royal College of Music.

Claude Debussy (1862–1918)

87 Debussy conducts in London, 27 February 1909 at Queen's Hall.

The famous French composer first came to London in 1902, when he was unknown here. In 1902 and 1903, he stayed at the Hotel Cecil in the Strand. In July 1902 he remarks in a letter home that it was impossible to find a reasonable cup of tea in London! He was not celebrated in London until his music began to be performed later in the Edwardian period, the first performance of *Prélude à l'Après-midi d'un Faune* coming in August 1904, almost ten years after the Paris premiere. On two later visits he stayed at 46 Grosvenor Street, home of Edgar Speyer (now the Japanese Embassy). He conducted two Queen's Hall concerts of his own music at the invitation of Sir Henry Wood – *La Mer* (which had been partly composed in Eastbourne) on 1 February 1908 and the following year the three *Nocturnes* and *L'Après-midi d'un Faune*, on 27 February, and 'Fêtes' was encored. That concert was at 3 p.m. and later in a letter (from the Hotel Cecil), Debussy indicated that he had to go to a reception organised by 'the Society of English Composers'. He was referring to the Music Club held at the Æolian Hall where Bax, substituting at short notice, accompanied an American singer in Debussy's songs including the *Ariettes Oubliées*, in a programme that Bax remembered as 'a fairly representative programme of the master's songs and instrumental works'. In the audience on that occasion was the Finnish composer Sibelius, who had been the Music Club's victim a couple of weeks before.

On 21 May 1909 *Pelléas* had its London premiere, but although in London for it, according to his letters Debussy declined to attend. Debussy's music became established to London audiences in the years before and during the First World War, but the composer did not visit England again.

Frederick Delius (1862–1934)

Delius, who was born in Bradford, attended at the age of sixteen the International College, Spring Grove, Isleworth, where he remained for two years, regularly travelling into London to attend concerts from the nearby Western Region station. Delius lived in France for most of his mature life. He became, however, a regular visitor to London in his forties once it grew to be the principal source of performances of his music.

Trying to promote his music, Delius travelled to London from Paris in the late autumn of 1898 and with the impresario R. Norman-Concorde (whose office, the Concorde Concert Control, was at 186 Wardour Street, on the corner of Oxford Street) was able to sponsor a concert devoted to his music in the following May. Delius wrote to Jelka Rosen (later his wife) in France from lodgings at 25 Montpelier Street, SW, reporting he had arrived safely but confessing 'I feel awfully out of my water here, and pretty hopeless'. Delius remained in London until early in the new year, having encountered various friends previously met in Germany. These included Percy Pitt, organist at Queen's Hall, who had been a fellow student at the Leipzig conservatoire years before, and the pianist Ferruccio Busoni, who wrote to his wife on 11 December 'The first person I met here was Delius. He was very delighted, and exceedingly warm'.

Perhaps his most valuable contact was R. Norman-Concorde, the agent with whom he would finally promote his concert on 30 May, which, in the end, would be held at St James's Hall, Piccadilly. In fact Delius had hoped for the new Queen's Hall with Henry Wood to conduct but had to settle for the old St James's Hall and Alfred Hertz, the newly appointed conductor of the Breslau Municipal Theatre, as by not going to the impresario Robert Newman to manage his concert he failed to get either the hall or conductor of his choice. Delius arrived back in London on 20 April 1899 to set up the arrangements for his concert and he must have spent some time at Norman-Concorde's offices. At least twenty-five cuttings of the concert survive, and so Delius's main objective, to put himself on the critical map, was met, though it was a financial disaster for him.

Delius looked to Germany for performances for the next few years and he did not return to London until April 1907 after Henry Wood had become interested in his music. He lunched with Wood on 12 April and wrote to Jelka on 14 April from 90

"HASSAN" AT HIS MAJESTY'S THEATRE.

Hassan: "And in the heart of each flower I will distil one drop of the magic of love."
HASSAN (HENRY AINLEY) PREPARES SWEETS, WITH THE AID
OF SELIM'S LOVE PHILTRE, FOR YASMIN.

88   James Elroy Flecker's *Hassan* was produced by Basil Dean
at His Majesty's Theatre, opening on 20 September 1923.

Oakley Street, Chelsea. He made many musical contacts and on 26 April found himself at the New Gaiety Theatre at the annual dinner of his old school in Bradford, the guest of an old school friend, the tenor John Coates. Delius's Piano Concerto was played by Theodor Szántó at the Proms at Queen's Hall on 24 October, Wood conducting. At this time Delius started staying with Norman O'Neill at 4 Pembroke Villas, W8, coming again in 1909 (for the premiere of the *Mass of Life*) in 1914, 1915, 1916, 1917 and 1920. He also stayed with Beecham at 8a Hobart Place, SW1, and after escaping from the German advance in 1914, from November 1914 to May 1915 at Watford (see p. 188). In September 1918 he stayed with the conductor Henry Wood at 4 Elsworthy Road, NW3. The story is told that Delius could not bear the sound of clocks ticking so they all had to be run down and stopped while he was there.

Subsequently Delius was from October 1918 to spring 1919 at Belsize Park Gardens and in February and March 1921 again in London and Hampstead. In September 1923 he and Jelka were in London for the final rehearsals of James Elroy Flecker's play *Hassan* for which Delius wrote an extensive score. Sumptuously produced by Basil Dean at His Majesty's, it opened on 20 September and became fashionable, enjoying a long run, earning Delius royalties of £25 a week. Delius was already physically in decline, now strongly exhibiting the symptoms of the syphilis contracted many years before that would ultimately kill him. At the final dress rehearsal Dean remembered 'Delius, carefully tended by his wife, sitting wrapped up in the stalls'. When Delius returned in 1929 the paralysis that was foreshadowed as early as 1923 was fully in evidence and he was a stricken figure in a wheelchair. This visit was for the Delius Festival, six concerts promoted by Beecham and held between 12 October and 1 November (at Queen's Hall and the Æolian Hall) for which the Deliuses stayed at the Langham Hotel. Augustus John sketched his familiar portrait there (now at the Royal College of Music).

Bernard van Dieren (1887–1936)

The Dutch-born composer Bernard van Dieren came to England in 1909, and lived here throughout the First World War. He had a wide circle of musical friends, including Cecil Gray, Philip Heseltine (Peter Warlock), Lambert, Moeran, the Sitwells, Sorabji and Walton, and he inspired great loyalty, particularly in Philip

Heseltine, who made various attempts to promote the music, notably in an unsuccessful concert in February 1917. After his marriage in 1910 van Dieren settled in Loudon Road, NW8, and in 1913 moved to 35a St George's Road in St John's Wood. After the war he returned to Holland in 1918, where he remained until 1921. He came back to England, and in 1932 he and wife Frida lived at 68 Clifton Hill, NW8.

Van Dieren inspired strongly conflicting views. Philip Heseltine's son, Nigel, in his biography of his father, *Capriol for Mother*, believed van Dieren to be the cause of his father's death. One faction remembers him as an evil influence and his music unlikely ever to inspire much of an audience. The other views him as a devout Catholic whose last years were wracked with pain owing to a kidney condition that eventually killed him. Sacheverell Sitwell remembered him as 'one of the five or six most remarkable persons I have known'. Epstein's sculpture of The Risen Christ was modelled on van Dieren in pain. He was cremated at Golders Green, and his ashes are buried at St Laurence's Church, West Wycombe, marked by a small flat stone.

Jacqueline du Pré (1945–1987)

The cellist Jacqueline du Pré enjoyed a spectacular but short-lived career in the 1960s. Her recital debut at Wigmore Hall in 1961 announced her as a young player of considerable charisma – a stature confirmed when she became associated with the Elgar Cello Concerto. Her appearance with this work at the Proms at the Royal Albert Hall, on 14 August 1962 when many people were turned away, sealed her popular reputation and also started the vogue for the concerto that today has made it possibly the most popular of all concertos by a British composer. She reappeared for the following three years with the Elgar and was also used by the BBC in 1964 to introduce the new Cello Concerto by Priaulx Rainier in the same concert as the Elgar, and in 1965 to play Bloch's *Schelomo* in a second Prom appearance that year. In 1967 she married Daniel Barenboim and in 1973 her career came to a premature end owing to the onset of multiple sclerosis. From 1967 to 1971 she lived at 27 Upper Montague Street, W1, and she subsequently bought a house at 5a Pilgrim's Lane, NW3, where she lived until 1975 (plaques at both). After her disease progressed she and Barenboim rented Margot Fonteyn's Knightsbridge house at 2 Rutland Gardens Mews, which had been specially adapted for the ballerina's disabled husband. In 1983 she moved to 36–38 Chepstow Villas, W11, where she died. She is buried at the Jewish Cemetery, Golders Green.

Thomas F. Dunhill (1877–1946)

The composer and writer Thomas Dunhill was born at 10 Swiss Terrace, NW6 (no longer there), and lived there till around 1897 when he took rooms in Bayswater. He went to the Royal College of Music in 1893 and studied with Stanford and Franklin Taylor. From 1899 to 1908 he was assistant music master at Eton College. He taught harmony and counterpoint at the College from 1905. In 1907 he founded a chamber concert series that featured new chamber music by British composers, and which for ten years achieved considerable celebrity.

His own concert music included the ballad cantata *Tubal Cain* (1908), and an orchestral song cycle *The Wind Among the Reeds*, which set words by W. B. Yeats. It was first performed at a Royal Philharmonic Society concert in November 1912, but has been little performed as a cycle, although it includes a widely sung setting of 'The Cloths of Heaven'. Later came a symphony – only once heard in London, in the 1930s – and the *Elegiac Variations* in memory of Parry. During the Second World War his *Triptych* for viola and orchestra was heard at the Proms, but all in all Dunhill's serious music has not made much impact on London music.

He wrote educational music and produced studies of Elgar, Mozart and Sullivan, and contributed many articles to W. W. Cobbett's *Cyclopedia of Chamber Music*. Dunhill's main success with the wider public came with his stage works of which the most celebrated was the light opera *Tantivy Towers* – a great success in 1931 at Nigel Playfair's Lyric Theatre, Hammersmith in 1931 (see Chapter 7).

He was married at St Luke's Chelsea in 1914 while John Ireland was resident organist and chorus master, and after a period in a Bayswater flat the couple moved into 74 Lansdowne Road, Notting Hill Gate. In 1924 Dunhill moved to Guildford. After his wife's death in October 1929 he lived successively in two houses in Platts Lane, Hampstead. He held appointments as Dean of the Faculty of Music, London University and as a director of the Royal Philharmonic Society, among others.

Antonín Dvořák (1841–1904)

The Bohemian composer Dvořák enjoyed an enormous vogue in the UK in the 1880s and '90s, and he visited London nine times, including one stay at the Langham Hotel. In 1883 the British premiere of his Piano Concerto took place at Crystal Palace, when he was the guest of Henry Littleton of Novellos at his nearby mansion, Westwood House, now demolished (see Chapter 7). In 1884 his base was 12 Hinde Street, home of Oscar Beringer, the German pianist and composer who was resident in London during the 1880s and '90s.

It was his choral works that established Dvořák's name in the UK, and his symphonies that maintained his reputation. The *Stabat Mater* was first performed at St James's Hall in 1883, conducted by Joseph Barnby and by Dvořák himself in May 1884 at the Royal Albert Hall. At the Philharmonic Society and Crystal Palace Dvořák had performances of his Symphony in D major (no 6), the *Husitska* overture, and other works. He conducted at the Philharmonic Society four times between 1884 and 1896. *The Spectre's Bride* was performed at one of Novello's Oratorio concerts at St James's Hall in 1886 and also in 1886 *St Ludmilla*. Dvořák conducted his Symphony in G major (no. 8) in 1890 and had two premieres in 1896, when on 19 March he conducted his *Five Biblical Songs* specially orchestrated for the occasion and sung by the now forgotten Katherine Fisk, and after Beethoven's

Emperor Concerto played by Emil Sauer (one had value for money in those days) there followed the first performance of Dvořák's Cello Concerto played by Leo Stern. Stern had previously visited Dvořák in Prague and had a big success with Dvořák's concerto.

Sir Edward Elgar (1857–1934)

Elgar was born in Worcester and his early life was spent there. Newly married, and in an attempt to establish himself, he and his wife Alice came to London in 1890 and lived at 51 Avonmore Road, W14, where there is now a blue plaque, but it did not work out and they returned to Worcester in 1891. As Elgar's fame grew he occasionally stayed at Basil Nevinson's house at 3 Tedworth Square, Chelsea after 1899.

The first performance of the *Enigma Variations* at St James's Hall on 19 June 1899, conducted by Hans Richter, established Elgar almost overnight. A few weeks before, on 24 May, he had had the satisfaction of having his part-song *To Her, Beneath Whose Steadfast Star* first performed at Windsor Castle before Queen Victoria.

Over the next few years Elgar's London premieres included *Cockaigne*, heard at Queen's Hall on 20 June 1901, and the first London performances of the *Pomp and Circumstance* Marches Nos 1 and 2, at Queen's Hall on 21 October 1901 conducted by Henry Wood. Arnold Bax, then a student, was there and remembered

> The hall was inspissated (a word one time dear to musical critics and ever associated with 'gloom') by one of London's most masterly fogs. The contrast between those slowly shifting nebulous veils choking the audience and the blare and glare of Elgarian brass was never to be forgotten. The famous and now much debated tune was greeted by thunders of applause and of course encored.

The Dream of Gerontius, after its unsuccessful premiere in Birmingham in October 1900, took three years to come to London, though Alice Elgar's books of newspaper cuttings, now preserved at the Elgar Birthplace Museum, include a handbill for 'Miss Holland's Choir' who presented part one on 8 May 1902, presumably with piano or organ accompaniment at St Andrew's Hall. The London premiere took place at the new and not quite finished Westminster cathedral on 6 June 1903 when Ludwig Wüllner, the Gerontius of the Düsseldorf performances in 1901 and 1902 sang the title role and Muriel Foster that of the Angel, with Elgar conducting. It was a triumph. Later it appeared again at Queen's Hall, on 15 February 1904, when John Coates sang Gerontius and Marie Brema (the soloist in the first performance at Birmingham) was the Angel. Perhaps the most interesting early performance was that conducted by Weingartner, when at Queen's Hall on 9 April 1904 Gervase Elwes sang Gerontius. Such was the scale of Edwardian programmes, *Gerontius* was sung in a double bill with Beethoven's *Choral* Symphony!

Elgar was established as a major draw on the London concert scene and his principal works henceforth appeared at frequent intervals until the First World War intervened. Possibly the one event that most notably signalled his success was the

Elgar Festival given at Covent Garden in March 1904, when Elgar conducted the Hallé Orchestra in his orchestral overture *In the South*.

In 1911 he took a short lease of 75 Gloucester Place, Portman Square, but his chief London home was Severn House, 42 Netherhall Gardens, NW3, where the family lived from the end of 1911 to 1918, at which time they moved to Sussex, to Brinkwells at Fittleworth, finally parting with Severn House in 1921. After the death of his wife, Elgar leased a flat at 37 St James's Place, Green Park, SW1, from 1921 to 1924, before finally retiring to the country. Elgar was the guest of honour at the opening of HMV's Abbey Road Studios in 1931, on which he is remembered by a plaque.

Manuel de Falla (1876–1946)

Falla first appeared in London at the Æolian Hall, as pianist with Franz Liebich, where on 24 May 1911, he played his *Piezas Españolas*, *Trois Mélodies* and the two-piano arrangement of Debussy's *Ibéria*. Unfortunately the concert was the same day as the premiere of Elgar's Second Symphony at Queen's Hall and it went unnoticed.

After the First World War, Falla returned to London at the end of June 1919 with Diaghilev's ballet company. This was for the premiere of his *Three-Cornered Hat* ballet at the Alhambra on 22 July 1919. Falla stayed at the house of the Swedish soprano Louise Alvar (Mrs Charles Copeley Harding) at 14 Holland Park, where Ravel also stayed. However on the day of the opening, Falla had already left for home as he had just learned that his mother was mortally ill. The story is told that he was seen off at Victoria by the Diaghilev troupe en masse.

Falla returned to London to play the solo piano part in his *Nights in the Gardens of Spain* in one of Edward Clark's concerts of modern music on 20 May 1921 at Queen's Hall. It was six years before Falla appeared again in London, when on the afternoon of Wednesday 22 June 1927 he was at the Æolian Hall for the premiere of his Harpsichord Concerto, which he gave on the piano at the beginning of the programme, and the harpsichord in the second half. Between them he conducted a concert version of his ballet *El Amour Brujo* and the concert ended with a 'concert version' of *Master Peter's Puppet Show* conducted by Falla. The concert is of particular interest for *The Scotsman's* critic's disclosure that Stravinsky was in the audience.

Falla's last visit to London was for a BBC broadcast of his music, his only personal appearance on the radio in the UK. The broadcast took place on 24 June 1931 in the BBC's series of late night Contemporary Music concerts, broadcast live. The programme was *El Amour Brujo* conducted by Sir Henry Wood, the Harpsichord Concerto in which Falla was soloist, and the composer returned to conduct *Master Peter's Puppet Show*.

Gabriel Fauré (1845–1924)

The name of the French composer Fauré was already known in London in the 1880s, his Violin Sonata in A being played at Steinway Hall by Ovide Musin and

Saint-Saëns on 1 June 1880. Fauré visited London many times, his first visit being in May 1882 to hear the *Ring* cycle at Her Majesty's Theatre. His second visit came in 1894, and in April 1896 he stayed at 12 Bruton Street, W1, with Earl de Grey. He returned to attend a concert of his own works in December 1896, when his *Fantaisie* for flute and piano was played by Louis Fleury, and he was the pianist in his own Piano Quartet No. 1 in a David Bispham concert. The Piano Quartet No. 2 appeared at St James's Hall in a Monday Popular Concert when Ysaÿe was the first violin.

At other times he was the guest of the painter John Singer Sargent at 31 Tite Street, SW3, and in March to April 1908 he stayed with Frank Schuster, friend of Elgar, at 22 Old Queen Street, SW1. He also visited London, and Schuster, in the autumn of 1908. On 21 June Fauré conducted his incidental music for Maeterlinck's play *Pelléas et Mélisande* at the Prince of Wales Theatre, given in the English translation by J. W. Mackail with Mrs Patrick Campbell as Mélisande and Forbes Robertson as Golaud. Fauré's score had already been heard in London, for Henry Wood had included it at a Queen's Hall Promenade concert on 18 September 1902. Schuster and Fauré were together in the stalls at Queen's Hall for the first London performance of Elgar's First Symphony on 7 December 1908. That evening Schuster gave a dinner party for Elgar and Fauré.

Howard Ferguson (1908–1999)

The Ulster-born composer and pianist Howard Ferguson stopped composing in 1960, though he lived for almost forty years more, telling his friends he had said all he wanted to say. He came to London in the summer of 1924 and attended Westminster School (where he had to wear top hat and Eton jacket), and moved to the Royal College of Music in 1925 at the early age of fifteen and a half. There he studied harmony, counterpoint and composition with R. O. Morris and conducting with Malcolm Sargent, while learning the piano privately with Harold Samuel.

His output was small, but perfectly conceived and sufficiently successful from the first for his Piano Sonata in F minor of 1940 to be quickly recorded by his friend and neighbour Myra Hess on 78s, as were his *Five Bagatelles* of 1944, both at Abbey Road for HMV. Similarly his Octet of 1933 was recorded by one of the top-line ensembles of the day based on the Griller Quartet and with Dennis Brain playing the horn, this time for Decca.

He had started to be noticed as his earlier works appeared, the First Violin Sonata played by Isolde Menges and Harold Samuel at Wigmore Hall in October 1932, the Octet at the Grotrian Hall in November 1933, the *Partita* for orchestra at the BBC Maida Vale studios in June 1937. The almost total neglect of his two large-scale choral works (about twenty-six minutes each), *Amore Langueo* (1956) and *The Dream of the Rood* (1959), his last works, may well have contributed to his decision to stop composing, though both were heard in London, in fringe concerts conducted by Arnold Foster, the first at Central Hall Westminster in December 1956, the latter at the Assembly Hall, Westminster Technical College on 8 December 1959.

They were not heard again until revived by Robert Tucker with the Broadheath Singers at Eton in 1985 and 1988. Ferguson was at those concerts, but would not be drawn when asked about composing again. Subsequently they were taken up by Richard Hickox and recorded on CD.

Ferguson made a notable reputation during the war in assisting Myra Hess to organise the wartime concerts at the National Gallery. All told, 1,698 concerts were given to a total audience of 824,152. After he stopped composing he turned to editing keyboard music. From 1948 to 1963 he taught composition at the Royal Academy of Music. He lived at 106 Wildwood Road, NW11, from 1937 for thirty-four years, only moving to Cambridge for his last years.

Kathleen Ferrier (1912–1953)

The contralto Kathleen Ferrier was discovered at a comparatively mature age when she had left school and was working as a telephone switchboard operator. She moved to London when taken on by the agents Ibbs and Tillett in 1942 in order to study with John Hutchinson and Roy Henderson. She took a flat at 2 Frognal Mansions, 97 Frognal, in Hampstead where she lived until the last months of her life, when she moved to a more accessible apartment, 40 Hamilton Terrace, NW8. She died of cancer in University College Hospital where there was a plaque to her in the Radiology Department – in the old building (now rebuilding). She was cremated at Golders Green and there is a memorial rose bed in the Garden of Remembrance.

John Field (1782–1837)

The Irish composer and pianist Field lived in London only at the beginning and end of his career. He moved to London in December 1793 when his father became a violinist at the Haymarket Theatre. He was apprenticed to Clementi in April 1794, where he was not only expected to develop as a piano virtuoso as a pupil of his celebrated master but also to demonstrate Clementi's pianos to prospective clients. He first appeared in London in May 1794 at a Barthélemon concert, where he played a sonata by Clementi. Haydn heard him and referred to 'Field, a young boy, which plays the pianoforte extremely well'.

Subsequently he studied the violin with G. H. Pinto and he performed his First Piano Concerto in E-flat on 7 February 1799 at Pinto's benefit concert at the Haymarket Theatre. Later he played his Three Sonatas Op. 1 at an oratorio concert at Covent Garden.

He left England with Clementi in August 1802 on a tour that would take them to Paris, Vienna and St Petersburg. He then lived in Russia for thirty years and did not return to London until September 1831. Arriving in London he appeared in Hummel's A-flat Piano Concerto at the Royal Academy of Music. His first and only appearance at the Philharmonic Society was on 27 February 1832 at the opening concert of the season, playing his Fourth Piano Concerto in E-flat, though it was thought to be 'a model of melodious symmetry of somewhat antiquated type'.

The musical London to which Field had returned was quite different from the one he had left, very extensive development having taken place, not least being the building of Regent Street. On leaving he had been a brilliant and good-looking young man; now he was white-haired, coarse in manners and playing in an idiom made outmoded by the latest youthful arrival, Mendelssohn. Moscheles, who entertained Field at his house on a number of occasions, paints a vivid portrait of him in London in 1832:

> His legato playing delights me, but his compositions are not at all to my taste; nothing can afford a more glaring contrast than a Field 'Nocturne' and Field's manners, which are often of the cynical order. There was such a commotion yesterday among the ladies, when at a party he drew from his pocket a miniature portrait of his wife, and loudly proclaimed the fact that she had been his pupil, and that he had only married her because she never paid for her lessons, and he 'knew she never would'. He also bragged of going to sleep while giving lessons to the ladies of St. Petersburg, adding that they would often rouse him with the question. 'What does one pay twenty roubles an hour for, if you go to sleep?' He played to us a good deal in the evening; the delicacy and elegance, as well as the beauty of his touch, are admirable, but he lacks spirit and accent, as well as light and shade, and has no depth of feeling.

Clementi died soon afterwards and Field attended his old master's funeral at Westminster Abbey on 28 March 1832. The following day he appeared at a concert in the Great Concert Room of the King's Theatre, and the day after that he played again at a dinner for the centenary of the birth of Haydn at the Albion Tavern. Engagements in Manchester and London and arrangements for publishing his music needed attention soon afterwards. On 31 July he found his old mother, who had welcomed him back from Russia, dead in bed at her house in Princes Street. His reasons for staying in London had now all passed and he left for Paris and eventually died in Moscow in 1837. His London lodgings from September 1831 until he left in 1832 were at 6 Beaufort Buildings in the Strand.

Henry Balfour Gardiner (1877–1950)

Balfour Gardiner came from a wealthy family and in the history of English music in the early twentieth century he is as important as a benefactor as he is a composer. A student of the Hoch'sche Konservatorium in Frankfurt, he is usually counted as one of the 'Frankfurt Gang'. (For a full list of the 'Gang', see the entry for Norman O'Neill.) His celebrated series of eight concerts of new music at Queen's Hall in

1912–13 were responsible for launching a new generation of composers, including Holst, Vaughan Williams and Bax. He first took rooms in London at 5 Paper Buildings, Temple in 1902. He lived at 7 Pembroke Villas from 1906 opposite his friend the composer Norman O'Neill, another member of the 'Frankfurt Gang', who with his wife lived at No. 4. Here Percy Grainger stayed between April and June 1914, but soon after Balfour Gardiner moved across Holland Park to 1 Hillsleigh Road, where Delius was a guest during the First World War. Balfour Gardiner was a much better composer than history has given him credit for, but above all he was a generous benefactor to less well-off composers and musicians. His memorial concert on 23 April 1951 was given at the French Institute, Queensbury Place, London, when his old friend Arnold Bax accompanied three of Gardiner's songs, in possibly Bax's last public appearance at the keyboard.

George Gershwin (1888–1937)

The American composer and pianist Gershwin first came to London in 1923 to write the music for the review *The Rainbow* which was wanted very quickly and which in consequence Gershwin thought was his poorest score. It opened at the Empire Theatre on 3 April 1923. Coming back to London in April 1924 he spent three months at 10 Berkeley Street, W1 ('one of the cheeriest flats'), working on a new show called *Primrose*, which contained a song about Berkeley Street and Kew.

89 Gershwin's *Lady Be Good* at the Empire Theatre in 1926 featuring Fred and Adèle Astaire.

FRED and ADELE ASTAIRE

Gershwin's London Recording Sessions

All recorded for Columbia (with original 78 issue numbers)
Reissued on World Record Club SH 144 and by Naxos, Pearl and other CD labels
26 April 1926: Gershwin accompanied Fred and Adèle Astaire in 'I'd Rather Charleston', 3870
6 July 1926, Numbers from *Tip-Toes*: 'When Do we Dance', 4066 'That Certain Feeling', 4066 'Sweet and Low-Down', 4065 'Looking for a Boy', 4065
8 June 1928: (3) Preludes, 50107-D*, Andantino moderato from *Rhapsody in Blue*; 50107-D*, My One and Only (from *Funny Face*), 5109 (*only issued in the USA)
12 June 1928: ''S Wonderful/Funny Face' (from *Funny Face*), 5109

It opened at the Winter Garden Theatre on 11 September 1924. Here he was visited by Lord Berners.

Gershwin came to England again in 1925 when he gave the first English performance of *Rhapsody in Blue* with the Savoy Orpheans and the Savoy Havana Band conducted by Debroy Somers in a BBC relay from the Savoy Hotel in the Strand on 15 June 1925. The composer William Walton remembered being taken to see Gershwin during this visit by the popular composer Vernon Duke, also known for his more serious works as Vladimir Dukelsky. Gershwin then had a flat in Pall Mall and Stephen Lloyd has pinpointed the date by noting that Walton gave Gershwin a copy of his Piano Quartet that he inscribed and dated 28 May 1925. Earlier he had appeared at a recital at the Æolian Hall on 22 May.

In 1926 Gershwin had a new show in London, *Tip-Toes*, which opened at the Winter Garden on August 31. In April he had accompanied Fred and Adèle Astaire in their recording of 'I'd Rather Charleston' heard in the London production of the show *Lady Be Good*. In July 1926 Gershwin had another Columbia recording session in London, and on 6 July he recorded piano solo versions of four numbers from *Tip-Toes*.

Gershwin made his final visits to London in 1928, his new show *Funny Face* opening at the Prince's Theatre on 8 November. Gershwin had earlier recorded three numbers from it on 8 and 12 June when he visited the studios of Columbia for the last time.

Orlando Gibbons (1583–1625)

Orlando Gibbons's life as a composer and musician was focused on the court and the Chapel Royal. He was possibly the leading English composer of the early reign of James I, writing music for organ and virginals, for ensembles and both liturgical and secular vocal pieces. He wrote arguably the best-known single vocal work of this period in the partsong *The Silver Swanne*. He lived at Woolstaple, Westminster, in the 1620s. This was broadly where Bridge Street is now, for the whole area has completely changed since the early seventeenth century. Gibbons's house would have been immediately outside the Palace of Whitehall. He was organist at the Chapel Royal from 1605 until his death, and a musician for the virginals to the king from 1619 to 1623. In 1623 he was appointed organist at Westminster Abbey for the last two years of his life, and conducted the funeral of James I in 1625. His bust is in Westminster Abbey and his son Christopher was also an organist there.

William Schwenk Gilbert (1836–1911)

Sullivan's partner in the 'G&S' operettas was a very successful writer of his day who occupied a succession of ample houses. From 1876 to 1883 he lived at 24 The Boltons, Kensington, a then new and very up-market development, where his neighbours included the singers Jenny Lind and Emma Albani. Here Gilbert wrote the early G&S operettas. *Patience* did so well financially that in 1883 he moved to a flamboyant house designed for him by Sir Ernest George and Harold Peto at 39

Harrington Gardens, SW7 (then numbered 19). His last permanent home, where he moved in 1890, was at Grim's Dyke, Old Redding, Harrow Weald, which is full of Gilbert and Sullivan memorabilia and is preserved much as it must have been in Gilbert's time. He died there of a heart attack while trying to rescue a young girl in difficulties swimming in his lake (see Chapter 7). He was cremated at Golders Green and his ashes buried at the church of St John the Evangelist in Great Stanmore.

Berthold Goldschmidt (1903–1996)

Goldschmidt was the rising new boy of German music in the 1920s, a short-lived celebrity crowned by his opera *Der gewältige Hanrei* (*The Magnificent Cuckold*) at Mannheim in 1932. The rise of the Nazis saw the end of his career. His only good fortune was in being interviewed by a sympathetic and musical SS officer, which resulted in his being told 'get out of this country, go tomorrow, take nothing'. He arrived in London in October 1935 and was soon followed by his future wife Elisabeth Karen Bothe. Goldschmidt lived in the same ground floor flat at 13b Belsize Crescent for almost exactly sixty-one years, from October 1935 until his death on 17 October 1996. Karen Goldschmidt died in 1979.

Goldschmidt's is a remarkable story of a life of endless musical frustrations, successive seeming breakthroughs coming to nothing, leading to the abandonment of composition for twenty-five years, in despair; but of eventual recognition and success in his final years. This was signalled for most London music-lovers by the concert performance of his opera *Beatrice Cenci* at the Queen Elizabeth Hall on

90   Berthold Goldschmidt at his desk at 13b Belsize Road, *c.* 1990.

Sunday 16 April 1988, and the composer's appearance to take a bow after Simon Rattle's performance of his *Ciaconna Sinfonica* at the 1993 Proms to an enthusiastic reception. Nearly thirty years before, in 1964, Goldschmidt had appeared at the Proms to conduct Deryck Cooke's performing edition of Mahler's unfinished Tenth Symphony, with which he had been intimately involved.

Sir John Goss (1800–1880)

In 1811 Goss was a chorister at the Chapel Royal, then a pupil of Thomas Attwood. Appointed organist at Stockwell Chapel in 1821, in 1824 he became organist at St Luke's Chelsea (a position later held by John Ireland). He is principally remembered, however, as being the organist at St Paul's cathedral from 1838 to 1872. From 1856 he was composer to the Chapel Royal, and was knighted in 1872. He enjoyed a substantial Victorian reputation as a composer of glees. Some of his sacred music is still sung, including various anthems. His pupils included Sullivan and Cowen. As one of the composers to the Chapel Royal he composed the *Te Deum* and an anthem for the thanksgiving service on the recovery of the Prince of Wales in 1872, music immediately upstaged by Sullivan's music, the vastly more flamboyant and popular *Te Deum* for the same event. There is a memorial tablet in the cathedral. He lived and died in Brixton.

Charles Gounod (1818–1893)

The French composer Gounod was a great favourite with the widest audience in mid-Victorian England, popular encores particularly from his opera *Faust* being arranged for every conceivable instrument and ensemble. He began to be known in the 1850s when excerpts from his *Petite Messe Solonnelle* were performed in London at St Martin's Hall in January 1851 and his opera *Sappho* appeared at Covent Garden. The latter was panned by the press despite a starry cast and a good reception by the audience. Chorley thought it had appeared too late in the season and blamed 'the pertinacious resistance of a portion of the English public to anything that is new'. The first night of *Faust* at Her Majesty's in 1863 with a 'name' cast was so successful it was followed three weeks later by a competing production at Covent Garden in Italian, and six months later, Her Majesty's mounted an English version with the leading British singers and ran it for a season without supporting productions. For this the baritone Charles Santley asked Gounod to put words to a tune from the orchestral prelude for him, which became 'Avant de quitter ces lieux' and was taken as part of the accepted text of the opera thereafter. Scholes reminds us that for 'nearly fifty seasons (to 1911), it never once missed including it in its programme [at Covent Garden], and by 1906 it had given it three hundred times'. This success was not entirely a musical one, for *Faust* had been incorrectly registered at Stationers' Hall and hence was not protected by copyright in Great Britain. From the opera companies' point of view it was also, therefore, the cheap option.

The censor objected to Gounod's opera *The Queen of Sheba*, and the plot where the Queen prefers a workman to a king hinted at anti-royalist sentiment. It was eventually heard at Crystal Palace as a dramatic oratorio, renamed *Irene*, on 24 February 1866. In this form it spawned a favourite concert encore of the Victorian period, the aria 'Lend Me Your Aid' extensively recorded in the earliest days of the gramophone. This was an English version of the aria 'Inspirez-moi, race divine!' When Caruso recorded the aria it was decided to do it in the original French. Unable to find a score it was translated as 'Prête-moi ton aide' and recorded thus.

In 1867 came *Roméo et Juliette* at Covent Garden, the decorated and coloratura role of Juliette attracting some of the greatest sopranos of the day. Gounod and his family came to London in September 1870 to escape the Franco-Prussian War and the Siege of Paris. His first address was in Greenwich at 17 Morden Road (plaque). He fulfilled a commission from the London International Exposition of 1871 for a work for the grand opening of the Royal Albert Hall on 1 May 1871. He produced the lament for soprano, chorus and orchestra he called *Gallia*, and it was so successful that it led to his being asked to conduct the newly formed Royal Albert Hall Choral Society. It did not enjoy financial success and Gounod soon resigned from the choir, which was merged with Barnby's Oratorio Concerts to form the Royal Choral Society.

Gounod lived in London, with occasional trips to France, from 1870 to 1875. On 26 February 1871 in the drawing room of his long-standing friend and supporter Sir Julius Benedict at 2 Manchester Square, W1 (plaque), Gounod was introduced to the thirty-three-year-old Mrs Georgina Weldon. Gounod was immediately strongly taken with her and by 21 May his wife had returned to France in a rage and Gounod moved into the Weldons' Bloomsbury home at Tavistock House, which then stood near Tavistock Square, and was once where Dickens lived.

Mrs Weldon gained Gounod's patronage for her musical orphanage and her singing and they became close friends for a time. She helped him in business and his autobiography was published by her husband. A court case against Littleton of Novello concerning royalty payments was brought in 1873, when she dominated the court hearing and Littleton's damages were nugatory. But Gounod began to find her intolerable and later fell out with the Weldons. Illness caused him to leave their house in 1874. The whole affair came to an acrimonious conclusion and Georgina for some time refused to return the composer's belongings, including the score of *Polyeucte*.

By the late 1870s Gounod had a major reputation in England and in 1879 the Birmingham Festival attempted to commission a substantial choral work, but were unable to agree to Gounod's demands for £4,000.

Eventually *The Redemption* was commissioned and Novello's agreed to purchase the copyright for £3,250, thus paying most of the fee. Gounod conducted the premiere at Birmingham and dedicated the score to Queen Victoria. Novello's printed a large number of vocal scores and it was said to be the 'most immediate and most complete success that any oratorio . . . has ever attained'. It was heard five times at

Crystal Palace, the first being on 2 December 1882. Yet Novello seems not to have reprinted the vocal score and the success did not outlive the century.

Gounod's succeeding choral work for Birmingham was the massive *Mors et Vita* in 1885, but Gounod was unable to conduct as Georgina Weldon had now sued him for libel and he faced arrest if he entered English jurisdiction. He never came to England again.

Percy Grainger (1882–1961)

The teenage Australian Percy Grainger arrived in London with his mother in May 1901. They had travelled from Frankfurt, where he had been a student at the Hoch'sche Konservatorium, and had been counted another of the 'Frankfurt Gang'. (For a full list of the 'Gang' see the entry for Norman O'Neill.) He was a few weeks short of his nineteenth birthday. The Graingers based themselves in London until the First World War.

His first appearance as a pianist came on 11 June at a concert at St James's Hall in Piccadilly given by the Australian soprano Lilian Devlin. At this time an unprecedented number of talented newcomers were attempting to launch themselves on the London musical scene and in the period up to the First World War this required not only public engagements but also success at concerts given by the aristocracy in London drawing rooms. Grainger's agent in London was Alice Joseph, who specialised in 'placing' Australian performers, and probably through her influence, on 3 July Grainger attended a recital by another Australian singer, Maggie Stirling, at the Park Lane home of Lady Brassey. When the conductor/pianist Theodore Flint failed to arrive, the audience saw the golden-haired young Grainger rise from amongst them and take over authoritatively. Other Australian artists with whom Grainger appeared were the celebrated singers Melba and Ada Crossley. On 29 October Grainger gave his first solo recital at Steinway Hall (15 Lower Seymour Street, Portman Square). During their first year in London the Graingers lived at 31 Gordon Place, South Kensington. It was close to Sir Charles Villiers Stanford's house at 50 Holland Street. Grainger later came to know Stanford well. Subsequently the Graingers had at least eleven further London addresses. We are indebted to Kay Dreyfus for deducing what these were.

Identifying one or two of these today is problematic, and 4 Hornton Street and 63 Oakley Street have been re-developed. 31a Kings Road, near Sloane Square, bears a GLC plaque. The contents of the music room at this address have been preserved in a reconstruction of the room in the Grainger Museum in Melbourne, Australia.

The Graingers' addresses in London

May 1901–May 1902: 31 Gordon Place, Kensington

May 1902–October 1902: 8 Hornton Road/4 Hornton Street, Kensington

November 1902–March 1903: 18 (also given as 88) Abingdon Road, Kensington

April 1903–22 June 1905: 26 Coulson Street, Chelsea

22 June 1905–23 December 1905: 63 Oakley Street, Chelsea

23 December 1905–20 December 1906: 14 Upper Cheyne Row, Chelsea

20 December 1906–15 July 1907: 5 Harrington Road, South Kensington

16 July 1907–31 December 1907: 26 Coulson Street, SW

31 December 1907–17 November 1913 [19 August 1914]: 31a Kings Road, SW

17 November 1913–*c.* 10 January 1914: 24, Cheniston Gardens, Kensington

10 February 1914–April 1914: 19 Cheniston Gardens, Kensington

April 1914–1 June 1914: 7 Pembroke Villas (Balfour Gardiner's home)

1 June 1914–19 August 1914: returned to 31a Kings Road

During his time in London Grainger fairly launched himself as pianist, composer, folk-song collector and musical character with a wide circle of friends and contacts. He appeared at the Philharmonic Society at Queen's Hall in Schumann's Piano Concerto in 1907, and the same year was in constant demand after his friend Edvard Grieg died in the autumn of 1907, particularly playing Grieg's Piano Concerto. From London Grainger, usually accompanied by his mother, travelled across Europe and launched one tour back to Australia, but on the outbreak of war they left for America and apart from occasional visits, notably appearing on BBC Television in 1956, they did not return. Grainger's archives and scores are preserved at the museum he established in Melbourne, Australia and at his last home at White Plains, New York.

Maurice Greene (1695–1755)

The composer and organist set out as a chorister at St Paul's and in 1714 became organist of St Dunstan-in-the-West, Fleet Street. In 1718 he also became organist of St Andrew's Church, Holborn, and that same year was appointed organist of St Paul's cathedral. As part of his work he composed much church music, of which the funeral anthem *Lord Let Me Know Mine End*, with two solo trebles, is still widely sung. Most of his output consists of Georgian anthems such as *O God is our Hope and Strength* and *How Long Wilt Thou Forget Me* and his organ voluntaries are still often heard. As a minor contemporary of Bach and Handel his distinctively lyrical voice in the Purcellian tradition has been made clear in a recording by Emma Kirkby (Music Oscura 070978) of his songs and vocal music including the solo cantata *The Ode to Beauty* and settings of Spenser sonnets.

He struck up a friendship with Handel, who was frequently at the cathedral and who was invited by Greene to play the organ, though later they fell out. In 1727 he was appointed organist and composer at the Chapel Royal, and in 1730 he became a doctor of music at Cambridge University and was awarded the honorary position of Professor of Music. In 1735 he succeeded John Eccles as Master of the King's Musick. He was buried first in St Olave's Jewry and after its demolition in 1888 he was reinterred in St Paul's, where he shares a grave with William Boyce.

Masters of the Music(k)

1660–1666	Nicholas Lanier
1666–1674	Louis Grabu
1674–1700	Nicholas Staggins
1700–1735	John Eccles
1735–1755	Maurice Greene
1755(57)–1779	William Boyce
1779–1786	John Stanley
1786–1817	William Parsons
1817–1829	William Shield
1829–1834	Christian Kramer
1834–1848	Franz Cramer
1848–1870	George Frederick Anderson
1870–1893	Sir William George Cusins
1893–1924	Sir Walter Parratt
1924–1934	Sir Edward Elgar
1934–1941	Sir Henry Walford Davies
1942–1953	Sir Arnold Bax
1953–1975	Sir Arthur Bliss
1975–2003	Malcolm Williamson
2004–	Sir Peter Maxwell Davies

Edvard Grieg (1843–1907)

The Norwegian composer Edvard Grieg made six visits to London. He first visited London with his parents in the summer of 1862 and stayed at 18 Norfolk Street off the Strand. Twenty years later he came as a leading pianist and composer and stayed with his publisher, the Augener family, at 5 The Cedars, Clapham Common (now

47 Clapham Common, north side, SW4; plaque), during April and May 1888. Nina Grieg wrote to Delius from there on 26 April reporting the weather to be 'atrocious, windy and cold almost like in winter, I can't tell you how frozen we are, and we long for our lovely Leipzig days again'.

Stanley Hawley, then a student at the Royal Academy of Music, was sent to meet Edvard Grieg at Waterloo Station. Grieg had promised to come to the Academy in Tenterden Street, where he had signified his intention of hearing Stanley Hawley play his concerto with Mackenzie and the Academy Orchestra. Eric Coates recalled Hawley's story of their passage across London:

> Could Hawley get Grieg across Waterloo Bridge? He refused to budge, standing there in his tweed cape, mushroom hat and leggings, fascinated by the shipping down towards Tower Bridge; talking, gesticulating, pointing, anything rather than bother about such trivial things as pianoforte concertos in A minor. After a good deal of persuasion, Grieg consented to continue the walk to the Academy, and, judging by the way Hawley said he stopped and looked at everything *en route*, it must have taken literally hours.

Grieg appeared at a Philharmonic Society Concert at St James's Hall on 3 May when he was soloist in his own Piano Concerto and Cowen conducted. In the same concert a Miss Carlotta Elliott sang two Grieg songs and the large string section of the orchestra played Grieg's *Two Elegiac Melodies* with the composer conducting. Lionel Carley tells us that Grieg 'was able to describe the evening of 3 May as a "colossal success" . . . When I showed myself in the orchestra doorway there was a roar of jubilation in the huge hall, which was filled to the last seat, and it was so intense and unending . . . I continued to bow in every direction, but it just wouldn't stop.'

Cowen, who was conducting that evening, remembered that:

> He was not a great pianist, but he could play his own music with much effect. The popularity of his compositions, too, made everyone curious to see him *in propria persona*, and added not a little to the success he achieved. He and his wife (who was a very capable singer) were an interesting couple. They were both quite short, with bright intellectual faces and rough grizzly hair, and looked more like brother and sister than husband and wife. They had simple, unaffected natures, and seemed as much attached to each other as they were to the art they both followed. He was perhaps the more simple-minded and ingenuous of the two.

The following day the Griegs dined with Delius and his parents at the Hotel Metropole in Northumberland Avenue. This was the occasion on which Grieg won over Julius Delius to admit that his son was talented musically and should continue as a composer; Julius duly continued his allowance. On 16 May Grieg appeared again at St James's Hall in a chamber concert at which the violinist Wilhelmina Norman-Néruda (Lady Hallé) with Grieg at the piano played his First Violin Sonata and the *Romance* and *Finale* of the third in C minor. (In 1874, Norman-Neruda had played Grieg's Violin Sonata in G at the same hall, with Hallé at the piano.) Grieg played two groups of his piano miniatures and Nina sang six of his songs. In an obituary tribute the *Musical Times* later remembered 'The fascinating manner in which Madame Grieg sang her husband's delightful songs to his delicate accompaniment forms a life-long memory.'

In 1889 he again stayed with Augener. Arriving on 16 February he appeared at the Philharmonic Society concert at St James's Hall on 14 March, when his wife sang three of Grieg's songs with the composer at the piano in the first half and two more in the second. In between, Grieg conducted his *Peer Gynt* Suite No. 1. He was back at the next concert, on 28 March 1889, this time conducting his Piano Concerto with Mme Backer-Gröndahl as soloist. There were two more chamber music concerts in which Nina Grieg was especially featured both as a singer and in piano duets with her husband. He left London on 4 April.

Grieg's final appearance at the Philharmonic Society came on 24 May 1895 when he conducted the first English performances of three pieces from his incidental music to *Sigurd Jorsalfar*. Again he stayed with Augener and left on 26 May. In 1897 he came in the autumn arriving on 6 October, and staying with Augener for the last time. First his wife Nina and then Grieg himself fell ill and finally his concerts for early November were cancelled, but they did not leave until 22 December.

Grieg did not travel to London again until 1906, when he arrived at Claridges Hotel in Brook Street on 5 October and later stayed with Edgar Speyer at 46 Grosvenor St. There were concerts at Queen's Hall on 17 May and also on the 24th. Grieg left for the last time on 31 May. He died on 4 September 1907, and immediately a Memorial concert was announced in the Promenade concert programmes which were then in progress at Queen's Hall.

Sir George Grove (1820–1900)

As the architect of what came later, Grove's influence on British musical life in the second half of the nineteenth century was remarkable, considering that not only was he not a trained musician, but also that he enjoyed a national reputation as an engineer and a Biblical scholar. He was born in Clapham, attended the recently established local grammar school, and studied music at Holy Trinity Church, Clapham. At the age of sixteen he was articled to a civil engineer with offices in Fludyer Street, Westminster. His early life as an engineer was spent outside London, and in his mid-twenties he went to Jamaica and Bermuda as the engineer during the building of two lighthouses. Grove returned to London and married in 1851, and the Groves moved to Sydenham in 1852. From 1860 to his death in 1900 he lived at 208 Sydenham Road, SE26.

Grove's achievements were manifold: as a founder of the concerts at the Crystal Palace, its secretary for many years, and virtually the inventor and author of their programme notes for forty years; as a Schubert scholar discovering the music for *Rosamunde* then thought lost; as organising financial secretary to the campaign for the founding of the Royal College of Music and as its first Director; and for conceiving his celebrated *Dictionary of Music*, first published in twenty-six parts between 1879 and 1882, and later reissued in four volumes. He was thus a strong determining force in our view of musical education, in concert life, in the development of repertoire, in writing about music and in musical reference books, and the view of history they contain.

George Frideric Handel (1685–1759)

Handel came to London as a young foreign musician and died here nearly fifty years later, one of the great English composers – a status that grew with succeeding generations. The London Handel came to was a city of change, where the layout of many of his centres of operation, notably Brook Street and Hanover Square, was just emerging, though modern Regent Street did not exist in his lifetime. Daniel Defoe wrote of 'New squares, and new streets rising up every day'. Handel's London, therefore, to him was new and exciting. In Brook Street his house and those adjacent to it survive, and his home is now the Handel House Museum. It is therefore comparatively easy to forget the traffic and imagine oneself back 250 years to Handel's time.

In 1710 Handel came to London, arriving in November and staying until the following May. Handel came from Italy and was thus able to respond to the recently established vogue for Italian opera with his *Rinaldo*, which he literally 'codged-up' in a fortnight from earlier works, and it was seen at the Queen's Theatre, later the King's Theatre, Haymarket, now known as 'Her Majesty's'. What we see today is not the theatre Handel would have known. Towards the end of the eighteenth century it was burned down, and the theatre has been rebuilt three times over the succeeding centuries, but it is still on the same site today, three hundred years after it was first built. It would become a favourite theatre for Handel where he would soon enjoy some of his most notable successes. *Rinaldo* opened on 24 February 1711 and received fifteen performances but Handel left in June 1711 before the last of them. The theatre would remain the regular venue for Handel operas until 1734.

Handel was not in England again until October 1712, almost immediately finding aristocratic patronage with the very young Lord Burlington, nine years his junior, and later with the Duke of Chandos. From 1713 to 1716 Handel lived at Burlington House in Piccadilly, then in the process of alteration. Soon after his arrival Handel ingratiated himself at court with his music, including his *Ode for the Birthday of Queen Anne* in January 1713, a score whose opening duet for trumpet and soprano ('Eternal source of light divine') was revived and recorded so memorably for the mid-twentieth century by the counter-tenor Alfred Deller. Handel was commissioned to compose the so-called *Utrecht Te Deum* to mark the end of the seven years war and the Treaty of Utrecht, written in 1713. It was given a public rehearsal at the Banqueting House in Whitehall in March and was formally performed at St Paul's in July. At the end of that year Handel was awarded a royal pension.

The Queen died in 1714 and Handel found himself brought face to face with his ostensible employer, the Elector of Hanover, now George I. Handel finally re-established himself with the king in 1717 when he composed the *Water Music*. This was heard on 17 July, an ambitious court entertainment on the River Thames, which was played by a band of fifty between Lambeth and Chelsea and back. Handel possibly embarked from Whitehall Stairs, and King George demanded three performances during the voyage. On a fine evening the whole river was covered with a press of the grandest boats and barges, everyone who considered themselves anyone wanting to be involved.

Immediately after this, in the summer of 1717, Handel moved to the estate of the Duke of Chandos to direct the duke's chapel at his mansion of Cannons at Stanmore, Middlesex (long gone). Here he wrote eleven anthems that were performed at the new church of St Lawrence, Whitchurch, which survives.

Between 1719 and 1728 a new opera-giving organisation, The Royal Academy of Music, flourished, with Handel having not only the role of principal composer but also being designated 'Master of the Orchestra'. This had nothing to do with the Royal Academy of Music, founded in the nineteenth century, but was a society of aristocratic opera lovers organising to 'secure for themselves a constant supply of operas' to be composed largely by Handel. It was focused on the King's Theatre and Handel was sent abroad to secure the best singers of the day. While it continued, Handel prepared one or two new operas for each year and in most seasons there were three or four of his own operas heard. Probably the greatest and most successful opera Handel produced at this time was *Giulio Cesare in Egitto*, nowadays called just *Giulio Cesare*, which first appeared at the King's Theatre on 20 February 1724 and was his fifth new score for the scheme. It is probably the most popular Handel opera to have been revived in modern times.

In August 1723 Handel moved to 25 Brook St, W1 (in Handel's day it was unnumbered, later numbered 57), where he lived for thirty-six years. A stone's throw away is St George's church, Hanover Square (which was completed in 1725), where in later years he often used to play the organ, and where the interior is still much as he would have known it in his last years. The house at Brook Street is now the Handel House Museum (see Chapter 3).

In 1727 Handel was naturalised, then customarily accomplished by Act of Parliament. Also in 1727 King George I died unexpectedly on 11 June. For the coronation of King George II in Westminster Abbey, on 11 October, Handel wrote four anthems including *Zadok the Priest*, which has been heard at every coronation since then. It would be Handel to whom the king would turn when state occasions demanded new music, including the weddings of his eldest daughter and his son, the funeral of Queen Caroline in 1737, and the celebrations after the Battle of Dettingen, and the Peace of Aix-la-Chappelle. During the 1730s the London opera scene changed, with competing companies, and the newly formed 'Opera of the Nobility' effectively ending Handel's operatic ascendancy, tempting away most of

Handel's principal attraction, his best singers. Handel sought a new market and inadvertently evolved the oratorio for which he would later be principally remembered. This began when *Esther* was heard at the Crown and Anchor Tavern in the Strand (on the right by St Clement Danes Church on the corner of Arundel Street), the building pulled down in 1790.

Handel fought back in the 1730s with new operas, first at Covent Garden, moving to the Haymarket and ending at the Theatre Royal, Lincoln's Inn Fields, then in Portugal Street. It was later a china warehouse, and was demolished in 1848.

Handel first suffered a stroke in 1737. In his last years his sight became increasingly poor and eventually he became blind. He came to rely increasingly on John Christopher Smith and his son of the same name, the son maintaining the performances of the oratorios after Handel's death and becoming the organist of the Foundling Hospital (in what is now Brunswick Square) in 1754.

Handel wrote *Messiah*, the work on which his fame was consolidated in the nineteenth century, in three weeks in 1741, though it was first performed in Dublin. Also in 1741 he wrote *Samson*, heard at Covent Garden the same year. His last oratorio, *Jephtha*, was produced at Covent Garden on 1 March 1752. Handel died on Easter Saturday, 14 April 1759, at the house in Brook Street where he had lived for thirty-six years and fifty years after he first came to London. His funeral was in Westminster Abbey on 20 April. Here, a quarter of a century later, *Messiah* was heard performed by huge forces and this stimulated similar festival performances round the country. Over the next fifty years this was the foundation of the nineteenth-century triennial festival movement, in London leading to the Handel Festivals at Crystal Palace that ran throughout the second half of the nineteenth century with massed performances and huge audiences.

Joseph Haydn (1732–1809)

Haydn was invited to London by Johann Peter Salomon, who was born in Bonn and had once shared a house with the Beethoven family. He came to London in 1780 as a violinist but soon established a role as an independent promoter. In alliance with Gallini, the owner of the Hanover Square Rooms, he sought an attraction to trump that of the then dominant Professional Concerts. Salomon travelled to Vienna and persuaded Haydn to come with him to London, where they arrived on 2 January 1791, and where Haydn remained for eighteen months, leaving towards the end of June the following year.

Haydn's first night was at the home of John Bland at 45 High Holborn. Haydn then stayed in rooms in the same house as Salomon at 18 Great Pulteney Street, near Golden Square (now demolished). He came as one of the most famous composers in Europe, and was an immediate celebrity, widely reported in the press, and at once the recipient of countless engagements, remarking that he had dined out six times in his first week.

Haydn's first concert took place at the Hanover Square Rooms on 11 March when his Symphony No. 92 was played before a glittering audience and was a sensation; the slow movement was encored. On 16 May there was a benefit concert for Haydn from which he earned £350.

In London Haydn composed an opera, *L'anima del filosofo*, for Gallini, but its staging was prevented at its first rehearsal at the King's Theatre by the established Italian Opera at the Pantheon in Oxford Street exercising their monopoly.

Haydn attended the Handel Festival at Westminster Abbey in May 1791, when William Gardiner tells us that for *Messiah* 'the band was a thousand strong'. Haydn was bowled over. During his first summer he was free to explore England, on one occasion being a guest at a party travelling on the Thames from Westminster to Richmond and dining on an island in the river, serenaded by a wind band. Haydn was a frequent visitor to Mrs Schröter, at 6 James Street, Buckingham Gate, who conducted a romance with him in the most affectionate terms.

The competition between Salomon's series and the Professional Concerts was responsible for Haydn increasing his rate of composition. At first trying to buy him out by offering enhanced fees, his rivals changed their tack and tried to discredit him by announcing that his pupil Pleyel had been secured as Haydn himself was no longer able to produce new major scores. Haydn responded with a string of new works performed in Salomon's twelve concerts in the early spring of 1792 and thus completed the first six of his *London* symphonies (Nos 93–8), great enthusiasm attending the first performance of the *Surprise Symphony* (No. 94) in March 1792.

On 4 June Haydn went to Vauxhall Gardens for the birthday celebrations of the king and before he left on the journey home travelled to Slough to meet William Herschel, astronomer and composer. Herschel's house in Windsor Road, Slough, survived until 1960, the plot now covered by a modern office block, Observatory House, which has a modern sculpture of Herschel by Frank Belsky.

Haydn returned to London, arriving on 4 February 1794, and his first concert for Salomon was on 10 February. Haydn was contracted to produce his second set of *London* symphonies and presided over their first performances from the piano. In the autumn of 1794 Salomon changed his concert-giving arrangements and promoted the Opera Concerts, given on a larger scale than hitherto with an orchestra of sixty players performing every fortnight at the King's Theatre, which had a great new concert hall. The series was extended and two extra concerts had to be given. Later Haydn was invited to Buckingham Palace by the queen, who gave regular 'musicales'. Major inducements were made to keep Haydn in England and the king had invited him to stay, but he decided to leave. After benefit concerts, Haydn departed, and by the end of August was back in Vienna. He did not return. Haydn kept four notebooks during his visits but alas only three of them survive. They consist of jottings, anecdotes, reminiscences and lists of musical events attended. Haydn's clavichord from his time in London is preserved at the Royal College of Music.

Myra Hess (1890–1965)

Myra Hess was one of a celebrated group of talented pianists, including several women who came from the Royal Academy of Music, and studied with Tobias Matthay in the early 1900s. She was born at 86 Alexandra Road, Hampstead, but the family moved to 78 Boundary Road soon after. They moved again to 50 Boundary Road in 1914, but from 1915 Myra lived at temporary addresses. During the Second World War she was the guiding spirit behind the National Gallery Concerts, which she ran with Howard Ferguson. She had three main London houses – 1915–36, 8 Carlton Hill, NW8; 1936–52, 48 Wildwood Road, Hampstead Garden Suburb (plaque); 1952–65, 23 Cavendish Close, NW8.

Gustav Holst (1872–1934)

Born von Holst in Cheltenham to a family of Baltic extraction, Gustav Holst came to London to study with Stanford at the Royal College of Music in 1893. In 1895 he conducted the Hammersmith Socialist Choir and became engaged to Isobel Harrison. After a brief early career as an orchestral trombonist, he lived in the area around Hammersmith for much of his life. On his marriage in 1901 they lived at 162 Shepherd's Bush Road, and in 1903 moved to 31 Grena Road, Richmond. In 1903 he taught at James Allen's Girls' School, Dulwich, and in 1904 he taught adult classes at the Passmore Edwards Settlement, Bloomsbury, later the Mary Ward Settlement. In 1905 he became Director of Music at the then newly established St Paul's Girls' School, Brook Green (plaque; see Chapter 7). Holst had been sought out by the pioneering first High Mistress, Frances Ralph Gray. Holst remained at St Paul's all his life, and a soundproof music room was specially built for him, which survives.

The Holsts moved to 9 The Terrace, Barnes, SW13, and lived there from 1908 to 1913, moving once more to 10 Luxemburg Gardens, Brook Green, within easy walking distance of the school. Holst is particularly associated with adult education, most notably at Morley College from 1907 to 1924, where he is commemorated by the Holst Room. Most of Holst's mature orchestral works were first heard at Queen's Hall in the last twenty years of his life.

Herbert Howells (1892–1983)

The composer Herbert Howells was born in the Severn-side town of Lydney, Gloucestershire, and having been articled to Sir Herbert Brewer at Gloucester cathedral came to the Royal College of Music as a student in 1912, remaining until 1917. He taught composition there from 1920 remaining until an advanced age, and he thus dominated the college for much of the twentieth century. His remarkably flamboyant First Piano Concerto, in which the pianism of Rachmaninov and the then new English pastoralism are synthesised into a remarkable wide-spanning canvas, was introduced at a concert at the Royal College of Music on 10 July 1914, with the student Arthur Benjamin as soloist and with Stanford conducting. It was not heard again until it was recorded in 2000.

Howells was so sickly while at the college that at one time it was feared he would not survive. However, in the 1920s he produced a succession of orchestral works that make him a significant figure of the period; but soon Howells suppressed his early orchestral scores and they have been performed and recorded only since his death. His fame in his lifetime rested on his church music and his visionary choral work *Hymnus Paradisi*, a requiem for his son Michael, who died aged nine in 1935. He succeeded Holst as Director of Music at St Paul's Girls' School from 1936 to 1962.

In 1916 he lived at 48 Aldridge Villas, and in 1920 at 44 Castelnau, Barnes. From 1928/9 he lived at Redmarley, Station Road, Barnes Common, but in September 1940 Howells's part of Barnes was devastated by an off-course German bomber and as Howells put it 'our house was blitzed and bashed and ruined one awful night'. Fortunately Howells's daughter Ursula, the actress, was in Scotland and Howells and his wife were visiting relatives. Subsequently Howells moved into 'a small furnished house' at 11 Beverley Close, Barnes, and after the war in 1946 moved nearby to 3 Beverley Close. He died in a Putney nursing home, and his ashes are buried in Westminster Abbey.

William Hurlstone (1876–1906)

One of Stanford's favourite pupils at the Royal College of Music in the mid-1890s, Hurlstone, composer, friend and fellow student of Coleridge-Taylor, was born at Richmond Gardens, West Kensington and showed early musical abilities. His first work, 'Five Easy Waltzes' for the piano, was published when he was nine. He taught piano while still very young to contribute to the family finances.

He was soloist in his own Piano Concerto at St James's Hall while he was still a student. His outstanding, though few, chamber works were heard at St James's Hall as well. His Fantasy String Quartet won the first Cobbett prize in 1905. He became Professor of counterpoint at the Royal College of Music in September 1905, and also taught at the Croydon conservatoire. In 1905 the family moved from Selhurst to Park Mansions in Battersea. Hurlstone was asthmatic, a complaint that was the cause of his sudden death, a shock to all. He is buried at Croydon Cemetery, Mitcham Road, and his college friend Fritz Hart told how Parry said to him as they left the graveside '*What* a tragedy, Hart, – *what* a tragedy!' The revival of his music, notably by Richard Itter of the Lyrita Recorded Edition, fully underlines Parry's regret.

John Ireland (1879–1962)

The composer John Ireland, when still a student at the Royal College of Music, and newly arrived in London from Bowden, Cheshire, at first had a post as assistant organist at Holy Trinity Church, Sloane Street, in 1896. In 1898 he lived in a flat in

Elm Park Mansions, and in the early 1900s he moved to 14 Gunter Grove where he lived until he left London in 1939, at first for the Channel Islands, from which he only just escaped in advance of the German occupation. Living outside London during the war, he later moved to Rock Mill at Washington, Sussex.

He became organist at St Luke's church, Sydney Street, in 1904, staying until 1926. From 1923 he taught composition at the Royal College of Music, one of his pupils being Benjamin Britten. After the John Ireland Society had been formed in 1960, a concert was given at the Arts Council Drawing Room, 4 St James's Square, at which Ireland's early Sextet was revived. At this well-dressed event, some of those present being in evening dress, there appeared Ireland's companion Norah Kirby dressed in gumboots and a man's trousers. Whispered Anna Instone to her husband Julian Herbage – 'have you seen Norah, she's wearing John's trousers!' He is commemorated in St Sepulchre's Church (see Chapter 2) by a memorial window.

August Jaeger (1860–1909)

The German-born editor and writer on music is widely remembered today only because he is Elgar's 'Nimrod' of the *Enigma Variations*. Jaeger was born in Düsseldorf and came to England with his family in 1878, living in the Caledonian Road, Islington. From an early age he sang in Richter's choir and in the Novello Oratorio Choir. He joined the music publishers Novello in 1890 in an administrative capacity, but soon became artistic adviser. He was friend, musical confidant and editor of Parry and Elgar and mentor to Coleridge-Taylor and Walford Davies. He recognised the talents of Walford Davies and recommended him to his employers. He had a strong influence on Elgar's music and was his contact at his publishers as new works were sent by Elgar for setting, usually against the clock.

After his marriage (in the same year as Elgar's *Enigma*) he lived at 16 Margravine Gardens, W6, from 1899 and moved to 37 Curzon Road, Muswell Hill, in 1902 where he lived for the rest of his life. There is a plaque on the house. He died on 18 May 1909 from tuberculosis and was cremated at Golders Green; accompanying music was sung by the choir of Temple Church with Walford Davies at the organ. His ashes were scattered in Coldfall Woods by Creighton Avenue in Muswell Hill.

A memorial concert was held at Queen's Hall on 24 January 1910, when Richter conducted a mixed programme of music associated with Jaeger, and Elgar produced the only three completed of his intended set of six songs by Sir Gilbert Parker, sung by Muriel Foster. Various composers who had benefited from Jaeger's editorial role conducted their own works. In addition to Brahms and Wagner and Elgar's *Enigma Variations* (conducted by Richter) three of Jaeger's other protégés conducted their own music: Parry his *Overture to an Unwritten Tragedy*, Coleridge-Taylor his *Ballade in A minor* and Walford Davies four songs from his song cycle *The Long Journey*, Op. 25.

Leoš Janáček (1854–1928)

The Bohemian composer Leoš Janáček visited London only once, and stayed at the Langham Hotel from 29 April to 7 May 1926, spending his last night at the Czech Embassy and leaving on 8 May. From his point of view his timing could not have been worse, because the General Strike broke out during his visit. Yet during his first days in London he was able to fit in extensive sight-seeing, including the House of Commons and the London Zoo. The invitation had come from Rosa Newmarch, representing a committee of the musical good and great, and he was hosted through a succession of activities including a reception at Claridges, which makes it disappointing so little of his music was played. He dined out with Sir Henry Wood and also, with Rosa Newmarch, visited Wood at 4 Elsworthy Road to discuss playing his music. He subsequently visited Wood's country home at Appletree Farm at Chorleywood on Sunday 2nd May. Other guests included Mrs and Miss Newmarch and the bass Herbert Hayner.

Wood had previously given the British premiere of *The Fiddler's Child* on 4 May 1924 and he subsequently gave the first British performances of the *Sinfonietta* (Queen's Hall, 10 February 1928), *Taras Bulba* (Queen's Hall, 16 October 1928) and the *Lachian Dances* (Queen's Hall, 19 August 1930). The *Sinfonietta* was later played at Queen's Hall by the London Philharmonic Orchestra conducted by Robert Heger on 16 October 1933. Wood conducted the first London performance of the *Glagolitic Mass* at the BBC Studios at Maida Vale in June 1935, having introduced it at the 1930 Norwich Festival.

Janáček's concert was given at Wigmore Hall on 6 May. Owing to the strike the audience was restricted to those who could walk to the hall, and, reported Eric Blom in the only review (the other papers were not published) in the *Manchester Guardian*, 'many music lovers walked long distances . . . [and] the press turned up almost in full force, although there were no papers to notice the concert'. He might have added that some of the performers also walked a long way to play (Léon Goossens, then the oboist of the London Wind Quintet, reported a three-hour hike). Four works were heard, the Violin Sonata, *Fairy Tale* for cello and piano, the first string quartet and the wind sextet *Mládí* (*Youth*), which Blom found 'a delightfully fresh and original work'. Intended for the concert had been the *Concertino* for piano and sextet, but this was dropped on the excuse that all the artists did not arrive, but actually because Janáček was very unenthusiastic about the proposed pianist, Fanny Davies (he called her 'an old scarecrow – beneath all criticism'), and it was later programmed at the Æolian Hall in a Gerald Cooper concert on 7 February 1928.

Joseph Joachim (1831–1907)

Born in Bratislava (then Pressburg) Joachim was a child prodigy violinist whose annual visits to England after 1866 became a national institution for nearly half a century. Moscheles recorded in his diary Joachim's arrival in London in 1844 at the age of thirteen with a letter of recommendation from Mendelssohn: 'his talent is his best introduction. We organised a small party expressly for him; I listened with delight to him and Emily playing in Mendelssohn's lovely D minor trio; after that I was fairly taken by surprise by Joachim's manly and brilliant rendering of David's Variations and De Beriot's Rondo. Mendelssohn is right, here we have talent of true stamp'. Joachim appeared at the Philharmonic Society a remarkable forty times between 1844 and 1899, and eight of his compositions were played there. In March 1844 he played at Drury Lane Theatre and in May at the Philharmonic Concerts, conducted by Mendelssohn. He also appeared at the Hanover Square Rooms and the Crystal Palace.

He visited England frequently – in 1847, 1849, 1852, 1858, 1859, 1862 and then annually. He founded the Joachim String Quartet in 1869 and it came to London in 1900 and played that April in St James's Hall. In 1899 at St James's Hall Joachim was presented with a Stradivarius violin and a Tourte bow. In 1903 he recorded five sides for the Gramophone and Typewriter Company preserving a distant shadow of what his playing must have been like in his prime. In Brahms's *Hungarian Dance* in G minor he is monumental, with the added bonus of his voice caught at the end. In May 1904 the diamond jubilee of his first appearance in England was celebrated with a reception at Queen's Hall at which he was presented with his portrait by John Singer Sargent; a concert was held and a eulogy given by Parry. In 1905 he had a series of concerts at the Bechstein Hall (now Wigmore Hall). In 1906 he gave a Brahms chamber music series at Queen's Hall.

Louis Antoine Jullien (1812–1860)

The French violinist and conductor who arrived in London in 1838 was a showman, and he made a huge if short-lived reputation with a succession of promenade concerts, most notably with sequences of quadrilles and popular dance music. These were the first concerts at which the general public could hear orchestral music for a shilling. Jullien first appeared at Drury Lane Theatre as conductor of summer concerts in June 1840, then conducted winter concerts in January 1841 and Concerts de Société at the English Opera House, Lyceum in February and March 1842. That December he began an annual series of concerts at the English Opera House, which continued until 1859.

Francesco Berger remembered Jullien on the podium for his flashy personal presentation: 'immaculately dressed, with a considerable display of ornamental shirtfront decorated with three dazzling diamond studs. Before the beginning of a concert, which he conducted facing the audience, a pair of white kid gloves were handed to him on a silver tray by a liveried attendant, and he put them on with ostentatious deliberation; and after each item he sank, apparently exhausted, into a gorgeous armchair without retiring.'

As music publisher Jullien opened a shop in Maddox Street, and then at 214 Regent Street, in the heyday of the craze for his dance music, with its lithographed

91   Jullien directing his orchestra and four military bands at Covent Garden, as seen by the *Illustrated London News*, 7 November 1846.

coloured covers, his 'elegantly appointed shop' sold it exclusively and did well. In 1847 he took a lease on the Theatre Royal, Drury Lane, to perform English operas, employing Berlioz as conductor. The venture bankrupted him the following year, but undaunted he planned monster concerts and fêtes using huge forces. The first two were held at Exeter Hall in June 1849 and at the Surrey Zoological Gardens, Kennington, in July, but ended badly again. He brought out his own opera *Pietro il Grande* at Covent Garden, but that failed too and was taken off after only a few performances. In March 1856 Covent Garden burned down and with it all his music, including the quadrilles manuscripts. He also lost financially through his involvement with the Royal Surrey Gardens Co., and he left England in 1858.

Zoltán Kodály (1882–1967)

Kodály first came to London in 1927. Possibly it was his nervousness and lack of English that at first may have been off-putting to some, but he met Arnold Bax who subsequently wrote to his friend the violinist May Harrison on 10 December: 'Kodály went back to Hungary the morning on which I received your letter . . . He is not at all pompous but extremely shy . . .' The BBC had broadcast the composer's performance of what they then called the *Hungarian Psalm* on 4 December, which is when he must have met Bax. The following year Kodály was guest at the Three

Choirs Festival at Gloucester, when *Psalmus Hungaricus* was again sung, technically the first UK public performance, on 6 September 1928. In order to make the trip worthwhile for Kodály, Sir Ivor Atkins persuaded the BBC that they should offer him a date at the same time, and he appeared at the Proms to conduct the suite from *Háry János* on 30 August.

It was 1932 before the BBC approached Kodály again and the composer replied in English for the first time, and conducted music from his new *Székely Fonó* (*Transylvanian Spinning Room*) in a contemporary concert in the then new Concert Hall at Broadcasting House on 26 May 1933, with rehearsals morning and afternoon the previous day and on the morning of the concert.

In 1935 the BBC proposed to include *Háry János* in a winter Prom in January 1936, and Kodály wrote throwing interesting light on what went on when he had first come in 1927: 'Háry János Suite I already conducted at Queen's Hall a few years ago, whereas I performed the Psalmus in 1927 only in a studio with small chorus and incomplete orchestra. This work is, as far as I know more rarely performed as the other, and would be more attractive.' In fact this trip did not mature as Kodály had a skiing accident and had to cancel at the last minute.

In 1937 he returned again combining appearances at the Proms and the Three Choirs. At Gloucester he conducted the *Dances of Galanta* and his new *Budavari Te Deum*. In those days the Three Choirs final rehearsals (orchestra and soloists) were in London, and Kodály was at the Royal College of Music to conduct these on 31 August and 1 and 2 September. The performance was on 6 September. He then returned to London where he appeared at the Proms on 9 September in his *Háry János* suite, which Kenneth A. Wright, BBC Deputy Director of Music later remembered as a 'riotous success'. On 12 September he was at Maida Vale for a BBC studio concert including *Summer Evening*, two songs with orchestra (in fact Op. 14 Nos 1 and 3) sung in English and the *Dances of Galanta* he had recently produced at Gloucester. Boult entertained Kodály and his wife to lunch at the Langham Hotel before they left London, not to return for nine years.

After the war the BBC Music Department tried to re-establish contact with a wide range of European composers. On 21 May 1946 Wright wrote to Kodály, the letter being personally delivered to Budapest by the BBC conductor Stanford Robinson. Kodály travelled to London from Vienna by British European Airways. During this trip he conducted the BBC Symphony Orchestra in the *Concerto for Orchestra* and *Missa Brevis*, and at Claridges Hotel on 10 October he was interviewed in Hungarian by Mátyás Seiber for the European Service. At this time Kodály was reported at a reception at the Hungarian Legation in London. In February 1947 he was back again for a BBC performance of his *Missa Brevis*. It was on this occasion that he met his future publisher at Boosey and Hawkes, Ernest Roth. It was Roth who wrote to the BBC in July that year a 'private and confidential' letter indicating that 'Kodály's life or at least his liberty may be in danger . . . Kodály . . . asked me to secure for him an invitation to this country which would, in case of need, secure him quickly a visa, so that he could leave Hungary at a very short notice'. The BBC responded on 5 August inviting Kodály to come to London to discuss the performance of the opera *Háry János* complete.

In 1948 Kodály conducted the *Missa Brevis* at the Three Choirs and in October 1949 arrived for what turned out to be an extended stay, for at least some of the time being at the Park View Hotel, Hyde Park Gate. In January 1950 he conducted BBC dates in Glasgow and London and on the 14th conducted *Háry János* at the Winter Proms when Kenneth Wright reported: 'Kodály had a spontaneous reception of great warmth. The applause continued for nearly 10 minutes and the final March had to be encored'. He returned to Budapest in mid-February.

Ten years later, after the death of his wife in 1959, on 3 May 1960 he received an honorary degree at Oxford, followed by a concert in London, where at Maida Vale he again conducted *Háry János*. It is an interesting reflection on concert mores that in 1960 the BBC found it necessary to state 'informal dress'. In August it was his *Te Deum* at that year's Three Choirs at Worcester. On 18 June 1965 the Aldeburgh Festival featured a 'Tribute to Zoltan Kodály' in the presence of the composer.

Constant Lambert (1905–1951)

Lambert was a brilliant shooting star on the London musical scene, where for twenty years he played a pivotal role in the development of the ballet. Lambert's career was very much centred on London, and in a period when many composers wrote music evoking a rural idyll, Lambert was quintessentially a metropolitan composer. Nevertheless his is a sad tale of youthful brilliance in several fields – as composer, writer and conductor – but also of overwork, excessive drinking and neglected diabetes, culminating in his death two days before his forty-sixth birthday.

Lambert was the leading light of a Fitzrovian bohemian circle that included Cecil Gray, William Walton, Alan Rawsthorne and Angus Morrison, the artists Michael Ayrton and Jacob Epstein, and later Dylan Thomas. They patronised the pubs and hostelries within easy reach of the BBC and Covent Garden, most notably the back bar of the Café Royal in Regent Street just off Piccadilly Circus (since much altered) and The George in Great Portland Street. Ayrton remembered that 'When Constant was present it was unparalleled conversation – I don't know I have ever known anybody who could so raise the spirits of a company by his mere presence'. In his *Who's Who in Music* entry for 1948 we find his posts given as 'Artistic Dir Sadler's Wells Ball; Pres Kensington Kittens & Neuter Cats Club.'

Lambert's professional life as a conductor and pianist centred at first on the Camargo Society ballet company at the Mercury Theatre in Ladbroke Road, W11, soon moving to Sadler's Wells Theatre in Islington as the Sadler's Wells Ballet, and later at Covent Garden, as well as at the BBC and Queen's Hall. Early concerts, often of his own music, were at the Æolian Hall in Bond Street. When Heseltine had been found dead in 1930 Lambert had organised the memorial concert, at which many of the leading musicians of the day gave their services. As a regular working musical journalist he would also have been a well-known character in Fleet Street, particularly at the office of the *Sunday Referee* where he had a regular column. His own music was notably performed at Queen's Hall and at Sadler's Wells and Covent Garden.

The family home from 1914 to 1926 was 25 Glebe Place, Chelsea, from where he launched his career, though he was at school at Christ's Hospital near Horsham in his teens. When Amy Lambert, his mother, returned to London from Australia in 1929, Constant went to live with her at 42 Peel Street, off Kensington Church Street. In 1931 Lambert married a very young Florence Chuter and they lived at first at 15 Percy Street in a flat belonging to Charles Laughton and Elsa Lanchester, who were off to the USA. In 1940, '41 and '42 he stayed at the cottage or gate house at Hanover Lodge in Regent's Park, where he conducted his affair with the ballerina Margot Fonteyn (Lambert called it 'Hangover' Lodge). In 1942 and again in 1946 he returned to 42 Peel Street and in 1947 lived at 39 Thurloe Square. In 1944–6 he also shared Michael Ayrton's house at 4 All Souls Place (behind All Soul's church, Langham Place, where Weber had worked on *Oberon* in 1826), and where Lambert continued his affair with Margot Fonteyn, though this house has not survived. He lived at 197 Albany Street, NW1, after his second marriage in 1947, and his ashes are buried in Brompton Cemetery. Lambert was a great cat lover and when, in January 1952, his *Eight Poems of Li Po* and his Piano Concerto were heard at Hampstead Town Hall, a large black cat is reported to have sat on the platform, vanishing after the concert.

Jenny Lind (1820–1887)

The celebrated soprano, known as the Swedish nightingale, lived in England from 1847. That year she sang in *Robert le diable* at Her Majesty's Theatre and also appeared in Verdi's *I masnadieri* among other stage performances. From 1856 in London again she sang in numerous concerts and oratorios. She was chosen by Grove for the newly opened Royal College of Music in 1883 and taught singing there until 1886. She is buried in Malvern. A memorial medallion is in Westminster Abbey, and a plaque is on her house at 189 Old Brompton Road, SW7, where she lived from 1876 to 1886.

Franz Liszt (1811–1886)

Liszt first came to London with his father in early May 1824 as 'Master Liszt' the child prodigy. He came for the last time in 1886 as the venerable 'Abbé Liszt' crowned by long white hair, his portrait adorning the whole front page of *The Graphic*. The young Liszt was brought to London by Erard the piano maker, arriving with one of the new pianos, and he was provided with rooms at Erard's London office at 18 Great Marlborough Street (plaque).

Liszt first appeared at the Argyll Rooms, then at Drury Lane in a mixed bill and then before the royal family at Windsor. At this time he also fulfilled two last-minute engagements in Manchester. The second visit was the following year and took a similar pattern, Liszt appearing again at Windsor, and a third journey took place in 1827 when he stayed in Frith Street, Soho. During Liszt's second visit to London the family went to St Paul's cathedral to hear the massed singing of several thousand children; these were the so-called Free Schools and Liszt responded emotionally, reacting as Haydn had done before him and Berlioz would do later.

Liszt did not return to London until 1840 and '41, when he again stayed at 18 Great Marlborough Street. His father had died soon after they had returned to France in 1827, and the Liszt who returned was now a towering virtuoso in his prime. Moscheles remembered:

> At one of the Philharmonic Concerts, he played three of my 'Studies' quite admirably. Faultless in the way of execution, but by his powers he has completely metamorphosed these pieces; they have become more his Studies than mine. With all that they please me, and I shouldn't like to hear them played in any other way by him. The Paganini Studies, too, were uncommonly interesting to me. He does anything he chooses, and does it admirably, and those hands raised aloft in the air come down but seldom, wonderfully seldom, upon a wrong key. 'His conversation is always brilliant,' adds Mrs. Moscheles: 'it is occasionally dashed with satire, or spiced with humour.' 'The other day he brought me his portrait, with his "hommages respectueux" written underneath, and, what was the best "hommage" of all, he sat down to the piano and played me the Erl-King, the Ave Maria, and a charming Hungarian piece.'

Liszt arrived in England on 6 May 1840, and on 8 May he appeared at the Hanover Square Rooms. The programme included opera fantasies on *I Puritani* and *Lucia di Lammermoor* and his *Grand Galop Chromatique*. His reception from a packed house was ecstatic. He appeared at the Philharmonic Society on 11 May and 8 June, in the first playing Weber's Konzertstück for piano and orchestra and in the second playing piano solos, Moscheles's *Studies* and his own *Marche Hongroise*. Audiences lionised him, and at the Philharmonic he was presented with a valuable piece of silver plate. The critics were not so sympathetic, not liking his flamboyant style of playing, which they equated with 'banging'. But the reception at Buckingham Palace and at various society houses was very cordial. During May, Liszt asked Marie d'Agoult to join him and they stayed at a hotel in Richmond. While on this tour Liszt established the future pattern of piano concerts with a series he announced as 'Liszt's Pianoforte Recitals', The first took place at the Hanover Square Rooms on 9 June 1840. Subsequently Liszt gave a second series, this time at Willis's Rooms, 55 (now 28) King Street. *The Times* reported 'Liszt leaves every other performer, whether on the pianoforte or any other instrument, at an immeasurable distance behind him.' In the summer Liszt came again, for a provincial tour, and in November returned for more touring and then to Ireland and Scotland, and appeared at the Philharmonic Society on 14 June 1841, when he played the piano part in Hummel's Septet.

Liszt in London

May–August 1824
June 1825
May–July 1827
May–June 1840
August–September 1840
September 1840–January 1841
June 1841
April 1886

These visits were followed by a long fallow period when Liszt's music was hardly heard in London at all. Eventually there was a revival, largely owing to the promotion of annual London concerts between 1869 and 1887 devoted to the music of Liszt by Walter Bache. At the end of his life Bache was able to persuade the composer to return to London. This was in 1886 when Liszt was widely fêted, and he stayed at Westwood House, Sydenham, as the guest of Henry Littleton, head of Novello's. During that crowded visit he went to St James's Hall, attended the inaugural ceremony for the Liszt Scholarship for young composers and pianists at the Royal Academy of Music, and visited Windsor Castle, the Grosvenor Gallery, Prince's Hall and Crystal Palace. He found time to see Henry Irving in W. G. Wills's adaptation of Goethe's *Faust* at the Lyceum Theatre; this was on 14 April when he was accompanied by the Littletons and his pupil Stavenhagen, Irving giving a dinner for Liszt in the Beefsteak Room when Liszt sat beside Ellen Terry. The party lasted until 4 a.m. The next day Liszt lunched with the Baroness Burdett-Coutts in Stratton Street and played for the company. Liszt's visit to London is remembered in a celebrated engraving published in *The Graphic* for 17 April in which Liszt is shown surrounded by the leading British musicians of the day (see p. 194).

George Lloyd (1913–1998)

George Lloyd was born in Cornwall and had his first success there, after his opera *Iernin* was given in Penzance in 1934. His family subsequently moved to London, for the London run of the opera at the Lyceum Theatre in June 1935. Living in Sydenham almost opposite the Crystal Palace (see Chapter 7 for his account of the building) he continued musical studies with Kidson at Trinity College of Music, and his second opera, *The Serf*, was produced by the British National Opera Company at Covent Garden in 1938 and subsequently toured. After the outbreak of the Second World War, in which he was very seriously shell-shocked, he did not live in London again until the late 1970s, when he and his wife Nancy sold their Dorset market garden and moved to a flat near Baker Street Station, at 199 Clarence Gate Gardens, Glentworth Street, NW1, from where he succeeded in establishing himself as a composer during the last twenty years of his life. Here he composed all his later symphonies, choral and other orchestral works.

Marie Lloyd (1870–1922)

The celebrated music hall entertainer Marie Lloyd was born at 36 Plumber Road, Hoxton. Marie Lloyd was the stage name of Matilda Alice Victoria Wood, who made her debut aged fifteen probably at the Eagle Tavern (see Chapter 1) in City Road or at the nearby Grecian Theatre. Marie Lloyd recorded with the Gramophone and Typewriter Company as early as 1903. From 1888 she lived at 55 Graham Road, E8, which bears a plaque to this effect. As she became more and more popular and successful, she moved to better and larger houses, all in London, starting at 54 Lewisham Road, New Cross, and in 1894 moving to 73 Carleton Road, Tufnell Park, and in 1898 Granville Lodge, 98 King Henry's Road, St John's Wood. In 1912 her address was Oakdene, Finchley Road, on the corner of Wentworth Road, and in 1922, shortly before she died, she moved to 37 Woodstock Road, Golders Green. She was buried in Hampstead Cemetery.

Elisabeth Lutyens (1906–1983)

The daughter of the architect Sir Edwin Lutyens, the composer Elisabeth Lutyens became well known as a pioneer of serial music in the UK and was a celebrated teacher of composition to a generation of avant garde composers in the 1960s and '70s.

Living in central London for most of her life, Lutyens was the archetypal Fitzrovian musician. Her childhood was spent in her parents' houses at first at 29 Bloomsbury Square, then at 31 Bedford Square, and finally an attractive Adam house at 13 Mansfield Street when aged fourteen. When Lutyens was first married to the singer Ian Glennie, in the 1930s, they lived in a flat in the basement of this house. At this time she was involved in the development of what became the Macnaghten-Lemare concerts at the Mercury Theatre in Notting Hill Gate (and later at Wigmore Hall). She was represented by new works in the first two concerts, though she soon rejected them both. The marriage was not successful and she was divorced.

In 1939 she lived with Edward Clark, who had been the BBC's champion of modern music but had left under a cloud in 1936. Clark was at 12 Fitzroy Street and after they were married they went to 6 Fitzroy Street while the composer Christian Darnton lived at the former flat at No. 12. Lutyens eventually left Clark and set herself up in a flat on her own at 1 Pond Road, Blackheath. Her subsequent addresses included 13 and 17 King Henry's Road and 76a Belsize Park Gardens. During the war and in the following years Lutyens kept body and soul together with a succession of commissions for radio incidental music and for documentary films, the commissions for which were allocated after apparently casual meetings with the relevant producers in pubs in the streets of Fitzrovia around the BBC (See Chapter 1).

Sir George Macfarren (1813–1887)

The composer and teacher Macfarren is remarkable not only for his celebrity at the height of his career but for how completely he was forgotten afterwards. He went to the Royal Academy of Music to study composition, piano and trombone, under Charles Lucas and Cipriani Potter, becoming a professor there when only twenty-one in 1834. He was one of the founders of the Society of British Musicians in 1834 and the Handel Society in 1843 and edited Handel's *Judas Maccabaeus*, *Jephtha* and *Belshazzar*. He was remarkably fertile as a composer, writing music in most forms, of which only the *Chevy Chase* overture (conducted by both Mendelssohn and

Wagner) and two of his nine symphonies have now been revived and recorded on CD. He wrote some twenty operas and operettas though not all succeeded, but *King Charles II* was seen at the Princess's Theatre in 1849 while in the 1860s *Robin Hood* and *She Stoops to Conquer* were given and the former was particularly successful. His chamber operas were possibly ahead of their time and were seen at the Gallery of Illustration in Marylebone in the 1860s. He was an interesting precursor of the later folksong school in his use of traditional tunes that he not only edited but also used in his music, most strikingly in the once-popular cantata *May Day* of 1857, which was published in vocal and full score, where the 'Staines Morris' appears in the movement called 'The Revels'. He also wrote prolifically on music.

Despite going blind in 1860 he continued with an amanuensis, Oliveria Prescott, and became principal of the Royal Academy of Music in 1876. He was knighted in 1883. He lived at 20 Hamilton Terrace, NW8 (plaque), and is buried in Hampstead Cemetery. Macfarren's wife, Natalia Macfarren (1828–1916), made many widely disseminated mid-century English translations of operas and songs and his brother Walter Macfarren (1826–1905) was also a well-known musician of his day who wrote orchestral and piano works in a more Mendelssohnian style than his brother.

Sir Alexander Campbell Mackenzie (1847–1935)

Mackenzie came from a musical family in Edinburgh. Sent to Germany at an early age, he subsequently played violin in the ducal orchestra at Sondershausen, where he found himself playing in premieres by composers such as Berlioz and Liszt. He entered the Royal Academy of Music in London at the age of sixteen to study violin with his father's teacher, Prosper Sainton, for which he was awarded a King's Scholarship, supporting himself by freelance work in London theatres. In 1865 he returned to Scotland and developed as both composer and performer, while teaching and conducting. He went to Italy in 1879 and became a full-time composer. He eventually moved to London in 1885 to become the conductor of the Novello Choir.

Mackenzie was an equal part of that Victorian compositional triumvirate that included Parry and Stanford, and held a dominant place in English composition in the twenty years before Elgar's ascendancy in the early 1900s. He wrote orchestral tone poems, a celebrated violin concerto, a piano concerto and a succession of festival choral works that have yet to be revived, though a BBC broadcast of the solos from his setting of the Biblical 'Song of Songs', *The Rose of Sharon* (1884) in 1995, revealed a delightfully atmospheric romantic score far removed from the presumed sabatarianism of such music.

He succeeded Macfarren to become the long-serving principal (1888–1924) of the Royal Academy of Music, and he also taught, conducted and oversaw the move to new premises in 1912 and its centenary celebrations in 1922. He conducted the Royal Choral Society and in 1892 was appointed conductor of the Philharmonic Society till he resigned in 1899. He had a great success when he introduced Tchaikovsky's

Pathétique symphony to London. He was knighted in 1895, and like his predecessor at the Academy he was another of those celebrated composers of late Victorian England who passed almost into oblivion after he died, though in Mackenzie's case today he is making a steady revival on CD. Mackenzie's London address was long at 15 Regent's Park Road.

Gustav Mahler (1860–1911)

Mahler came to London once only, from May to July 1892 to conduct Wagner operas at a six-week German opera season at Covent Garden and Drury Lane, with the leading German singers of the day, and also *Fidelio* at Drury Lane which was given in German for the first time in London. He stayed first at Keyser's Royal Hotel (now demolished), 69 Torrington Square, WC1, and later at 22 Alfred Place, WC1. Mahler's rehearsals started at the beginning of June, and he wrote to a German friend, trying out his newly learned English: 'I have found the circumstances of orchestra here bader [*sic*] than thought and the cast better than hoped'. Mahler was very well received by the public, and the *Morning Post* critic wrote about *Tristan*: 'only the word "perfect" can describe the orchestra, which achieved wonders under the direction of Herr Mahler'.

Sir August Manns (1825–1907)

The German-born conductor was long associated with the Crystal Palace and created with George Grove the popular Saturday concerts that ran there from 1855 to 1901. By attracting thousands to listen to classical music at reasonable prices, he was one of the mainsprings of the enormous development of the audience for music in the second half of the nineteenth century. Manns was instrumental in bringing many of the iconic works of today's repertoire to London soon after they were written. In 1861 he accepted an invitation to conduct a series of promenade concerts at Drury Lane Theatre. In 1883 he succeeded Michael Costa as conductor of the triennial Handel Festival, also held at Crystal Palace since 1857. In the 1890s he was a regular visitor to Glasgow and Edinburgh, and his series of Patterson's Concerts in the latter city were clearly modelled on the Crystal Palace, even to the extent of recycling the programme notes. He was naturalised in 1894, made Doctor of Music at Oxford University in 1903 and knighted the same year. He lived at 'Cleadale', Harold Road, Norwood, and the year before he died he moved to White Lodge, Beulah Hill, Norwood. He is buried at West Norwood Cemetery. (See also Crystal Palace, Chapter 7.)

Tobias Matthay (1858–1945)

Composer, pianist and teacher, Matthay was regarded by many as the originator of a distinctive piano school, though his method was waspishly remembered by

Bax in his autobiography and discredited by his pupil Alan Bush, later a student of Schnabel, who told one of the present authors that Matthay was 'the ruination of pianism in England'. Matthay was a student at the Royal Academy of Music in 1871 under Sterndale Bennett, Sullivan, Prout and Macfarren. He became a professor there from 1880 to 1925, when he left to develop his own piano school, which he had founded in 1900. He lived at 21 Arkwright Road, NW3 (plaque), where a succession of pupils including Myra Hess, Irene Scharrer, Arnold Bax, York Bowen, Arthur Alexander and Harriet Cohen called regularly for lessons. Bax said of him:

> It nearly always happened that just as I would begin to forget my self-consciousness and begin to play something like freely, 'Tobs' would bump my forearm from beneath and cry excitely, 'What's this? Key-bedding? To the sound and no further, remember! And now! Don't think of yourself! Think of the music! Beethoven!! (and he would assume an expression and attitude of sublimity). 'Beethoven's messenger!!!' (in a thrilling voice). 'That's *you*!' and he would poke a long forefinger hard into one's midriff. Another trick he had was to charge one off the piano-stool like a heavy-weight footballer, and play the passage quite unintelligibly himself.

Nicolas Medtner (1879/1880–1951)

Born in Moscow, the pianist-composer Medtner had the misfortune to emerge at much the same time as Rachmaninov, who tended to eclipse him. He settled in London in 1935 and lived for the rest of his life at 69 Wentworth Road, NW11 (plaque). His house was a meeting place for Russian émigré composers and musicians. Medtner is known for a large portfolio of piano music and three piano concertos that were championed on 78rpm records with the financial support of the Maharajah of Mysore.

Dame Nellie Melba (1861–1931)

Melba was the stage name of the Australian-born soprano Helen Porter Mitchell. She made her first appearance in London at Prince's Hall in Piccadilly, but she did not sing in London again or become celebrated until she took the title role in *Lucia di Lammermoor* at Covent Garden in 1888. From then on she sang regularly at Covent Garden and in 1894 at the Handel Festival. In 1904 she organised a charity concert at Queen's Hall and sang for royalty at Buckingham Palace. She made her final farewells at Covent Garden and the Royal Albert Hall in 1926; extracts from her Covent Garden Farewell Concert on 8 June 1926 were recorded by HMV, including arias from Verdi's *Otello*, Puccini's *La Bohème* and her emotional farewell speech (see pp. 161 and 167). She lived at Coombe Hill, Beverly Lane, Coombe Lane West, Kingston upon Thames (plaque), and is celebrated by a memorial window in the Musicians' Chapel in St Sepulchre's.

Felix Mendelssohn (1809–1847)

Mendelssohn made ten visits to London as performer and composer; despite his youth he was generally regarded as a visiting musical luminary, and was accepted by the musical establishment from the outset. He first arrived in London on 21 April 1829, the nineteen-year-old entrusted to Moscheles's protection by Mendelssohn's father. Moscheles found him lodgings at 203 Great Portland Street where his landlord was a German ironmonger called Heincke (on the corner of Riding House Street, since renumbered 79 and rebuilt). He conducted his Symphony in C minor in the seventh concert of the Philharmonic Society at the Argyll Rooms nearby. This was on 25 May when J. B. Cramer led him to the piano. The applause was reported as 'very strong' and the scherzo was encored. He also appeared as a pianist and at the age of twenty made such a strong and charming impression that he was commissioned to write an opera for Covent Garden.

In July he left for a tour of Scotland and returned in September, finishing a String Quartet at 35 Bury Street, St James's. After a coach accident and convalescence at Thomas Attwood's house in Norwood, he left for Berlin towards the end of November. His overture to *A Midsummer Night's Dream* was given its first British performance on 24 June 1829. Earlier he had given the manuscript to Thomas Attwood to look after but Attwood accidentally left it in a cab and it was never found – Mendelssohn had to write the whole score out again from memory!

He returned to London in April 1832, staying until June. That May the *Hebrides Overture* was premiered by the Philharmonic Society and he gave several piano concerts. Moscheles chronicled this musically brilliant time:

> 28th,-Rehearsal of the Philharmonic Concert, where a regular Art Congress assembled, including Mendelssohn, Lablache, Field, and J. B. Cramer; in the evening we joined Meyerbeer in his box at the Opera, and saw 'Il Barbiere' with Cinti and Lablache; it was a first-rate performance.

> 30th,-Today Mendelssohn played us his Cantata 'Die Erste Walpurgisnacht,' which I had heard and admired in former days in Berlin. Now that he has completely re-written it, I admire it still more. He also played me that charming Liederspiel, 'The Son and Stranger,' written for the silver wedding of his parents, and lastly his overture to the 'Hebrides.' My wife's invitation for this evening he answered in the following way, 'I thank Mr. Moscheles exceedingly for wishing to see something of my new compositions, and if he promises to tell me when he has had too much of me, I will bring a whole cab-load of manuscripts to your house, and play everyone of you to sleep.'

> May 1st (Sunday).-Mendelssohn and Klingemann came to the children's one o'clock dinner. The former gave me the score of his overture to the 'Hebrides,' which he had finished in Rome on 16th December, 1830, but afterwards altered for publication. I often thought the first sketch of his compositions so beautiful and complete in form that I could not think any alteration advisable, and during our stroll in the Park we discussed this point again and again.

Mendelssohn did not return to London for five years. On 27 August 1837 he arrived back at Klingemann's house at 4 Hobart Place, Pimlico. He appeared as organist at city churches – St Paul's, Christ Church, Newgate Street – dazzling his audiences with his improvisations. He took three rehearsals of his oratorio *St Paul* in Exeter Hall but at the Sacred Harmonic Society concert on 12 September he could not conduct because his contract with Birmingham forbade it. He was impressed and his response was cordial, writing: 'I can hardly express the gratification I felt in hearing my work performed in so beautiful a manner . . . The power of the choruses – this large body of good and musical voices – and the style in which they sang . . . gave me the most heartfelt treat'. He left for Birmingham the next day and then went home.

Three years later he came again, this time for the British premiere of the *Lobgesang* at the Birmingham Festival. Arriving in London on 8 September 1840 he stayed with Klingemann again and renewed contacts with all his London friends and acquaintances before going to Birmingham. He returned on 30 September and appeared at St Peter's, Cornhill, as organist before leaving for Dover almost immediately.

His seventh visit to London came in May 1842 for the London premiere of the *Scottish Symphony*, dedicated to Queen Victoria, at the Philharmonic Society on 13 June. There were two invitations to Buckingham Palace that sealed Mendelssohn's place in British music. He also appeared as soloist in his D minor Piano Concerto. Cécile Mendelssohn came on this trip and they stayed with her relatives, the Beneckes, at Denmark Hill. Mendelssohn again appeared as organist, at St Peter's in Cornhill, Christ Church, Newgate Street and at Exeter Hall. They left on 10 July.

For the 1844 season the directors of the Philharmonic Society invited him back to London to conduct the last six concerts of the season. He first appeared at the Philharmonic at the Hanover Square Rooms on 13 May, his programme including his protégé Sterndale Bennett's Piano Concerto in C minor and the first British performance of Beethoven's overture *Leonora No 1*. Other concerts featured the thirteen-year-old Joachim (another of his protégés) playing Beethoven's Violin Concerto from memory on 27 May and the British premiere of *Die Erste Walpurgisnacht* in the last concert on 8 July. Mendelssohn was very warmly received and the concerts were packed. He was the soloist in Beethoven's Fourth Piano Concerto improvising the cadenzas. He appeared at a huge number of other concerts, and writing to his sister Fanny on 19 July he reported he had 'made more music in these two months than I do elsewhere in two years'.

Other visits to London and Birmingham were made in 1846 and 1847. On 18 August 1846 he arrived again in London for the premiere of *Elijah* at the Birmingham Festival. After a piano rehearsal with Moscheles and the band rehearsals – most of the nineteenth-century provincial festivals rehearsed the orchestra in London if London players were being used – at the Hanover Square Rooms. The premiere in Birmingham would cast its shadow over British music for the remainder of the century. Mendelssohn returned to London and stayed briefly with Moscheles and his wife's relatives, the Beneckes, and left England on 6 September.

92 Thomas Attwood's House at Norwood where Mendelssohn stayed. Attwood lived here from 1821 to 1834.

Mendelssohn made his final visit to England in April and May 1847, staying once more with Klingemann. He conducted four performances of the revised version of *Elijah* at the Exeter Hall with the Sacred Harmonic Society. On 23 April, Queen Victoria and Prince Albert attended the performance, and on 26 April Mendelssohn appeared at the Philharmonic Society to conduct his own *Scottish Symphony* and *A Midsummer Night's Dream* music. He was also soloist in Beethoven's Fourth Piano Concerto where again he improvised the cadenzas.

Mendelssohn died on 4 November 1847 in Leipzig. In the first edition of *Grove*, the editor's book-length article records the impressions of his London contemporaries:

> In London the feeling, though naturally not so deep or so universal as in his native place, was yet both deep and wide. His visits had of late been so frequent, and the last one was so recent, and there was such a vivid personality about him, such force and fire, and such a general tone of health and spirits, that no wonder we were startled by the news of his death. The tone of the press was more that of regret for a dear relation, than of eulogy for a public character. Each writer spoke as if he intimately knew and loved the departed.

Yehudi Menuhin, Baron Menuhin (1916–1999)

The violinist Yehudi Menuhin was born in New York and first visited London in 1929 as a child prodigy, playing to packed audiences in the Royal Albert Hall. He performed Elgar's Violin Concerto with the composer at Queen's Hall aged fifteen and they recorded it for HMV at Abbey Road Studios. He returned every year until 1936 when he briefly retired. He came again in 1938.

He commissioned Bartók's solo violin sonata in 1944 and in July 1945 he and Britten played at the Belsen concentration camp. Two years later he was the first Jewish soloist to appear with the Berlin Philharmonic and Furtwängler after the war. Menuhin was a typical example of a musician who was long based in London, having homes there and in Switzerland. He lived in Highgate until the early 1980s and his home for the rest of his life was 65 Chester Square, SW1. The huge house, on a corner, was designed in 1838 by Thomas Cubitt. With an imposing white stucco façade, it was used as an office and music studio as well as a home. (Plaque in Chester Square gardens.)

Olivier Messiaen (1908–1992)

Messiaen first appeared in London during the 1938 International Society for Contemporary Music Festival, when, on 22 June, he played the organ of the BBC Concert Hall, Broadcasting House in his 'Les Mages' and 'Le Verbe' from *La Nativité du Seigner*. On 25 June he played the complete *Nativité* at St Alban's, Holborn. During this visit Messiaen stayed at the home of the First Secretary of the French Embassy, Roland de Margerie, in Eaton Square.

Messiaen returned to London in December 1945. The BBC was keen to catch up with what had been going on musically in Europe, and there was also an initiative in the French Embassy in London to promote French culture. There Le Conseiller Culturel was Tony Mayer, whose British interlocutors were Edward Lockspeiser at the BBC and Felix Aprahamian, friend of Messiaen and adviser to United Music Publishers. Although Lockspeiser did not like Messiaen's music, Aprahamian did. Even as early as 13 August 1945, Mayer was writing to Lockspeiser trying to arrange a London hearing for the *Trois Petites Liturgies*, which had been first heard in Paris in April. In December, Messiaen and Yvonne Loriod – later his second wife – stayed at the Bayswater Hotel, 60 Princes Street, W2.

Felix Aprahamian has described how Messiaen and Loriod played *Visions de l'Amen* for two pianos at his house at 10 Methuen Park, N10. That was on 19 December 1945. The next day Messiaen gave a complete performance of *La Nativité* at St Mark's, North Audley Street, at 6.30 p.m., and afterwards Messiaen and Loriod went to Broadcasting House and gave an audition performance of *Visions de l'Amen* to an audience of the musical good and great. Messiaen returned to St Mark's the following morning for a half-hour broadcast organ recital.

Messiaen was a case in point at the BBC in internal debates on the new music. In January 1946 Julian Herbage (for many years the principal planner of the Proms programmes) wrote to the Director of Music remembering 'that before the war we were extremely doubtful of his qualities as a composer. What we have heard recently – at this recital, at a special recording heard by several of us the other day [probably a French Radio recording of *Chant des Déportés*] . . . seems to indicate that these doubts were fully justified . . . I feel it was very unfortunate that such strong political pressure was put on us to engage Messiaen as organist and composer . . .'

In 1946 the ISCM Festival was again held in London, where Messiaen was the pianist in his *Quatour pour la Fin du Temps* on 10 July at Goldsmith's Hall, Foster Lane, EC2, where the composer experienced the innumerable bombsites that were the City of London in 1946. The British Embassy in Paris had reported to the BBC that Messiaen's new work was the cycle *Harawi*, but it does not seem to have been given in London until 1952 when Messiaen was the pianist at Wigmore Hall.

Messiaen returned to London with Loriod in May 1947. They appeared at Oxford and Cambridge and on 18 May Loriod played in the *Trois Petites Liturgies* conducted by Roger Désormière at Wigmore Hall in the afternoon and that evening appeared at Maida Vale for a BBC broadcast of the same piece. (Felix Aprahamian recalls Constant Lambert phoning afterwards and remarking somewhat satirically '. . . and when the choir came in with 'Little Grey Home in the west' for the seventh time, I thought all the audience would join in!')

Thus Messiaen's music and the composer himself gradually appeared in London and the UK. Some of his works were submitted to the BBC's score reading panel (in December 1949 William Alwyn found the new *Cinq Rechants* 'a repellent work') and in 1951 Leonard Isaacs did 'not know whether this was music or not: it was none the less a quite fascinating experience, hovering on the borders of insanity'.

In June 1952 Messiaen and Loriod again appeared in London, in *Les Visions de l'Amen* at Hampstead Town Hall, *Harawi* at Wigmore Hall. It was *Turangalîla* that caused much soul-searching, not least because of the cost of performing it. As early as May 1950 John Lowe at the BBC was 'urgently seeking judgement' on it. Eventually the BBC performed it twice, promoting the London Symphony Orchestra on 26 and 27 June 1953, when Walter Goehr conducted it at Maida Vale. Felix Aprahamian remembers Messiaen and Loriod at a party afterwards at his house when Goehr brought his young son Alexander, who subsequently studied with Messiaen in Paris.

At the Festival Hall on 12 April 1954 the BBC gave *Turangalîla* again in a pioneering series of 'Third Programme Concerts', but it was far from an established work and Robert Simpson, for example, at the BBC was representative of an unsympathetic constituency. During the 1950s Messiaen was played occasionally, perhaps the high-point being on 26 January 1956 when Loriod was the pianist in *Cantéyodjayâ* for the BBC. But he was not yet an accepted big name with the wider public. In 1958 Alexander Goehr wrote to the BBC reminding them that Messiaen would be celebrating his fiftieth birthday that year. Maurice Johnstone's reply admitted that the occasion had been noted but that no special plans had been made to mark it 'because Messiaen is one of the many distinguished foreign composers who has not yet been accepted by the general run of English listeners'.

William Glock's period as the BBC's Controller, Music (1959–72) marks the wider acceptance of Messiaen in the UK and the composer's appearances in London, usually with Yvonne Loriod who would be playing his music. Thus on 1 June 1961 it was *Oiseaux Exotiques*, on 24 June 1962 *Réveil des Oiseaux* at the Festival Hall and on 25 March 1962 excerpts from *Catalogue d'Oiseaux*. Messiaen had a rapidly increasing exposure, notably during Boulez's time as Chief Conductor of the BBC Symphony Orchestra (1971–5). His music was played at the Proms – *Turangalîla* attracting a popular following. Big occasions included *La Transfiguration de Notre-Seigneur Jésus-Christ* in which Loriod appeared at the Proms on 17 July 1970 and *Des canyons aux étoiles*, a Royal Philharmonic Society concert at the Festival Hall with Loriod and Boulez on 12 November 1975 after which Boulez presented Messiaen with the Gold Medal of the Royal Philharmonic Society.

One of the chief British champions of Messiaen was the organist Jennifer Bate, who for the last seventeen years of the composer's life was his organist of preference in his music. Bate met Messiaen when the composer was in London in November 1975, and first played for him privately in a freezing St James's, Muswell Hill. Subsequently she met Messiaen frequently, and on many occasions in London.

Messiaen's seventieth birthday was celebrated with performances in the composer's presence, and on 29 March 1978 it was *Hymne au Saint Sacrément* at the Festival Hall conducted by Serge Baudo. In 1985 LWT's *South Bank Show* produced a television portrait of Messiaen for which Jennifer Bate was artistic adviser. On 26 March 1986 came the first UK performance of three tableaux (Nos. 3, 7 and 8) from

93   Felix Aprahamian greeting Messiaen and Jennifer Bate in his garden at Muswell Hill. Photograph by Yvonne Loriod.

Messiaen's opera *St François d'Assise* given by BBC forces conducted by Seiji Ozawa at the Festival Hall. The *Financial Times* reported 'the composer was present and received a standing ovation at the end: it was a genuine occasion'.

On 7 October 1986 Jennifer Bate gave the premiere of *Livre du Saint Sacrément* at Westminster cathedral and subsequently recorded it, though at La Trinité in Paris. The work was completed long before the performance but at the time of the London performance of three tableaux from *St François*, Messiaen was unable to leave rehearsals and Bate played it straight through, recording it for him on Felix Aprahamian and Peter Dickinson's 'ghetto blaster' for the composer's advice. Two days before, Felix Aprahamian had given a dinner for Jennifer Bate, George Benjamin and Loriod and Messiaen at his home at Methuen Park, and the day before the performance a dress rehearsal in full evening dress had allowed Channel 4 to film as input to their tele-recording of the actual performance.

Messiaen had no on-going teaching relationship with any London conservatoire, but from 16 to 22 March 1987 the Royal Academy of Music presented an unprecedented festival of his music at which the composer was present throughout, including the earlier rehearsals and all performances, and thirty-three of his works were performed. During this event Messiaen judged an organ competition at St Pancras Parish Church featuring his music, at which Jennifer Bate was present, though she reports he found the organists disappointing (in contrast with the pianists heard earlier at the Academy who had been 'exciting').

On 23 January 1988 Messiaen was given the Honorary Fellowship of the Royal College of Organists and soon after he received an Honorary Degree from City

University. Returning in February he was with Jennifer Bate when she gave the second performance of *Livre du Saint Sacrément* at the Royal Festival Hall, on 21 February, both receiving a twenty-minute standing ovation.

Messiaen's eightieth birthday came in 1988, and it was widely noted that he had chosen to celebrate the occasion in London rather than Paris. On his actual birthday, 10 December 1988, Messiaen was at the Festival Hall for a complete performance of *St François d'Assise* given by the London Philharmonic Orchestra, soloists and the London Philharmonic Choir conducted by Kent Nagano. At that time the BBC broadcast a television film 'Messiaen at 80' followed by the third Act from *St François*.

Thomas Morley (1557/8–1602)

Morley was born in Norwich, the son of a brewer. He studied under Byrd, probably in the 1570s. He became Choirmaster at Norwich cathedral from 1583, and organist of St Paul's cathedral in 1591. By 1592 he was a Gentleman of the Chapel Royal. From 1596 he lived in the Parish of St Helen's, Bishopsgate. Earlier he had worshipped at St Giles, Cripplegate. When Byrd's monopoly over music-printing expired in 1596 he sought the new monopoly that he was granted in 1598. Morley was able to publish lute and consort music as well as vocal music. He became the architect of the English-language madrigal and published his *A Plaine and Easie Introduction to Practicall Musicke* in 1597, and a celebrated book of songs in 1600.

Ignaz Moscheles (1794–1870)

Born in Prague, Moscheles came to fame as a travelling pianist and he first appeared in London at the Philharmonic Society on 11 June 1821 when he played his own First Piano Concerto. Newly married, he settled in London in 1825 where for sixteen years he was established, first at 77 Norton Street and subsequently at 3 Chester Place, Regent's Park, leaving after the first performance of Mendelssohn's *Elijah* at Birmingham in August 1846. He left England, taking up Mendelssohn's invitation to accept the post of professor of piano and composition at the newly founded Leipzig Conservatoire, where he arrived on 21 October.

Moscheles is especially remembered for hosting Mendelssohn in London over several years, and for his published diaries and correspondence, which provide many thumb-nail sketches of his musical friends and contemporaries. He appeared at the Philharmonic Society twenty-two times between 1821 and 1861. At his final appearance on 24 June 1861 he played his Third Piano Concerto in G minor, not having appeared in London for fifteen years, when his wife told of 'the storm of cheers and waving of handkerchiefs . . . and he played so finely that his friends eagerly congratulated him on a performance quite on a level with those of his best days'.

Wolfgang Amadeus Mozart (1756–1791)

Mozart came to Britain in his eighth year on 22 April 1764, with his father Leopold and family. After one night in an inn they stayed first at 19 Cecil Court, WC2, from April to August and from August to September, owing to Leopold's illness, at Dr Randal's house at the quieter location of 180 Ebury Street – that section of the street between Bourne Street and Eaton Terrace is now called Mozart Terrace. This was then semi-rural and Leopold commented favourably on the view. The family was presented to George III within a week of their arrival and the children performed three times in Buckingham House, while Mozart played at four other concerts. They met J. C. Bach in London, visited Westminster Abbey, Westminster Hall and St James's Park. They gave concerts at Spring Gardens, by Admiralty Arch, and the Little Haymarket Theatre, which was next to what is now the Theatre Royal Haymarket. A concert was also given at Hickford's Rooms in Brewer Street and there were several performances at the Swan and Harp Tavern, Cornhill, in July 1765. From September 1764 to July 1765 the family resided at Frith Street (then known as Thrift Street) at the home of Thomas Williamson, corset maker. (A plaque on a later house marks the site.) The Mozart family sailed from Dover on 1 August 1765 and had a calm crossing. They did not return.

Vincent Novello (1781–1861)

The founder of the music publishing firm that bears his name was also a composer, conductor and organist. This musical family settled in London before Vincent was born. He became a chorister at the Sardinian Embassy chapel and learned to play the organ. He was appointed organist at the Portuguese Embassy chapel off Grosvenor Square and remained there for twenty-five years. He was a member of the Philharmonic Society from its foundation in 1813 and he directed concerts from the keyboard. He also acted as conductor/accompanist at the King's Theatre. His first publishing venture was a two-volume *Collection of Sacred Music*, which was followed by other music to which he added accompaniments.

From 1829 he operated from 67 Frith Street. Vincent played an active role in the proceedings of the Classical Harmonists and Choral Harmonists. He also published *The Fitzwilliam Music* and sacred music by Purcell. From 1840 to 1843 he was organist at the Roman Catholic chapel St Mary Moorfields, in Eldon Street, where Weber's funeral was held. He lived in Meard Street, Soho. In 1849 he left London and retired to Nice.

His son Joseph Alfred Novello (1810–1892) established the publishing climate that would drive the business (and music publishing in England) later in the nineteenth century. He established the standard octavo format for vocal scores of choral works, he pioneered music that all could afford (initially publishing *Messiah* in sixpenny parts), he looked for massively enlarged markets yet with high quality printing, and he successfully campaigned for the abolition of newspaper stamp duty, advertisement duty and paper duty. The business was for many years at 69 Dean Street, with a City Branch at 24 Poultry (at the Sign of the Golden Crochet), and subsequently at Wardour Street where the magnificent premises remain, for some years occupied by the British Library Board but now under commercial management. (See Walk 1 and Chapter 5)

Norman O'Neill (1875–1934)

Norman O'Neill was one of the five composers who, having studied at the Hoch'sche Konservatorium, Frankfurt, became known as 'The Frankfurt Gang' (the others were Balfour Gardiner, Cyril Scott, Roger Quilter and Percy Grainger), and O'Neill became celebrated as a theatre composer. He was resident conductor of the Theatre Royal, Haymarket, from 1909 to 1932, with a brief interlude at St James's Theatre immediately after the First World War.

O'Neill was born at 'the house with bow windows' – 16 Young Street (once numbered 13), Kensington, near Kensington Square, the house in which Thackeray had written *Vanity Fair* and other novels. The family later moved to 6 Pembroke Gardens near the O'Neills' house, at 4 Pembroke Villas. Before that, when first married, O'Neill had lived at 7 Edwardes Square. At Pembroke Villas Norman and Adine entertained all the celebrated English musicians of the day, and here Delius spent some time during the First World War (see p. 230). O'Neill died as a consequence of a road accident while he was on his way to Broadcasting House for a recording session. He left the bus at Oxford Circus and while crossing Holles Street was struck by the wing mirror of a passing van. As a result of this he developed blood poisoning from which he eventually died. Usually 1934 is thought of as the year in which three great English composers died – Elgar, Delius and Holst – Norman O'Neill was the fourth.

Sir Charles Hubert Hastings Parry (1848–1918)

Coming as he did from Gloucestershire, Parry's introduction to London was doubtless during his time at Eton. After Oxford he took a post at Lloyd's Register of Shipping Directory in the City, in 1870 renting rooms at 5 Chapel Street off Gloucester Place. Later he moved to 7 Cranley Place and Lincoln House, Phillimore Place, South Kensington in 1876.

Many of Parry's first performances were focused on provincial music festivals, but they all had London performances, initially at St James's Hall and the Royal Albert Hall, later at Queen's Hall. The revised versions of the Second Symphony, for example, were introduced by Richter at St James's Hall in June 1887 and May 1895, and the Fourth Symphony was heard on 1 July 1889, also conducted by Richter. Parry's early chamber music performances came at his teacher and mentor Edward Dannreuther's private concerts at 12 Orme Square, Bayswater (see p. 228) between 1879 and 1886. Soon these works were also heard at St James's Hall, the Trio in E minor, for example at one of 'Mr Charles Hallé's Pianoforte Recitals' on 4 June 1880, and the Piano Quartet in A-flat at a Monday Popular Concert on 3 December 1883.

Parry was invited to become Professor of Music History at the new Royal College of Music at the end of December 1882, and he did so from the opening of the College on 7 May 1883. He became Director in 1895 on Grove's retirement. For the rest of his life his daily round was based on the journey from 17 Kensington Square, where he lived from 1887 to 1918, to Kensington Gore and back. Kensington Square was an artistic locale; other residents included the painter Edward Burne-Jones who lived at No. 41, Parry's pupil Arthur Somervell, the publisher Kegan Paul, Thackeray's daughter Mrs Richmond Ritchie, and Dr John Merriman the Royal Physician. Parry had a family estate in Gloucestershire and a seaside house at Rustington, but his working life was focused on Kensington Square and the Royal College of Music. He is buried in St Paul's cathedral.

Cipriani Potter (1792–1871)

Although the composer of ten symphonies, until late in the twentieth century Cipriani Potter was remembered only as a pianist and teacher, who had met Beethoven in Vienna and who later had a piece conducted by Wagner. Potter's florid piano *Enigma Variations*, has been noted as anticipating Elgar's variations by over eighty years. He became a member of the Philharmonic Society in 1815, and the Society commissioned two works the following year. He made his debut as a pianist at the Philharmonic Concerts with a performance of his Sextet for piano, flute and strings in April 1816. He left England for Vienna at the end of 1817 and returned in 1819, having met Beethoven while away. Until 1836 he appeared as a piano soloist giving English premieres of many Mozart and Beethoven concertos, and he became the conductor of the Philharmonic Concerts until 1844. He taught piano for many years at the Royal Academy of Music from 1822, and was its principal from 1832 to 1859. He lived at 3 Craven Hill, W2, and is buried at Kensal Green, although the grave is now very hard to find.

Sergey Prokofiev (1891–1953)

Prokofiev first visited London in the summer of 1913 as a tourist doing the circuit, including Windsor Castle, but felt inhibited by his lack of English. In the summer of 1914 he returned, arriving on 22 June and leaving in late July. He attended the Ballets Russes at Drury Lane and on 3 July he was introduced to Diaghilev. After playing his music to the impresario – including his Second Piano Concerto and Second Piano Sonata – he was commissioned to write a new ballet that became *Ala and Lolly* (later known as the *Scythian Suite*), though it was not well received by Diaghilev nor danced by the Ballets Russes.

Prokofiev had arrived with a letter of introduction to Otto Kling at Breitkopf and Härtel in Great Marlborough Street, who provided him with a studio with piano, and it was here, on 26 June, that he met the British composer Granville Bantock. Prokofiev played him his first two piano sonatas and First Piano Concerto. A week later Bantock met Delius and Prokofiev – significantly on the day Prokofiev would be lunching with Diaghilev. On Saturday 4 July Prokofiev left with Bantock for Birmingham to stay the weekend, and on arrival at Bantock's home beat his host at chess. Prokofiev arrived back in Russia the day before Germany declared war on Russia. When he next travelled to London the world had changed.

In the spring of 1920 Prokofiev briefly visited London, but made an impact only with his ballet-comedy *Chout* (*The Buffoon*), his first successful ballet for Diaghilev, which opened at the Prince's Theatre on 9 June 1921, and was enthusiastically received but was not a critical success. It was 1924 before he came again, on a concert tour. In 1927 Prokofiev's second successful ballet for Diaghilev, *Le Pas d'Acier*, appeared at the Prince's Theatre on 4 July, but the composer does not seem to have been present. In 1930 Prokofiev briefly visited London to record his Third Piano Concerto for HMV with the London Symphony Orchestra conducted by Piero Coppola, though it was not issued until June 1933. Prokofiev's final visit to London came on 19 October 1934 when he appeared conducting his Third Symphony at Queen's Hall. After Prokofiev returned to Russia in the summer of 1936 he had his passport withdrawn and was not able to visit London again.

Henry Purcell (1659–1695)

Probably born in Tothill Street, SW1, near Westminster Abbey, Purcell's short life was set against the background of Westminster, the abbey and royal music and the theatre. The city Purcell would have known was Westminster, and the Palace of Whitehall, which he must have frequented on a daily basis, covered the area now given to Parliament Street and Whitehall from the River Thames to the edge of St James' Park. It was destroyed by fire in 1698, three years after Purcell died, and the only building remaining that he would have known, apart from the abbey and Westminster Hall, is Inigo Jones's Banqueting House, which was then in the centre of the Palace area.

The abbey building was much as it is today, except that the great west towers had not yet been built, and did not appear until well into the eighteenth century. The city of London was the commercial and financial centre as now, but to get there would have been a journey through the ribbon development that separated it from the Palace, or else, the safest way, by boat. The Fire of London took place when Purcell was seven so the city with which he was familiar was very much new-built, the old medieval buildings being completely destroyed, including St Paul's.

On the Restoration, King Charles II reached London on 29 May 1660 and was warmly received. Purcell's father was 'Musician in Ordinary for the voice and lute' and a musician of the Chapel Royal (which had been in abeyance during Cromwellian times). However, his father died suddenly and was buried in the East Cloister of Westminster Abbey; the young Purcell was five. He was a chorister at the Chapel Royal and attended Westminster School at the mature age of nineteen, becoming an organist at the abbey. He was made one of three organists at the Chapel Royal.

In his late teens Purcell was writing ambitious music for both the abbey and the Chapel Royal. Assistant to his godfather John Hingeston (the keeper of the royal instruments) at the age of fourteen, Purcell was tuning the Westminster organ at the age of sixteen. Purcell's world in his mid-twenties was dominated by Whitehall and his music includes a series of 'welcome odes' written to greet the king on his return to the palace, and occasional works for royal occasions including wedding odes and an anthem for the coronation of the Roman Catholic James II, *My Heart is Inditing*. Starting in 1683 there was an annual celebration of St Cecilia's Day in London when Purcell produced his ode *Welcome to all the Pleasures*; in 1692 it was his ode *Hail, Bright Cecilia*. After the Glorious Revolution in 1688 the new rulers, the Protestant William and Mary were far less interested in royal music, though paradoxically it was for Mary that Purcell wrote some of his greatest works in his series of birthday odes, crowned by his music for her funeral in the year of his own death 1695.

Purcell's other musical achievement in London focused on the theatre. There were two in Purcell's day, at Drury Lane and Dorset Gardens, the latter approached by many of its patrons by river. The increasing use of music and lavish spectacle in what were otherwise straight plays resulted in a new genre sometimes called 'semi-opera'. Purcell produced a succession of such scores for Dorset Gardens in the 1690s – *Dioclesian*, *King Arthur*, *The Fairy Queen* and *The Indian Queen*. *Dido and Aeneas*, Purcell's only true opera, was performed at 'Mr Josias Priest's boarding-school at Chelsey by young Gentlewomen', as the printed libretto tells us. This would have been located near where the present-day Battersea Bridge reaches the north shore of the River Thames. He is buried in the abbey and a striking recent memorial to him has been erected in Victoria Street (see p. 121).

Roger Quilter (1877–1953)

Quilter was educated at Eton and the Hoch'sche Konservatorium, Frankfurt, as a result of which he has been regarded as one of the 'Frankfurt Gang' of British composers who studied there. (For the 'Gang' see the entry for Norman O'Neill.) Quilter, whose opulent family home was at Bawdsey Manor, Suffolk, came to London in 1901 as an unknown composer and secured his first success at the Crystal Palace that year when his *Four Songs of the Sea* were sung by a now forgotten baritone, Denham Price, with Quilter accompanying. Soon other songs were heard. Between 1903 and 1907 Quilter had rooms at 27 Welbeck Street. On 2 June 1904 the then celebrated Australian soprano Ada Crossley sang Quilter's subsequently famous song *Now Sleeps the Crimson Petal* at St James's Hall, with Quilter accompanying, and later that month Gervase Elwes sang it again, also with Quilter accompanying at the Bechstein (now Wigmore) Hall. On 15 December that year Quilter accompanied a Mrs Duncan Gregory in a group of his songs in a private concert at 37 Cheyne Walk, Chelsea. Quilter's song cycle *To Julia* first appeared at the Æolian Hall when it was sung by Gervase Elwes accompanied by the composer. On 27 August 1907 Quilter's first orchestral work, his *Serenade*, Op. 9 appeared at a Promenade concert at Queen's Hall for its first of only two performances, and in June 1910 Henry Wood included Quilter's *Three English Dances* in another Promenade concert at Queen's Hall. Inheriting a substantial sum in 1911, for twenty-five years from just before the First World War to the outbreak of the Second, Quilter lived at 7 Montague Street. Throughout the inter-war period he was a familiar name in the musical world, particularly associated with the children's play *Where the Rainbow Ends*, first produced at the Savoy Theatre in 1911. This started a fifty-year tradition of Christmas productions, first at the Garrick Theatre, and variously at the King's Theatre, Hammersmith, the Globe, Victoria Palace, and in the 1920s and '30s in the long-vanished Holborn Empire. Altogether *The Rainbow* lasted until the late 1950s. There was also his one light opera, to which Quilter gave a variety of titles in different versions: *The Blue Boar*, *Julia*, *Rosmé*, *Love and the Countess*, *Love at the Inn* and *The Beggar Prince*. *Julia* appeared at Covent Garden in 1936 and was not a success. As *Love at the Inn* it was seen in a production by the John Lewis Partnership Opera Company in 1977 but proved to be a disappointment. In his later years Quilter lived and subsequently died at 23 Acacia Road, St John's Wood, NW8.

Maurice Ravel (1875–1937)

London audiences gradually became aware of the French composer Ravel in the early 1900s, the Promenade concert performance of *Introduction and Allegro* in 1907 and the Société des Concerts Français concert of music by Ravel at Bechstein (now Wigmore) Hall on 26 April 1909, at which Ravel was present, being perhaps the two most significant early straws in the wind. From 1909 onward new works by Ravel came regularly to London, and significantly Vaughan Williams was sufficiently aware of the French composer (recommended by M. D. Calvocoressi) to seek to study with him in Paris early in 1908. In April 1909 Vaughan Williams invited Ravel to stay at 13 Cheyne Walk, SW3, and he escorted Ravel round London, introducing him to steak and kidney pudding, among other things. In his letter of thanks dated 5 May 1909, Ravel confessed himself 'a Parisian home-sick for London'. In January 1911 Ravel returned to London, also appearing in Newcastle and Edinburgh in support of programmes of his music. In December 1913 he was again in London, appearing in a series of recitals sponsored by the Classical Concert Society and the Music Club.

In July 1922 Ravel came back to London, where Georges Jean-Aubry, the editor of J. and W. Chester's house journal *The Chesterian* had arranged several concerts.

Leigh Henry, their critic, reported Ravel's cordial reception by the leading society hostesses:

> [Ravel's] visit brought about two of the most charming events, the reception in his honour given by Mme. Alvar, on June 30th, and the chamber music concert at Lady Rothermere's a few days later, organised by Jean-Aubry. The first took a leading place among the most important events of last season, inasmuch as it provided the first performance of the *Sonata* for violin and cello by Jelly d'Aranyi and Hans Kindler, a memorable rendition. Ravel himself played piano pieces, including a performance of the original version of *Ma Mère l'Oye* for piano duet, assisted by Eugene Goossens; and a remarkable impression was created by the splendid rendition of *Gaspard de la Nuit* by Robert Casadesus, a master-artist, despite his not yet being twenty-six. Particular interest attached to the admirable rendering by Fleury of Debussy's unpublished flute solo for *Psyché*.
>
> At Lady Rothermere's the *Sonata* was repeated, and Ravel again appeared as soloist, playing the *Sonatine* and pieces from *Miroirs*. The Défauw Quartet gave one of the most spirited renderings of the *Quartet* which I have ever heard; and a *tour de force* of artistry was presented in Mme. Alvar's singing of Ravel songs, *Sur l'herbe* being an amazing presentation of the spirit of Verlaine's poem by vocal means, without any adventitious aid of gesture or facial expression. The programme concluded with the *Introduction and Allegro* for harp and seven instruments, in which the harp-playing of Gwendoline Mason was marked by fine subtlety. The flute obligato of Louis Fleury in *Asie* was also another delight in an evening distinguished by its artistry.

Early London Performances of Ravel	
2 May 1904	*Jeux d'Eau* Bechstein Hall, Evelyn Suart
4 Sept. 1907	*Introduction and Allegro* Queen's Hall/Alfred Kastner (hp)/Wood
6 Dec. 1907	*String Quartet* Leighton House/Parisian Quartet
7 Nov. 1908	*Pavane our une Infant défunte* (pf) Bechstein Hall/Evelyn Suart
26 April 1909	*Shéhérazade* Bechstein Hall/Jane Bathori
26 April 1909	Sonatine (pf) Bechstein Hall/Mary Vadot
26 April 1909	*Cinq mélodies populaires grecques* Bechstein Hall/Jane Bathori/Emile Engel/ Mary Vadot
26 April 1909	*Histoires Naturelles* (1, 4 and 5) Bechstein Hall/Jane Bathori/Emile Engel/Mary Vadot
21 Oct. 1909	*Rhapsodie Espagnole* Queen's Hall/QHO/Wood
2 Dec. 1909	*Alborada del gracioso* (pf) Queen's Hall/ErnestSchelling
8 Dec. 1910	*Le Gibet (Gaspard de la Nuit)* Bechstein Hall/Evlyn Howard-Jones
16 Aug. 1911	*Pavane pour une infante défunte* (orch) Queen's Hall Wood
4 May 1912	*Ma Mère l'Oye* Queen's Hall/Wood
25 Sept. 1913	*Valses Nobles et Sentimentales* (orch) Queen's Hall/QHO/Wood
13 Dec. 1913	*Daphnis et Chloë* Queens Hall/Beecham
4 Feb. 1914	*Gaspard de la Nuit* Æolian Hall/Ricardo Viñes
11 Feb. 1914	*Valses Nobles et Sentimentales* (pf) Æolian Hall/Leonard Borwick
9 Feb. 1914	*Daphnis et Chloë* Drury Lane/Ballets Russes/Monteux
23 March 1914	*Gaspard de la Nuit* Æolian Hall/Ricardo Viñes
27 March 1914	*Valses Nobles et Sentimentales* (orch) Queen's Hall/QHO/Geoffrey Toye

On 19 October 1923, Mason was the harpist, with Ravel conducting, when Columbia recorded his *Introduction and Allegro*. Between 1922 and 1932 Ravel stayed with his friend the singer Louise Alvar-Harding at 14 Holland Park, W11. After the enthusiastic reception in 1922 he came again in 1923 and 1924, and returned in 1928, 1929 and 1932. In 1924 the world premiere of *Tzigane*, Ravel's only London premiere, given by Jelly d'Aranyi on 26 April, was at an all-Ravel concert. The critics were cordial to Ravel the composer and pianist, but not to Ravel the conductor. When Ravel's Piano Concerto had its first London performance by Marguerite Long, on 25 February 1932, conducted by Ravel himself, the *Musical Times* reported 'M Ravel moved the stick'.

Hans Richter (1843–1916)

When the Austro-Hungarian conductor Hans Richter first came to London in April 1877, the hero of Bayreuth the year before, to conduct the Wagner Festival, he first put up at the Charing Cross Hotel and then took rooms at 46 Petersburgh Place in the Bayswater Road. One imagines this may well have been arranged by Edward Dannreuther (see p. 228) who was heavily involved with the arrangements for the Festival and who lived nearby in Orme Square. In 1879 Richter stayed at the home of the parents of the critic Herman Klein at 11 Bentinck Street during the first annual series of 'Richter Concerts' at St James's Hall, which continued until 1902. Probably Richter needed to feel he did not have to stand on ceremony, for in 1880 he arrived on 4 May and took a flat in Cavendish Square; in 1881 a different flat in Vere Street.

94   *Punch* (5 February 1908) salutes Richter for the first complete cycles of Wagner's *Ring* in English, in 1908. At Covent Garden, *The Ring* was sung in Frederick Jameson's translation, with the majority of the singers being English artists.

PUNCH, OR THE LONDON CHARIVARI.—February 5, 1908.

RICHTER THE RING-MASTER.

Mr. Punch begs to congratulate Dr. Richter on the brilliant success with which he has conducted the first complete performance of Wagner's "Ring" in English.

After his 1879 success he was immediately lionised and much in demand in society artistic circles, and at this time he came into the orbit of Marie Joshua. Mrs Joshua was one of the well-off patronesses of the arts who encompassed a wide circle of leading painters and musicians of the day. He was soon a regular guest at her informal Sunday lunches at Westbourne Terrace, Hyde Park. Richter's celebrity unlocked doors and his visits included most of the well-known London musicians of the day, especially those of German extraction. These included Edward Speyer at Denmark Hill, Jenny Lind, Charlotte Moscheles (the widow of Ignaz) and Charles Villiers Stanford.

In 1882 Richter conducted the first English performance of *Die Meistersinger* at Drury Lane and *Tristan und Isolde*. He gave many first performances of works by Stanford, Parry, Mackenzie and Cowen, and was the first to conduct Elgar's *Enigma Variations* in 1899. He conducted the 1900 performance of *The Dream of Gerontius* in Birmingham, for which the orchestral rehearsals (without the choir) were in London at Queen's Hall a week before the premiere and drew a large audience. He conducted the first concert given by the London Symphony Orchestra in 1902. In 1904 he put on an Elgar festival in London and in 1908 Elgar dedicated his first symphony to Richter: 'To Hans Richter, Mus. Doc. True artist and true friend'. The symphony was first heard in Manchester on 3 December 1908 and on 6

December the London Symphony Orchestra assembled to rehearse the symphony under Richter, who, according to W. H. Reed addressed the orchestra: 'Gentlemen, let us now rehearse the greatest symphony of modern times, written by the greatest modern composer, and not only in this country'. Richter retired to Bayreuth in 1911, but was very sorry to leave England, and even more distressed at the outbreak of war, which resulted in a polarisation of attitudes and the growth of strong anti-German sentiment in British music.

Camille Saint-Saëns (1835–1921)

The French composer Saint-Saëns was known in London not only as pianist and composer, but also as organist and conductor. In 1871 he visited London for the first time, giving organ recitals at the Royal Albert Hall, where he represented France at the celebrations for the opening of the new organ. In July 1874 he appeared for the first time at a Philharmonic Society concert playing Beethoven's G major Piano Concerto, where he used his own cadenzas. When he was seen again, on 2 July 1879, not only did he play his own Second Piano Concerto but was also organist in Bach's Prelude and Fugue in A minor. In May 1886 he played the Beethoven G major once more and also introduced the world premiere of his *Organ Symphony*, which had been commissioned by the Philharmonic Society, when he stayed at 49 George Street, W1. In June 1893 he repeated his own G minor Piano Concerto (in a concert which included Tchaikovsky conducting his own Fourth Symphony, see p. 300). On 7 June 1895 he conducted the *Organ Symphony* and in the second half conducted his Third Violin Concerto with an unknown violinist, Drida Scotta. In June 1898 he also appeared in three capacities, first playing his own Organ Fantasie in D-flat, then conducting when Blanche Marchesi sang his ballade *La Fiancée du Timballer* and finally conducting his Symphony in A minor. The Organ Fantasie was then topical for its dedication to Queen Elizabeth of Romania, then better known among London literary circles as Carmen Sylva, the author of *The Bard of the Dimbovitza*, supposed Romanian peasant verse collected by her.

Outside the Philharmonic Society, he often played in London, giving concerts of his own work and of Mozart in particular. He played at Wigmore Hall and visited Sir Julius Benedict at 2 Manchester Square. In 1887 he played all four of his then extant Piano Concertos. In 1902 he was a guest of Sir Henry Wood at 4 Elsworthy Road. In his autobiography Wood recalled:

> During the London Festival of 1902 I came to know Saint-Saëns very well as he was in London for some considerable time. I remember how regularly he would go over to Queen's Hall as early as 8.30 in the morning to enjoy an hour on the organ before the orchestral rehearsals began. I often went there myself in order to listen, unseen, to his unique extemporization.

A very hilarious lunch we had when Saint-Saëns and Ysaÿe came to us at Elsworthy Road. Saint-Saëns was in a vocal mood and declared he ought to have been a *tenore*

The programme on 15 June 1908

Suite Algérienne, Op 60 (1880)
Concerto No 5, in F, for piano and orchestra, Op 103
    (1896) (soloist Saint-Saens)
Recit and Aria 'Printemps qui commence' (*Samson et
    Dalila*) (soloist Julia Culp) (1892)
Rhapsodie d' Auvergne for piano and orchestra, Op 73
    (1884) (soloist Saint-Saens)
Symphonic Poem – *Le Rouet d'Omphale*, Op 31 (1871)
Songs: La Cloche; Reverie; Aimons-nous (Julia Culp
    accompanied on the piano by the Composer)
Wedding Cake (for piano and string orchestra), Op 76
    (1885) (soloist: Saint-Saens)
Symphonic Poem – *Danse Macabre*, Op 40 (1874)

robusto instead of a composer. He insisted on displaying his stentorian voice in all kinds of *solfeggi*. He made grand opera of everything that day. When Olga apologized because the drawing-room curtains had not come back from the cleaners he dashed to the piano and proceeded to improvise a free *fantasia* to express the horror of his feelings at being asked into a drawing-room without curtains. We laughed heartily at what was extremely clever musical fun.

Saint-Saëns's standing with the London audience can be seen when on 15 June 1908, at the age of seventy-three, he appeared at Queen's Hall with the Queen's Hall orchestra. The *Musical Times* is worth quoting at length:

> The season was brought to a brilliant conclusion on June 15. On that occasion the entire programme was devoted to the compositions of Dr Camille Saint-Saëns, the famous French composer himself playing the pianoforte solos and accompaniments. A very large audience gave the hero of the day a great ovation. The *Suite Algérienne*, which displays the composer at his best, was superbly played under Mr Henry J. Wood, who conducted throughout. The three concerted pieces for the pianoforte were performed with extraordinary vim, delicacy, and masterful ease by Dr Saint-Saëns.

In 1910 Saint-Saëns promoted the then almost unknown Mozart piano concertos by playing twelve of them in three concerts. In 1913 a committee patronised by Queen Mary organised a Jubilee Festival to celebrate the seventy-fifth anniversary of his music career, which had begun at the age of three, consisting of a concert mainly of his own music and a performance at Covent Garden of *Samson and Delilah*.

Sir Malcolm Sargent (1895–1967)

The conductor Malcolm Sargent was very much a self-made man from a modest family from Stamford, Lincolnshire, who was articled to the organist of Peterborough cathedral and emerged as a brilliant young musician, taking a music degree at Durham by private study, all before the age of nineteen. Sargent made his London debut on 11 October 1921 to conduct his own overture *Impressions of a Windy Day* at a Promenade concert, and was well received. Malcolm Sargent introduced this work on television in the late 1950s, and asked by a commentator what it was like quipped: 'I'm afraid that chap Mendelssohn rather cribbed from it!' After Sargent's death it was forgotten, apparently lost. For Robert Tucker's revival in a Broadheath Singers concert at Eton in 1993, forgotten transparencies were found in the BBC television music library from which the score could be reconstructed and it has subsequently been played and recorded.

Sargent moved to London from Melton Mowbray at the age of thirty and lived variously at Brompton Road, St Petersburgh Place, Wetherby Place, and during the war at Chesham Place. His final home was at 9 Albert Hall Mansions, Kensington Gore, SW7, from 1947 to 1967 (plaque). Sargent's early career in London was focused on the Royal College of Music, where he taught conducting, and the Savoy Theatre in the Strand, where he achieved celebrity for bringing a new élan to a by then faded Gilbert and Sullivan tradition. On 14 July 1924 Sargent conducted the cash-strapped British National Opera Company in their under-rehearsed first performance of Vaughan Williams's opera *Hugh the Drover* at His Majesty's Theatre. Having recently conducted it at the Royal College of Music he brought in some of their performers to stiffen the company and as Ralph Vaughan Williams observed he 'pulled the chestnuts out of the fire in a miraculous way'. HMV decided to record it in what we now know were the closing months of the acoustic recording era, and Sargent found himself with the company in the cramped recording studio at Hayes making a remarkably successful job of it as we can still hear, and with the American soprano Mary Lewis and Tudor Davies creating one of the great pioneering recordings of British music.

All this spread Sargent's reputation as a charismatic and technically accomplished musician who was not afraid of the modern music of the day, nor of taking on jobs at short notice and in difficult circumstances. This soon had its reward when he was called in by Diaghilev at His Majesty's Theatre where Eugene Goossens had fallen ill. Sargent conducted the ballets *Firebird* and *Les Biches* at five hours notice and then spent a week conducting ballets, keeping one day ahead as he studied the scores. Sargent was asked back in 1928 and on 25 June shared the podium with Igor Stravinsky himself on the night of the stage premiere of *Apollon Musagète*, conducting Respighi's *Cimarosiana*. In 1931 he would share the podium with Stravinsky again when, at Queen's Hall, the Russian conducted his new *Symphony of Psalms* and Violin Concerto, and Sargent conducted the supporting programme consisting of Haydn's Symphony No. 86 and Schubert's Great C major Symphony.

Sargent was also the architect of the renewal of the Royal Choral Society between the wars, and was particularly fond of Coleridge-Taylor's *Hiawatha,* which was performed by the Society at the Royal Albert Hall in full costume every summer for a long period. Sargent was a notable choral conductor and choirs always loved him and responded to his – as they thought – aristocratic good sense, particularly in his favourite British choral repertoire by Delius, Walton and Elgar. Orchestras became increasingly less charitable.

He was conductor of the Courtauld–Sargent concerts at Queen's Hall in the 1930s, which set ticket prices to appeal to wider audiences. He became the conductor of the BBC Symphony Orchestra after Boult, from 1950 to 1957, and most famously of the Promenade concerts. His end of season speech in 1967, though he was dying of cancer, has become a legendary occasion and can be seen on video. The blue carpeting, kneelers and an altar frontal in the Sanctuary at St Sepulchre's church were given in his memory in 1969.

Cecil Sharp (1859–1924)

Although remembered as a key folk dance and song collector in the early 1900s, Cecil Sharp's first exposure to folk song came when he was in his forties. From 1896 to 1905 he was principal of the Hampstead Conservatoire of Music, where Arnold Bax was once a pupil. He was born on Denmark Hill, Camberwell, and later lived in Hampstead at 183 Adelaide Road (now gone) from 1905 to 1911, and at 4 Maresfield Gardens from 1918 to 1924. From the early 1900s he spent his time collecting and preserving folk songs and dances and writing about them. He gave lectures and demonstrations and organised holiday schools. In 1911 he founded the English Folk Dance Society. The folk song and folk dance societies later amalgamated. His memorial is the headquarters of the English Folk Dance and Song Society at Cecil Sharp House, 2 Regent's Park Road (see Chapter 3). The foundation stone was laid in 1929 and the original building opened in 1930.

Dmitri Shostakovich (1906–1975)

Shostakovich did not visit the UK until after the Second World War, but the 1936 BBC concert performance of his opera *Lady Macbeth of Mtsenk* was a remarkable opportunity for his music to impinge on a London audience, and it certainly impressed the young Benjamin Britten.

Shostakovich actually first came to London in June 1958 to be awarded an honorary degree at Oxford University. There was also a ceremony at the Royal Academy of Music in London where the lauded visitor was made an honorary member. In the autumn of 1960 Shostakovich visited London again and on 6 October he was introduced by Rostropovich to Britten. Shostakovich had come for the Leningrad Philharmonic's Promenade Concert at which Mravinsky conducted Shostakovich's Eighth Symphony at the Royal Albert Hall on 23 September.

In 1963 Shostakovich returned to London, this time for the Covent Garden premiere on 2 December of the new version of *Lady Macbeth of Mtsensk* now called *Katerina Ismailova*, conducted by Edward Downes.

Jean Sibelius (1865–1957)

Early interest in the Finnish composer Sibelius in England was almost entirely due to the championship of Granville Bantock in Birmingham and Liverpool and Henry Wood in London. Henry Wood introduced a succession of new works by Sibelius at the Proms in the early years of the twentieth century, and at Queen's Hall successively gave the first English performances of *King Christian II* suite (26 October 1901); the First Symphony (13 October 1903); *The Swan of Tuonela* (31 August 1905); *En Saga* (4 October 1906); *Finlandia* (13 October 1906); *Karelia Suite* (23 October 1906); Violin Concerto (1 October 1907) and the *Karelia* Overture (25 October 1907).

Sibelius came to London to give the first performance of his Third Symphony at Queen's Hall on 27 February 1908 and 'met with a hearty reception'. In telling us so the *Musical Times*'s critic also reminded readers that Sibelius's first appearance in the UK had been in Liverpool on 2 December 1905.

In 1909 Sibelius conducted a sold-out concert at Queen's Hall on 13 February including his *En Saga* and *Finlandia*, having seven recalls after *En Saga* and more after *Finlandia*. On this visit Sibelius found himself on the London social circuit, lunches, a reception, a soirée hosted by Lady Bective, and a dinner with Lady Wakefield and Lady Burton. He met Bantock, Siloti, Ernest Newman, Busoni, Vincent d'Indy and the young Benjamin Dale. In 1909 he stayed at 15 Gloucester Walk, W8 (plaque), lodgings found for him by his friend Rosa Newmarch, and where she believed he completed the string quartet *Voces Intimae*. During this visit Sibelius also heard Elgar's First Symphony and Bantock's vast choral setting of *Omar Khayyam*. He was in the audience on 27 February when Debussy conducted his *Nocturnes*. It was on this visit that Sibelius was made guest of honour by the Music Club at Suffolk Street Galleries. Arnold Bax was called in from time to time as stand-in pianist when their regular accompanist let them down, and he remembered it with thinly disguised mirth:

In 1908 or thereabouts was founded the 'Music Club', a dressy concert-cum-supper affair presided over by Alfred Kalisch, critic of the *Star*, and a pious thurifer before the altar of Richard Strauss. Kalisch was a lovable little man; in person – with his barrel-like trunk, thick colourless skin, squat features, and habitual cigar, suggesting the gentleman constructed entirely of motor tyres who used at one time to figure in M. Michelin's advertisement.

The Club members were mostly elderly, and notable for wealth, paunchiness, and stertorous breathing. Bulging pinkish bosoms straining at expensive decolletages, redundant dewlaps, and mountainous backs were generously displayed by the ladies, whilst among the men ruddy double-chins, overflowing their collars at the back of the neck and boiled eyes were rife. The assemblage indeed was very inclined to bring to mind Beardsley's famous drawing – *The Wagnerites*. In 1909 Kalisch and the Club, seized with overweening ambition, decided to invite several eminent foreign composers as their guests, and to glut them with copious food, strong wines, and selections from their own works.

In describing how Sibelius reacted to this process Bax expresses his bafflement at the lack of character of Sibelius's lighter works:

Of all the human beings with whom in the course of my life I have become acquainted none, I should say, has altered more, during the last thirty years, than Sibelius. Physically he has changed much, but this apart, comparison of my impression of him in 1909 with that of 1936 might be of two totally different men. The massive, bald-headed titan of the later years, suggesting an embodiment of one of the primeval forces that pervade the 'Kalevala', can at whim transform himself into a purveyor of farcical fun and Rabelaisian joviality. But the earlier Sibelius gave one the notion that he had never laughed in his life, and never could. That strong taut frame, those cold steel-blue eyes, and hard-lipped mouth, were those of a Viking raider, insensible to scruple, tenderness, or humour of any sort.

Such was his outward semblance, but can it be that on that evening of his London reception he was hag-ridden by an artistic conscience? Now we do not know, and no one will ever dare ask him, what he himself thinks of that endless series of short instrumental pieces and songs which all his life he has poured out in *opus* numbers interlarded with those of such mighty monuments of an utterly individual mind as the Fourth Symphony, – 'Luonnotar,' and 'Tapiola'. With undeterred hope we continue to turn over these hundreds of pages, discovering nothing with the hallmark of the master upon them. These trifles are, with scarcely an exception, entirely undistinguished and characterless.

In 1912 he came to England for the premiere of his Fourth Symphony at the Birmingham Festival, when he was noted sitting with Bantock and Delius for Elgar's *The Music Makers* with the composer conducting. Sibelius had spent 24 and 25 September at the Langham Hotel, days of a 'dingy yellow fog'. On the second day he attended the rehearsal for Birmingham at Queen's Hall and then travelled up with Rosa Newmarch.

Sibelius made his last visit to London from 6 February to 9 March 1921. There were four Queen's Hall concerts, the first on the afternoon of Saturday 12 February featuring the new Fifth Symphony conducted by Sibelius with Sir Henry Wood supporting, in a mixed programme including Jelly d'Aranyi in Beethoven's Violin Concerto. The *Daily Express* described how Sibelius 'a tall, clean-shaven man, elderly and quite "unmusical" stepped on the conductor's podium at Queen's Hall on Saturday afternoon, and, with a wide sweep of his baton began the opening bars of his new symphony'. The *Daily Mail* noted the 'exceedingly warm welcome' and that 'as a conductor he is not showy'. Several papers noted the hall was packed, and he had rousing applause at the end. Yet the tone of the papers is puzzled; the later popularity of the Fifth needed a few performances to establish itself.

Sibelius had conducting dates in Manchester, Birmingham and Bournemouth, but appeared at Queen's Hall for two ballad concerts that included the *Karelia Suite*, *Valse Triste* and the Romance in C, and later on 26 February conducted the Fourth Symphony, when Busoni was present to play his *Indianische Phantasie* and received more applause than Sibelius had for the symphony. On 27 February came the *Oceanides, King Christian II* and *Valse Lyrique*, and after a flying visit to Manchester he reappeared at Queen's Hall at short notice with *The Swan of Tuonela*, *Andante Festivo* and *Finlandia*, which was encored.

John Christopher Smith the younger (1712–1795)

The English composer John Christopher Smith, son of the composer of the same name, was assistant and amanuensis to Handel. A plaque commemorates him as having lived and died at 6 Carlisle Street, W1. When Handel's eyesight deteriorated Smith began to help him more and more with performances of his works, making cuts, additions and corrections to the music. Handel bequeathed his large Ruckers harpsichord to J. C. Smith who in turn left it to George III. It is now in Fenton House, Hampstead (see p. 172).

Edward Speyer (1839–1934) and Edgar Speyer (1862–1932)

There were two Speyers – cousins – both substantial benefactors to London music. Sir Henry Wood differentiated between them by saying 'Edward Speyer in Elstree' – generally known as the 'Elstree Speyer', and cousin to Sir Edgar. The two did not quite hit it off musically: Edgar was all out for the modern, Edward for the strictly classical. Edgar was the Head of a Frankfurt bank and his wife was Leonora von Stosch, a pupil of Ysaÿe who appeared at Queen's Hall, whose syndicate was headed by Speyer. They lived at 46 Grosvenor Street, now the Japanese Embassy, and there he entertained, among others, Debussy, Elgar, Joachim and Richard Strauss. Thus he financially underpinned much of London musical life until he emigrated to the USA after being harassed as a German during the First World War.

Edward Speyer was German by extraction and a banker and benefactor. He settled in London in 1859 and was naturalised in 1869. After his marriage in 1869 he lived in Denmark Hill, then remarkable for the number of well-off German families who had settled there. He was thus part of the large local audience for the Crystal Palace concerts, and got to know Sir George Grove. Speyer's second wife was the pianist Antonia Kufferath. They later became known for their forty-year occupancy of Ridgehurst, a large house and estate at Shenley, Hertfordshire, only seventeen miles from London, where many musical aquaintances were invited. He was a generous benefactor to the Queen's Hall promenade concerts in the 1920s, a patron of orchestral music in London and founder and chairman of the Classical Concert Society.

Louis Spohr (1784–1859)

In the first half of the nineteenth century Spohr was regarded as one of the great composers, widely mentioned in the same breath as Beethoven, and Spohr's oratorio *The Last Judgement* was one of the cornerstones of the oratorio repertoire. However, this reputation faded towards the end of his life and did not outlast his period.

Spohr visited England six times, the first in 1820 when he came to London at the invitation of the Philharmonic Society and appeared throughout that year's season. Spohr and his then wife arrived at the end of February and he first performed on 6

March; his last appearance was on 19 June. This was a financially attractive deal for him, being paid 250 guineas plus all facilities to give a benefit concert at the end of the season. At the first concert Spohr played his own violin concerto billed as *Nello Stilo Drammatico* (No 8). Spohr's role during this season was varied and at the second concert on 20 March he appeared as first violin in one of his own string quartets. At the following concert Spohr took the role of both leader and conductor, when he conducted his own Second Symphony in D minor, which was warmly received. It was at this concert that he established the practice of using a baton, for the first time in London. At the rehearsal he took his baton from his pocket and caused a brief protest from the directors but, as Spohr put it, 'the triumph of the baton as a time-giver was decisive'. Spohr was in four further Philharmonic Society concerts that season, ending with a repeat of the Symphony plus his Nonet for strings and wind in which he appeared as first violinist. Spohr's benefit concert was due to be given with his wife on 20 June 1820. It was then he found himself inadvertently involved in a riot as it was the day on which Queen Caroline returned to London to face Parliament on an accusation of adultery, and opposing factions clashed next to the concert hall.

In 1839 he made his second visit to England to conduct his new oratorio *Calvary* at the Norwich Festival. This was a success with the public but to respond to religious objections the words of Jesus were given to St John in the third person. Presumably Spohr travelled through London, but seems not to have appeared in public.

In 1843 Spohr again played for the Philharmonic Society, and the last Philharmonic Society programme of the season contained four works by him including his Fourth Symphony *The Consecration of Sound* (3 July). By special permission of the Queen and Prince Albert a further concert was given on 10 July, when Spohr played one of his violin concertos, an aria from his opera *Jessonda* was sung by Joseph Staudigl and Spohr conducted his new overture *Macbeth*.

That summer of 1843 Spohr twice conducted his oratorio *The Fall of Babylon.* This was written for the Norwich Festival of 1842 when Spohr had been prevented from attending by his employer, the Elector of Hesse Cassel. Thus on 7 July 1843 he conducted his new oratorio at the Hanover Square Rooms, finding only a small audience. Stung by this failure the Sacred Harmonic Society proposed a second performance with bigger forces at Exeter Hall, when it attracted a much larger audience and was so well received that people stood on their benches to applaud. Spohr was recalled at the end and presented with an engraved silver salver as a tribute.

In 1847 Spohr returned to London, where the Sacred Harmonic Society announced a series of three concerts on 9, 16 and 23 July at Exeter Hall devoted to major choral works. This was to have included the first London performance of his oratorio *Calvary*, his success at Norwich in 1839. However, owing to opposition by religious zealots who objected to his musical personification of the Saviour, it was dropped. *Calvary* was actually performed by the Sacred Harmonic Society in 1852 when Spohr came again, though then the main focus of his visit was his opera

Faust, which he had been commissioned to turn into an Italian opera, and it was produced on 15 July.

In 1853 he came to England for the sixth and last time. This was to fulfil an invitation from the New Philharmonic concerts – when he conducted many of his own works and Beethoven's *Choral* symphony. Spohr's reputation as the conductor of this then rarely performed work was considerable after a pioneering performance at the 1845 Bonn Beethoven Festival, and he must have generated much interest following Berlioz's revelatory performance the previous year. John Francis Barnett described how he made his debut in Spohr's series on 4 July in Mendelssohn's Concerto in D minor with Spohr conducting, and he left us an impression of 'a massive style of man, both tall and stout, but his face was intellectual, without, however, the poetical expression of features that I noticed in Berlioz'. Spohr's opera *Jessonda* was at Covent Garden that summer but Spohr was unable to conduct it as he had to return to his post in Germany.

Sir John Stainer (1840–1901)

Principally organist and choir trainer, Stainer was also noted as a composer and musicologist. He was born in Southwark and in 1847 became a chorister at St Paul's. He became organist and choirmaster at St Benedict and St Peter, Paul's Wharf, Upper Thames Street, while continuing to study the organ with George Cooper at St Sepulchre's. In 1872 he succeeded Goss as organist at St Paul's and made many reforms, adding to the choir and giving them better pay and holding weekly choral Eucharists. He dedicated his Passion Music *The Crucifixion* to the choir of St Marylebone Parish Church. He was a driving force behind the founding of the Musical Association in 1874. In 1876 he became professor of organ and in 1881 principal of the National Training School for Music. He held many posts in the musical world, and was knighted in 1888; that year he had to resign as organist of St Paul's because of his failing eyesight. There is a memorial to him at St Paul's.

Sir Charles Villiers Stanford (1852–1924)

Stanford was born in Dublin, and his early musical life was centred on Cambridge with several periods spent in Germany. In 1876 he wrote incidental music for Tennyson's play *Queen Mary* at the Lyceum, and in 1879 his First Symphony was heard at the Crystal Palace. Stanford only became a familiar figure on the London musical scene once he was appointed to the Royal College of Music as Professor of Composition and conductor of the orchestra in 1883. His only regular London performing appointment was as conductor of the Bach Choir from 1886 to 1902, though he occasionally appeared as a conductor, notably for the Philharmonic Society on some eleven occasions. Many of his works were first performed at Cambridge or at provincial festivals, but his Third Symphony was first heard at St

95   The first teaching staff at the Royal College of Music. Stanford wears a grey top hat, third row, centre. Behind him, above, sits Sir George Grove, and in front in top hats Parratt and Parry (in profile). Other celebrated names include: Algernon Ashton (back row, second from left); Albert Visetti (third on Ashton's left); Frederic Cliffe (in front of Visetti, sixth in the second row); Franklin Taylor (next to Parratt) and Charles Wood (third from right second row). In the front row the third from the left is Gustave Garcia, and in sequence to his left: G. Watson (Registrar); Ernst Pauer (with umbrella); Miss Mayfield; Henry Lazarus and (Sir) Frederick Bridge.

James's Hall, while the last three were premiered at Queen's Hall. Stanford's music was often programmed at Queen's Hall, particularly before the First World War, but was much less in favour at Crystal Palace where Manns programmed him only seven times. Five of his operas appeared on the London stage in his lifetime, of which only one, *Shamus O'Brien*, was a popular success, while his incidental music for four plays was also heard.

He lived at 50 Holland Street on the corner with 56 Hornton Street, W8, from 1894 to 1916. In 1916 he moved to 9 Lower Berkeley Street (now Fitzhardinge Street), Portman Square, W1, where he remained until his death. He is buried near the tomb of Purcell in Westminster Abbey (see Chapter 4).

Leopold Stokowski (1882–1977)

The celebrated conductor Leopold Stokowski was born at 13 Upper Marylebone Street, which later became 146 New Cavendish Street (by the corner of Cleveland Street); the building is still an apartment block. There is a plaque on the wall of St Marylebone School at the top of Marylebone High Street, where he studied and sang in the choir. He was a chorister at St Marylebone Parish Church, attended the Royal College of Music in 1895 and gained his FRCO diploma. He formed a choir at St Mary's, Charing Cross Road (now the site of the Central St Martin's College of Art and Design). He was also assistant organist to Walford Davies at the Temple Church. He became organist at St James's Piccadilly from 1902 to 1905 and took lodgings at 76 Jermyn Street, nearby. He travelled widely from 1905, leaving London and making his home in the USA as a conductor. A flying visit to London brought him to conduct the Royal College of Music orchestra under very secretive conditions. He visited his alma mater and conducted Wagner's *Meistersinger Overture* with a startled orchestra of students on 29 May 1933 and left.

Discounting his flying visit to the Royal College of Music in 1933, he reappeared publicly in the UK for the first time in around forty years to conduct at the Festival of Britain in 1951 when he again made a brief visit to conduct students at the RCM. He returned to England in 1972 and gave concerts until 1975, making his home at Nether Wallop, Hampshire, and was still recording until his death. His appearance in January 1973 at a rehearsal at the Bishopsgate Institute with the New Philharmonia Orchestra is a remarkable tribute to his musical longevity. The work was Elgar's *Enigma Variations*, and 'Stoky' appeared, very frail and helped by two minders, one at each arm. He looked as if he would be incapable of conducting. However once on the podium and ready to start it seemed to those present as if he had clicked into life, as if some hidden puppet-master had taken up the strings. He was the old Stokowski, imperious, wise-cracking, playing tricks on the players. As soon as it was over he seemed to slump and the two minders rushed forward to support him. He died four years later and is buried at St Marylebone Cemetery, East Finchley. (See also Chapter 4 and p. 114.)

Richard Strauss (1864–1949)

The British vogue for Richard Strauss's orchestral music developed in the late 1890s after August Manns had conducted *Till Eulenspiegel* at the Crystal Palace on 21 March 1896. In a speech afterwards Manns announced it was the most difficult piece he had ever conducted, and he then played it again. Within two years it had enjoyed five performances in London.

Strauss made his first appearance in London in 1897 at the last of the Wagner concerts in Queen's Hall that December. In 1899 he conducted his *Tod und Verklärung*. In this he was championed by Edgar Speyer, whose guest he was at 46 Grosvenor Street, W1, also staying there in 1902, 1903, 1905, 1910 and 1914. In 1903 a Richard Strauss Festival consisting of eight symphonic poems and some songs was held in St James's Hall, played by the visiting Concertgebouw Orchestra. Strauss's Berlioz concert in 1903 was poorly attended. He was co-conductor of Beecham's opera performances in 1910, which included the UK premiere of his opera *Elektra*, Strauss demanding a fee of £200 a night.

In the summer of 1914 Strauss attended the London premiere of Diaghilev's ballet *La Légende de Joseph*, with music by Strauss, which generated enormous press coverage and opened at Drury Lane on 23 June. Strauss conducted and was called many times. This was also the visit on which he was received by the Music Club at the Grafton Galleries, where Alfred Kalisch welcomed him on 21 June. Strauss later received an honorary doctorate from Oxford University.

During the First World War Strauss was little heard – music by living German composers being frowned on – but although in 1922 he conducted a concert of his own works at the Royal Albert Hall he found it did not elicit the support of pre-war appearances. Strauss also conducted the London Symphony Orchestra at Columbia's Petty France Studio on 18 and 19 January that year, returning in April, when he recorded *Salome's Dance*, the *Rosenkavalier* waltzes and *Don Juan*.

In 1925 he was in London for the recording of extracts from *Rosenkavalier* for a silent film, a recording that was issued on 78s. In 1926 Strauss appeared at the Albert Hall in a BBC programme that included the *Alpine* Symphony (the second performance in London) and the *Festival Prelude*. In the symphony E. J. Moeran was seen by the audience 'diligently exhibiting numbers corresponding to the explanations in the programme'. It was not entirely successful. 'The Albert Hall was little more than half full', reported the *Star*, and in the storm in the *Alpine* Symphony the thunder machine was seen slowly to topple over and crash into the orchestra. Several critics complained that in the important organ part in the *Festival Prelude* there was an 'excruciating difference of pitch between the organ and the orchestra'.

Strauss's invitation from the BBC was renewed in 1931 and he was interviewed on 1 February and appeared as conductor in October. On 18 October he conducted *Macbeth*, *Don Juan* and *Tod und Verklärung* with the then new BBC Symphony Orchestra at that now forgotten temporary hall, Studio 10. This was a huge disused warehouse, the Red Lion Warehouse, not far from the present day Southwark tube station, though then far less salubrious. Three days later, but this time at Queen's Hall he appeared again, the programme including the first British performance of Strauss's *Three Hymns of Hölderlin*, Op. 71, sung by Margarete Teschemacher.

Strauss's last London visit before the war, in 1936, saw him presented with the Gold Medal of the Royal Philharmonic Society by Sir Hugh Allen on 5 November. He had come to London in support of the Dresden State Opera, conducting their production of *Ariadne auf Naxos* at Covent Garden on 6 November and was seen at Covent Garden in a box with von Ribbentrop when the latter gave a Nazi salute during the National Anthem. Strauss also appeared at Queen's Hall conducting the Dresden State Orchestra in a concert that included *Don Quixote* (preserved on Aphan CD APR 5527).

After the Second World War, with his world in ruins, in 1947 Strauss flew to London (arriving at Northolt) and conducted *Don Juan* and waltzes from *Rosenkavalier*, among other works, at the Theatre Royal, Drury Lane. This was the brainchild of Sir Thomas Beecham who launched a Strauss Festival with the Royal Philharmonic Orchestra. Strauss attended concerts and rehearsals conducted by Beecham, the *Die Frau ohne Schatten* Fantasia conducted by Norman del Mar, and a now celebrated concert performance of *Elektra* conducted by Beecham in conjunction with the BBC. Del Mar, who was then Beecham's assistant, describes how Strauss came forward and embraced Beecham at the end, remarking 'I had not realized that Beecham was so small or that Strauss was so large'. Subsequently Strauss conducted the recently formed Philharmonia Orchestra at the Royal Albert Hall giving *Don Juan*, the *Burlesque* and the *Sinfonia Domestica*.

Strauss had died by the time the *Four Last Songs* had their first performance on 22 May 1950. They were given by the Philharmonia Orchestra at the Royal Albert Hall, with Kirsten Flagstad, conducted by Furtwängler, closing a remarkable London link with one of the major composers of his time.

Igor Stravinsky (1882–1971)

The Russian composer Igor Stravinsky came to London with the Diaghilev Ballet in June 1912 on the first of three visits before the First World War. This visit was for the London stage premiere of *The Firebird* on 18 June by Diaghilev's Ballets Russes and was very favourably received. He returned for *Petroushka* in February 1913 when he was interviewed by the press and effusively praised Beecham's orchestra in his music. However he was not able to visit London for the scandalised reception of *The Rite of Spring* in July 1913 as he was suffering from typhoid fever, and he next came in 1914 for the opening performance of *Le Chant du Rossignol* at Drury Lane on 18 June. This was the occasion when he stopped the taxi he was travelling in with the critic Edwin Evans to listen to the bells of St Paul's cathedral change ringing, an experience that some feel could have contributed to his later ballet *Les Noces*.

The Ballets Russes were unable to come back until near the end of the First World War, next appearing in London in 1918, though Stravinsky did not return until 1920, arriving on 7 June, and with Massine and Diaghilev creeping into their seats in the Queen's Hall dress circle, straight from the train, just as the first British concert performance of *The Rite of Spring* conducted by Eugene Goossens started playing. *Le Chant du Rossignol* and *Pulcinella* were both danced on 10 June 1920, and the same night the composer was present when Koussevitzky presented the disastrous first London performance of the *Symphonies for Wind Instruments* at Queen's Hall. On this occasion the rest of the orchestra left the platform for the Stravinsky, but there was no platform reorganisation, the twenty wind players just remained in their seats creating an unfocused effect in what was anyway a strange-sounding work. Ernest Newman reported 'a good deal of laughter and some hissing'.

During 1920 the more modernistic short chamber works of Stravinsky were promoted to a fashionable London audience seeking the latest outrage. Arthur Bliss's chamber concert at Æolian Hall in April included the only Stravinsky world premiere to be given in

96   Members of the Diaghilev Ballet's *Sleeping Princess* with Stravinsky outside the Alhambra, November 1921. Lubov Egorova, Marie D'Albaicin, Vera Soudeikin, Lydia Lopokova (in front), Igor Stravinsky and Bronislava Nijinska.

London with *Ragtime,* which the *Daily Mail* noted under the headline 'Anthropoid Music'. Worse was to come when Ernest Ansermet presented his concert at Wigmore Hall on 20 July devoted to Stravinsky's chamber music. It is worth noting the leisured audience these concerts were aimed at, for both took place on a weekday afternoon, and the press commented on the fashionable audience for Ansermet. The *Daily News* noted: 'One of the largest and most dazzlingly fashionable audiences on record assembled at Wigmore Hall yesterday to hear M. Ansermet's Stravinsky concert. Such frocks and hats rarely delight the eye of the mere musical critic.' Before the concert Ansermet gave a preliminary lecture that one paper noted as lasting twenty-five minutes, and another made clear was delivered in French. Yet most of the critics discussed his remarks without highlighting the language in which they were delivered.

Stravinsky had not yet launched his annual (or more frequent) appearances in London to introduce his latest music which characterised the later inter-war period, but in May 1921 Charles B. Cochran brought Diaghilev back to London to the Prince's Theatre, a smaller space than those used by the company previously; but it was a summer that was bad for the theatre owing to the sunny weather, and the heatwave went on and on. The high point was a new production of *The Rite of Spring,* which Stravinsky opened on 27 June to a rapturous reception, and the July issue of *Musical Times* published a group photograph of Ansermet, Diaghilev, Stravinsky and Prokofiev. In October 1921 he returned to London for the rehearsals at the Alhambra for Diaghilev's sumptuously dressed production of Tchaikovsky's *The Sleeping Princess.* This opened on 2 November and the first night was not a happy occasion for Diaghilev and Stravinsky owing to a succession of failures by the stage machinery, which jammed during the transformation after the 'Lilac Fairy' dance of Olga Spessiva as Aurora; and then the curtain failed to rise for the new act. All was eventually resolved but it ended nearly an hour late and the press coverage was cooler than it might have been for a slicker first night.

Stravinsky does not seem to have been in London again until 1927, when on 19 June he broadcast the first English performance of his concerto for piano and winds with the Wireless Symphony Orchestra conducted by Edward Clark. On 27 June at the Prince's Theatre Stravinsky conducted the Diaghilev company in *Petroushka, Pulcinella* and *The Firebird.* If by then the public suspected that the Diaghilev company had slightly lost its edge, when Stravinsky appeared everyone sat up. The *Observer* noted: 'in the most businesslike but least showy manner, [he] electrified three of his popular ballets. . . . It was as though father had paid a purposeful visit to the nursery. Every dancer from A to Z was on the tiptoe of form.' Stravinsky had many curtain calls. On 18 July the company introduced the third version of *Le Chant du Rossignol,* but by then Stravinsky had left for the continent.

He returned to London in 1928, when on 12 May, exactly a year after its first performance in Paris, he conducted the first English performance of *Oedipus Rex* in a BBC broadcast and on 25 June conducted the London premiere of *Apollon Musagète* at His Majesty's Theatre, on its second night with the Diaghilev company.

In the summer of 1929 he came to London for a Queen's Hall concert on 19 June in which he was soloist in his Piano Concerto, with Eugene Goossens conducting, and then took the baton for *Apollo*. He also conducted a broadcast concert of *The Fairy's Kiss* and *Apollo and the Muses* (as *Apollon Musagète* was then known to English audiences) for the BBC from Kingsway Hall on 27 June. This was before an invited audience and was widely reviewed. 'It was in fact one of the best concerts the BBC has arranged', said 'RLM' in the *Daily Herald*, and the *Evening Standard* critic gave us a vivid pen-picture of Stravinsky at the rostrum: 'Every conductor has his mannerisms. Mr Stravinsky crouches behind his score during a quiet passage, and then reappears as suddenly as some of his most effective passages'. During this visit he met Willy Strecker of the music publishers Schott.

Stravinsky had several dates in London in 1931, and in days when a winter visit to London from the Continent usually meant a rough crossing, his approach of a succession of short visits may not have been all that comfortable for him. On 28 January he appeared at a BBC Symphony Concert at Queen's Hall devoted to his music, conducted by Ansermet, at which Stravinsky played the Piano Concerto. In March he was back again for two performances of the *Capriccio*, on 21 March at Queen's Hall at a Courtauld-Sargent concert conducted by Dr Malcolm Sargent. Then in November he was back in Queen's Hall, conducting the London Symphony Orchestra when the new *Symphony of Psalms* and Violin Concerto had their first performances in London. There were two performances on 16 and 17 November. 'Igor Stravinsky had a great reception from a very large attendance at Queen's Hall last night', noted the *Daily News*, but the *Daily Telegraph* reported that the *Symphony of Psalms* had only 'half-hearted applause'.

Stravinsky and the violinist Samuel Dushkin returned in 1933 and 1934. On 13 March 1933 they played a wide-ranging programme of Stravinsky's violin music, including the *Duo Concertante*, *Suite Italienne* and transcriptions from *The Firebird*, *Petroushka* and *The Nightingale*. Eric Blom wrote:

> After an unbearably stuffy London day, it was refreshing to sit in the beautiful concert hall at Broadcasting House last night and to breathe the healthy fresh air that was being artificially produced there. This is not to say, however, that artificiality is always pleasing. It was certainly not in the music of Stravinsky when it becomes too consciously manufactured . . . All the intelligent people, of course, were there and enthusiasm ran almost as high . . . as the Russian Ballet.

He went on to note that Stravinsky 'handles his own very difficult keyboard writing very well indeed in that rather aggressive percussive way it requires.'

In February 1934 Dushkin and Stravinsky ended a rare provincial British tour with a concert at Queen's Hall on 27 February with almost identical repertoire. They were not so fortunate with the weather and the conductor Boyd Neel tells how on a day of a London 'pea-souper' fog he was asked by the agent Wilfred van Wyck to go to Queen's Hall and turn for Stravinsky at the first London performance of the *Duo Concertante*. The hall was full of fog and Neel remembered 'propped on the piano was a very thick mass of music manuscript sheets, which at first appeared to be quite blank. Peering closer, however, I could just discern some faint pencilled outlines of ghostly note shapes on the staves . . . from what I could see of the ghostly shapes through the fog, the manuscript appeared to be a series of shorthand symbols, which conveyed everything to the composer but nothing to anyone else.'

Stravinsky's visits to London

June 1912	In audience for *Firebird* on 18 June
February 1913	In audience for *Petroushka*
June 1914	In audience for *Le Chant du Rossignol* on 18 June (Drury Lane)
7 June 1920	In audience for *The Rite of Spring* (Queen's Hall)
10 June 1920	*Chant du Rossignol & Pulcinella*
October 1921	*Sleeping Beauty* (Alhambra)
19 June 1927	Concerto for piano and winds, Stravinsky Piano/ WirelessOrch/Clark
27 June 1927	Conducts *Petroushka/Pulcinella/Firebird* (Princes Theatre)
12 May 1928	Conducts *Oedipus Rex* BBC
19 June 1929	Concerto for piano and winds, *Apollon Musagète*, Goossens/Stravinsky (Queen's Hall)
27–28 July 1928	Records *Petroushka* suite for Columbia (6 sides)
27 June 1929	Conducts *Apollon Musagète*, *Le Baiser de la Fée* BBC
28 January 1931	Conducts *Apollon Musagète*, *The Rite of Spring*, *Four Studies*, Violin Concerto BBC
21 March 1931	*Capriccio*, Stravinsky, piano: Queen's Hall/Sargent
16 November 1931	Conducts *Symphony of Psalms* and Violin Concerto Queen's Hall
27 January 1932	*Capriccio*, Stravinsky, piano: Queen's Hall/Ansermet '6th appearance in 12 months'
13 March 1933	Stravinsky and Dushkin broadcast: *Song of the Nightingale* and *Chinese March*; *Suite Italienne*; *Duo Concertante*
27 February 1934	Stravinsky and Dushkin at Queen's Hall – end of tour with Dushkin
28 November 1934	*Perséphone*: Ida Rubinstein/BBC conducted by Stravinsky
18 November 1937	*Jeu de Cartes* Queen's Hall conducted by Stravinsky
27 May 1954	Stravinsky presented with gold medal of RPS by Bliss; Stravinsky conducted *Scènes de Ballet*
December 1956	To London, though not well enough to appear in public. BBC Concert (*Symphony of Psalms* & Symphony in C) conducted by Sir Malcolm Sargent. Robert Craft conducted *Canticum Sacrum* and *Variations on Vom Himmel Hoch* at St Martin-in-the-Fields
10 December 1958	BBC Home Service concert from RFH/BBCSO/Stravinsky *Agon*; Symphony on Three Movements; *Apollon Musagète*; *Firebird* – three extracts
12 December 1958	BBC Third programme BBCSO/Stravinsky *Apollo*; *Agon*; Symphony in Three Movements
9 November 1959	RFH *Oedipus Rex* (with Jean Cocteau, narrator)
18 Oocber. 1961	Stravinsky present at staged performance of Oedipus Rex at *Sadler's Wells*
21 October 1961	Stravinsky at rehearsal at Maida Vale
25 and 29 October 1961	*Perséphone* with Vera Zorina
29 May 1963	Attends Royal Albert Hall for Monteux's 50th anniversary performance of *The Rite of Spring* and takes a bow
June 1964	Stravinsky only appeared at Oxford, but was photographed laughing with Rostropovich in London
14 September 1965	*Fireworks*; *The Firebird* (1945 suite) (Craft conducted *Huxley Variations*; *The Rite of Spring*

In the summer of 1934 Stravinsky came again, this time to record *Les Noces*. This was for Columbia and took place at the Abbey Road Studios with an English team consisting of Kate Winter, soprano, and Linda Seymour, contralto, neither of whom are now remembered, together with two celebrated British male singers of the time, the tenor Parry Jones and the baritone Roy Henderson. The four pianists were Berkeley Mason, Leslie Heward, Ernest Lush, and C. E. Benbow. The recording took place on 10 July and was completed in one day.

On 28 November 1934 there was a large audience in Queen's Hall when Stravinsky returned to conduct a concert performance of his latest work, *Perséphone*, with Ida Rubinstein as the narrator with BBC forces. In the rest of an all-Stravinsky programme Sir Henry Wood took the baton and Stravinsky was the soloist in his own *Capriccio*. The many press notices found the critics puzzled and Richard Capell noted that Stravinsky's piano playing 'rather failed to do justice' to the *Capriccio*.

Stravinsky does not seem to have been in London again until 18 November 1937, when he conducted *Jeu de Cartes* on two successive nights at Queen's Hall. A gap of seventeen years then elapsed until he returned, when at the Royal Festival Hall on 27 May 1954, Stravinsky was presented with the Gold Medal of the Royal Philharmonic Society by his early champion Sir Arthur Bliss, and conducted *Scènes de Ballet*, *Orpheus* and the *Petroushka* suite, a concert preserved in the BBC Archives and accessible through the National Sound Archive.

In December 1956 Stravinsky travelled to London to conduct a BBC concert of his recent music, but he was not well enough to appear in public, and the programme was shared between Malcolm Sargent (*Symphony of Psalms* and Symphony in C) and Robert Craft, who conducted *Canticum Sacrum* and *Variations on Vom Himmel Hoch* at St Martin-in-the-Fields.

On 10 December 1958, Stravinsky again appeared at the Festival Hall, conducting *Agon*, the Symphony in Three Movements and *Apollo*. Broadcast live, the programme was circulated worldwide on BBC transcription discs, copies of which may be heard in the National Sound Archive. For these postwar visits to London Stravinsky stayed at Claridges Hotel, Brook Street.

Stravinsky's performance of *Oedipus Rex* with Jean Cocteau as narrator and BBC forces was at the Festival Hall on 9 November 1959 starting at the unusual time of 11 p.m. It was packed. The conductor Leslie Head tells us that it was the night of his own successful Albert Hall performance of Verdi's *Requiem*, after which he went to the Festival Hall along with the cream of musical London to find a crowded hall. Two days previously Stravinsky had made a studio recording with the same forces including his Symphony in C.

After the financial and artistic success of *Oedipus Rex*, the BBC Director of Music, William Glock, floated the idea of a repeat occasion a year later to perform *Perséphone*. Eventually it changed to October 1961 when there was a public performance and a BBC studio performance broadcast on 25 and 29 October. Stravinsky was paid enormous

Various live London performances conducted by Stravinsky in his later years which were broadcast and survive in the BBC or National Sound Archive or have been subsequently issued on LP or CD.	
27 May 1954	RFH Orpheus; *Petroushka* suite Royal Philharmonic Orchestra National Sound Archive/BBC Archives
10 Dec. 1958	RFH *Agon*; *Symphony in* Three Movements; *Apollo*; *The Firebird* (1945 suite) BBC Transcription Service 98562–66
9 Nov. 1959	RFH *Oedipus Rex* (with Jean Cocteau, narrator) BBC Chorus/ BBC Symphony Orchestra Fonit-Cetra DOC 11
29 Oct. 1961	RFH *Perséphone* (with Vera Zorina speaker) Schola Polyphonica Boys Choir; BBC Chorus; BBC Symphony Orchestra National Sound Archive
14 Sept. 1965	*Fireworks*; *The Firebird* (1945 suite) New Philharmonia Orchestra National Sound Archive. The *Firebird* sequence is now issued on DVD as a filler to a programme featuring Igor Markevitch on EMI Classic Archive 7243 4 90110 9 0.

fees for these appearances, and it must seem strange to us today that they were willing to pay two fees when a recorded repeat broadcast must have been cheaper. During this visit Stravinsky was seen in the audience at the Mermaid Theatre where Denis Stevens was conducting a series of concerts with the then fashionable practice of presenting very old and very new together.

Stravinsky was next in London on 29 May 1963, but does not seem to have appeared as a conductor. However he attended a sold out Royal Albert Hall for Pierre Monteux's fiftieth anniversary performance of *The Rite of Spring* and, reported *The Times*'s critic, 'it was a moving experience to watch these octogenarian partners in a 50-year old crime receiving their ovation for it'.

In June 1964 Stravinsky again visited the UK. He conducted only in Oxford, but was photographed exchanging a joke with Rostropovich in London.

The final appearance in London came on 14 September 1965 when with the New Philharmonia Orchestra he conducted *Fireworks* and *The Firebird* 1945 suite, and Robert Craft conducted the brief new *Huxley Variations* and *The Rite of Spring*. The ticket prices were enormously high and Craft received a bad press. *The Firebird* was televised and the archive footage has been issued on DVD as a filler to a programme featuring Igor Markevitch.

Sir Arthur Sullivan (1842–1900)

Born at 8 Bolwell Terrace, off Lambeth Walk, the future theatrical partner of W. S. Gilbert lived at 6 Cheyne Walk as one of the choristers of the Chapel Royal until 1856 when, at the age of fourteen, he won the competition for the first Mendelssohn Scholarship to the Royal Academy of Music. He subsequently went to the Leipzig Conservatoire in 1858 where one of his fellow students, a year his junior, was Grieg. While at Leipzig Sullivan wrote his music for Shakespeare's *The Tempest*, and when it was performed at the Crystal Palace on 5 April 1862 his reputation was made, almost overnight; he was still only nineteen. Needing to earn his living, Sullivan taught at the Chapel Royal and became organist of St Michael's, Chester Square, a very fashionable church, and from 1867 to 1871 was director of music at St Peter's, Cranley Gardens. His friendship with George Grove had already secured him his performance at Crystal Palace. He conducted at the Royal Aquarium from 1874 to 1876, and then had a rather unsatisfactory role as principal of the National Training School for Music (predecessor of the Royal College of Music) and Professor of Composition until resigning in 1881. Long remembered chiefly for the operettas he created with Gilbert for the Savoy Theatre, his other works are increasingly being revived and recorded. From 1881 until his death he lived at 1 Queen's Mansions, 58 Victoria Street (now demolished). Sir August Manns conducted a concert in his memory at the Crystal Palace, reflecting his associations with its musical life. He was buried in St Paul's cathedral at Queen Victoria's insistence, although he had wanted to lie in the family grave at Brompton Cemetery.

Pyotr Il'yich Tchaikovsky (1840–1893)

The Russian composer first visited London in August 1861 when he went with a friend of his father's acting as interpreter and stayed for about a week. He did the tourist sites but disliked the gloom and rain. During this stay Tchaikovsky visited the newly refurbished Cremorne Gardens, which then covered a huge site between the King's Road and the river. Like Haydn, Berlioz and Liszt before him he was enchanted by the massed singing of the charity children at St Paul's.

Over a quarter of a century later Tchaikovsky came as an established composer. In March 1888 he stayed at the French-speaking Dieudonné Hotel in Ryder Street (off St James's Street), and made his debut at the Philharmonic Society at St James's Hall on 22 March with the *Serenade for Strings* and the *Theme and Variations* from his *Suite No. 3*. William Apthorp's essays *By the Way* give us a vivid picture of Tchaikovsky's striking appearance at the head of an orchestra:

> Tall and slim of figure, with short, thick iron-grey hair, moustache, and imperial, there was something military in his bearing, in the grave, dignified response he bowed to his reception by the audience . . . His beat . . . was unostentatious, he used his left arm but little. But his down-beat was admirably clear and precise . . . It soon became evident that the man was positively an electric battery, launching lightning-flashes right and left from that terrible bâton, egging his men on to the utmost fury of fiery intensity.

Frederic Cowen, who was also conducting, remarked that 'the reception they [the *Theme and Variations*] met with was favourable enough, [but] there were few if any signs of the phenomenal success his music was destined later to obtain'. Cowen points out that Tchaikovsky did not speak English and therefore he had to 'stand at his side all the time and translate his wishes to the members of the orchestra. This I had to do with nearly all the foreign composers who came over.'

Tchaikovsky returned to the Philharmonic a year later, and on 11 April 1889 he appeared as conductor at St James's Hall in his Piano Concerto in B-flat minor with Wassily Sapelnikov as soloist and what was billed as 'Suite in D' – the First Suite, Op. 43–, the latter having its English premiere. After the rehearsal on the morning of 10 April Tchaikovsky had his first encounter with a really bad London fog, finding it dark when he left the hall at noon.

Tchaikovsky returned to London for the last time in May 1893. On 1 June he appeared at St James's Hall to conduct his Fourth Symphony and in the same concert Saint-Saëns played his G minor Piano Concerto and conducted the symphonic poem *Le Rouet d'Omphale*. On this visit Tchaikovsky was lionised, attended innumerable concerts and received invitations to lunch, dinner or tea. He ended by receiving an honorary doctorate at Cambridge when he conducted *Francesca da Rimini*. A. C. Mackenzie remembers Tchaikovsky on this occasion:

When the famous Peter Ilitsch came to conduct his *Fourth Symphony* in '93 he seemed already a spent man, nor did he live very long after his visit; the weak voice, intense nervousness, and exhaustion after rehearsal, plainly indicated failing health. His unaffected modesty, kindly manner and real gratitude for any trifling service rendered, all contributed to the favourable impression made by a lovable man. Truth to tell, Tchaikowsky possessed no gifts as a conductor, and knew it; nevertheless, thanks to the assistance of an attentive and sympathetic orchestra, *No. IV* scored a complete success. I fear to have unwittingly provided an uncomfortable hour for him when, honouring the R.A.M. by a quite unexpected visit at a time when I happened to be exceptionally busy, I placed the baton in his hand and called upon a student to play his *B Flat Minor Concerto* at an orchestral practice.

The day after the concert, Tchaikovsky and Saint-Saëns were invited by the Philharmonic Society to dinner at the St. Stephen's Club, on the corner of the Embankment and Bridge Street facing the Houses of Parliament. Here, sitting between the two distinguished guests, was Francesco Berger who records in his memoirs how they conversed in French and that Tchaikovsky was more subdued, less voluble while Saint-Saëns was 'far more animated, more voluble, with much gesture and vehemence to emphasise his conversation'. Approaching midnight they left and Mackenzie walked Tchaikovsky back to his hotel:

He and I started on a long ramble through the streets until past one o'clock in the morning. I then learned that he was neither a perfect Wagnerite nor a devout worshipper at the shrine of Brahms, and gathered that his reception at Vienna had not been a pleasant one. Probably friend Hanslick had been at his courteous tricks again: '*Stinkende Musik*' was not a pretty expression to use in connexion with the popular Violin Concerto. He stated to me that the fight for recognition had been a hard one everywhere but in England. Without showing discontent or bitterness, the amiable Russian appeared melancholy and lonely; devoid of self assertion and giving no sign of the passion and force revealed in his music.

Four months later Tchaikovsky was dead, but this was the beginning of the Tchaikovsky craze in England, and when Mackenzie played the *Pathétique* symphony for the first time in England on 28 February 1894 it was such a success it had to be repeated at the next concert on 14 March.

Ralph Vaughan Williams (1872–1958)

Vaughan Williams is one of so many who became a Londoner during his student days. He studied at the Royal College of Music, and in 1895 became organist at St Barnabas, South Lambeth. He married Adeline Fisher in 1897 and in 1898 resided briefly at 16 North Street and then 5 Cowley Street, both in Westminster, and at 10 Barton Street in 1899. They moved to 13 Cheyne Walk in 1905 and left London for Dorking in 1929. Vaughan Williams was, of course, a leading light of the English Folksong Society, later English Folk Dance and Song Society.

Vaughan Williams enjoyed first performances throughout the country, but most of his major orchestral works were first heard at Queen's Hall. Many of his most notable chamber music and several of his songs were heard at the Æolian Hall where *On Wenlock Edge* and the First String Quartet were premiered in November 1909, the *Phantasy Quintet* in March 1914 and *Merciless Beauty* in October 1921. This was a hall that could accommodate a small orchestra and Vaughan Williams's violin concerto the *Concerto Accademico* was first given there in November 1925 played by Jelly d'Aranyi. Vaughan Williams was also heard at the Bechstein (now Wigmore) Hall. These were not all firsts, and after an early performance of his *Songs of Travel* in December 1904, these tended to be later performances. The Second String Quartet was written during the Second World War and it was natural that it should appear at the National Gallery on 12 October 1944, in one of the celebrated National Gallery lunchtime concerts. Vaughan Williams also contributed to great occasions at Westminster Abbey, and his *Festival Te Deum* was a feature of the coronation of King George vi, his triumphal setting of the *Old Hundredth* at the coronation of Queen Elizabeth ii in 1953.

Vaughan Williams's wife Adeline died in 1951, and in 1953 he married Ursula Wood, and spent his last years in London at 10 Hanover Terrace, NW1. His ashes are buried in Westminster Abbey.

Giuseppe Verdi (1813–1901)

Verdi's only opera written for London was *I Masnadieri*, which he conducted at Her Majesty's Theatre on 22 July 1847. Verdi enjoyed a gala reception with the Queen, the Prince Consort and Prince Louis Napoleon present, and received a quarter-hour ovation before the performance started. He was repeatedly called for what, now, has become regarded as one of his lesser scores. The opera had a mixed reception by the critics, many of whom had still not accepted Verdi as a major composer, but it was well received by the public.

In London Verdi disliked the climate and the smoky atmosphere but admired the buildings. There were four performances of *I Masnadieri* but Verdi conducted only the first two, Balfe the others. The cast was a brilliant one with Jenny Lind (the *Illustrated London News* told how 'bouquets innumerable were thrown to the Swedish songstress'), Gardoni and Lablache, and Verdi was offered a lucrative contract to return each year, but declined because he worried that his health could not stand the climate.

He briefly returned in the summers of 1854, 1855 and 1856, always on business trips relating to the copyright of his works. In August 1855 the *Musical Times* reported that Verdi had been in London recently with his wife and publisher, Ricordi, and had visited 'all the sights of London during the week and paid a visit to the Crystal Palace'. The 1850s were the time at which Verdi's operas were widely performed, *Rigoletto* in 1853, *Il Trovatore* in 1855, *La Traviata* in 1856, *Luisa Miller* in 1858, *Sicilian Vespers* in 1859, *Un Ballo in Maschera* in 1861. While in London in 1855 the Verdis attended the premiere of *Il Trovatore*, a triumph for Pauline Viardot as Azucena. Verdi had lost copyright protection in his works published in Great Britain up to 1855 owing to the House of Lords decision in *Jeffreys v Boosey*, where the court held that a foreigner could have copyright in Great Britain on first publication as long as he was resident at the time. Verdi had come to London to secure the rights of *Il Trovatore*, which reappeared in English the following year. When he and his publisher registered *Jérusalem* in 1855, they gave their address as 6 Arundel Street, Coventry Street.

In 1862 he came again and stayed at 43 Alpha Road, Regent's Park (later referred to by the conductor Luigi Arditi as 'his quiet retreat in St John's Wood'). This was for the London International Exhibition, a disastrous attempt to revisit the Exhibition of 1851, less than six months after the death of Albert the Prince Consort. For the opening ceremony special music was commissioned to represent leading participating countries, including Sterndale Bennett for England with a short cantata (his *Exhibition Ode*), Auber for France with a march and Meyerbeer for Germany with an overture. Verdi came to conduct his short cantata for tenor, chorus and orchestra, *Hymn to the Nations* (*Inno delle Nazione*), which later became celebrated when championed by Toscanini at the end of the Second World War. This is of particular significance for Verdians as it was his first partnership with Boito. In fact Verdi's music was not performed at the opening concert, as a result of unsubtle politicking by the conductor Sir Michael Costa. Verdi wrote to *The Times* making clear its non-performance was not down to him. This was no unknown composer making waves, and one newspaper referred to him as 'the famous Guiseppe Verdi, the most popular composer in Europe'. Subsequently the opera impresario Mapleson offered to give it at Her Majesty's after *The Barber of Seville*, where conducted by Arditi, on 24 May it had a rousing reception and was encored, Verdi having six curtain calls. Over the following weeks it was given five further performances.

Verdi briefly visited London in June 1874 for discussions concerning his *Requiem*, which was due to appear for the first time in 1875, and he happened upon an amazed Alberto Randegger, singing teacher, composer and conductor who had known the composer in Trieste, when he attended Handel's *Israel in Egypt* at the Handel Festival at Crystal Palace, as Verdi entered the hall ostensibly incognito.

Verdi came to London for the last time to conduct the *Requiem* at the Royal Albert Hall on 15 May 1875 (there was a semi-public rehearsal on the 12th) which was given by a choir of twelve hundred that had been trained by Barnby, with Stainer at the organ. Massed performances on that scale can still be heard from time to time at the Albert Hall, and the effect of so large a choir in this music is always remarkable. It had a good reception by the press and had to be repeated on 19, 22 and 29 May, the composer appearing on each occasion. Herman Klein recalled the composer at the dress rehearsal in his memoirs: 'his closely cut beard was fast turning grey; but he was as active and robust as a youth'. During a break Verdi mingled with the invited audience greeting old friends and suddenly recognised Klein's companion who had been a fellow student with Verdi in Milan, 'then followed a close embrace that I thought would never end. It would be hard to say which of the two former classmates evinced the fuller measure of joy.' Verdi left England soon afterwards.

Richard Wagner (1813–1883)

Wagner came to London three times. His first visit was in the summer of 1839 when, escaping from his creditors, he sailed from Riga to London, a voyage of three weeks, with his wife, Minna, and his St Bernard dog, Robber. They arrived in the Pool of London on 13 August, and first went to the Hoop and Horse Tavern near the Tower of London, but finding the district unbearably insalubrious they went by cab to Old Compton Street, which, Wagner tells us, in the traffic took an hour, and there they stayed at the King's Arms, since demolished. Before they left for France on the 20th Wagner had witnessed a debate in the House of Lords, then in temporary premises after the fire of 1834. They endured a 'ghastly London Sunday' and travelled by train for the first time.

That was the visit of an unknown musician without an entrée to London musical society. The next time he came it was at the invitation of the Philharmonic Society in the capacity of conductor. He arrived at London Bridge Station on 4 March 1855 and spent his first night at Ferdinand Praeger's house at 31 Milton Street (now 65 Balcombe Street, NW1). Wagner then took rooms at 22 Portland Terrace, no longer extant, now North Gate, Prince Albert Road, NW1. This is near Regent's Park and London Zoo, which became favourite places. He stayed for nearly four months, leaving on 27 June. During that time he conducted the whole season, eight concerts, for the Philharmonic Society at the Hanover Square Rooms, the first on Monday 12 March, the last on Monday 25 June.

Wagner's London friend Karl Klindworth in old age recalled Wagner's objections to the London practice of giving enormously long programmes on minimal rehearsal.

He used to grumble tremendously at the length of the programmes. He found it impossible to properly prepare such an amount of work with the too limited time at rehearsal. I remember how distressed he was at the lethargy of the orchestra. He said, with arms uplifted to the band: 'You are the famous Philharmonic orchestra. Raise yourselves, gentlemen; be *artists*!' He waged war with the

97   The Hoop and Horse, 10 Queen Street, Tower Hill, where Wagner spent his first night in England.

98   Silhouette of Wagner conducting in his prime.

Directors for doing such absurd things as putting down an operatic air quite unsuitable to the artistic standard which the Philharmonic Society should follow and to the singer to whom it was assigned. '*Where* are the Directors?' he furiously asked at the rehearsal. Wagner said that, outside his immediate circle of friends, there were only two people in England who cared anything about him, and they were the Queen and the Prince Consort.

Queen Victoria and Prince Albert were present at the seventh concert when the *Tannhäuser* overture was repeated at Prince Albert's request. Wagner protested that the overture did not worthily represent him to royalty. Wagner's own music was not well received by the critics, who hated it, *The Musical World* critic saying: 'We hold that Herr Richard Wagner is not a musician at all . . . Look at "Lohengrin" . . . it is poison, rank poison . . . an incoherent mass of rubbish, with no more pretension to be called music than the jangling and clashing of gongs, and other euphonious instruments.'

At the end of this visit Wagner met Berlioz, who reported in a letter to their mutual friend Liszt that Wagner had had to suffer from 'a hostility born of prejudice'. Berlioz enthused that Wagner's 'passion, warmth and enthusiasm are superb'.

Wagner returned to London in 1877 for the Wagner Festival at the Royal Albert Hall. He was met at Charing Cross Station on 1 May by Hans Richter, and a deputation from the orchestra. Richter in the end would conduct most of the Festival. Wagner lodged with Edward Dannreuther at 12 Orme Square, Bayswater. The orchestra arranged for this event was enormous, numbering 169 players. The woodwind were trebled, the brass doubled after the tradition of the great choral festivals. Hubert Parry, then aged twenty-eight, was an habitué of 12 Orme Square, and had been to Bayreuth for the first *Ring* the previous year. Parry's diaries, still held by the family, are at Shulbrede Priory, Hampshire. Here Parry recorded his view of Wagner's visit, and gives a vivid portrait of events:

> May 4th: All the morning at the rehearsal at the Albert Hall. The hero was there and in good humour, and pleased with the band. They chiefly practised Siegfried second act and finale. Richter conducted wonderfully and drilled the incompetents with vigour.
>
> May 5th: (Evening) . . . to Dannreuther's, where there was a goodly company of artist folk to see Wagner, who was in great fettle and talked to an open-mouthed group in brilliant fashion. He talks so fast that I could catch but very little of what he said.
>
> May 7th: All the morning at the rehearsal at the Albert Hall. Wagner's conducting is quite marvellous; he seems to transform all he touches; he knows precisely what he wants, and does it to a certainty. The *Kaisermarsch* became quite new under his influence, and supremely magnificent. I was so wild with excitement after it that I did not recover all the afternoon. The concert in the evening was very successful and the Meister was received with prolonged applause, but many people found the *Rheingold* selection too hard for them.

May 9th: Rehearsal in the morning, not very satisfactory as far as I heard it . . . The concert in the evening was very successful and the Meister was well received. Hill singing as the Hollander was superb. The long first act of *Walkure* was a severe test on the public, without the assistance of the scenery or dramatic action, and many went out; but the applause at the end was great nevertheless.

May 12th: Went to the *Valkurie*, it was a triumphant success. The great last act of *Walkure* was overwhelming and very few went out before the end. And the cheering and clapping was prolonged and enthusiastic. The *Walkurenritt* was encored bodily. That last scene is soul subduing and many people that I saw afterwards were as moved at it as I could have wished.

May 14th: We had the great Telramund and Ortrud scene from *Lohengrin*, in which Hill let himself out and surpassed everything I ever heard before for dramatic singing . . . He half-acted it throughout and made me quite wild with wonder. He is a real genius – Materna also worked up at the end and gave us

---

Works conducted by Wagner in his 1855 series
(vocal works are cited in the language in which they were sung)

Beethoven: *Fidelio* 'A qual furor' ('O tu, la cui dolce possenza') 30 April
Beethoven: Overture *Leonora* (number not given), 28 May
Beethoven: Piano Concerto in B-flat Op. 19, 16 April
Beethoven: Symphony No. 3, 12 March
Beethoven: Symphony No. 4, 25 June
Beethoven: Symphony No. 5, 16 April
Beethoven: Symphony No. 6, 14 May
Beethoven: Symphony No. 7, 30 April
Beethoven: Symphony No. 8, 11 June
Beethoven: Symphony No. 9, 26 March
Beethoven: Violin Concerto, 28 May
Cherubini: *Anacreon* Overture, 11 June
Cherubini: *Ave Maria* (aria), 11 June
Cherubini: *Les Deux Journées* overture, 16 April
Cherubini: *O Salutaris Hostia* (aria), 26 March
Chopin: Piano Concerto No. 1, 14 May
Handel: *Acis and Galatea* ('O Ruddier Than the Cherry'), 28 May
Haydn: *The Spirit Song* (Song), 25 June
Haydn: Symphony No. 7 [No. 104 *London*], 12 March
Hummel: Piano Concerto No. 5 in A-flat, 15 June
Lucas: Symphony No. 3 in B-flat, 30 April
Macfarren: *Chevy Chase* Overture, 11 June
Marschner: *Der Vampyr* ('Oh. My father'), 12 March
Mendelssohn: *The Hebrides* Overture, 12 March
Mendelssohn: *Midsummer Night's Dream* Overture, 25 June
Mendelssohn: Italian Symphony,. 16 April
Mendelssohn: Scottish Symphony, 28 May
Mendelssohn: Violin Concerto, 26 March
Meyerbeer: *Le Prophète* (Duet: 'Della Mosa'), 25 June
Meyerbeer: *Les Hugenots* ('Più bianca'), 30 April
Mozart: 'Bald schlägt die Abschieds stunde' (aria), 16 April

Mozart: *Così fan tutte* (Trio: 'Soave sia il vento'), 12 March
Mozart: *Così fan tutte* (Duet: 'Fra gl'amplessi'), 30 April
Mozart: *Don Giovanni* ('Crudele – Non mi dir'), 28 May
Mozart: *Il Seraglio* (Aria: 'Martern aller arten'), 14 May
Mozart: *Il Seraglio* (Aria: 'Questi avventurieri'), 28 May
Mozart: Symphony No 39 in E-flat, 14 May
Mozart: Symphony No 41 *Jupiter* , 11 June
Mozart: *Die Zauberflöte* Overture, 12 March
Onslow: Overture *L'Alcalde de la Vega*, 30 April
Paër: *I Fuorosciti* (aria: 'Agitato di smania funesta'), 14 May
Paër: *Agnese* ('Quel sepolcro'), 11 June
Pergolesi: *Siciliana* (aria) , 28 May
Potter: Symphony in G minor, 28 May
Spohr: *Der Berggeist* overture, 28 May
Spohr: *Faust* 'Im Wechsel – Ja, ich fühl' es', 16 April
Spohr: *Jessonda* (aria: 'Di militari onori'), 11 June
Spohr: Nonet, 30 April
Spohr: Symphony No. 3 in C minor, 25 June
Spohr: *Faust* ('Va sbramando'), 16 April
Spohr: Violin Concerto No 8 'Dramatic', 12 March
Wagner: *Lohengrin* (extracts), 26 March
Wagner: *Tannhäuser* Overture, 14 May and 11 June
Weber: *Oberon* Overture, 25 June
Weber: *Euryanthe* Overture, 16 April
Weber: *Der Freischütz* Overture, 26 March
Weber: *Der Freischütz* ('Wie nahte mir der Schlummer'), 25 June
Weber: *Oberon* ('Ocean, thou mighty monster'), 12 March/11 June
Weber: *Preciosa* Overture, 14 May
Weber: *Ruler of the Spirits* overture, 30 April

In addition there was an unidentified duet sung by soprano Jenny Ney and baritone Giovanni Belletti on 14 May

some fine bits of singing and warmth. Then Unger and Sadler-Grün followed with the lovely scene 'Das slisse Lied' and failed rather, Unger seeming quite out of voice and shambling. We had also the opening scenes of *Gotterdammerung* which were splendid. Wagner has compressed it for the occasion, curtailing the Norns' bit and cutting out Tagesgrauen and fitting it so into one scene, which is very effective. We had the introduction to *Lohengrin* which he takes very slow and quite teased the band. At the concert in the evening Unger shortly showed that his voice had utterly collapsed. The beautiful scene in *Lohengrin* was quite painful, and at the end of the first part a general change of the programme was determined on – all *Siegfried* had to be missed out; and the short second part consisted only of the *Walkürenritt*, which was again encored, and the opening scenes of *Gotterdamerung* as in the morning, in which Unger cut a very poor figure after that Wagner cut short the proceedings by taking Materna by the arm and walking straight out.

May 15th: To rehearsal. The last scenes of *Gotterdammerung*. Didn't go well and the wind had to be drilled alone. Unger did not appear at all.

May 16th: A day to have lived for. The concert was a perfect triumph. They were in great difficulties about it as Unger and Hill were both unable to sing.

At the end of Parry's diary entry for 4 June he noted 'saw Wagner and his wife off at Victoria Station'.

In fact, despite Parry's enthusiasm, he was guilty of seeing Wagner's role as conductor through rose-tinted spectacles, for as recounted by Hermann Klein and others, Wagner's rapport with the orchestra, which may well have been in evidence at the early rehearsals, quickly faded. Klein described it as 'a bad attack of Albert Hall stage fright'. Miles Birket Foster reflected the observation of many contemporary critics when he remembered 'taking part in that Festival, and well recalled the all-controlling power of Hans Richter, hidden behind Wagner's conducting desk. But really conducting everything: for Wagner, in the enjoyment of his own splendid creations, frequently forgot the baton altogether'.

Sir William Walton (1902–1983)

The composer William Walton came from Oldham and was 'discovered' at Oxford by Osbert and Sacheverell Sitwell, with whom he lived for many years when a young man. This was first at 5 Swan Walk (1919) and, from 1920 to 1929 and again briefly in 1932 and 1934, at their home at 2 Carlyle Square (plaque), both in Chelsea. In the latter, in a double first-floor room the first performance of *Façade* took place in June 1922. Walton did not achieve financial independence until the mid-1930s, at first as the consequence of a bequest from Elizabeth Courtauld and subsequently on the proceeds of his film music commissioned by the Hungarian Director Paul Czinner for films starring Elisabeth Bergner. Walton's first film score was *Escape Me*

Never for which he was paid £300. He moved to 56a South Eaton Place, Belgravia, in 1935, the year in which he took up with Alice Wimborne, who was twenty-two years his senior, precipitating a final and sudden break with the Sitwells. This house was her London cottage and it was destroyed in the Blitz in May 1941. After the death of Alice's husband, Lord Wimborne, in 1939, Walton lived at her home at Ashby St Legers, Rugby, a house celebrated for being the location of the hatching of the Gunpowder Plot. When Alice died in April 1948 she left Walton Lowndes Cottage, Lowndes Place, SW1. It was here that Walton and Susanna Gil lived until 1955, after marrying on 13 December 1948. Curiously a plaque has been placed at 10 Holly Place, Holly Walk, Hampstead, NW3, but not on his other London residences. There is a memorial stone in Westminster Abbey.

Peter Warlock (Philip Heseltine) (1894–1930)

The composer, writer and editor Philip Heseltine adopted the pseudonym 'Peter Warlock' in his mid-twenties in order to achieve an objective assessment by the publisher Winthrop Rogers, with whom he was not on good terms, and who successfully published Warlock's early songs in 1919. Heseltine was born in the Savoy Hotel, and as a baby his parents lived in a house in Hans Place (where Harrods Food Hall has since been built), and he first went to school at 35 Cliveden Street.

Heseltine did not serve during the First World War, living variously in Cornwall and Ireland. In 1916 he was at 14 Whitehead's Grove, and then stayed with Cecil Gray at 2 Anhalt Studios, Battersea. On 27 December Heseltine married Minnie Lucy ('Puma') Channing at the Chelsea Register Office, now the Workhouse Art Gallery. This marriage proved disastrous for Heseltine and by May 1917 he was back in Cornwall.

In London Heseltine lived in a succession of rented rooms or apartments, and as they were within a comparatively small area, mainly in Chelsea, SW3, they are easily visited on foot (with possibly one or two tube excursions) in one trip. After the First World War and through 1919 he was at 35 Warrington Crescent, Paddington, W9. Early in 1920 Winthrop Rogers agreed to fund a new journal to be called *The Sackbut*, edited by Heseltine. Heseltine launched on this task with enthusiasm, and during this time he wrote from the publisher's address, 18 Berners Street, W1, when he took new rooms at 35 St George's Road, Kilburn, NW6. However, so independent was Heseltine's editorial view, Rogers became unhappy at the controversial material he was publishing and after nine issues (May 1920 to March 1921) he withdrew his funding. Heseltine tried to continue alone but was unsuccessful.

In May 1921 he was at 122 Cheyne Walk, Chelsea, and then had a period in France, later returning to the family home in Montgomeryshire. In 1923 he was at 125 Cheyne Walk, and from there went to 6a Bury Street, Chelsea in 1924. From 1925 to 1928 Heseltine lived in a cottage at Eynsford, Kent (see Chapter 7) when his female companion was Barbara Peache, who remained with him for most of the rest of his life. In the summer of July 1929 Heseltine's address was 78 Denbigh Street, Pimlico, SW1, soon changing to 15 Gloucester Street, Pimlico, SW1, and he was working from the offices of Sir Thomas Beecham's Imperial League of Opera at 90 Regent Street, W1, whose magazine, known by the acronym *MILO*, was edited by Heseltine. At the Promenade concerts at Queen's Hall on 29 August Heseltine and his friend Constant Lambert each appeared as conductors, Heseltine, not one of music's great maestros, worried at the BBC's demands that he conduct. The *Daily Express* critic reported: '"Peter Warlock" (whose real name is Philip Heseltine) . . . is tall and fair, with a slight beard. He raised his hand in the air as though about to dive and brought it down energetically some three beats ahead of the orchestra. They proceeded (by his instructions) to play his sixteenth-century dance suite in a manner devoid of any expression at all, which was singularly effective for this type of music.' In October 1929 came the London Delius Festival, organised by Beecham, into which Heseltine was drawn, and which was focused on Queen's Hall, where Beecham conducted the opening concert on 12 October and ending there with the sixth concert featuring Delius's ecstatic *A Mass of Life* on 1 November. The two concerts requiring smaller forces were at the Æolian Hall in Bond Street. Heseltine met Delius at the Langham Hotel, and the celebrated image of the stricken composer in his wheelchair, in one case the chair pushed by Heseltine, had musical London mesmerised.

The critic Felix Aprahamian described Heseltine's 'artistic' appearance in the late 1920s as a 'strikingly handsome bearded figure . . . black sombrero, red tie, russet-coloured raglan top-coat, his left hand holding a slim brown-leather attaché-case with brass locks, and in the other hand, an ash walking-stick'. The last year of his life found Heseltine and Barbara Peache living in a basement flat at 30 (then 12a) Tite Street, Chelsea, now marked by a plaque. Here Heseltine died of coal gas poisoning on the night of 16/17 December 1930 and then lay in the local mortuary (no longer extant), the site of which was at Dovehouse Green, Kings Road, SW3. Whether it was misadventure, suicide or murder (as suggested by his son) has never been established, though the fact that he put out the cat and that the flat was bolted from the inside many have found significant. Close by is his favourite hostelry, the Antelope Tavern, 22 Eaton Terrace, SW1, while other nearby pubs he frequented include the Wellesley Arms, 70 Sydney Street, SW3.

Carl Maria von Weber (1786–1826)

Weber made one visit to London, over the last three months of his life, and died there. He arrived at Dover on 4 March 1826 and was in London the following day. He resided at the house of Sir George Smart, 91 Great Portland Street (later renumbered 103, just above Portland Chapel, and later in the nineteenth century replaced by Nelson's Hotel, itself since demolished). On 7 March he appeared in the audience at

Covent Garden and as soon as he was recognised he received an ovation from the audience. He made his first public appearance at Covent Garden on 9 March when *The Times* reported 'every seat in the pit was occupied' and that he 'did not preside at the piano-forte . . . but stood in the front of the stage, provided with a music desk and a *bâton de mesure* to regulate the time'. Moscheles was there and reported:

> What emotion he must have felt on his first appearance yesterday, before the English public, in Covent Garden Theatre! The thundering applause with which he was greeted affected us deeply, how much more himself, the honoured object of all this enthusiasm! The performance consisted of a selection from the Freischütz, conducted by himself; the overture was encored with acclamation. Braham, Miss Paton, and Phillips sang the chief numbers of the opera; they seemed inspired by Weber's presence. During the peals of applause, Weber shook hands with the singers, to express his pleasure and satisfaction; at the end of the performance the whole pit stood up on the benches, waving hats and handkerchiefs, and cheering the composer. I saw him later on in the evening, sitting in the green-room, and completely exhausted; he was too ill fully to enjoy this signal triumph in a land of strangers, but we, I mean the poet Kind, the fluteplayer Fürstenau, the good old harp-player Stumpff, the publisher Schulz, and myself, as being his fellow-countrymen, felt honoured in our friend's reception.

Moscheles was there again on 12 March when Weber improvised at the house of John Braham, one of the leading singers of the day who would be taking the role of Sir Huon de Bordeaux for whom Weber had specially written a scena: 'Although it was not a remarkable exhibition of his powers, he made his performance deeply interesting by introducing some subjects from "Freischütz". Unfortunately his physical weakness makes any great exertion dangerous, and yet at eleven o'clock he hurried off to a large party given by Mrs Coutts, as he was to be handsomely paid for his services. How we grieved at his thus overexerting himself!' Weber's ill-health became increasingly evident. On 13 March he was invited to dinner at Moscheles's house: 'What a treat! And yet even here the sight of him moved us to intense pity! for he could not utter a word when he entered our room; the exertion of mounting the small flight of stairs had completely taken away his breath; he sank into a chair nearest the door, but soon recovered, and became one of the most delightful and genial of guests. We took him to the Philharmonic concert, the first he ever heard.'

As soon as Weber had arrived in London he had been voted a free pass to the Philharmonic Society for the season, and on 3 April he conducted the third concert of the series at the Argyll Rooms.

> The concert-room was crowded to the doors with a brilliant assembly of people not only distinguished in music, but well known in art and literature. Weber had

99   103 Great Portland Street in 1894 – it had long been the home of Sir George Smart, where Weber spent his last three months in 1826.

a grand reception, and showed, by expressive gestures, how pleased and gratified he was. He had a clear and graceful mode of conducting. The Programme included four of his compositions: Mr Sapio sang the big Scena for tenor from *Der Freischütz*; the Overture to that Opera was played, and, the Overture to *Euryanthe*, while Mille Caradori-Allan sang his Italian Scena, *La Dolce Speranza*.

On 11 April Moscheles attended the dress rehearsal of *Oberon* at Covent Garden directed by Weber, which was before a full audience. The first night was the following evening and it was a triumph, the overture and many numbers being encored, though early in the second act Mary Ann Paton, who was singing the role of Reiza, was hit on the head by a stage flat and her part had to be read by the prompter, though she was back for the remainder of the run, which ran for twelve consecutive evenings. Twice Weber encountered bad London fogs that adversely affected his health. A benefit concert arranged for 26 May was not successful as, on a day of torrential rain, it was Derby Day at the Epsom Races and a competing concert drew away the aristocratic audience.

Weber was planning to leave but he died at Sir George's house on 5 June. Moscheles described how he was summoned at an early hour:

Early this morning I was summoned in all haste to Sir G. Smart's. At eleven o'clock last night Fürstenau had conducted Weber to his bedroom; his friends went to his door at an early hour, but found it locked inside, contrary to Weber's promise. To do this he must have got up during the night. It was in vain to knock or call for admission; no answer came. So Sir George sent to me and other friends, and the door was broken open in our presence. The noise did not disturb the sleeper; it was his sleep of death. His head, resting on his left arm, was lying quietly on the pillow.

The burial service was at the Roman Catholic chapel at Moorfields on 21 June, where Mozart's *Requiem* was sung. Years later Wagner organised the removal of the coffin to Dresden.

Anton Webern (1883–1945)

The composer Anton Webern came to London six times in the 1930s at the invitation of the BBC, but always as a conductor, altogether giving nine concerts. His own music appeared in only three of them. These invitations were doubtless inspired by Edward Clark and were not sustained once he had left the BBC in 1936. Webern's first visit to London was to conduct a short concert consisting of Milhaud's *Little Symphony* No. 1, Webern's own *Five Pieces for Orchestra*, Op. 10, and Brahms's *Serenade* in A, Op. 16. This involved his travelling to Ostend from where the sailing at 3.30 p.m., presumably to Harwich, took four and a half hours, including a storm. The train to London arrived at 10.30 p.m. and Webern was met by Clark and taken to the Strand Palace

Hotel. Webern stayed here on each visit but doubtless neither he nor his host realised they were on the site of the Exeter Hall and Berlioz's triumphs of eighty years before.

Webern had three rehearsals for this first concert, which was in a small (unspecified) theatre before an invited audience, all concerts then going out live. Webern's *Pieces*, then thought immensely difficult, were repeated for the studio audience after the broadcast was over. When Webern returned in 1931 a pattern began to develop in which he gave two concerts on consecutive days at an inclusive fee less than two separate fees. This became a favourite BBC ploy during the 1930s to contain expenditure while making it worth the while of European musicians to come to London. Webern came each year from 1933 to 1936, crowned by the second performance of the Berg Violin Concerto with Louis Krasner as soloist, a performance that has survived, for the soloist had it recorded by a studio on acetates off-air and these were the source of its issue on CD in 1991. At that time there was criticism among BBC staff of Webern's conducting technique and with the departure of Edward Clark from the BBC in 1936 he was never asked again.

> ### Webern's BBC concerts
>
> 2 December 1929: Milhaud, Little Symphony No. 1 *Printemps*; Webern, Five Pieces for Orchestra, Op. 10; Brahms, Serenade in A, Op. 16
> 7 May 1931: Schubert, *Rosamunde* Ballet Music (II); Johann Strauss, Waltz, *Roses in the South*; Wolf, *Italian Serenade*; Johann Strauss, Waltz, *Vienna Woods*
> 8 May 1931: Webern, *Five Movements for String Orchestra*; Schoenberg, *Song of the Wood-Dove*; Schoenberg, *Music for Cinema Scene*, Op. 34
> 21 April 1933: Berg, Two Pieces from *Lyric Suite*; Krenek, *Durch Die-Nacht*; Berg, *Kammerkonzert*
> 23 April 1933: Beethoven, Overture *Prometheus*; Schubert, *German Dances*; Mahler, Symphony No. 4
> 25 April 1934: Schubert, Symphony No. 4; Mahler, *Two Nachtstücke* from Symphony No. 7
> 25 April 1935: Schubert, Symphony No. 8; Bach-Webern, *Ricercare*; Webem, Six Pieces, Op. 6; Webern: Passacaglia, Op. 1
> 1 May 1936: *Berg Memorial Concert*; Berg, Two Pieces from *Lyric Suite*; Berg, Violin Concerto (issued on CD Testament STB 1004)
> 3 May 1936: Bruckner, Symphony No. 7

Samuel Sebastian Wesley (1810–1876)

Wesley was a composer and organist, the natural son of Samuel Wesley, also an organist and composer and nephew of Charles Wesley. He became a chorister at the Chapel Royal, St James's Palace, from the age of nine, and he was later organist there. In 1826 he became organist at St James's, Hampstead Road, in 1829 organist at St Giles, Camberwell, and St John's, Waterloo Road, in 1830 at Hampton. Assessed by *New Grove* as 'the greatest composer in the English cathedral tradition between Purcell and Stanford', he was instrumental in the revival of music in the Anglican church. In 1832 he left London and became one of the most celebrated cathedral organists of his time, as well as a striking composer, though inconsistent and eccentric in behaviour.

Sir Henry Wood (1869–1944)

The future founder and conductor of the Proms was very much a local man, born in Oxford Street, at No. 413a over his father's jewellery business, then moving to 7 Pond Street, Hampstead in 1873. In 1875 the family moved again, to 355 Oxford Street, and to Langham Place in 1878. In 1895 he became the founder conductor of the Proms at Queen's Hall, within a short walk of his home.

100   Sir Henry Wood conducts at Queen's Hall for the fortieth anniversary of the Proms in 1935.

From 1905 his London house was 4 Elsworthy Road, NW3, and that he retained until 1937. In about 1915 he bought Appletree Farm in Chorleywood, Hertfordshire. When he was separated from his second wife in 1935, she became the owner and from then Sir Henry lived at 19 Adam Street and from 1942 at 63 Harley House in the Marylebone Road (the block of flats where Beecham would die in 1961). His career from 1895 was centred on Queen's Hall until its destruction in 1941.

As the founder of the Proms Wood was a significant figure in the development of the audience for what he called 'great music' in the first thirty years of the twentieth century, and also in promoting the concept that British artists could be pre-eminent in their field. His was an enormous repertoire, and while early in his career he was widely associated with Russian music and the promotion of Sibelius, he became a champion for the new British composers of his day.

Wood was a notable pioneer of orchestral recording, standing astride the change from acoustic recording to the new electrical process. In a speech at the Connaught Rooms on 16 September 1926 to launch Columbia's new 'Viva-tonal' electrical recording system he compared the two:

> Of course, making orchestral records is one of the most trying things you can ask any musician to do. The conditions are so entirely different from the ordinary concert world. To begin with we made orchestral records in a small room – so small, in fact, that I have many a time given some of the dear members of my orchestra little raps on the top of the head whenever I desired certain effects and it was the reverse of encouraging [laughter]. Anyhow, the acoustics I always noticed because I found if I tapped a bald pate I got a different resonance, from those with a full thatch [laughter] . . . We have made enormous strides and advances since those times and I want to tell you what pleasure it gave me a few months ago when I was asked to make some orchestral records under the new conditions. Since we have been making the new electric records the whole scheme of things has changed. Not only do we work in a fine large studio instead of an attic, but the players have room to bow and I need not tell you how important it is that members of an orchestra should have room to bow. I have suffered all my life from people who will try to jam an orchestra into a square yard. You must have room to expand if you want to play your instruments [laughter].

His ashes are buried in St Sepulchre's church, where there is a memorial window to him designed by Gerald Smith and Frank Salisbury. Dedicated in 1946, it portrays St Cecilia (see Chapter 2).

Part III

Five Musical Walks

London is too large to explore comprehensively on foot, but musical life has tended to focus first on one district, then another. Linked by the underground or buses, the following walks underline how five characteristic areas of interest were once (and still may be) vibrant musical areas, because the many musical activities and personalities were but a step from each other. Although the London known by many of those described in this book was bombed during the Second World War, and extensively rebuilt and modernised in the 1960s, many original buildings still survive. During the writing of this book (2002–4) many celebrated musical centres have been refurbished, making this a time of renewal. Walking around these districts it is still possible to obtain a good idea of what it must have been like to live and work there over the past two or three centuries, as well as to enjoy the very active and diverse musical scene of today. The itineraries below should be followed with reference to the more extended accounts of the musicians and places concerned that appear elsewhere in this book, notably in Chapters 1 and 2 and Part II.

Walk 1: Music Publishers' London

For two centuries London's burgeoning music publishing and instrument trade focused largely on a few city blocks off Oxford Street. Music publishers came and went over the decades, but most twentieth-century publishers survived the bombing of the Second World War, only to be dispersed by changes in the publishing industry in the 1960s, which resulted in most of them leaving premises in which they had been resident for many years, in one or two cases for over a century. This resulted in significant losses of archives and of scores and performing materials of music then considered to be out of fashion but now of interest again. A painting by Sir Lawrence Alma-Tadema was once reported thrown in a skip as worthless but is now sold for a significant sum. So too was the music of Victorian England once rejected, but the music of Stanford, Parry, Mackenzie and their contemporaries is now played, and valued, again. Today music publishing is primarily concerned with performing and mechanical fees, and printed music has taken a much lower profile. Nevertheless musicians still need copies from which to play, but they are now

101 Sir John Barbirolli's birthplace in Southampton Row on the corner of Cosmo Place. (Inset: the plaque that appears on the wall by the door.)

1 Chappell's of Bond Street
2 Sotheby's
3 Façade of the Æolian Hall
4 St George's, Hanover Square
5 Former location of the RAM
6 Site of Hanover Square Rooms
7 Location of Zumpe's shop, at No. 7 Princes Street
8 Site of Argyll Rooms
9 Former location of Oxford University Press
10 Location of Cramer, Beale and Co. in the mid-nineteenth century
11 Boosey and Hawkes' showroom
12 BBC Broadcasting House
13 Site of Queen's Hall (plaque)
14 Guivier's Violin Shop
15 The George
16 Site of Pagani's restaurant
17 Schott of Mainz
18 Harold Moore's record shop
19 Site of Augener's music shop, Liszt plaque
20 Former premises of Novello and Co.
21 Site of Theresa Cornelis's 'Temple of Festivity' now at St Patrick's Church
22 Mozart plaque
23 Site of The Pantheon
24 Performing Right Society
25 Denmark Street

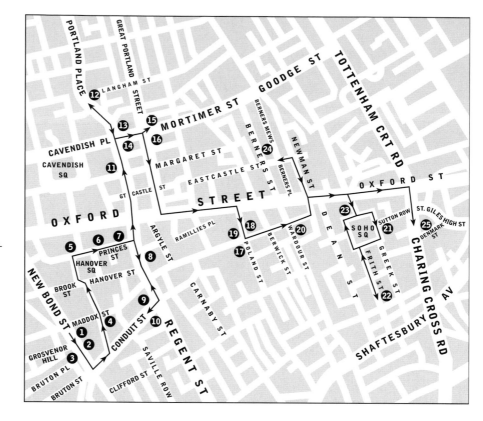

not always obtained by simply walking into a London publisher's showroom and purchasing them.

Until the mid-1960s a notable feature of the trade was the fact that these publishers all maintained trade counters at their central London premises, and early every morning what were called 'collectors' would make the rounds of these from wholesalers and music shops, fulfilling their customers' orders within 24 hours – something unheard of later. We describe the trade counters in Chapter 5.

Probably the best place to start a music publishers' walk is in Bond Street where 50 New Bond Street was long the home of Chappell and Co. Still trading as 'Chappell of Bond Street' it is now the home of Kemble pianos, though with a much less grand shop front than they once enjoyed. At nearby premises other music publishers and suppliers once prospered. Warner-Chappell no longer have a dedicated West End retail outlet. In the nineteenth century Rudall, Rose, Carte and Co. were at 100 New Bond Street. As well as being publishers of music and the nineteenth-century annual musical directory, they were concertina manufacturers, instrument retailers and agents for Adolphe Sax, of saxophone fame. Before the First World War the agent Concorde Concert Control, run by R. Norman-Concorde, was at 82 New Bond Street. Here Delius would have visited Concorde to finalise the details of the concert of his music at St James's Hall, his first in London, in June 1899. In the 1930s J. B. Cramer were at 139 New Bond Street. In the mid-twentieth century Keith Prowse, music publishers, retailers and ticket agents were at 159 New Bond Street. Before moving on, note Sotheby's auctioneers at 34 New Bond Street and, almost opposite, the façade of what used to be the Æolian Hall.

Walking down Bond Street left into Conduit Street and left again towards Hanover Square. The musical antecedents of Hanover Square derive from St George's church, on the right as one approaches the square, long associated with Handel. The Royal Academy of Music was in Tenterden Street (in the top left-hand – northwest – corner) for most of the century preceding the First World War, while the Hanover Square rooms were on the northeast side of the square, demolished in 1900, the site now occupied by anonymous office buildings and a sushi bar. In a similar building at the top northeast corner of the square was BBC Radio London in the 1970s. The music publisher long associated with the square was Ashdown, first as Ashdown and Parry at 18 Hanover Square (1860–67) and 19 Hanover Square (1868–82), and as Enoch and Ashdown at the same address (1928–60). In the earlier nineteenth century Patterson's were at 43 Hanover Square (1826–30).

Walking through Princes Street to Regent Street we pass No. 7, one of the few houses remaining from the eighteenth century, where from 1761 to 1780 Johann Christoph Zumpe started an enormous vogue for square pianos. In Regent Street we again pass a location where an active concert hall – the Argyll Rooms, on the corner of Argyll Street – helped generate supporting musical infrastructure nearby in the first quarter of the nineteenth century. However, south of Oxford Street nothing remains today, with the removal of the Oxford University Press Music Department from 44 Conduit Street to Oxford in 1980, and the closure of Bosworth and Co., at 8 Heddon Street (an alley off Regent Street) in the late 1990s. *The Architectural Panorama*, published in 1849, shows Cramer, Beale and Co., music sellers and publishers on the corner of Conduit Street at 201 Regent Street. Founded there in 1828, Francesco Berger remembered the shop in its hey-day as 'the *rendez-vous* of the elite of the musical profession'. He continued:

102   Cramer, Beale and Co. at 201 Regent Street on the corner of Conduit Street, 1849.

> Here I have chatted with Bottesini, the great (and tall) contrabassist, worthy successor of the earlier Dragonetti; and with that delightful violinist Sivori ... Henry Smart, the composer of so many fine songs, and the distinguished organist of St Pancras Church ... the Dutchman Silas, the Irishman Duggan, the Frenchman Sainton ... the German Blumenthal ... Sims Reeves might look in ... one might catch a glimpse of the jovial Balfe, or the smiling Arditi, or, if

they happened to be visiting England, the aristocratic Thalberg, the lion-headed Rubinstein or the rotund Jaëll.

At this date Addison, Hollier and Lucas, publishers, were at 210 Regent Street, while the flamboyant Jullien's sheet music, with its brilliant engraved coloured covers was at 214 Regent Street. Going north, in the mid-twentieth century Ricordi were at 271 Regent Street, while Boosey and Hawkes can still be found at 295 Regent Street where they have been (at first as Boosey and Son) since 1874. Though today without their former extensive shop front, the classical architecture of the salesroom is worth inspection.

Again we are in a locality where active musical centres generated local infrastructure. At the top of Regent Street is the BBC. To its right is the site of Queen's Hall (plaque). Turning left into Cavendish Place would eventually bring us to Wigmore Hall, but turning right into Mortimer Street brings us to J. P. Guivier's violin shop at 99 Mortimer Street, striking for its old-fashioned shopfront. Guivier's, founded in 1863, was at 2 Great Marlborough Street for the first half of the twentieth century, moving to its present address after the Second World War. Conductors needing a baton will find a varied selection here.

Going on brings us to Great Portland Street and those musical hostelries, The George, which still stands, and Pagani's Restaurant, which does not. Left up Great Portland Street would bring us to Yalding House on the right, formerly the home of BBC Radio Three and the once great BBC Music Library, since removed and much diminished and reduced. The continuation of Mortimer Street would take us towards the Middlesex Hospital and the present day premises of music publishers Josef Weinberger Ltd at 12–14 Mortimer Street.

Heading south we are back in Oxford Street, where turning left and then taking the third right leads us to Poland Street and, subsequently, Great Marlborough Street (where, onthe corner of Argyll Street until 1830 were located the Argyll Rooms). Great Marlborough Street has long been a noted centre of music publishing, though only Schott and Co. remains, in a showroom now jointly owned with Universal Edition at 48 – premises purchased in 1908 by Charles Gottlieb Volkert for Schotts. Here a number of premises have been in the music business for well over a century, though with a succession of owners or tenants. Guivier and Co. and Bayley and Ferguson were at 2 Great Marlborough Street in the 1930s, subsequently occupied by Musica Rara and now the premises of the specialised record shop Harold Moores, though Harold Moores himself retired in 2003 and sold the business. However, the shopfront with its canvas awning remains almost unchanged from the earlier twentieth century, giving a good idea of how the whole of that side of the street once looked.

Swan and Co. were successively at 3 Great Marlborough Street (1875–7), 4 Great Marlborough Street (1878–1906) and 9 Great Marlborough Street (1913–14). Number 11, long associated with J. and W. Chester, was previously the premises of

Scrutton (1873–5). For thirty years Enoch were at 14 or 14a (1887–1917), moving to 58 before going out of business in 1927. All who were music students in the 1950s, will remember Augener at 18 (1913–59), where the friendly reception and the conspiratorial question 'music students' discount?' created an instant rapport. In the nineteenth century S. and P. Erard, agents for the French piano makers, were at this address, where Sébastien Erard acquired 18 in 1794 and Pierre Erard amalgamated it with No. 17 in 1833. Liszt stayed with them on several occasions, a connection now marked by a self-effacing panel set into the wall. On the first floor the Salle Erard hosted concerts between 1898 and 1910. Hopwood & Crew were at 25 between 1900 and 1906, an address perhaps better known for Howard and Co., publisher of the musical song *Oh! Mr Porter*, with its lithographed cover. Hutchings and Romer were at 39 (1891–1916), premises shared with Metzler, piano manufacturers and publishers (who were at 42 in the 1880s).

Although active for less than a quarter of a century, before the First World War brought its closure, the London office of Breitkopf and Härtel of Leipzig was at 54 Great Marlborough Street from 1892–1916. Headed by its charismatic manager Otto Kling, Breitkopf was a significant publisher in its day, offering British composers publication by the leading German house, with worldwide offices. Kling became a personal friend to many composers, including Bantock, who published all his biggest works of the time with them. It also offered the best quality printing and engraving in Leipzig at very competitive rates and was widely used by the London trade. With the excellent and dependable pre-First World War postal service, using Breitkopf was as reliable as visiting Novello's printing works in nearby Wardour Street, where we should walk now.

Novello occupied premises at Novello House, 160 Wardour Street, the most prestigious home of any London music publisher, from 1906 to 1964. Designed by Frank Pearson with stone and white stucco dressings it is still a very distinctive building whose exterior has been referred to as 'Hanseatic', owing to its modelling on the German Renaissance town hall in Bremen. Subsequently occupied by the British Library, it has since been a shopping centre, and as such again accessible by the public, where one could see all the original panelling and mouldings still *in situ*, albeit obscured by the impedimenta of the then occupants. It was empty in the late summer of 2004. Wardour Street was long the home of the celebrated violin dealers and restorers Beare and Son (or Beare, Godwin and Co.) at 186, later 164 Wardour Street. Since 1929 they have been at 7 Broadwick Street (the third right off Wardour Street). North of the former Novello building we go through to Dean Street and pass the former London premises of Universal Edition of Vienna at 2–3 Fareham Street.

Dean Street was the home of various popular music publishers, and specialist shops selling pop and jazz CDs can still be found. Here was Henry Stave's, for many years London's leading showroom of classical LPs, and also the publishers Paxton's at 36–8. At 69 Dean Street, Novello developed in the mid-nineteenth century before the building of their Wardour Street showrooms. It would be possible for energetic readers to continue down Dean Street at this point and take up Walk 4 (below).

Cut through to Soho Square, the site of Carlisle House where in the 1760s and '70s the flamboyant adventuress Theresa Cornelys ran her 'Temple of Festivity' and was a significant pioneer of concert life. In a house adjoining the north side of Carlisle House lived C. F. Abel. The pianoforte showrooms of J. and J. Hopkinson were at 18 Soho Square in the mid-nineteenth century; Kirkmans at No. 3 from 1830 to 1892, as were other piano makers at the time. Out of the south side of the square run Frith Street and Greek Street. At 20 Frith Street (then Thrift Street) in 1764–5 the eight-year-old Mozart lodged with the corset-maker Thomas Williamson and performed for half a guinea (plaque). At 67 Frith Street Vincent Novello opened his first music publishing business, the firm (as part of Music Sales) is now at No. 11.

We exit Soho Square on the north side and return to Oxford Street. To the left near Ramillies Street the large branch of Marks and Spencer is on the site of the Pantheon that so revolutionised concert-giving in the late eighteenth century. The superscription 'The Pantheon' is still visible high on the wall. Here music publishing developed in one or two of the turnings on the north side of the street, notably Berners Street, where at 29–33 the Performing Right Society, the financial cornerstone of most composers' careers today, maintain their offices. In the nineteenth century the publishers Novello were long established at 1 Berners Street (1867–1906), while in the twentieth, Lengnick were at 14, Curwen at 24 (1902–69), Forsyth at 34 and Stainer and Bell at 58.

Continue walking east down Oxford Street to the junction with Tottenham Court Road (left) and Charing Cross Road (right). On the left, on the corner of Oxford Street was the Oxford Music Hall at the back of the Tottenham public house. Cross the road and turn right into the Charing Cross Road, the home of 'tin pan alley'. Probably the principal street to be thus designated was Denmark Street, a short way down on the left, from where many popular music publishers still operate. Here the basement Tin Pan Alley Studios (TPA), founded in 1954 by session musician Ralph Elman, saw many later celebrated pop groups making their first recordings. It is also worth remembering that in the late 1930s at 99a Charing Cross Road, the pioneer of acetate disc recording, Cecil Watts, operated his MSS Recording Service which made high quality off-air disc recordings for the music profession and rich enthusiasts.

Walk 2: Purcell, Handel and Ceremonial London

Those who frequent the area between Whitehall and Buckingham Palace will have a constant awareness of military music and ceremonial. Marching down the Mall, associated with the Changing of the Guard we hear music. There are occasional events such as a Guard of Honour for a visiting head of state, and for the regular state occasions such as The Queen's Speech for the opening of Parliament, in

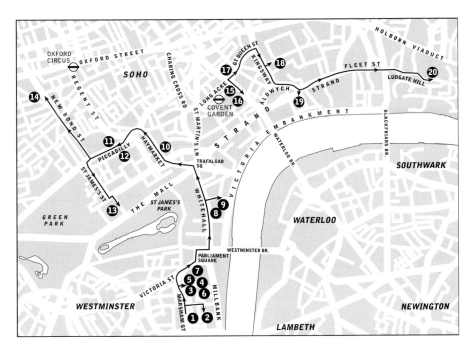

1 Marsham Street, where Purcell was living at his death
2 St John's, Smith Square
3 Entrance to Dean's Yard
4 Westminster School
5 Entrance to the Abbey Cloisters
6 College Gardens
7 Westminster Abbey
8 Banqueting House
9 Queen Mary's Steps
10 Theatre Royal, Haymarket
11 Burlington House
12 St James's, Piccadilly
13 Chapel Royal, St James
14 Handel's House (and museum), No. 25 Brook Street
15 Royal Opera House, Covent Garden
16 Site of Evan's Supper Room, Covent Garden
17 Site of St Martin's Hall
18 Site of Theatre Royal, Lincoln's Inn
19 Arundel Street, location of Crown and Anchor Tavern
20 St Paul's

November. From time to time there will be one of the great state events, including royal weddings and funerals. At the time of writing the most widely remembered funerals are those of H.M. The Queen Mother and Diana, Princess of Wales. The latter, on Saturday 6 September 1997 (see video clips on the CNN website, cnn.com), was the first such state occasion at which pop music was heard integrated into traditional musical proceedings in the Abbey, through the participation of Elton John singing *Candle in the Wind*. During the twentieth century there were also four coronations here, in 1902, 1911, 1937 and 1953.

The London of the late seventeenth century, in which Purcell worked, was a completely different place to today, dominated as his life would have been by the Palace of Whitehall, which was burned down three years after he died. All that remains of the Palace is the Banqueting House in Whitehall, and other contemporary buildings such as St James's Palace, where the Chapel Royal was located after his death, and Westminster Abbey (then without the west towers), which was the focus of Purcell's working life. Westminster, as the City of London, was then a maze of small streets. The great thoroughfares such as Whitehall and Victoria Street were not to begin to emerge for over a century, and Westminster Bridge was not built until 1750. The sites of the present imposing structures of the Foreign and Commonwealth Office and the Treasury were likewise a warren of narrow lanes, up against the Palace of Whitehall, the last of which were demolished only at the turn of the nineteenth into the twentieth century. However, in Purcell's day these sometimes squalid streets were surrounded by open country.

When the good and the great needed to get about they would have gone by boat, and Purcell would have been familiar with the elaborate barges of the nobility. Purcell himself would have probably travelled by boat down the River Thames when he needed to visit the City of London, which was newly built during Purcell's lifetime, after the Great Fire of 1666. The practical day-to-day reality of his life would have been very much as described by Samuel Pepys in his diary, which might be read for background. In the winter of 1683/4 the Thames froze, so severely that a frost fair was held on the ice; during the two hundred years after 1620 it froze on twenty-three occasions.

The most considerable buildings remaining from Purcell's time are, of course, the Abbey, Westminster Hall and the Banqueting House, and No 10. Downing Street and the adjacent frontage, which was built in the 1680s. We start our walk in Marsham Street, said to be the location of Purcell's death, and in 2004 very much the scene of reconstruction after the demolition of the three concrete towers of the 1960s Department of the Environment. Turning into Great Peter Street we take the second or third turnings on the right and find ourselves in Smith Square, where St John's church, built between 1713 and 1728, dominates the centre of the Square and offers a full programme of evening and occasionally lunchtime concerts.

Returning to Great Peter Street, the first turning on the left out of Marsham Street is Tufton Street, which takes us up towards the Abbey. This may well have been the line of Bowling Alley East where Purcell moved in 1684, his address possibly being the bottom half of the street south of Great Peter Street. A door at the top lets us into Dean's Yard, where on the left is situated Westminster Choir School and to the right is Westminster School, the only other building from Purcell's lifetime that survives in the vicinity. Purcell, a pupil in the Chapel Royal since the age of eight, attended the School in his late teens when he was already established as a musician and while still a student there became Abbey Organist. Other celebrated musicians who were pupils in later times include Charles Wesley, Sir Adrian Boult and Andrew Lloyd Webber, as had been Purcell's friend and collaborator Dryden. Indeed here probably uniquely, one can still imagine Purcell and Dryden together in premises that they would have known.

We enter the Abbey cloisters through the door at the top of the square on the right (incidentally, free, whereas the main Abbey now charges visitors) and walk through the cloisters (where we find many of the musical memorials described in Chapter 4, including, in the floor, the adjacent tablets for William Shield, Johann Peter Salomon and Muzio Clementi). Continuing to the end and turning right we emerge into College Gardens, where in the summer a band sometimes plays and visitors eat their sandwiches in the sun. Here we get a good idea of how the Abbey must have appeared to Purcell, the white building looming above the domestic scale of the surrounding architecture, and with those eighteenth century additions, the west towers, not in evidence (see p. 70). We need to visit the Abbey itself for the Purcell memorial and to hear the organ and Abbey choir, perhaps at a service or concert.

During Purcell's day the Chapel Royal was in Whitehall Palace and did not return to St James's until the palace was burned down after his death. Purcell had several addresses in the area around the palace of Whitehall and the abbey, within a few minutes walk of the abbey; these included Great Ann's Lane (probably the present day St Ann's Street, which joins Abbey Orchard Street and Great Peter Street) which he left in 1684. He moved to Marsham Street in 1692 or 1693 and died there in 1695.

Purcell was also associated with the theatre, providing music for the Duke of York's Theatre in Dorset Gardens, which opened in 1671. This does not survive but was off Fleet Street between the street and river, and typical of its time it faced the river so that its patrons could arrive by boat. Here, Nathaniel Lee's *Theodosius* with music by Purcell was first produced in 1680. He contributed a song to Nahum Tate's *Cuckold-Haven* in 1685 and eight songs to d'Urfey's *A Fool's Preferment* in 1688. Later came *Dioclesian* in 1690 and *King Arthur* in 1691. Purcell was very active at the Drury Lane Theatre, later the Theatre Royal, Drury Lane, and between 1690 and his death in November 1695 he wrote or contributed songs or instrumental music to some two dozen productions. After he died *A Collection of Ayres, Composed for the Theatre, and upon Other Occasions* appeared, a substantial collection of pieces from the theatre.

Purcell's most celebrated stage work was the opera *Dido and Aeneas*, performed at 'Mr Josias Priest's boarding-school at Chelsey by young Gentlewomen'. There is nothing left to see, but to understand how far Purcell would have had to go, walk down Marsham Street, across into John Islip Street, passing behind Tate Britain, and out onto the Embankment. Priest's school was near the present day Battersea Bridge.

As the organist of Westminster Abbey, Purcell would have been a prestigious figure, in demand to demonstrate new organs. At the Temple church in 1683, in the celebrated 'battle of the organs' between the leading builders of the day, two organs were installed, Purcell demonstrated the new organ by Renatus Harris but 'Father' Smith won. In 1684 Purcell tried the organ at the rebuilt church of St Michael Cornhill which then did not have its spire, where the organ was also by Renatus Harris. In 1686 at St Lawrence Jewry Renatus Harris's new one manual organ was tried by both Blow and Purcell. In 1686 Purcell was at St Katherine Cree, Leadenhall Street, notable because it survived the fire, and the first organ, by Bernard Smith, was tried by Purcell and others in September 1686.

Also at the Temple we need to remember that Purcell's publisher, John and Henry Playford, had a shop 'in the Inner Temple neere the Church doore', also at Arundel Street (which runs from Temple tube to the Strand). Purcell is buried in the Abbey and a striking recent memorial to him has been erected in Victoria Street, opposite New Scotland Yard.

When we investigate Handel we find a quite different situation, for many of the major buildings associated with him, including his house, have survived. The main locations (in a suitable sequence for walking) are as follows, but readers should refer to the section on composers and musicians to fill in the biographical and historical background.

Starting at Westminster Abbey, we remember Handel's many associations with the place, not only during his lifetime, including the coronation of George II in 1727, but also the Handel Festivals that were held between 1784 and 1791. The construction of the west towers took place during Handel's lifetime and scaffolding was doubtless a longstanding feature of his experience of the place. Handel is buried in the Abbey near Poets' Corner. One of the two Roubiliac memorials of Handel will be found here, and in 1784 it was sufficiently celebrated to be the subject of one of the illustrations in Burney's account of the 1784 Handel Commemoration.

We now go up Whitehall to the Banqueting House, where Handel enjoyed various performances during his lifetime, notably the *Utrecht Te Deum* and possibly also the *Ode for the Birthday of Queen Anne*, the first of these being billed as 'rehearsals', though an entrance fee was charged. We now need to walk through to the River Thames, and turn right into Horse Guards Avenue. Turn right again to find Queen Mary's Steps. Queen Anne died in 1714 and was succeeded by the Elector of Hanover, who became George I. In 1717 Handel composed the *Water Music* for which the King processed up the river from Whitehall to Chelsea and back while some fifty musicians played the music in one of the large decorated barges owned by one of the City Livery Companies. The present Thames Embankment was not built until the 1870s, and so in Handel's day the tidal River Thames was much more unpredictable. The only feature to survive from that time is Queen Mary's Steps, designed by Wren and built in 1691. There, a terrace projected about 70 feet into the river with a curved flight of steps at each end. Part of this can be seen now behind the Ministry of Defence building on the landward side of the present-day Victoria Embankment. Once the river is imagined it is easy to persuade oneself that the king may have boarded his ceremonial barge here.

Returning into Whitehall, we continue to Trafalgar Square, turn left and walk through to Haymarket, which is on the right. Here we find the Theatre Royal, Haymarket, the scene of most of Handel's operatic triumphs in the 1720s. What we see today is not the theatre Handel would have known. Towards the end of the eighteenth century it was burned down, and the theatre was subsequently rebuilt three times, but is still on the same site.

We continue to Piccadilly, where we find Burlington House (now the Royal Academy of Arts) on the right opposite St James's Church, Piccadilly. Burlington House has been changed over the years, and the building Handel would have known is the main building that faces one on entering the courtyard; but we should remember the top floor, with its facing of statues of artists in niches, was only added in 1867. St James's Piccadilly is across the road, and it seems probable that Handel would have played the organ there, in what was then a fashionable new church. However, the church was bombed in the Second World War (see Chapter 2).

Continuing down Piccadilly we should remember that on Sundays in winter one can attend a service at the Chapel Royal at St James's Palace, and for this we need to turn left down St James's Street. The *Dettingen Te Deum* was first performed here in

November 1743 to celebrate George II's victory over the French during the War of the Austrian Succession. Returning, we turn right into Piccadilly, then left into Old Bond Street and walk up to Brook Street on the left. Handel purchased No. 25, then newly built, in 1723 and lived there until his death on 14 April 1759 (plaque). Visitors can now visit the Handel House Museum, which brings Handel and his London vividly alive (see p. 106). If one can ignore the traffic, the scale of Brook Street, perhaps early on a Sunday morning, is very much as it would have been in Handel's day. Turning right down Brook Street we come to Hanover Square, and turning right see St George's church far down on the left. Newly built in Handel's day, he was particularly associated with it in his last years when he rented a pew and regularly played the organ. The interior today is not dissimilar to what it must have been like to Handel.

We now need to take the tube to Covent Garden for the second part of this walk. John Rich opened his new theatre in Covent Garden in December 1732, on the site of today's opera house. Handel's operas *Alcina* and *Berenice* were produced here in the mid-1730s, but in fact Handel's principal association with the opera house was as the location for the production of his oratorios in English. These included *Alexander's Feast* in 1736, the first London hearing of the *Messiah* in 1743, and later *Judas Maccabaeus* and *Jephtha*. Here Handel's oratorio season in the spring became a regular feature of the musical life of London, with ticket prices that many outside the rich could afford, the cheapest in Handel's lifetime being three shillings and sixpence, falling to one shilling later in the century.

While in Covent Garden it is worth remembering that in the north-east corner in the colonnade that skirted the market, in the mid-nineteenth century was Evans's Supper Room and music hall. That tireless chronicler Francesco Berger remembered 'if you wanted the best grilled kidney or mutton chop with potatoes served in the jacket or Welsh rarebit, with the best-sung glees in London, it was to Evans's you went'.

From Covent Garden we walk east down Long Acre, passing the site of another nineteenth-century landmark, St Martin's Hall, into Great Queen Street, cross Kingsway into Lincoln's Inn Fields. Here at the south-east corner on the corner of Portugal Street, on the present day site of the Royal College of Surgeons, a theatre had operated since 1661. At this Theatre Royal, Rich produced Gay's *Beggar's Opera*, which was the sweeping hit from 1728. Early in 1740 Handel's *Ode for St Cecilia's Day* and *L'Allegro, Il Penseroso ed Il Moderato* were performed here, and a year later Handel's last opera, *Deidamia*. The building was finally demolished in 1848.

Continuing down Portugal Street we emerge on Kingsway and turn left towards the east end of the present-day Aldwych, where on the corner of Arundel Street and Strand was the location of the Crown and Anchor Tavern, facing St Clement Danes church. This was the home of the Academy of Vocal Music, founded in 1726, who performed 'old masters' as well as, later, Handel's oratorios. This was the location for the performance of Handel's *Esther* in February 1732. We continue walking down the Strand into Fleet Street, and eventually up Ludgate Hill to St Paul's cathedral. The official first performance of the *Utrecht Te Deum* was at the newly built St

Paul's in July 1713. Handel could often be heard playing the organ in St Paul's and regularly attracted a substantial informal audience.

For the energetic a short detour may be interesting here to visit the location of the concerts given by Thomas Britton. During his early years in London Handel patronised the concerts given by the 'musical small coals man' Thomas Britton (see p. 217) and Handel played for him. The house was in Jerusalem Passage, EC1, off Aylesbury Street, though as a result of war damage, where Britton lived has been rebuilt since his day and is now called Britton Street, Clerkenwell, EC1 (behind Farringdon Station.) A plaque carries the message 'here stood the house of Thomas Britton 1644–1714 the musical coalman'. Britton died in 1714 and was buried at St James's church, Clerkenwell, itself also rebuilt in 1792.

Two other locations of particular interest may justify a special journey. First the Foundling Hospital which stood in Brunswick Square at Coram Fields (tube: Russell Square), which in Handel's day was almost into the country but is now beyond a 1960s concrete development. The Hospital was founded to care for abandoned children and opened in 1741. Handel's association with the charity resulted in him giving his services in money-raising concerts, and he also presented an organ. Here an annual performance of *Messiah* became a celebrated event. All that remains today is the Foundling Museum at 40 Brunswick Square (see pp. 104–5) which contains three restored rooms from the Foundling Hospital whose 1740 building was demolished in the 1920s – the Court room, the Committee room and the picture gallery, with paintings from the original collection on the walls. Here also will be found the Handel Study Centre.

St Lawrence, Whitchurch, is an essential part of a Handel tour, although because of its distance from the centre it will need a half day to accomplish. Go to Canons Park tube and turn left out of the station along Whitchurch Lane. The sports ground to the left is Canons Park, once part of the grounds of James Brydge's (later Duke of Chandos) mansion of Cannons. The stately home is long demolished but here Handel lived between the summer of 1717 and the end of 1718. The church, which survives, was used by Brydges as a chapel and Handel certainly played there and wrote his *Chandos Anthems* in 1717 (see p. 186). With its Handel memorabilia it is very redolent of the period.

Walk 3: Stanford, Parry and the South Kensington Hegemony

Set out from Notting Hill Gate tube station. Emerge on the southern side of Notting Hill and turn east towards Kensington Church Street. Dr William Crotch (1775–1847), celebrated child prodigy, composer, teacher, scholar and keyboard virtuoso, was the first Principal of the Royal Academy of Music. Crotch was also a talented artist and on 5 August 1829, sketched the view from his bedroom window looking down Church Street. He lived at 1 Notting Hill High Street, now Notting Hill Gate, facing down Kensington Church Street (the building survives above today's brash shopfronts), down which one should now turn.

The third turning on the right is Peel Street, where at 42 lived Constant Lambert's mother, Constant frequently also finding himself there in the 1930s. Returning to the main road, two turnings further down on the right is Bedford Gardens and here at No. 4 lived Frank Bridge, composer, conductor, viola player and teacher of Benjamin Britten (plaque). Returning to Kensington Church Street, across the road at No. 128 is the house (plaque) where Muzio Clementi lived in the early nineteenth century when he was celebrated as composer, publisher and piano manufacturer. Subsequently the house was owned by the Horsley family who were visited here by Mendelssohn in the early 1830s.

Re-crossing the road we turn down Gloucester Walk where Jean Sibelius stayed in

103   The view Dr William Crotch painted from his bedroom window from the north side of present-day Notting Hill Gate, then 1 Notting Hill High Street, to the top of present-day Kensington Church Street, dated 5 August 1829.

1909 (plaque) and probably completed his String Quartet *Voces Intimae*. Continuing down Gloucester Walk one emerges into Hornton Street. Turn left and follow down to the junction with Holland Street, where in the corner house at 56 lived Sir Charles Villiers Stanford (in Stanford's day it was numbered 50 Holland Street, plaque). Percy Grainger also lived briefly in Horton Street in 1902. Continuing up Holland Street one returns to Kensington Church Street. Here, across the road, at 80 was Dobson Books run by Dennis Dobson (1919–1978) and his wife, whose postwar list of books on music was a notable and pioneering one.

We now walk on, down to the very busy three-way junction with Kensington High Street. Crossing to the south side we turn left and then the first on the right is Young Street where No. 16, the house where Thackeray had written *Vanity Fair*, was the birthplace of theatre composer and friend of Delius, Norman O'Neill. A little further down the street we reach Kensington Square, where 17 was the London home of Sir Hubert Parry from 1887 to 1918. Also nearby off the square (at Albert Place) lived composer Arthur Somervell, from 1901 Inspector of Music to the Board of Education for twenty-seven years.

An optional additional loop at this point is to walk out of the south side of the square and passing through Stanford Road reach 15 Cottesmore Gardens where Sir Arthur Bliss and his family lived from 1948 to 1955. Two turnings further down Stanford Road we reach Cornwall Gardens where at 32b lived Sir William Glock, BBC Director of Music and revolutionary director of the Proms.

It would have been possible for Bridge, Stanford, Parry and Somervell to walk to work at the Royal College, or they may have taken a bus the two or three stops involved. We can do the same, returning to Kensington High Street and turning

1 Surviving eighteenth-century house where Dr William Crotch drew Kensington Church Street in 1829
2 No. 42 Peel Street, Constant Lambert's House
3 Frank Bridge's house
4 Clementi's house
5 Where Sibelius completed *Voces Intimae* in 1909
6 Stanford's house
7 Location of Dobson Books
8 16 Young Street, birthplace of Norman O'Neill
9 Parry's house at 17 Kensington Square
10 Somervell's house at 1 Albert Place
11 Bliss's house at 15 Cottesmore Gardens
12 William Glock's flat at 32b Cornwall Gardens
13 The Albert Memorial
14 Royal Albert Hall
15 former home of the NTSM, RCM and Royal College of Organists
16 Plaque for Sir Malcolm Sargent
17 Royal College of Music
18 former premises of the British Institute of Recorded Sound
19 Victorian and Albert Museum
20 Brompton Oratory
21 Site of Catalani's house
22 Site of Brompton Grange
23 Site of J. R. Planché's house
24 Bartók statue
25 Bartók plaque
26 4 Pelham Place, home of Henry Lazarus
27 Jenny Lind's house
28 Sargent/Schnabel house
29 W. S. Gilbert's house

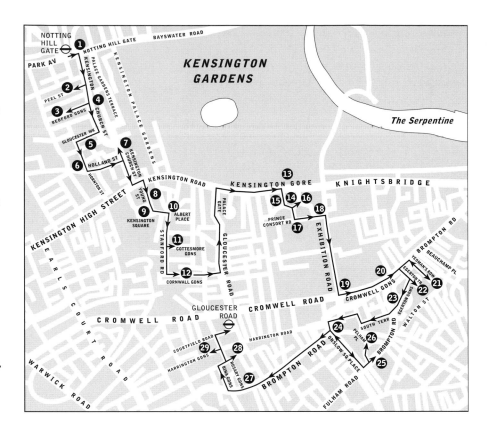

right then left up Chester Road. (If already tired turn left for High Street Kensington tube.) Soon we can see the green of Kensington Gardens opening out on the left and ahead the dome of the Royal Albert Hall on the right.

When the Royal Albert Hall was opened in 1871, it was faced to the north by the Albert Memorial standing in Kensington Gardens. The Royal College of Music building appeared in the 1890s and was built on a greenfield site that was formerly a public park, which occupied the whole South Kensington site now dominated by the Museums and Imperial College. This area has been the subject of much renovation at the end of the twentieth century.

If we stand at the Albert Memorial, with its many sculptures of composers along the plinth (see p. 122), and face the Royal Albert Hall, to the right of the hall is the ornate façade of the former Royal College of Organists, the first home of the Royal College of Music. In the summer the Albert Hall is the home of the Proms, and daily in July and August a queue of music-lovers forms for the arena or gallery promenades. Everyone should enjoy the experience of the arena promenade at least once, for its unique atmosphere, and the remarkable impact the music has from such proximity. Having visited the Albert Hall either for refreshment or one of their regular official tours go to the opposite side of the hall to Albert Hall Mansions for the plaque that marks where for twenty years No. 9 was the home of Sir Malcolm Sargent, where he died on 3 October 1967.

Walking round the Albert Hall the descending flight of steps brings us to the Royal College of Music. Here in term time, students present free concerts in the well-appointed portrait-lined concert hall or in the upstairs recital room. Termly opera productions in the Britten Theatre are usually very reasonably priced. On entering the building one is faced with the First World War memorial listing the names of those from the college who were killed, including composers George Butterworth and Ernest Farrar. Inside, often there will be a small exhibition of documents from the unsurpassed Centre for Performance History.

Turning right out of the college and continuing to walk towards Exhibition Road, the corner building on the left is the former premises of the British Institute of Recorded Sound, now the National Sound Archive. The national collection of sound recordings moved to the British Library at Euston Road when that building opened in 2000. Turning right down Exhibition Road we soon come to the Victoria and Albert Museum on the left. It is easy to forget that the Victoria and Albert Museum has extensive musical holdings, not only of instruments but also a variety of documentation and images in the library. The collection of musical instruments is in Room 40A and the museum is notable for its collection of keyboard instruments, including examples dating back to the sixteenth century. Both popular and scholarly guides to the collection have been published, together with, on cassette, examples of them being played. Music also appears in a variety of other locations around the museum, where will be found Queen Elizabeth I's virginals, a music stand once belonging to Marie Antoinette and the Roubiliac statue of Handel from Vauxhall Gardens, once in the front hall of Novello's former Wardour Street showroom.

If one leaves the museum by the front door, in Cromwell Road, and turns left, next door is situated Brompton Oratory fronted by a statue of Cardinal Newman to whom it was a tribute. Cross the road and the second on the right past Brompton Road is Yeoman's Row, where at a house called 'The Hermitage' lived the soprano Angelica Catalani from 1835 to 1839. The parallel road on the way back to South Kensington station is Egerton Terrace, the line of the former Michael's Grove at the bottom of which on the left was Brompton Grange, demolished in October 1843, where lived the celebrated tenor and composer John Braham (1774–1856). Running out of Egerton Terrace is Egerton Gardens, formerly Brompton Crescent, where at No. 20 lived the playwright and librettist J. R. Planché from 1822 to 1844, and the librettist of Weber's *Oberon*. We are now near to South Kensington tube and the tour could end there, with the new Bartók statue (see p. 204). For those still enthusiastic walking round the station into Onslow Square brings us to Sydney Place, where at No. 7 during his London visits in the 1930s Béla Bartók stayed with Duncan Wilson (plaque). Turning right on returning to the station station is Pelham Street where half-way down on the right we find Pelham Place, where at No. 4 (then No. 2) lived the celebrated Victorian clarinettist Henry Lazarus from 1860 to 1871.

Returning to the Old Brompton Road we turn left and walk along to the home of the singer Jenny Lind from 1875 to 1887 at 189 (plaque), formerly No. 1 Moreton Gardens. We eventually come to Bina Gardens, on the right, at the top of which is Wetherby Place, where Sir Malcolm Sargent lived in the 1930s, a house that he rented to the great pianist Artur Schnabel. Walking back along Wetherby Place and right into Ashburn Place takes us to Harrington Gardens, where at 39 W. S. Gilbert built a spectacular house designed by himself with a Dutch style gable and engineered by the architects Sir Ernest George and Harold Peto, who were specialists in brick and terracotta. From here it is only a short distance to Gloucester Road and (left) Gloucester Road tube.

Walk 4: From Soho via the Café Royal to Great Portland Street

This walk, or sections of it, could be integrated into Walk 1 at almost any point. (See Chapter 1 for details of the locations described.) We start in Dean Street at St Anne's church, Soho (Tube: Tottenham Court Road or Leicester Square) thanks to wartime bombing now only a tower in a small grassed garden. Here two notable musicians were organists: William Croft, whose hymn tune *St Anne* ('O God Our Help') is named after the church. The Parish archives refer to him as 'Phillip Crofts' and his appointment as organist in 1700. Over 150 years after Croft, in 1871, Joseph Barnby became the organist. Another composer of hymn tunes, we probably remember him best for 'For All the Saints'. Briefly in 1890 the young Henry Walford Davies was organist.

Dean Street is associated with the composer, harpsichordist and music publisher Jan Ladislav Dussek (1760–1812) who lived in London for eleven years between 1789 and 1799. A refugee from the French revolution, he married the singer and pianist Sophia Corri at St Anne's Westminster in 1792. With his father-in-law he established the music publisher Corri, Dussek and Co., at 90 Dean Street, but eventually fled the UK to escape his debtors. At different times he lived at 8, 32 and 68 Dean Street, the last surviving as it was in his day.

While in Dean Street we should note at 73 an office block called Royalty House built on the site of the Royalty Theatre (previously the Royal Soho Theatre), which had closed in 1938 and was demolished in 1953. Here W. S. Gilbert had various plays and burlesques produced, including his parody of Balfe's popular opera *The Bohemian Girl* ('The Merry Zingara') in 1868. It later saw the first production of *Trial by Jury* and an early revival of Sullivan's *The Zoo*.

Towards the top of Dean Street at No. 21 will be found the Soho Theatre and Writers' Centre, formerly the West End Great Synagogue. Here a notable early public concert room was established in 1751, known as the Great Room, with entrances in Dean Street and Thrift (now Frith) Street. It was celebrated for performances of Handel's music, but ceased being a concert room in 1763. It became a synagogue during the Second World War and in 1961 it was demolished and replaced by the present building.

Walking up Dean Street, Old Compton Street bisects it, and has a significant musical history. Turning right into Old Compton Street, in 1839 Wagner stayed in

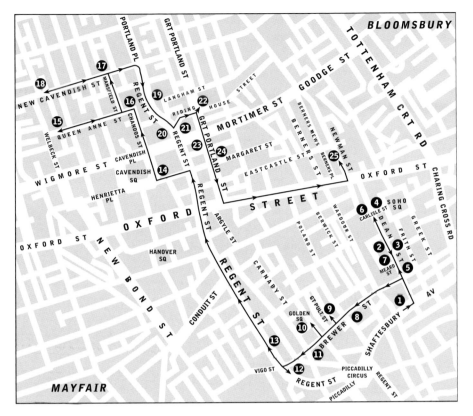

an inn – long gone – a short way down. Continuing up Dean Street we come to Carlisle Street where a plaque tells us Handel's amanuensis John Christopher Smith (1712–1795) lived and died, though the date given for his death is wrong. Here too lived J. C. Bach and Carl Friedrich Abel, who lived together at various addresses in Soho from 1762 until Bach's marriage twelve years later. Returning down Dean Street we find the narrow entrance to Meard Street on the right, now pedestrianised; this is one of the few where eighteenth-century houses still stand. At No. 1 the harpsichord builder Burkat Shudi worked from 1738 to 1742, where he was visited by Handel. At No. 18 (which does not survive) the first occupant was J. C. Schmidt, father of Handel's J. C. Smith. Meard Street also saw J. C. Bach and Abel living and working in the 1760s. Here, too, later lived Vincent Novello at whose house both Mendelssohn and Chopin played in public – albeit to a very limited audience.

Further down Dean Street we turn into the other half of Old Compton Street, which becomes Brewer Street, Here at No. 18 lived the eighteenth-century impresario J. C. Salomon, with whom Haydn stayed. This part of London was the centre of piano and harpsichord building at that time. Next door lived Jacob Kirkman, harpsichord maker, described by Fanny Burney as 'the first harpsichord maker of the times'. In the street in 1774 could also be found James Lyneham, organ builder.

We have already mentioned the great harpsichord maker Burkat (or Bukhardt) Shudi (or Tschudi). From 1 Meard Street in 1742 he moved to 33 Great Pulteney Street, where we will shortly walk. John Broadwood worked for Shudi after 1761 and married his daughter. The son-in-law eventually took over the business. C. M. Tuscher's painting *Burkat Shudi and his Family* was set at this address and can be seen at the National Portrait Gallery. In 1855 the firm of Broadwood was still at 33 Great Pulteney Street, and remained until 1904.

Great Pulteney Street, on the right, was clearly a centre of musical activity in the late eighteenth century; at 17 lived Jacob Kirkman from 1739 to 1750, while Abraham Kirkman resided at 40 (which survives) from 1759 to 1770; at 18 lived Salomon where Haydn first arrived to stay on the first day of 1791, and remained until the following year. In his *Third London Notebook*, Haydn notes collecting Mrs Bindon and her two daughters from 19 Great Pulteney. Proceeding to the top of this street we turn left and second left again into Upper James Street and thus into Golden Square. This route gives a strong feeling of the narrowness of many of the streets in eighteenth-century London and the placing of squares at regular intervals. This square was the location of many small residential hotels used by visiting musicians in earlier times. Here we can still find Foote's musical instrument dealer at No. 10. While there it is worth noting that No. 11 was the long-standing address of Rye and Eyre, solicitors to the Bax estate. Elsewhere in the square resided the pianist Vladimir de Pachmann between the wars; he died here in 1933. The statue of George II in the square is said to have originated from the gardens at Cannons, the Duke of Chandos's short-lived mansion at Edgware. Emerging again into Brewer Street we come to the back of the Regent Palace Hotel, the annex to which stands on the site of Hickford's Rooms (then 41 Brewer Street, it was later renumbered 65 before demolition in the 1930s). Here on 13 May 1765 the nine-year-old Mozart and his sister appeared in a public concert. Any of the turnings on the left or in front will bring us out into the bottom of Regent Street.

This leads us to the Café Royal, a short distance up Regent Street from Piccadilly Circus, on the right. In its earlier life the back bar at the Café Royal was a celebrated meeting place for the artistic and Bohemian community of its day. During the 1940s it was frequented by Constant Lambert, Michael Ayrton, Dylan Thomas, Cecil Gray and their circle. As the 'Café Royal by Le Meridien' the front of house is much changed with a tightly controlled lobby, but it is worth calling in for a drink or snack to gain some feeling of what it once was, before starting the second part of this tour.

Continuing up Regent Street note 90 where, in the early 1830s probably the most important and famous opera composer of his time, Rossini, and his wife, the celebrated soprano Isabella Colbran, stayed on their only visit to London, between December 1823 and July 1824. This would have been very soon after Regent Street was developed, but unfortunately nothing of the original colonnading remains, and the address is now Moss Bros the outfitters. The Rossinis specialised in playing at grand private gatherings or giving music lessons at high fees, earning a sufficient sum to finance the remainder of Rossini's career. After they arrived, the King's Theatre promoted a Rossini season, but it was comparatively unsuccessful, and Rossini failed to produce his promised new opera. Futhermore his wife was a disappointment with audiences as her voice was in decline. While in London Thomas Lawrence drew Rossini's portrait in chalks, and the composer negotiated a contract with the French government, moving to Paris, never to return.

We continue up Regent Street (see Walk 1) through Oxford Circus, and then take the second road on the left, Margaret Street, which leads us thus into Cavendish Square. Here at 7 lived the parents of Arnold Bax (and at times the composer himself) between 1911 and 1918, in one of the most sumptuously appointed central London residencies of the day. Continuing north we go up Chandos Street. The road turns left as Queen Anne Street where at 58 (just before Welbeck Street) Berlioz stayed during his 1851 visit to London (plaque). Turning north from Queen Anne Street we come to Mansfield Street, where in a flat at No. 2 Eric Coates died in 1957. Moving on into New Cavendish Street we find at No. 58 one of Elgar's London addresses, and at 146 the birthplace of the conductor Leopold Stokowski.

New Cavendish Street emerges into Portland Place just above Broadcasting House, to the right on the other side of the road. The arrival of the BBC so near to the Queen's Hall, the Langham Hotel, the Wigmore Hall and the infrastructure of music publishing in 1931 gave the surrounding area a special character in the decade before the wartime destruction of Queen's Hall. Various pubs, restaurants and hotels became the places where musicians met their cronies, did deals and found work.

Possibly, if we're feeling rich, we should start with a drink at The Langham Hotel, where so many famous musicians stayed during its heyday, now completely renovated. Or we can go to the top floor bar at the opposite St George's Hotel – on the site of Queen's Hall – from which one can appreciate the juxtaposition of Queen's Hall, All Souls and the Langham Hotel. If we look out for postwar buildings placed among the older property from this vantage point, we realise how the Luftwaffe's bomb-aimer was intending to hit the BBC, but in the event straddled it, the Queen's Hall's loss and Broadcasting House's salvation being a matter of a second's error.

Leaving the BBC and the hotel by walking down Riding House Street, we emerge into Great Portland Street. The building on the corner at 79 is on the site of the former 203 Great Portland Street, where on 21 April 1829 the nineteen-year-old Mendelssohn was found lodgings with a German ironmonger called Heincke. To the left is the location of Sir George Smart's house at 103 (then 91) where Weber died in 1826. Turning right we come, on the corner of Mortimer Street at 55, to The George, a pub frequented by BBC musical people in the past. Elisabeth Lutyens (see Chapter 1) has described how she had to spend her evenings in this bar, rather than with her children, because that was where she met the producers, conductors and entrepreneurs who would give her work over a drink, which they would not do on the telephone or in writing. Diametrically across the road from here would have been Pagani's restaurant, its architectural impact still faintly recognisable from the arch-like shape of the decoration on the surviving adjacent building. Continuing into Oxford Street we should imagine it in the 1860s, lined with small family-owned shops on both sides, their awnings usually pulled down. Then numbered as 413a, a little east of Oxford Circus, the father of the future conductor Henry J. Wood was established as a master jeweller, later optician and engineering modeller, and it was for his model engines that Wood's father became celebrated. The business (and family) later moved to 355 now numbered 185.

We turn left. Marks and Spencer on the other side of the road occupies the site of the Pantheon (see Walk 1). Continuing to Newman Street on the left, at No. 80, near the corner with Eastcastle Street, lived J. C. Bach after 1774. In the same street lived Salomon during his final years, dying in 1815. At a long-gone St Andrew's Hall in Newman Street, in 1881 'Master Henry J Wood' appeared as the pianist in an amateur concert in which his father also appeared as cellist.

Walk 5: From the Wigmore Hall to the Royal Academy of Music

The walk going west from Harley Street brings us past the homes of many of the most influential performers and musical personalities of the late nineteenth and early twentieth centuries. We turn down Harley Street, remembering that the ear, nose and throat specialist Dr George Cathcart had consulting rooms here in the late nineteenth century at No. 35, later at No. 52. It was he who agreed to fund the Promenade Concerts in 1895 on the proviso that high pitch would be abandoned, and he was thus instrumental in making this the standard in the UK. Reaching the corner of Cavendish Square we remember the pre-Wigmore Hall chamber music venue of the Beethoven Concert Rooms was at 27 Harley Street during the late nineteenth century. Turn right into Wigmore Street and walk along to the Wigmore Hall on the right, still looking much as its lobby must have looked when it first opened. The next turning on the right is Welbeck Street, where at 47, on the corner of Bulstrode Street, lived the celebrated Victorian pianist Arabella Goddard during her early celebrity, before she married the critic J. W. Davison in 1860. Her house has been replaced by a later Victorian development, but one can get a feel for what it would have been like by comparing it with the adjacent original properties. Two of them bear blue plaques so it was clearly then a good address. Nearby at 63 Welbeck Street (long gone) during the 1850s lived John Ella, founder of the elite chamber music society the Musical Union. Continuing down Bulstrode Street we go left into Thayer Street and soon turn right into Hinde Street, where at the home of the pianist Oscar Beringer, No. 12, Dvořák stayed during March 1884. Beringer is remembered as the pianist in the first London performances of Brahms's Second Piano Concerto in October 1882 and Dvořák's Concerto almost exactly a year later, both at the Crystal Palace under Manns. Beringer's own now forgotten *Andante and Presto Agitato in E* for piano and orchestra had been heard at the same hall in 1880.

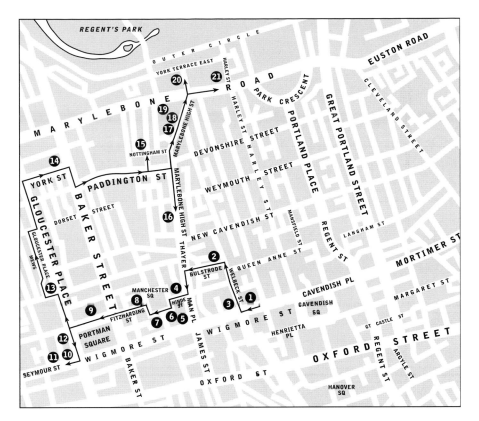

We could briefly return to Thayer Street at this point to find Mandeville Place and the former premises of Trinity College of Music, which stand almost unchanged on the left hand side just before Hinde Street. Unfortunately the various internal commemorative windows and fixtures not taken to Greenwich cannot be seen from the street.

Continuing the few yards from Oscar Beringer's house into Manchester Square, and turning left, the third door along is Julius Benedict's house at No. 2 (plaque), for forty years the centre of his wide spanning musical activities and, between 1845 and 1885, many of the leading musicians of the day must have visited him here. These would have included the soprano Jenny Lind with whom he toured the USA as accompanist. Composers who would have called on him at the square included Berlioz, Meyerbeer, Gounod and Saint-Saëns. In a later age, also in the square at No. 20, was once the headquarters of EMI records, perhaps most widely associated with The Beatles in the 1960s when they recorded for Parlophone, an EMI company. Since EMI left, the building has been replaced. Continuing across the square we find Fitzhardinge Street, formerly Lower Berkeley Street, where at No. 9 (since developed) Sir Charles Villiers Stanford lived from 1916. In the context of the twenty-first century rise in rents – which in recent years drove the publisher B. T.

Batsford from No. 4 – it is piquant to realise that Stanford moved here from his longstanding residence in Kensington because this was cheaper.

Emerging onto Baker Street from Fitzhardinge Street we cross the road to the north side of Portman Square, where at 20 lived Samuel and Mrs Courtauld, notable backers of concerts in the 1930s. Mrs Courtauld ('Lil'), particularly through the Courtauld-Sargent concerts, intended to widen the audience with subsidised ticket prices. Their mansion is one of the few that have not been redeveloped. On into Seymour Street where at 12 the opera composer and conductor Michael Balfe, composer of *The Bohemian Girl*, lived from 1861–5 (plaque). Opposite at 17 Seymour Street (now part of The Leonard Hotel) stayed Eduard Hanslick, the celebrated Viennese critic, in the summer of 1886, the *Musical Times* reproducing, with great indignation, English translations of Hanslick's account in the *Neue Freie Presse*, in which he characterised Sullivan as 'a drowsy fellow'. 'That large close-cropped head on a firm neck, that dark face with its black eyes, give one an impression of a passionate man whose anger might explode suddenly like a cannon. Instead of this we have unequalled phlegm. The G minor symphony of Mozart is performed. Sullivan conducts it without lifting his eyes from from the full score . . . The heavenly piece is played badly, without feeling or elegance.'

Retracing our steps to Gloucester Place, the main road running up the west side of the square, we turn left to find at 76 the site of the flat that Elgar briefly occupied during 1911, the year of the coronation season and the first performance of his Second Symphony at Queen's Hall. Left into George Street takes us (first right) to Gloucester Place Mews where No. 8, the white corner cottage on the right as the

104   Harriet Cohen's last house at 8 Gloucester Place Mews (on the corner).

road wriggles slightly to the right, was the residence of the pianist Harriet Cohen for the last twenty years of her life. She was here when she developed the pneumonia in November 1967 from which she unexpectedly died. To keep away from the traffic, walk up Gloucester Place Mews to the top. Turning right at the top we are back in Gloucester Place. Continuing north, with the traffic flow, the second on the right is York Street, where at No. 6 (at the far end on the left) lived Francesco Berger, long the Secretary of the Philharmonic Society, and his wife, the soprano Annie Berger-Lascelles. (In his autobiography Berger records that she had an enormous three-octave range, from the E an octave below the stave to the E an octave above it.) A few doors along at No. 20, for fifty-three years during the second half of the nineteenth century, lived the portrait painter George Richmond (plaque). Berger was here for over forty years and, like Benedict nearby, must have received many of the leading musicians of the day. Here he entertained Saint-Saëns to lunch and dinner, remembering him as 'a man of middle stature, square-set, with a finely chiselled nose, and a wonderful pair of alert, penetrating eyes. He has a remarkable speaking-voice, loud and very shrill, and he utters so rapidly that it is difficult to follow him'. Another visitor was the twenty-one-year-old Rachmaninov on his first visit to London in 1899, when the Russian conducted his early orchestral fantasia *The Rock* at the Philharmonic Society at Queen's Hall. Perhaps the most interesting of these visitors must have been Tchaikovsky, who, in 1893, Berger tells us, 'invited himself to dine with me at my house, stipulating that there should be "no party" and "no evening dress". Accordingly we were only four: Madame Berger, myself, and one young lady (a talented pupil of mine, Phoebe Hart)'. Berger noted that 'His conversation, carried on in French and German . . . was easy without being brilliant, and in all he said there was apparent the modest, gentle spirit which was so characteristic of the man.'

A few doors down York Street we emerge in Baker Street, cross the road and turn right and take the first left into Paddington Street. Walking down here the third on the left is Luxborough Street, and the first on the right here is Nottingham Street, where in the corner Victorian block, at No. 10, the conductor Leopold Stokowski lived with his parents as a young man. The building has been converted into flats as Nottingham Mansions, but the exterior is much as Stokowski would have known it. From here on 10 March 1902 Stokowski wrote to his teacher, Henry Walford Davies, 'I am sure you will be glad to hear that I was appointed to St James Church [Piccadilly] this morning. I can never, of course, repay in any way your kindness to me, I can only hope to have an opportunity of passing them on to another.' Stokowski left for the USA in June 1905.

Back into Paddington Street we turn left and walk through to Marylebone High Street. Here we need to note that the BBC Third Programme was long at 35 Marylebone High Street, which long before then was the site of Marylebone Music Hall, and before that was the location of the entrance to Marylebone Gardens, which closed in 1778. Going back up Marylebone High Street we move into the upper, narrower, part of the road (a slight twist to the right) and pass on the left the former premises of St Marylebone School, bearing a plaque recording that Leopold Stokowski went to school there. Next we reach the Wesley Memorial Gardens, and St Marylebone Parish Church, where Stokowski was a choirboy. We might remember that Stainer dedicated *The Crucifixion* to the choir.

We emerge into the very busy Marylebone Road and cross at the traffic lights. Diametrically opposite is the Royal Academy of Music, where in the first (new) entrance is an exhibition of instruments, and a public counter selling souvenirs. Moving further east along Marylebone Road we come to a large block of flats on the left. This is Harley House where flat No. 21 was Thomas Beecham's last home, and it was here that he died in 1961. From here we can either return to the tube at Great Portland Street (entrances on either side of the road), or we can turn left into Regent's Park, where in summer we may well find a band playing at the bandstand.

QUADRILLE FOR ALL NATIONS,

COMPOSED & RESPECTFULLY DEDICATED TO

HIS ROYAL HIGHNESS

PRINCE ALBERT,

IN COMMEMORATION OF THE

GRAND EXHIBITION OF 1851.

BY

HENRY FARMER.

ENT STA HALL — Op. 5¹ — Pr. 3⁄

LONDON, J. WILLIAMS, 123, CHEAPSIDE

THE HYDE PARK GRAND REVIEW MARCH

BY

HENRY FARMER.

LONDON J WILLIAMS 123 CHEAPSIDE
WHOLESALE WAREHOUSE H HOLBORN BARS

LONDON BY NIGHT

QUADRILLE.

INTRODUCING

"OUT FOR THE EVENING" "THOSE TASSELS ON HER BOOTS" "THE CITY SWELL"
"WHERE THERE'S A WILL THERE'S A WAY" "A MOTTO FOR EVERY MAN"
"THOROUGH-BRED" "DON'T STAY OUT TOO LATE AT NIGHT" "HANSOM CAB"
"PRETTY LITTLE FLORA" "SHE WAS VERY FOND OF DANCING"

THE HOUSES OF PARLIAMENT

BY

CHARLES COOTE JUNR

LONDON

HOPWOOD & CREW 42 NEW BOND ST W

PERFORMED AT **HER MAJESTY'S** STATE BALL,

BUCKINGHAM PALACE.

THE VERY LAST POLKA.

BY

FRANCOIS BERNARD.

LONDON

PUBLISHED BY DUFF & HODGSON,
65, OXFORD ST.

ENT. STA HALL   Pr. SING 2⁄6
DUET 3

SOLD BY
PATERSON & SON
EDINᵍ

Musical Compositions Evoking London

As early as the sixteenth century various composers occasionally produced music programmatically related to London, of which Thomas Weelkes and Orlando Gibbons both wrote fantasias called *The Cryes of London*, elaborating London street traders' sales calls, and similar works were written at the time by Ravenscroft and Deering. In the twentieth century Luciano Berio emulated them in his *The Cries of London*, in which the sixteenth-century street traders' cries are used as the basis of extended musical elaborations, the words being taken as the starting-point of dramatic and humorous excursions in colour and sound. Victorian London saw a pale reflection of these, doubtless using then contemporary street cries, in Frederick Scotson Clark's sheet music *London Streets: fantasia on popular cries* of 1866. Later Herbert Oliver produced a series of *Songs of Old London*, the material recycled in his choral suite *The Cries of London* published in 1913, the movements comprising 'The Cries of London', 'Fine Seville Oranges', 'The Bellman', 'The Pieman', 'The Lavender Girl' and 'Buy My Crumpling Codlings'.

At the end of the seventeenth century, Purcell and his contemporaries produced works, usually with voices, for state occasions, for the nobility and for the theatre, though none of them can really be described as programmatic. Purcell's *Music for the Funeral of Queen Mary* (more formally *Funeral Sentences for the Death of Queen Mary*) of 1695, and John Blow's *Ode on the Death of Mr Henry Purcell*: 'Mark How the Lark and Linnet Sing' of the same year are extended works for specific occasions that still retain their immediacy and sense of place and occasion.

In the eighteenth century Handel's *Water Music* and *Music for the Royal Fireworks* were both associated with celebratory occasions in London, while Haydn's *London Symphonies* and Mozart's childhood First Symphony, sometimes called his *London Symphony*, merely record the place the music was written for and where it was first played. Such associations continued into the twentieth century, Gustav Holst, for example, calling his two suites for school orchestra the *St Paul's Suite* after the school where he worked and for which he wrote it, and the *Brook Green Suite* after the locality where St Paul's Girls' School is situated.

In the nineteenth century, programmatic and illustrative music became increasingly the norm, though until the last quarter of the century London pieces tended to be domestic light music for piano, written to celebrate a particular place or occa-

105 Contemporary lithographed sheet music covers from the mid-nineteenth century on London subjects. *The Very Last Polka* illustrates a familiar but now forgotten scene from any concert, opera or social gathering before the provision of good public transport and the arrival of the car, the line of carriages waiting to pick up well-off members of the audience.

Some Victorian sheet music about London with lithographed covers

(Publishers, where named, are in London unless otherwise stated)

W. T. Abbott: *The Sydenham or the New Crystal Palace Polka*. Panormo, 1854.

Charles Louis Napoleon d'Albert: *The Court of St James Quadrilles*. Chappell and Co., 1865.

Charles d'Albert: *Iolanthe Lancers* [after Sullivan, with an engraved cover of the Palace of Westminster] Chappell, 1883.

C. C. Amos: *Al Fresco – Polka*. London, 1861.

C. C. Amos: *Colosseum Polka*. London, 1862.

Barling: *The Crystal Palace Quadrille*. Sydenham, 1869.

Baudouin, Adrien: *The Oxford Galop*. [Oxford Music Hall] Williams, 1861.

F. Bell: *The Coffee Shop at Pimlico*. Watts, 1865.

George Bicknell: *The Streets of London Quadrilles*. London, 1874.

T. Clare: *The Greenwich Royal Naval School Boys* (song). Webb, 1842.

Frederick Scotson Clark: *London Streets: fantasia on popular cries*. London, 1866.

H. C. Cole: *Royal London Quadrilles*. Goddard, 1875.

Michael Connelly: *The Lights O'London – galop*. London, 1882.

Charles Coote, the elder: *London in 1851: mélange for the ball-room*. Coote and Tinney, 1852.

Charles Coote, jnr: *Covent Garden Quadrille*. Hopwood & Crew, nd.

Charles Coote, jnr: *London by Night Quadrille*. Hopwood & Crew, 1885.

Gaston de Lille: *London – Polka*. Paris, 1860.

A. Desblins: *Sydenham Palace Quadrille*. London, 1881.

Henry Farmer: *The Hyde Park Grand Review March*. J Williams, nd.

J. E. Field: *New Crystal Palace Polka*. Harry May, nd.

Léonard Gautier: *On the Thames Polka*. F Pitman, 1884.

Chas. W Glover: *Partant Pour la Syrie* [cover illustration of interior of Crystal Palace]. Addison & Hollier, 21 Regent St [1855].

Stephen Glover: *I Met Her in the Crystal Halls*. Duff and Co., 1851.

William Grossmith: *Twelve Easy Original London Polkas*. London, 1851.

Joseph Halberstadt: *Crystal Palace Polka Mazurka*. London, 1862.

Charles Hall: *Streets of London Quadrilles*. H. D'Alcorn, 1865, 1873.

T. G. B. Halley: *Royal Aquarium Galop*. Wood, 1876.

Joseph Labitzky: *Souvenir de Londres – polka*. Mayence, 1863.

J. R. Ling: *The Crystal Palace Polka*. 1851, 1859.

August Manns: *Marian Redowa* as performed by the Crystal Palace Company's Band [cover illustrates the Egyptian Hall at the Crystal Palace]. Jullien [1854].

August Manns: *Prince Alfred's March* [black and white cover illustration of Crystal Palace] Universal Circulating Music Library, 86 Newgate Street, nd.

G. Mather: *St Bride's Bells*. Longman & Bates, nd.

Olive May: *London Musical Gems*. Brooks, 1889.

J. F. Mitchell: *That's the Way to the Zoo*.

Capellmeister Oser: *Gay London Society: polka*. Ascherberg, 1886.

Henry [T.] Parker: *The Burlington Waltz*. C. Sheard [1871].

Albert Parlow: *Covent-Garden-Klänge: waltzer für piano*. Breslau, 1872.

Adolphe Schubert: *The Real Crystal Palace Quadrilles*. London, 1856.

Angelo Vananzi: *Venice in London Polka (Waltz)*. London, 1892.

Theo Ward: *How London Lives*. London, Francis, Day and Hunter, 1897.

Friedrich Anton Weber: *The Buckingham Palace Quadrilles*. Set 2. George & Manby, *c*. 1840.

Warwick Williams: *Old London Quadrilles*. Francis Bros and Day, 1884.

Warwick Williams: *Songs of London Lancers*. Francis, Day and Hunter, nd.

Julius Wittenberg: *Rotten Row Galop*. London 1853, 1861.

---

sion, often in the popular dance forms of the day, such as the galop or polka. A typical early example is the piano rondo *The Delights of Greenwich*, by Gustav Holst's grandfather, published by G. Walker of 106 Great Portland Street. Many of these dating from the mid-century and later have become better known for the coloured lithograph covers of the sheet music than for the pieces themselves.

A London background might also be evoked in an opera or stage work, the Gilbert and Sullivan operetta *The Yeomen of the Guard* being among the first noteworthy early examples. Later, Albert Coates's opera *Samuel Pepys*, Alan Bush's *Wat Tyler* and his children's opera *The Ferryman's Daughter* and Britten's coronation opera *Gloriana* all featured scenes set in various parts of London with suitably evocative music. Phyllis Tate's two-act *The Lodger* (1960) is set in the London of Jack the Ripper, but, with its divided set showing two rooms simultaneously, it only provides the atmosphere of a foggy Victorian London, rather than depicting any specific places. We also need to mention Iain Hamilton's 1992 'lyric comedy' in two acts, *London's Fair*, which had first appeared ten years before as *Dick Whittington*.

Specific London references also appear in various musicals, of which Eric Maschwitz's 'A Nightingale Sang in Berkeley Square' (words by Manning Sherwin) is probably the best-known. Notable among such numbers is Gershwin's 'Berkeley and Kew' in his 1924 show *Primrose*; the song 'A Foggy Day in London Town' introduced by Fred Astaire in the film *A Damsel in Distress* in 1937 (for British audiences perhaps best remembered in Gracie Fields's recording of 1938), and Albert Ketèlbey's waltz song 'A Mayfair Cinderella' (1937) for which he wrote both words and music. George Black's and Bert

Lee's *London Rhapsody* was a vehicle for Flanagan and Allen at the Palladium in the autumn of 1937 and included numbers such as 'Sing a Song of London' and 'Along the River with You'. After the war, Van Heusen and Burke's *London Town*, yielded an overture of that title recorded by Decca (10″ 78 rpm, F 8672). The jazz pianist Fats Waller's *London Suite*, recorded in 1939, included movements evoking Limehouse and Whitechapel, both transformed by the bombing that soon followed.

In film music too there are many occasions where music is used to evoke London, even if only in passing. This often relates to scenes of departure or arrival – Gladys Aylward sets out for her journey to China in *The Inn of the Sixth Happiness* with expectant and almost heroic music, ideas that Malcolm Arnold grows into the symbol for her heroism and compassion later in the film. Elisabeth Lutyens's *En Voyage* film music includes an evocative movement celebrating the departure of the *Golden Arrow* boat train from Victoria. This was more of a documentary, and, of course, there are many documentaries whose film scores have since become very familiar. Vaughan Williams's *The England of Elizabeth* is a distinguished example, another being Arnold Bax's for *Journey into History*. By using a model of London in 1600, made up from Visscher's celebrated engraving, as the backcloth for the title music for Olivier's wartime film of Shakespeare's *Henry V*, Walton also created indissoluble associations in his celebrated score for the film.

106 The illustrated cover of the first issue of Elgar's *Cockaigne* underlines its subtitle 'In London Town', with its variety of landmarks and activities.

Edwardian London was widely depicted in music, Elgar setting the tone with his concert overture (really more an orchestral tone poem) *Cockaigne*, subtitled *In London Town* and first heard at Queen's Hall in June 1901. Taking their cue from Elgar's achievement, others followed, ranging from the light music of Eric Coates and Haydn Wood to John Ireland's evocative piano writing in his *London Pieces* and *A Ballad of London Nights*. Sir Alexander Campbell Mackenzie's light music suite in four movements, *London Day by Day* ('Under the Clock', 'Merry Mayfair', 'Song of Thanksgiving' and 'Hampstead Heath'), first heard in 1902, opens with what its composer called 'a series of snapshots over the persistently repeated chimes of the Westminster chimes'. As he ruefully noted in his autobiography 'the whole point . . . was missed at the first performance by the refusal of Big Ben to strike at the right moment. The gong-artist evidently found the single-stroke expected from him too much to remember.' This movement, which is subtitled 'humoresque', was later recorded by its composer, albeit by the acoustic process (HMV, D 190). At the time of the 1937 coronation, in his capacity as Master of the King's Music, Sir Henry Walford Davies produced his children's suite for orchestra, *Big Ben Looks On*, which achieved some celebrity when, arranged as a piano duet, it was played by the princesses Elizabeth and Margaret Rose. Bax, too, contributed to the 1937 Coronation celebrations with his *A London Pageant*. Also new at this time was John Ireland's *A London Overture*, with its striking string motif evoking the cry of a London bus conductor: ''dilly. Piccadilly' which ensured it a popular following at the time.

The work that crowned the genre with a new and more adventurous harmonic palette, also featuring the Westminster chimes, was Vaughan Williams's *A London*

Symphony, first heard at Queen's Hall in 1914 in a version (now recorded by Chandos) that was soon withdrawn by its composer, who by a succession of cuts eventually arrived at the score that is generally played today. Other works to feature the Westminster chimes include Dyson's *In Honour of the City*, Louis Vierne's *Carillon de Westminster* from his work for organ *Pièces de Fantasie*, Suite No. 3, Op. 54, and Ernst Toch's orchestral tour-de-force *Big Ben, a Variation on the Westminster Chimes*, Op. 62, written while crossing the Atlantic in 1935 after a year living in London as a refugee from Nazi Germany.

Several composers have pictured the August Bank Holiday fair on Hampstead Heath, the first example possibly being the finale of Mackenzie's suite already mentioned. Certainly the most uproarious was the opening scene of Havergal Brian's burlesque opera *The Tigers*, written during the First World War, which demands a live elephant on stage. This survives into the concert hall as an almost exact transcription in Brian's *Symphonic Variations* on the popular song 'Has anyone here seen Kelly', and provides a constant thread through the music. In 1924 Albert Ketèlbey portrayed Hampstead Heath and its bank holiday fair in the final movement of his *Cockney Suite*, subtitled ''Appy Ampstead': by providing a kaleidoscope of passing images, mouth organs, a cornet playing snatches of popular tunes, a band comes into hearing playing Rossini's *Semiramide* Overture, shouts of a showman (in his recording he has an actual voice) with his rattle and a steam engine and roundabout. Later the Dutch composer Paul von Klenau did it again in *Souvenir of Hampstead Heath*, and much later Phyllis Tate took a lighter view of the same scene in her 'Hampstead Heath', subtitled 'Rondo for Roundabouts' from her suite *London Fields*. (Other movements are 'Springtime at Kew', 'Hampton Court – the Maze' and 'St James' Park: a lakeside reverie'.)

Eric Coates was probably the most assiduous composer of light music celebrating London. Some of these scores were general in effect, such as 'Evening in Town' from the suite *Meadow to Mayfair*, 'The Man About Town' or *London by Night*. But he is best-known for familiar scores depicting specific landmarks, such as the *London Suite* ('Covent Garden', 'Westminster' and 'Knightsbridge March', the latter very familiar to British audiences as for many years the theme music for the popular radio show 'In Town Tonight') and *London Again* ('Oxford Street', 'Langham Place: Elegie' and 'Mayfair Valse'). Coates is especially remembered for his marches and in addition to those that appeared in one or other of his suites he also produced the *Holborn* and *London Bridge* marches.

Haydn Wood almost out-Coateses Eric Coates with his similar London light music in his suite *London Cameos* ('The City', 'St James' Park' and 'State Ball at Buckingham Palace') and elsewhere he also produced *London Landmarks* ('Nelson's Column', 'Tower Hill' and 'Horse Guards Whitehall') and *Snapshots of London* ('Sadler's Wells', 'Regent's Park' and 'Wellington Barracks'). Another similar movement is *The Bandstand in Hyde Park*. There were other such composers, including Montague Phillips with his overture *Hampton Court*, Thomas F. Dunhill's *The Way to London*, Robert Farnon's *Westminster Waltz* and Gordon Langford's *London*

Miniatures ('London Calls', 'Soho', 'Green Park', 'Trafalgar Square', 'Cenotaph' and 'Horseguards'). (For another atmospheric evocation of the Cenotaph see the fourth movement of Ketèlby's Cockney Suite.) Francis Chagrin's brief *London Sketches for Light Orchestra* dates from that high-point of BBC light music, the 1950s. London means a theatre-show for many visitors, and Eric Rogers's *Palladium Symphony* reflects his working experience as the Music Director of the London Palladium, each movement self-evidently evoking the different aspects of a variety bill. Another composer of musical picture-postcards was Percival Garratt, whose *London Fantasies* Op. 50 for piano included such subjects as 'The Chamber of Horrors (Madame Tussaud's)' and 'The Monkey House (The Zoo)'.

Composers for brass and military band also wrote London pieces, and these include Frank Wright's *Old Westminster* and *Whitehall*, Eric Ball's *Kensington Concerto* and Peter Cork's *London in the Thirties* ('Bowler Hats and City Pavements', 'Koffee at the Kardoma', 'Afternoon in Limehouse', 'Teatime Tango at the Ritz', 'First House at Hackney Empire', 'Westminster Bridge at Sunset' and 'Morning on Horse Guards Parade').

The catalogue of the publisher Bosworths, now part of Music Sales, was once a source of an extensive selection of light music, and among evocatively London pieces listed several other titles by Ketèlbey including *Bow Bells* foxtrot (1920) and, under the pseudonym of Geoffrey Kaye, *In the Shadow of St Pauls* (1921). Similar descriptive pieces include *The Ghosts of Berkeley Square* by Hans May, *A London Day* suite ('Dawn', 'Daytime' and 'Dusk') by Michael North (1948), *Thames Castles* suite ('The Tower Beefeaters', 'Hampton Court' and 'Windsor Castle') by Graeme Stuart (1947), *Shaftesbury Avenue* by Jack Strachey, orchestrated by Augustus Franzel (1947), and Bert Martland's *Piccadilly Prelude*. Finally in the spirit of Eric Coates and Haydn Wood there is Graeme Stuart's *Up for the Day* ('Excursion Train', 'Round the Shops' and 'At the Theatre').

The River Thames provides a constant thread in any view of London, and particularly in the music of Holst and Vaughan Williams we find the use of low sustained notes in an atmospheric and impressionistic texture uniquely compelling in evoking the conjunction of the flow of the river and a philosophical musing on the longer view. Vaughan Williams did this first in *A London Symphony* but some fifteen years later his friend Gustav Holst was even more successful in his musical evocation *Hammersmith*, in which the contrast between the great forces of nature with the river's timeless and inexorable flow and the tawdry brilliance and human vitality of the market traders is brilliantly depicted. Other composers took the river as their subject, but they tended to treat it as a motif for a historical panorama of incidents associated with it, and for which it may well have been the most convenient means of transport in times past, in works such as Elizabeth Maconchy's overture for the coronation in 1953, *Proud Thames*, and Andrzej Panufnik's children's cantata *Thames Pageant*, setting specially written words by Camilla Jessel. Nigel Hess's wind band tone poem *Thames Journey* evokes the passage of the River Thames from Kemble in Gloucestershire to the open sea. Britten's 'Marine' from his cycle *Les Illuminations*, in evocative water music, is a musical impression of the nineteenth-century Pool of London.

The First World War does not seem to have generated any major works associated with London per se rather than the country at large. However, in the Second World War it was a different story, and with the capital more widely threatened by bombing, and indeed with much of it destroyed, the nostalgia was more intense, the mood of defiance more immediate, an emotional reaction that gave added resonance to the creation of forceful images usually associated with music from documentaries such as *Fires Were Started* at one extreme to *Shakespeare's London* at the other. Sidney Gilliat's film *London Belongs to Me* featured music by Benjamin Frankel. It was Sir Noël Coward though, who most probably reached the widest audience in works relating to London in the war, with the popular song 'London Pride' not only alluding to the spirit of London but also referring to the delicate flowers of the widely seen weed that grew on bombsites throughout the metropolis. However, Coward's two extended London scores, the review *London Calling* and the ballet *London Morning*, were not associated with the war, the review being one of his first stage successes in 1923 and the ballet long after, in 1958. Possibly the most typical wartime score is the *London Fantasia* for that popular wartime form of the short romantic piano concerto, written and recorded by Clive Richardson in 1940. Later, Gordon Langford's 1965 *Spirit of London* is a nostalgic memory of Londoners' response to the bombing, albeit through rose-tinted spectacles.

Remembering the rich literature of poetry and prose about London it is not surprising that many composers have set such words to music. Possibly the first two choral works that come to mind are first Dyson's *In Honour of the City* setting seven verses of Dunbar's poem in modern English. That was in 1928. Later, in 1937, Walton set these same words for similar forces. The Scottish poet is believed to have written his poem around 1500 when a member of the embassy from the court of James IV of Scotland came to negotiate the king's marriage to Margaret Tudor, though some recent scholars have thrown doubt on Dunbar's authorship. Dyson wrote several vocal works celebrating London in one way or another. These include his overture *At the Tabard Inn*, a quodlibet of themes from his celebrated choral work *The Canterbury Pilgrims*, evoking the gathering of the pilgrims at the celebrated Southwark Inn, *Sweet Thames Run Softly*, and the short choral setting *To the Thames*, words by Sir John Denham (1615–1669). Sir Richard Rodney Bennett (in his *London Pastoral*) and Walton (in *Songs for the Lord Mayor's Table*) have also set London texts evocatively for solo voice and orchestra.

More recent London events remembered by London composers include George Lloyd's *Royal Parks*, the commissioned work for the European Brass Band Championships in 1985, whose middle movement 'In Memoriam' deals with more serious matters, and remembers 20 July 1982 when young bandsmen were killed in their bandstand by terrorists. Finally Paul Patterson's *Royal Eurostar*, for brass, percussion and organ, which was written for the official opening of the London Eurostar terminal at Waterloo. The music, designed to be played in a large space, incorporates *Rule Britannia* and the *Marseillaise*.

Dealers

The number of London dealers in second-hand and antiquarian music has declined over the last twenty years, and now there remains only one dealer with a retail shop in central London. This is Travis and Emery at 17 Cecil Court, WC2N, next door to where Mozart is reputed to have stayed in 1764. Cecil Court is a small street linking Charing Cross Road with St Martin's Lane just above and opposite the Coliseum. Its shops comprise a variety of dealers selling books, engravings, posters and prints, many of which may well have material relevant to musical interests. Travis and Emery was founded by Valérie Emery at No. 16, across the court from the present premises, in January 1960 and moved to No. 17 in September 1976 where it remains. Valérie Emery achieved wider celebrity shortly before her death in 2000 when she revealed her wartime role as a codebreaker at Bletchley Park, during a BBC interview. Regular book and music catalogues are issued, and the stock is one of the contributing dealers on Abebooks.com, which can be searched via the internet.

Three other notable London dealers issue regular lists, but should only be approached by appointment: H. Baron, 121 Chatsworth Road, London, NW2 4BH; Decorum Books, 24 Cloudesley Square, London, N1 0HN; and Martin Eastick, 42 Craignish Avenue, Norbury, London, SW16 4RN. All issue regular catalogues, but only Decorum Books can be found via the second-hand book website Abebooks.com.

Bibliography

All published in London unless otherwise stated.

Abbott, John: *The Story of Francis, Day and Hunter*. Francis, Day and Hunter, 1952.

The ABC Guide to London: twentieth-century edition. 1901.

Aprahamian, Felix: 'Remembering Messiaen', *Choir and Organ*. January/February 1999, p. 72; March/April 1999, p. 72; May/June 1999, p. 72.

Apthorp, William Foster: *By the Way*. Vol. II. Boston: Copland and Day, 1898.

Austin, Ernest: *The Story of Music Publishing*. Lowe and Brydone, nd [*c*. 1920].

Baedeker, Karl: *London and its environs 1900: a handbook for travellers*. Moretonhamstead. Facsimile reprint, Old House Books, 2002.

Baker, Margaret: *Discovering London statues and monuments*. Princes Risborough: A Shire Book, 5th edition, 2002.

Baldwin, David: *The Chapel Royal, ancient and modern*. Duckworth, 1990.

Barnett, John Francis: *Musical Reminiscences and Impressions*. Hodder and Stoughton, 1906.

Barty-King, Hugh: *GSMD: a hundred years' performance*. Stainer and Bell for the Guildhall School of Music and Drama, 1980.

Bashford, Christina, and Leanne Langley, eds: *Music and British Culture 1785–1914*. Oxford: Oxford University Press, 2000.

Bax, Arnold: *Farewell, My Youth*. Longmans, Green and Co., 1943.

Beaver, Patrick: *The Crystal Palace*. Chichester: Pillimore, 1970, 1977.

Beckson, Karl: *London in the 1890s: a cultural history*. New York and London: W. W. Norton and Co., 1992.

Bennett, Joseph: *Forty Years of Music, 1865–1905*. Methuen, 1908.

Berger, Francesco: *Reminiscences, Impressions and Anecdotes*. Sampson Low: Marston and Co., 1913.

Berger, Francesco: *97*. Elkin Mathews and Marrot, 1931.

Berlioz, Hector: *Evening in the Orchestra*. Harmondsworth: Penguin Books, 1963.

——: *La Voix du Romanticism*. [Exhibition Catalogue.] Paris: Bibliothèque Nationale de France/Fayard, 2003.

Berry, Patricia Dee: *Theatrical London (Britain in Old Photographs)* Stroud: Alan Sutton Publishing, 1995.

Boalch, Donald H.: *Makers of the Harpsichord and Clavichord 1440–1840*. Oxford: Clarendon Press, 2nd edition, 1974.

Booth, J. B.: *Palmy Days*. The Richards Press, 1957.

Borer, Mary Cathcart: *Covent Garden*. Abelard-Schuman, 1967.

Brian, Havergal: *Havergal Brian on Music Selections from his Journalism*. Vol. 1, *British Music*, edited by Malcolm Macdonald. Toccata Press, 1986.

Bridge, Sir Frederick: *Samuel Pepys – lover of musique*. Smith, Elder and Co., 1903.

Brooks, Chris, ed.: *The Albert Memorial: the Prince Consort's National Memorial: its history, contacts and conservation*. New Haven and London: Yale University Press, 2000.

Burden, Michael: *Purcell Remembered*. Faber and Faber, 1995.

Burke, John: *Musical landscapes*. Exeter: Webb and Bower, 1983.

Burney, Charles: *An Account of the Musical Performances in Westminster-Abbey and the Pantheon May 26th, 27th, 29th; and June the 3rd and 5th 1784 in Commemoration of Handel*. Printed for the Benefit of the Musical Fund; and sold by T. Payne and Son, at the Meuse-Gate; and G. Robinson, Paternoster-Row, 1785.

Busoni, Ferruccio: *Letters to his wife*, translated by Rosamond Ley. Edward Arnold, 1938.

Carley, Lionel: *Delius – a life in letters.* 2 vols: vol. 1, 1862–1908; vol. 2, 1909–1934. Scolar Press, 1985; 1988.

Carley, Lionel: *Grieg and Delius – a chronicle of their friendship in letters.* Marion Boyars, 1993.

Carpenter, Edward: 'Music in the Abbey' in *A House of Kings: the history of Westminster Abbey.* John Baker, 1966.

Carse, Adam: *The Life of Jullien.* Cambridge: W. Heffer and Sons, 1951.

Chancellor, E. Beresford: *The XIIIth century in London: an account of its social life and arts.* Batsford, 1933.

——: *The pleasure haunts of London during four centuries.* Constable, 1925.

Christiansen, Rupert: *The visitors: culture shock in nineteenth century Britain.* Chatto and Windus, 2000.

Coates, Eric: *Suite in four movements: an autobiography.* Thames Publishing, 1986.

Colles, H. C., and J. Cruft: *The Royal College of Music: a centenary record 1883–1983.* Prince Consort Foundation, 1982.

Collins' Guide to London and Neighbourhood. William Collins, 1885.

Collins, Chris: 'Falla in Britain', *Musical Times.* Summer 2003, pp. 33–48.

Coover, James, ed.: *Music Publishing, Copyright and Piracy in Victorian England: a twenty-five year chronicle, 1881–1906* . . . London and New York: Mansell Publishing, 1985.

Corder, Frederick: *Royal Academy of Music: Souvenir centenary 1822–1922.* Royal Academy of Music, 1922.

Cowen, Sir Frederic H.: *My Art and My Friends.* Edward Arnold, 1913.

Cox, David: *The Henry Wood Proms.* British Broadcasting Corporation, 1980.

[Cox, John Edmund]: *Musical Recollections of the Last Half-Century.* 2 vols. Tinsley Bros, 1972.

Croker, Thomas Crofton: *A Walk from London to Fulham* . . . revised and edited by his son T. F. Dillon Croker. William Tegg, 1860.

Crystal Palace: *Catalogue of the Principal [works played]* . . . *in the Saturday Concerts.* Crystal Palace: Evans, 1895.

Culbertson, J., and T. Randall: *Permanent Londoners: an illustrated biographical guide to the cemeteries of London.* Robson Books, 2000.

Culshaw, John: *Putting the Record Straight.* Secker and Warburg, 1982.

David, Hugh: *The Fitzrovians: a portrait of Bohemian Society 1900–55.* Michael Joseph, 1988.

De Lara, Adelina: *Finale.* Burke, 1955.

Dibble, Jeremy: *C. Hubert H. Parry.* Oxford: Clarendon Press, 1992.

Dibble, Jeremy: *Charles Villiers Stanford – man and music.* Oxford: Oxford University Press, 2002.

Dickens, Charles: *Dickens's Dictionary of London 1888: an unconventional handbook.* Facsimile edition. Moretonhampstead: Old House Books, 1993, reprinted 2001.

Dreyfus, Kay: 'Percy Grainger's London addresses: Part I: The historical background', *The Grainger Society Journal,* vol. 16, no. 1, Winter 2002, pp. 24–29. Part II is by John Bird. pp. 29–31.

Dreyfus, Kay, ed.: *The Farthest North of Humanness – letters of Percy Grainger 1911–14.* Melbourne, Australia: Macmillan, 1985.

Edwards, Christopher, ed.: *The London Theatre Guide, 1576–1642.* Royston, Herts: The Burlington Press, 1979.

Edwards, F. G.: *Musical Haunts in London.* Curwen and Sons, nd [1895].

Ehrlich, Cyril: *The Music Profession in Britain Since the Eighteenth Century: A Social History.* Oxford: Clarendon Press, 1985.

——: *The First Philharmonic: A History of the Royal Philharmonic Society.* Oxford: Clarendon Press, 1995.

Elkin, Robert: *The Old Concert Rooms of London*. Edward Arnold, 1955.

——: *Queen's Hall 1893–1941*. Rider, nd [1944].

——: *Royal Philharmonic*. Rider, nd [1946].

Fagg, Edwin: *Old 'Sadler's Wells'*. Vic-Wells Association, 1935.

Fletcher, Geoffrey S.: *London overlooked*. Hutchinson, 1964.

Ford, Boris: *The Cambridge Guide to the Arts in Britain*. Cambridge: Cambridge University Press, 1989. Vol. 3: 'Renaissance and Reformation'; vol. 4: 'The Seventeenth Century'.

Foreman, Lewis: *Bax – a composer and his times*. Scolar Press, 2nd edtion, 1988.

——: *Music in England 1885–1920, as recounted in Hazell's Annual*. Thames Publishing, 1994.

——: 'Music's Crucible – Recordings made in Queen's Hall' *International Classical Record Collector*. Vol. 3, no. 10, Autumn 1997, pp. 64–71.

——: 'Watford sur Gade – Delius in Watford during the First World War', *Delius Society Journal*, no. 130, Autumn 2001, pp. 8–18.

——: 'Crystal Palace on Shellac', *Classical Record Collector*, vol. 8, no. 26, Autumn 2001, pp. 30–36.

Foreman, Lewis, ed.: *Lost and Only Sometimes Found – a seminar on music publishing and archives*. Upminster: British Music Society, 1992.

Foreman, Susan: *From Palace to Power: an illustrated history of Whitehall*. Brighton: Alpha Press, 1995.

——: *H M Treasury in Whitehall: an exhibition of pictures principally from the Lister Collection*. Catalogue by Susan Foreman. H M Treasury, September 1998.

Friends of Highgate Cemetery: *Highgate Cemetery*. 1978.

Friends of Highgate Cemetery: *In Highgate Cemetery*. 1992.

Friends of Kensal Green Cemetery: *Paths of glory – or – a select alphabetical and biographical list, illustrated with line drawings of their monuments, of persons of note commemorated at the Cemetery of All Souls at Kensal Green*. 1997.

Galatopoulos, Stelios: *Bellini: life, times, music 1801–1835*. Sanctuary, 2002.

Ganz, A. W.: *Berlioz in London*. Quality Press, 1950.

Ganz, Wilhelm: *Memories of a Musician: reminiscences of seventy years of musical life*. John Murray, 1913.

Gillies, Midge: *Marie Lloyd the one and only*. Orion, 1999.

Glinert, Ed: *A Literary Guide to London*. Harmondsworth: Penguin Books, 2000.

Goodman, Andrew: *Gilbert and Sullivan's London*, edited and presented by Robert Hardcastle. Faber and Faber, 2000 [first published 1988].

Gotch, R. B., ed.: *Mendelssohn and his friends in Kensington: letters from Fanny and Sophy Horsley*, written 1833–36. Cambridge: Cambridge University Press, 1934.

Griffiths, Paul: *Bartok*. (Master Musicians series) Dent, 1984.

Grove, Sir George, ed.: *A Dictionary of Music and Musicians*. 4 vols. Macmillan, 1883. Fifth edition, edited by Eric Blom, 1954. *The New Grove Dictionary of Music and Musicians*, edited by Stanley Sadie, 2nd edition, 2001.

Hall, Barrie: *The Proms and the men who made them*. Allen and Unwin, 1981.

Hammond, Audrey, and Brian Dann. *Crystal Palace Norwood Heights: a pictorial record*. Crystal Palace: Triangle Community Association, 2nd edn 1989.

Harley, John: *Music in Purcell's London – the social background*. Dennis Dobson, 1968.

——: *William Byrd Gentleman of the Chapel Royal*. Aldershot: Scolar Press, 1999.

Head, Louise, ed.: *British and International Music Yearbook 2003*. Rhinegold Publishing, 2 vols, 29th edition, 2003.

Heathcote, Edwin: *Theatre London: an architectural guide*. Ellipsis, 2001.

Huntley, John: *British Film Music*. Skelton Robinson, nd [1947].

Hurd, Michael: *Vincent Novello – and company*. Granada, 1981.

Jacobs, Arthur: *Henry J. Wood Maker of the Proms*. Methuen, 1994.

Jones, David Wyn: 'London' in *Haydn*. Oxford: Oxford University Press, 2002, pp. 217–24. (Oxford composer companions).

Jones, Peter Ward: *The Mendelssohns on Honeymoon*. Oxford: Clarendon Press, 1997.

Kenyon, Nicholas: *The BBC Symphony Orchestra: The First Fifty Years, 1930–1980*. British Broadcasting Corporation, 1981.

King, Robert: *Henry Purcell*. Thames and Hudson, 1994.

Klein, Herman: *Musicians and Mummers*. Cassell, 1925.

——: *Thirty years of Musical Life in London, 1870–1900*. Heinemann, 1903.

Knight, David S.: 'The organ in Westminster Abbey at the Restoration and its subsequent history.' *The Organ Yearbook*. Vol. 27 (1997) Laaber: Laaber-Verlag, pp. 25–39.

——: 'Westminster Abbey organ in the Twentieth Century' *BIOS Journal*. Vol. 23. 1991. Oxford: Positif Press, 1990, pp. 76–104.

Landon, H. C. Robbins: *The Collected Correspondence and London Notebooks of Joseph Haydn*. Barrie and Rockliffe, 1959.

——: *Handel and His World*. Weidenfeld and Nicolson, 1984.

——: *Haydn in England 1791–1795*. Thames and Hudson, 1976, 1983.

Latham, Alison, ed.: *The Oxford Companion to Music*. Oxford: Oxford University Press, 2002.

Laurence, Dan H., ed.: *Shaw's Music – The Complete Music Criticism in Three Volumes*. Second revised edition, The Bodley Head, 1981, 1989.

Lebrecht, Norman: *Music in London*. Aurum Press, 1992.

Lee, Edward: *Musical London. (Thirteen guided walks to the fascinating music landmarks of London)*. Omnibus Press, 1995.

Lee-Browne, Martin: *Nothing so charming as musick! The life and times of Frederic Austin, singer, composer, teacher*. Thames Publishing, 1999.

Ley, Rosamund, trans.: *Ferrucio Busoni, Letters to his Wife*. Edward Arnold, 1938.

Lloyd, Stephen: *H Balfour Gardiner*. Cambridge: Cambridge University Press, 1984.

——: *William Walton: Muse of Fire*. Woodbridge, Suffolk: The Boydell Press, 2001.

Macdonald, Nesta: *Diaghilev Observed by Critics in England and the United States 1911–1929*. New York, Dance Horizons; London, Dance Books, 1975.

Macqueen Pope, W.: *Goodbye Piccadilly*. Michael Joseph, 1960.

——: *Theatre Royal Drury Lane*. W. H. Allen, 1945.

MacRae, Julia, ed.: *Wigmore Hall 1901–2001: a celebration*. The Wigmore Hall Trust, 2001.

McVeigh, Simon: *Concert life in London from Mozart to Haydn*. Cambridge: Cambridge University Press, 1993.

Mair, Carlene: *The Chappell Story, 1811–1961*. Chappell and Co., 1961.

Martland, Peter: *Since records began: EMI, the first 100 years*. Batsford, 1997.

Matthews, Betty: *A history of the Royal Society of Musicians 1738–1988*. Royal Society of Musicians, 1988.

Meller, Hugh: *London cemeteries: an illustrated guide and gazetteer*. Amersham: Avebury, 1981.

Melling, John Kennedy: *Discovering lost theatres*. Princes Risborough: Shire Publications, 1969.

Monson, Craig: 'Elizabethan London', in *The Renaissance from the 1470s to the end of the sixteenth century*, edited by Iain Fenlon. Basingstoke: Macmillan, 1989, pp. 304–40.

Moore, Gerlad: *Furthermore: Interludes in an accompanist's life*. Hamish Hamilton, 1983.

Moscheles, Ignatz [*sic*]: *Recent music and musicians, as described in the diaries and correspondence of Ignatz Moscheles*, edited by his wife and adapted from the original German by A. Coleridge. New York: Henry Holt and Company, 1873.

Musgrave, Michael: *The Musical Life of the Crystal Palace*. Cambridge: Cambridge University Press, 1995.

Music at St Paul's: the story of the choir, organ and school. St Paul's, nd [?2002].

The Music Trades Pocket Directory, 1894. G D Ernest and Co. nd [1894].

Musical Directory, Register and Alamanack, for the year 1856. Rudall, Rose, Carte, and Co., nd [1856].

Nalbach, Daniel: *The King's Theatre 1704–1867: London's first Italian Opera House*. The Society for Theatre Research, 1972.

Näslund, Erik: Överdådets konst II [The Art of Extravagance II] Kostymer från Diaghilev Ryska Baletten I Paris. Stockholm: Dansmuseet, 2004.

Nettel, Reginald: *The orchestra in England: a social history*. Cape, 1946, 1948.

New, Anthony: *Historical Buildings Register*. Vol. 2. *London*. PSA, Architectural Services Division, 1983.

Newman, Ernest: *The Life of Wagner: Vol IV, 1866–1883*. Cassell, 1947.

Nichols, Roger: *Mendelssohn Remembered*. Faber and Faber, 1997.

Noble, Peter, ed.: *British Ballet*. Skelton Robinson, nd.

Norris, Gerald: *A musical gazetteer of Great Britain and Ireland*. Newton Abbot: David and Charles, 1981.

Northcott, Richard: *Records of the Royal Opera Covent Garden 1888–1921*. The Press Printers, 1921.

Novello: *A Century and a half in Soho – a short history of the firm of Novello, publishers and printers of music, 1811–1961*. Novello, 1961.

Osborne, Richard: *Till I end my song: English music and musicians 1440–1940, a perspective from Eton*. The Cygnet Press, 2002.

Parkinson, John A.: *Victorian Music Publishers – an annotated list*. Warren, Michigan: Harminie Park Press, 1990.

Pascoe, Charles Eyre: *London of to-day: an illustrated handbook for the season 1897*. Bemrose and Sons Ltd, 1897.

Pentelow, Mike, and Marsha Rowe: *Characters of Fitzrovia*. Chatto and Windus, 2001.

Petersen, Peter, ed.: *Berthold Goldschmidt – Komponist und Dirigent ein Musiker-Leben Hamburg, Berlin und London*. Hamburg: von Bockel Verlag, 1994.

Picard, Liza. *Dr Johnson's London: life in London 1740–1770*. Weidenfeld and Nicolson, 2000.

Piggott, J. R.: *Palace of the People – The Crystal Palace at Sydenham, 1854–1936*. Hurst and Co., 2004.

Pine, Edward: *The Westminster Abbey Singers*. Dennis Dobson, 1953.

Pirouet, Edmund: *Heard Melodies are Sweet. A history of the London Philharmonic Orchestra*. Lewes, Sussex: Book Guild, 1998.

Plumley, N., and A. Niland: *The organs of St Paul's Cathedral*. Positif Press, 2001.

Plumley, Nicholas M.: *The organs of the City of London: from the Restoration to the present*. Positif Press, 1996.

Pollard, Anthony: *Gramophone: the first 75 years*. Sudbury Hill, Harrow: Gramophone Publications Ltd, 1998.

Popkin, J. M.: *Musical monuments*. Munich: K. G. Saur, 1986.

Pudney, John: *Music on the South Bank: an appreciation of the Royal Festival Hall*. Published in association with the London County Council, Max Parrish, 1951.

Purcell's The Fairy Queen as presented by Sadler's Wells Ballet and The Covent Garden Opera. A Photographic Record by Edward Mandinian . . . and article by Constant Lambert and Michael Ayrton. John Lehman, 1953.

The Queen's London: a pictorial and descriptive record of the Great Metropolis in the year of Her Majesty's Diamond Jubilee. Cassell and Co. Ltd, 1897.

Reed, Nicholas: *Crystal Palace and the Norwoods*. Tempus, 1995. (Images of London series).

Reynolds, David, ed.: *Weber in London 1826: selections from Weber's letters to his wife and from the writings of his contemporaries, London in 1826*. Oswald Wolff, 1976.

Richards, Jeffrey: *Imperialism and Music: Britain 1876–1953*. Manchester: Manchester University Press, 2001.

Ridgewell, Rupert: *Concert Programmes in the UK and Ireland – a preliminary report*. IAML (UK and Ireland) and the Music Libraries Trust, 2003.

Rowell, George: *Queen Victoria Goes to the Theatre*. Paul Elek, 1978.

Royal Academy of Music: *Musical Directory, Register and Almanack, for the year 1856*. Rudall, Rose, Carte and Co., 1856.

Royal College of Music, Museum of Instruments: Catalogue Part IA: European Wind Instruments, addenda by E. A. K. Ridley. RCM, 1998; Part II: Keyboard Instruments, ed. Elizabeth Wells. RCM, 2000.

Russell, John: *London*. New York: Harry N. Abrams, 1994.

Rust, Brian: *London Musical Shows on Record, 1897–1976*. Kenton: General Gramophone Publications, 1977.

Rutland, Harold: *Trinity College of Music: the first hundred years*. Trinity College of Music, 1972.

Ryan, Thomas: *Recollections of an Old Musician*. Sands and Co., 1899.

Saint, A. et al.: *A History of the Royal Opera House Covent Garden 1732–1982*. Royal Opera House, 1982.

Sandeman, R.: *Grand Architectural Panorama of London* [1849]. Reprint, Lympne Castle, Kent: Harry Margary in association with Guildhall Library, London, nd.

Savage Club: an introduction. Savage Club, nd [2002].

Saxe Wyndham, H.: *August Manns and the Saturday Concerts: a memoir and a retrospect*. Walter Scott Publishing Co., 1909.

Scholes, Percy A.: *The mirror of music 1844–1944: a century of musical life in Britain as reflected in the pages of the Musical Times*. 2 vols. Novello and Co. Ltd and Oxford University Press, 1947.

Schouvaloff, Alexander: *The Theatre Museum*. Scala Books, 1987.

Scowcroft, Philip L.: *British Light Music – a personal gallery of 20th-century composers*. Thames Publishing, 1997.

Seldon, Anthony: *10 Downing Street The Illustrated History*. Harper Collins, 1999.

Simeone, Nigel. *Paris – a musical gazetteer*. New Haven and London: Yale University Press, 2000.

Simon, Jacob, ed.: *Handel: a celebration of his life and times, 1685–1759*. National Portrait Gallery, 1985.

Southall, Brian, et al.: *Abbey Road: the story of the world's most famous recording studios*. Omnibus Press, 2002.

Speyer, Edward: *My life and friends*. Cobden-Sanderson, 1937.

Spink, Ian, ed.: *The Seventeenth Century*. Oxford: Blackwell, 1992, 1992. (Music in Britain 3.)

Stevens, John: *Music and Poetry in the Early Tudor Court*. Cambridge: Cambridge University Press, 1961, 1979.

Stoker, Bram: *The Personal Reminiscences of Henry Irving*. 2 vols. William Heineman, 1906.

Stone, Jonathan, ed.: *The Royal Albert Hall – a Victorian Masterpiece for the 21st Century*. Fitzhardinge Press, 2003.

Stuart, Philip, comp.: *The London Philharmonic Discography*. Westport, Conn.: Greenwich Press, 1997 (Discographies No 69).

Sumeray, Derek. *Discovering London plaques*. Princes Risborough: Shire publications, 1999.

Summers, Judith: *The Empress of Pleasure. The Life and Adventures of Teresa Cornelys – Queen of Masquerades and Casanova's Lover.* Viking, 2003; Penguin, 2004.

Summers, Judith: Soho. *A History of London's Most Colourful Neighbourhood.* Bloomsbury, 1989.

The Survey of London. 38 vols. London: Joint Publishing Committee, LCC and others, 1900–1975.

Taylor, Chas: *The Handy Handbook of London.* Geo Falkner, nd [1907].

Thackrah, J. R.: *The Royal Albert Hall.* Lavenham, Suffolk: Terence Dalton, 1983.

Thompson, Robert: *The Glory of the Temple and the Stage: Henry Purcell 1659–1695.* The British Library, 1995.

Thorold, Peter: *The London Rich – The Creation of a Great City, from 1666 to the present.* New York: St Martin's Press, 1999.

Tooley, John: *In House – Covent Garden, 50 years of opera and ballet.* London: Faber and Faber, 1999.

Vickers, Graham. *Classical music landmarks of London.* Omnibus, 2001.

Walford, Edward. *Old and new London: a narrative of its history, its people and its places . . .* new edition. Cassell, ?1888–1893, 6 vols. (Vols 1 and 2 by Walter Thornbury.)

——: *Old London – Westminster to St James's.* The Alderman Press, 1989.

Walsh, Stephen: *Stravinsky – a creative spring.* New York: Knopf, 1999.

Warwick, Alan R. *The Phoenix suburb: a south London social history.* The Blue Boar Press in association with the Beulah Group, 2nd edition, 1982.

Weber, William. *Music and the middle class: the social structure of concert life in London, Paris and Vienna.* Croom Helm, 1975.

White, Eric Walter: *A Register of First Performances of English Operas and Semi-Operas from the 16th Century to 1980.* The Society for Theatre Research, 1983.

Who's Who in Music. [Various imprints.] 1915, 1937, 1949, 1969 editions.

Wignall, Harrison James. 'London (and Chelsea)' in *In Mozart's footsteps.* Paragon House, 1991, pp. 85–96.

Wlaschin, Ken: *Encyclopedia of Opera on Screen. A Guide to more than 100 years of opera films, videos, and DVDs.* New Haven and London: Yale University Press, 2004.

The Year's Music 1896, being a concise record of British and Foreign Musical Events, Productions, Appearances, Criticisms, Memoranda, etc. J. S. Virtue and Co., 1896.

The Year's Music 1899, being a concise record of all Matters Relating to Music and Musical Institutions Which Have Occurred During the Season 1897–8 with information respecting the events of the season 1898–9; edited by A. C. Carter. J. S. Virtue and Co., 1899.

Young, Geoffrey: *Walking London's Parks and Gardens.* New Holland, 1998.

Some Useful Websites

All web addresses are preceded by www. Other web addresses are given in the text.

Abbey Road Studios: abbeyroad.co.uk
Alexandra Palace: alexandrapalace.com
Banqueting House: hrp.org.uk/
Barbican: barbican.org.uk
Blackheath Concert Halls: blackheathhalls. com
Bonhams: bonhams.com
Brompton Cemetery; royalparks.gov. uk/ brompton
Brompton Oratory: brompton-oratory. org.uk
Chapel Royal, St James's Palace: royal. gov.uk/
Christchurch, Spitalfields: christchurchspitalfields.org
Conway Hall: conwayhall.org.uk
Crystal Palace: crystalpalacefoundation. org.uk
English National Opera: eno.org
Eton College: etoncollege.com
Fenton House: nationaltrustorg.uk
Grave tracing: findagrave.com
Grim's Dyke: grimsdyke.com
Guildhall School of Music and Drama: gsmd.ac.uk
Highgate Cemetery: highgate-cemetery.org
Horniman Museum: horniman.ac.uk
Kensal Green Cemetery: kensalgreen.co.uk
Kenwood House: english-heritage.org.uk
Kneller Hall: usite.army.mod.uk
Lyceum Theatre: lyceum.org.uk
Lyric Theatre, Hammersmith: theatre.works.co.uk/individualtheatres/lyricHammersmith
Methodist Central Hall: c-h-w.com
Musical Museum, Brentford: musicalmuseum.co.uk
Royal Academy of Music: ram.ac.uk
Royal Albert Hall: royalalberthall.com

Royal College of Music: rcm.ac.uk
Royal Festival Hall: rfu.org.uk
Royal Opera House: royalopera.org
Sadlers Wells Theatre: sadlers-wells.com
St Alfege, Greenwich: st-alfege.org.
St Andrew's, Holborn: cityoflondonchurches.com/standrewsholbom
St Bride's: aboutbritain.com/stbrides
St George's, Hanover Square: stgeorgeshanoversquare.org
St George's Chapel, Windsor Castle: stgeorges-windsor.org
St Giles, Cripplegate: stgilescripplegate.com
St James's, Piccadilly: st-james-piccadilly.org
St John's, Smith Square: sjss.org.uk
St Lawrence, Little Stanmore: pmr.dircon.co.uk
St Martin-in-the-Fields: stmartin-in-the-fields.org
St Mary le Bow: cityoflondonchurches.com/stmarylebow
St Mary Woolnoth: cityoflondonchurches. com/stmarywoolnoth
St Michael's, Cornhill: st-michaels.org.uk
St Paul's, Covent Garden: covent-garden.co. uk/Histories/stpaul
St Paul's cathedral: stpauls.co.uk
St Sepulchre's: cityoflondonchurches.com/ stsepulchre
Sotheby's: sothebys.com
Southwark cathedral: dswarkorg/cathedral/
Temple church: templechurch.com
Theatre Royal, Drury Lane: londontheatre. co.uk
Theatre Royal, Stratford East: stratfordeast. com
Trinity College of Music: tcm.ac.uk
Victoria and Albert Museum: vam.ac.uk
Wesley's Chapel: wesleyschapel.org.uk
Westminster Abbey: westminster-abbey.org/
Westminster cathedral: westminstercathedral.org.uk
Wigmore Hall: wigmore-hall.org.uk

Index

Other Books by the Authors

Lewis Foreman

Havergal Brian: a collection of essays (1969)
The British Musical Renaissance: a guide to research (1972)
Discographies: a bibliography (1973)
Archive Sound Collections (1974)
Systematic Discography (1974)
Factors Affecting the Preservation and Dissemination of Archive Sound Recordings (1975)
British Music Now (1975)
Havergal Brian and the Performance of his Orchestral Music (1976)
Edmund Rubbra: composer (1977)
Dermot O'Byrne: poems by Arnold Bax (1979)
Arthur Bliss: catalogue of the complete works (1980)
The Percy Grainger Companion (1981)
Bax: a composer and his times (1983; 2nd edn 1988; 3rd edn in preparation)
Oskar Fried: Delius and the late romantic school (1984)
From Parry to Britten: British music in letters (1987, 1988)
Farewell, My Youth and other writings by Sir Arnold Bax (1992)
Lost and Only Sometimes Found: a seminar on music publishing and archives (1992)
British Music 1885–1921 (1994)
Koanga: the 1935 production of Frederick Delius's opera (1995)
Vaughan Williams in Perspective (1998)
Elgar & Gerontius: the early performances (1998)
Oh My Horses! Elgar and the Great War (2001)
British Choral Music (2001)
Information Sources in Music (2003)

Susan Foreman

Shoes and Ships and Sealing-Wax: an illustrated history of the Board of Trade 1786–1986 (1986)
Striking a Balance: the role of the Board of Trade 1786–1986 (1986)
Consumer Monitor: an annotated bibliography of British Government and other official publications relating to consumer issues (1987)
Loaves and Fishes: an illustrated history of the Ministry of Agriculture, Fisheries and Food 1889–1989 (1989)
From Palace to Power: an illustrated history of Whitehall (1995)
Consumer Monitor 2 (1996)
H M Treasury in Whitehall: an exhibition of pictures . . . Catalogue (1998)
Back to Work: a guide for women returners (With Diana Wolfin) (2004)